Marxist Inquiries

Marxist Inquiries: Studies of Labor, Class, and States

Edited by
Michael Burawoy
and
Theda Skocpol

American Journal of Sociology
Volume 88, Supplement 1982

The University of Chicago Press
Chicago and London

American Journal of Sociology

EDWARD O. LAUMANN, Editor

JOHN A. Y. ANDREWS, WENDY GRISWOLD, and JOHN F. PADGETT, Associate Editors

PAUL M. HIRSCH and SALLY B. KILGORE, Book Review Editors

GAY-YOUNG CHO, STEVEN C. DUBIN, STUART MICHAELS, and DENNIS R. WHEATON, Associate Book Review Editors

WINIFRED HUNT BENADE, Editorial Manager

JANE MATHER, Editorial Assistant

The AMERICAN JOURNAL OF SOCIOLOGY (ISSN 0002-9602) is published bimonthly in July, September, November, January, March, and May by The University of Chicago at The University of Chicago Press, Journals Division, P.O. Box 37005, Chicago, Illinois 60637. Subscription rates, U.S.A.: institutions, 1 year $55.00, 2 years $99.00; individuals, 1 year $30.00, 2 years $54.00. Student subscription rate, U.S.A.: 1 year $25.00 (letter from professor must accompany subscription). ASA and BSA members, 1 year $25.00. All other countries add $5.00 for each year's subscription to cover postage. Single copy rates: institutions $9.25, individuals $5.00. Back issues available from 1962 (vol. 68). Subscriptions are payable in advance. Subscriptions will be entered to start with the first issue to be published after receipt of order. *Claims for missing numbers* should be made within the month following the regular month of publication. The publishers expect to supply missing numbers free only when losses have been sustained in transit and when the reserve stock will permit. *Postmaster:* Send address changes to The University of Chicago Press, Journals Division, P.O. Box 37005, Chicago, Illinois 60637

American Journal of Sociology

Volume 88   Supplement 1982

CONTENTS

Preface

The idea for this Supplement to the *American Journal of Sociology* developed in 1977 and 1978, during the editorship of Charles Bidwell. As many who have followed the *Journal* over the years will know, Bidwell's leadership served to broaden the appeal of the *AJS*, ensuring its continued preeminence as the leading journal in American sociology. The launching of this Supplement was intended not as an endorsement of a particular theoretical perspective, but as part of the *AJS*'s effort to keep abreast of major theoretical and substantive developments in the discipline.

The present editor of the *AJS*, Edward O. Laumann, asked the two of us —Michael Burawoy and Theda Skocpol—to edit the Supplement jointly, in part because both of us are members of the cohort of sociologists, now in its mid-thirties, that has been most influenced by Marxist perspectives. More important, however, the pair of us was recruited because, while we are both sympathetic to the Marxist presence, we hold different views on its significance. For Burawoy, Marxism offers a powerful theoretical framework for understanding the past and future of capitalist societies, in particular, changes in the organization of work, community, social inequalities, state structures, and transnational relations, as well as the social movements these changes stimulate. He is committed to working within the Marxist tradition, pursuing its motivating questions, trying to elucidate its anomalies and contradictions, insisting on its diversity, while at the same time remaining true to its political and philosophical premises and to its critical perspectives. He sees this tradition as requiring continual reconstruction as history unfolds and, as part of that reconstruction, seeks to incorporate insights, findings, and methodologies developed in sociology. Skocpol's views are somewhat different. She values the Marxist resurgence in contemporary sociology for the big questions it has prompted Marxists and others to investigate and debate with renewed vigor. She also believes that Marxists have helped to increase the historical awareness of sociologists and to strengthen their concern to explain historical patterns and transformations. However, not being enthusiastic about totalistic macrotheoretical frameworks of any sort, Skocpol does not care whether the best explanatory answers turn out to be Marxist. She simply feels strongly that Marxist questions are important, and she wants to see Marxist hypotheses fully researched and debated alongside hypotheses from the other classical sociological traditions founded by Max Weber, Alexis de Tocqueville, and Émile Durkheim.

Working at the meeting point of these orientations, the two of us agreed to focus the Supplement on Marxist-inspired contributions to current social research. Our "Call for Papers" deliberately left room for a wide range of substantive topics and methodologies but stressed an exclusive interest in empirical studies designed to build on—or react to—Marxist ideas. Some of the more than 150 submissions we received had to be set aside as inappropriate, but we were left with a profusion of interesting papers to review. In this task we were fortunate to have the help of 10 editorial advisors and 10 additional referees, all of whom gave us written comments on submissions we sent to them anonymously. We gratefully acknowledge the assistance of all these advisors and referees. Of course, the editors alone are responsible for the final shape and content of the volume.

When we began work on the Supplement we never supposed that we would be able to cover all the areas of Marxist research. Nor did we aim to "survey" or "represent" alternative Marxist perspectives or schools. We simply wanted to demonstrate to a broad audience the fascination and fruitfulness of Marxist ideas in contemporary social research. In this aim we now feel we have succeeded. This volume assembles nine examples of some of the most interesting work being done today by younger sociologists who are seriously pursuing the rich and provocative arguments to be found in one or another strand of the ongoing Marxist tradition.

MICHAEL BURAWOY
THEDA SKOCPOL

April 1982

Introduction: The Resurgence of Marxism in American Sociology[1]

Michael Burawoy
University of California, Berkeley

> The court has been sitting in judgement upon historical mate-
> rialism for one hundred years, and it is continually being ad-
> journed. The adjournment is in effect a tribute to the robust-
> ness of the tradition; in that long interval the cases against a
> hundred other interpretive systems have been upheld, and the
> culprits have disappeared "downstairs." That the court has not
> yet found decisively in favour of historical materialism is not
> only because of the ideological *parti pris* of certain judges (al-
> though there is plenty of that) but also because of the provi-
> sional nature of the explanatory concepts, the *actual* silences
> (or absent mediations) within them, the primitive and unre-
> constructed character of some of the categories, and the in-
> conclusive determinacy of the evidence.　　[E. P. THOMPSON]

> It would be strange if Marxist theory eternally stood still.
> 　　　　　　　　　　　　　　　　　　　　　　[NIKOLAI BUKHARIN]

The renewed interest in Marxism within American sociology is only the latest revitalization of that discipline by European thought. Between the two
world wars, the Chicago School was inspired by German thought as filtered
through Louis Wirth and Robert Park. The two decades after World War
Two were dominated by Talcott Parsons's grand synthesis of Weber, Durkheim, Pareto, Marshall, and, subsequently, Freud. *The Structure of Social
Action* (1937) set new parameters and directions in the heyday of an expanding field. It was during this period that Parsons, together with a number of eminent colleagues and students, developed and consolidated the
basis of structural functionalism, lending American sociology at least the
appearance of an overarching coherence. Structural functionalism provided
an intellectual framework for celebrating the virtues of American society
and fighting the evils of totalitarianism: fascism and communism. It inspired major studies in comparative and historical sociology—such as those
of Neil Smelser, Robert Bellah, and Reinhard Bendix—although Bendix

[1] I should like to thank Gretchen Franklin, Harriet Friedmann, Carol Hatch, and David
Plotke for their detailed comments on earlier drafts. Requests for reprints should be sent
to Michael Burawoy, Department of Sociology, University of Wisconsin, Madison, Wisconsin 53706.

was very much opposed to Parsons's systems analysis. Seymour Martin Lipset played a pioneering role in political sociology, drawing on De Tocqueville as well as Weber, Michels, and Marx. Robert Merton and his students—Peter Blau, Alvin Gouldner, and Philip Selznick—drew out underlying implications of Weber's theory of bureaucracy, welding it to functionalist theory and laying the basis for organizational analysis. Another of Parsons's students, Harold Garfinkel, drew on the work of Alfred Schutz to develop his ethnomethodology. Industrial sociology became a burgeoning field of inquiry at all the major centers. Toward the end of the period, the "new nations" of the Third World temporarily caught the sociological imagination, and structural functionalism was harnessed to modernization theory. Barrington Moore's momentous work *Social Origins of Dictatorship and Democracy,* published in 1966, signaled a major departure and the dawning of a new period.

Where did Marxism figure in these two decades? Obviously Soviet Marxism constituted a major point of opposition. But there were also subterranean legacies from the past. During the turbulent 1930s, a number of these leading sociologists had developed a serious relationship with Marxism. Although their turn away from any Marxist allegiance was often as striking as it was rapid, some have continued to debate with strands of the Marxist legacy. I am thinking here of such figures as Daniel Bell and Seymour Martin Lipset. Both have spurned the systematizing efforts of "grand theory." Their industrial, political, and cultural sociologies have examined class conflict and its demise, the destiny of the working class, the formation of interest groups, intellectuals and their relationship to social movements of the left and right, and the political and cultural implications of long-term economic change. If their analysis is indelibly marked by their dialogue with Marxism, their conclusions—like their premises—are anything but radical. Indeed, Lipset (1981) recently endorsed the development of an apolitical sociological Marxism. They embraced the self-congratulation and self-assurance of a sociology of the "American Century." Together with Edward Shils, they developed theories of the "end of ideology," symbolized by what they saw as the collapse of Marxism via Stalinism.

The "end of ideology" thesis constituted a major challenge to Marxism, but there were few around to meet the challenge. This is perhaps not surprising. With the exception of the works of Leon Trotsky and a transmuted Frankfurt School, the powerful European Marxism that grew up in opposition to the orthodoxies of Soviet Marxism and the Comintern remained largely unknown in this country. And often those, like Bell and Hook, who were familiar with such writers as Lukács and Korsch were also the very ones proclaiming the end of ideology (see, e.g., Bell 1960, chap. 13; 1981). In the face of anti-Communist repression and the absence of a strong socialist movement or Marxist intellectual tradition in the United States, there were few Marxists able to sustain a creative dialogue and critique to counter the euphoria of 1950s sociology. In particular, structural functionalism pursued its totalizing mission unhindered by an intellectual opposition that might have brought its premises into line with the emerging political realities and social movements of the 1960s.

The year 1965 saw the first teach-ins on the war in Vietnam. In the same year, Talcott Parsons captured both the triumph and the limits of structural functionalism in a paper he delivered at a plenary session of the American Sociological Association's annual meeting. He dismissed Karl Marx as a social thinker "whose work fell entirely within the nineteenth century . . . he belongs to a phase of development which has been superseded. . . . [His] predictions about the course of the socioeconomic system have been deeply invalidated by the course of events in most advanced industrial societies. . . . [J]udging by the standards of the best contemporary social-science . . . Marxian theory is obsolete" (1967, pp. 135, 109–10, 132). Accordingly, Marxism is reduced to a dogma of "certain categories of intellectuals, who have professed to speak for the masses of the underprivileged in their respective societies and, in their latest phase, for the underprivileged society as a whole" (p. 127). Parsons advances telling criticisms of Marx, claiming that he overgeneralized from "the structure of the early capitalist firm and its market involvements" (p. 109); that he overlooked the possibility of diverse power relations between "ownership-management and workers" (p. 110); that he postulated a false tendency for "the status of the worker component to become progressively homogenized and separated drastically from the proprietary status" (pp. 110–11); that he was "virtually oblivious to the elements of what may be called pluralization" (p. 113); that he missed the role of the state in "directly supporting trade-union organization and welfare legislation, both of which strengthen the position of the proletariat in class struggle" (p. 114); that he attempted to "rule the ideal and normative factors out of 'basic' significance in the determination of social processes" (p. 123); and that he predicted that "the revolutionary situation would develop most clearly and rapidly in the most advanced industrial countries," whereas in fact there has been a "shift in the socialist-communist movement from the advanced industrial societies to the more or less 'underdeveloped' areas" (pp. 124–25).

Parsons's conclusions do not appear to have been based on a careful or systematic reading of the works of Marx and Engels; every footnote is to a non-Marxist source. Nevertheless, his critique hits home at major weaknesses in the writings of Marx and Engels, some of which are directly addressed in the papers collected in this volume. What is remarkable, however, is Parsons's obliviousness to the Marxist literature after Marx,[2] a

2 Parsons therefore overlooks the convergence of his own systems analysis with, e.g., that of Nikolai Bukharin—the leading official Soviet theoretician in the 1920s. Both Par-

Burawoy

literature whose *raison d'être* was to transcend the shortcomings of Marx's own analysis, developing it in new directions while remaining true to its philosophy of history, ethical imperatives, and methodology.[3] By ignoring 20th-century Marxism, Parsons betrayed not only an unfortunate parochialism but also a fundamental misconception of Marx's epistemology. Its central tenet of the link between theory and practice implies at the very least that social theories—and particularly Marxism itself—must undergo continual reconstruction. Marxism cannot be its own exception; it too succumbs to the forces it claims to be dominant.

Parsons's attempt to hermetically seal Marxism as an intellectual tradition within the 19th century betokens his own pursuit of theoretical closure—a pursuit which led structural functionalism away from the new historical forces being unleashed on its own doorstep. In its isolated and abstract character, social theory proved to be out of phase with the burgeoning collective disaffection of the 1960s: the civil rights movement, the antiwar movement, and the critique of the mass university. Vilified by C. Wright Mills, and later given a more nuanced critique by Alvin Gouldner (who sought to recover the emancipatory potential, the voluntaristic moment of structural functionalism), mainstream sociology came under relentless assault. "Conflict theory" replaced "consensus theory"; contradiction replaced equilibrium; critiques of capitalism replaced its celebration. But in its concern for issues of the moment, this radical sociology of the 1960s often lost the historical and comparative perspective that had characterized some of the best work of the 1950s.

It was only in the 1970s, when the attack on complacent politics and consensus theory had run its course and the experiences of the New Left had to be assimilated, that a new wave of specifically Marxist thought surfaced. It appeared in at least four guises. The first was the widening appeal of the *Monthly Review* School, which had begun its journal in 1949 as a vehicle for developing Marxist theory independent of the Communist party. *Monthly Review* survived the "McCarthy era" to pioneer a Marxist analysis of the Third World, analyzing the imperial role of the United States

---

sons and Bukharin were to develop theories of societal equilibrium and evolutionary change, and they both faced criticisms for downplaying conflict and internal contradictions. Seymour Martin Lipset again demonstrates his familiarity with certain strands of Marxism when he writes of Bukharin's *Historical Materialism:* "It represents the one sophisticated attempt by a major Marxist to come to terms with the emerging body of sociological theory and research" (Lipset 1962, p. 27).

[3] In 1906 Trotsky wrote: "Marxism is above all a method of analysis—not analysis of texts, but analysis of social relations. Is it true that, in Russia, the weakness of capitalist liberalism inevitably means the weakness of the labour movement? Is it true, for Russia, that there cannot be an independent labour movement until the bourgeoisie have conquered power? It is sufficient merely to put these questions to see what a hopeless formalism lies concealed beneath the attempt to convert an historically relative remark of Marx's into a supra-historical axiom" (1969, p. 64).

and championing the Cuban and, at times, the Chinese revolutions. As early as 1957, Paul Baran published his path-breaking critique of modernization theory, *The Political Economy of Growth,* which imported Frankfurt School pessimism into an analysis of the dynamics and interdependence of advanced and backward economies. This was followed in 1966 by Baran and Sweezy's *Monopoly Capital* and by a series of timely studies of U.S. imperialism. Immanuel Wallerstein's more recent analysis of the world capitalist system has affinities with this school.[4]

A second stream of thought, concerning the exceptional character of U.S. society, was developed by Marxist historians. Associated with the journal *Studies on the Left* (and its heirs, *Socialist Revolution* and *Socialist Review*) and with the history department of the University of Wisconsin, William Appleman Williams, Gabriel Kolko, James Weinstein, and others mounted an assault on American liberalism as the ideology of an "enlightened" ruling class preempting popular struggles at home while imposing domination abroad.

A third strand of Marxism drew its inspiration from the Frankfurt School and the tradition of Hegelian Marxism, in particular the writings of Georg Lukács, Karl Korsch, Antonio Gramsci, Max Horkheimer, Walter Benjamin, Theodor Adorno, and, above all, Herbert Marcuse. The journal *Telos* has been most closely associated with the development of this critical theory, exploring such themes as psychoanalysis, feminism, council communism, existentialism, and the legacy of the Frankfurt School in the work of Jürgen Habermas. With only a few exceptions, the contributors to *Telos* share an unmistakable hostility to all forms of Soviet and scientific Marxism. They shrink from treating society as an "object" to be examined, an object with its own "laws of motion" whose unfolding is independent of human will. Instead they insist on restoring "subjectivity" to human endeavors, the capacity of people to shape their own destiny, and the potential for rational and collective regulation of society—although the most pessimistic would argue that capitalism has penetrated the human psyche so deeply as to erode even the potential for an emancipated society. The pursuit of the themes of domination and resistance, particularly in the realm of culture, established affinities with social historians such as E. P. Thompson, Herbert Gutman, Eugene Genovese, and David Montgomery,

[4] A close relative of the *Monthly Review* School is the work of radical economists who began the journal *Review of Radical Political Economics* in 1969. Apart from being concerned with traditional Marxist debates, their contributions have been shaped by opposition to neoclassical orthodoxies. Thus, the work of Samuel Bowles, Richard Edwards, Herbert Gintis, David Gordon, Heidi Hartmann, William Lazonick, William Tabb, Tom Weisskopf, and many others seeks to bring a sociological and historical dimension to the analysis of such economic institutions as the labor process, labor markets, and schools, as well as patterns of racial and gender discrimination. In a different mold are those, such as John Roemer, who have taken the sophisticated mathematical apparatus of orthodox economics to construct equally sophisticated Marxist models.

all of whom stress the authenticity of struggles by the oppressed. Critical theory's concern with resistance resonates with populist themes in U.S. culture and social movements, also captured by the journal *Radical America.*

Finally, a fourth strand of Marxism, drawing on French structuralist thought, sought to revitalize historical materialism as a social science. Locked in battle with existentialism and Marxist humanism, Louis Althusser, Nicos Poulantzas, Maurice Godelier, Etienne Balibar, and others constructed what is now known as "French structuralist Marxism." They tried to create a space within scientific Marxism, hitherto dominated by Communist party orthodoxy, for original theorizing, what they called "theoretical practice." In its emphasis on the conditions for the reproduction of capitalism, considered as a system of social relations with distinctive contradictions and dynamics, this French Marxism exhibited definite affinities with structural functionalism—affinities which critical theorists and humanist scholars have been quick to exploit (see, e.g., Thompson 1978, pp. 262–76, 340). But for this very reason French structuralism was also a natural medium for Marxist academics to adopt in their debates with American sociology. It led to concrete studies of the state, class structures, the labor process, and urban political economy. Through its close connections with European Marxism, the British journal *New Left Review* was largely responsible for purveying the revamped scientific Marxism. In the United States, *Kapitalistate* and at times the *Insurgent Sociologist* played an important role in disseminating the structuralist perspective.

These four strands of Marxism—the *Monthly Review* School, the corporate liberal school, critical theory, and Marxist structuralism—have all been influenced, although in different degrees, by European Marxism. They are part of a broader shift from the classical Marxism of Kautsky, Luxemburg, Lenin, Trotsky, and Bukharin to the Western Marxism of Gramsci, Korsch, Lukács, Horkheimer, Adorno, Reich, Marcuse, Lefebvre, Della Volpe, and Althusser.[5] Perry Anderson (1976) characterized this shift as a movement from a dialogue between theory and working-class struggles to one between Marxist theory and bourgeois theory. The major Western Marxists, with the notable exception of Gramsci, all finally became academics, most often philosophers. Thus, Western Marxism is the Marxism of working-class defeats, of socialism in retreat. Given the extent of anticommunism within the working class and the weakness of the Communist party, it is not surprising that this retreat has gone furthest in the United

---

[5] "Western Marxism" originally referred to the body of Marxism which emerged in response to the optimism of classical Marxism and the orthodoxy of Soviet Marxism. It opposed scientific Marxism with a critical, humanistic Marxism. See Merleau-Ponty (1973), Arato and Breines (1979), and Jacoby (1981). Perry Anderson (1976) redefines "Western Marxism" to include both Hegelian and scientific works that reflect the separation of theorizing from working-class struggles. It is in this latter sense that I use the term here.

States, where the university is virtually the only refuge for Marxists. American Marxism has, therefore, a particularly pronounced academic character, being separated not only from the working class but from social movements in general. As David Plotke (1982) has argued, this has led to contradictory impulses toward immersion in social movements, on the one hand, and a critique of their limitations, followed by withdrawal, on the other. The tension is reflected in divergent theoretical tendencies toward pessimism (drawn from the Frankfurt School or the "iron laws of history") and toward a populist romanticism (drawing on certain American cultural traditions and at times the triumphalism of the Communist movement).

Even if few are now able to straddle the divide between university and social movements on the back of Marxist theories, the impetus for the revival of interest in Marxism in the United States did come from the protests and disillusionments of the 1960s and early 1970s. Sustaining that revival without a permanent base outside the university will depend on forging links with an international movement and winning a place for Marxist ideas within academic discourse. Both have been occurring. The international character of the New Left has brought with it the translation of Marxist classics into English. Monthly Review Press and New Left Books have been responsible for opening Marxist legacies to the English-speaking world. With the availability of original works, there has also been an explosion of secondary analyses, situating the different phases and branches of Marxism in their historical contexts, subjecting them to internal critique, and rebuilding Marxist traditions. This has been further encouraged by the proliferation of journals, the development of networks and collectives, and the staging of conferences. That is, during the last decade Marxists have begun to develop rudimentary institutional bases from which they can talk to one another and question the assumptions underpinning academic disciplines. If the 1960s involved the rejection of mainstream sociology and the 1970s saw the emergence of Marxisms, often in isolation from debates in sociology, then the 1980s will test their capacity to address problems more powerfully than alternative theories without losing their critical stance toward contemporary society.

The assimilation of contemporary Marxism into sociology has already begun. Sociologists are experimenting with Marxist ideas and testing Marxist theories of class structure, work organization, the state, and the international division of labor. The contents of the *American Sociological Review* and the *American Journal of Sociology* testify to the growing appeal of Marxist concepts.[6] At the same time, American Marxists have

---

[6] Contemporary sociological dialogue with Marxism has advanced much further in England, where a distinctive "neo-Weberian" school has coalesced around the writings of Anthony Giddens, Frank Parkin, David Lockwood, Michael Mann, Howard Newby, Steven Lukes, and others.

begun to recover sociology's preoccupation with normative orders, socialization through family and school, the resilience of bureaucracy, and the
conditions for authoritarianism. Where appropriate, Marxists have begun
to adopt sociology's techniques of analysis in order better to evaluate
their theories. We can observe these embryonic tendencies in journals of
Marxist inspiration such as *Politics and Society, Theory and Society,* and
Political Power and Social Theory (which takes its name from Barrington
Moore's book of the same title).

This volume is intended to demonstrate the fruitfulness of both forms
of convergence: sociology's appropriations from Marxism and Marxist appropriations from sociology. Thus, there are essays that self-consciously
build within the Marxist tradition, taking one or another of its defining
problems as a point of departure, yet bear the marks of dialogue with sociology. There are other essays that borrow from Marxism to enrich their
sociology. But all engage Marxist or Marxist-inspired theory with empirical
analysis, using a wide variety of techniques, from participant observation
to time-series analysis, from interviews to archival work. Some evaluate the
relative merits of different Marxist theories, while others compare the explanatory power of Marxist theories with that of contemporary sociological
theories. While the essays do not deal directly with such topics as culture
and ideology, Marxism and feminism, urban political economy and social
movements, race and nationalism, the Marxian appropriation of psychoanalysis, or issues of philosophy and methodology, they do tackle issues at
the intersection of Marxist and sociological discourse: the organization of
work, the state, class structure, and economic development. In the remaining pages of this Introduction, I will explore the linkages among these diverse papers and between them and other Marxist works. What I will offer
is less a summary of each paper than a loose framework within which their
interrelations can be understood.

WORK, POLITICS, AND SOCIETY

It is difficult to comprehend the enormous transformation that the Russian
Revolution brought to Marxism, not only in the writings of Lenin and
Trotsky but also in the Western Marxisms they stimulated. There is no
shortage of Marxist theories explaining why early capitalism gave way to
advanced capitalism rather than to socialism and why socialist revolutions
have taken place in predominantly peasant societies rather than advanced
capitalist societies. Indeed, much of 20th-century Marxism can be understood as an attempt to come to terms with such facts. But as Marxists
continually modify and sometimes even transform their theories to take
into account unanticipated developments, it is also necessary to reinterpret
the past in accordance with those transformed theories. In short, history

continually compels its own reconstruction. In the case of Marxism, this must begin with a critique of Marx's understanding of early capitalism in Britain.

Marx warned those of his German compatriots who shrugged their shoulders at the conditions of the English working class, *"De te fabula narratur"*—of you the future is told. "The country that is more developed industrially only shows, to the less developed, the image of its own future" (Marx 1967, pp. 8–9). There can be no disputing the essential truth of Marx's prognosis. Capitalism has penetrated the furthest corners of the globe. But that penetration has been uneven, occurring at different times, at different rates, and in different forms. Moreover, it has combined with preexisting social formations in a variety of ways. This combined and uneven character accounts for the diverse political responses to the development of capitalism.

Marx himself claimed in *Capital* that the political consequences of capitalist development are inherent in the capitalist mode of production itself, irrespective of its historical and societal context. He saw the modern factory as a despotic regime made necessary by the competitive pressures of the market, which continually compelled technological innovation and work intensification, and made possible by the availability of workers dependent for their survival on the sale of their labor power. But the factory was also the crucible of revolution. The undisputed domination of capital over labor was to turn into its opposite, "the revolt of the working class." But the mechanisms for the transformation of subordination into resistance remained obscure.

As social historians have been clamoring for some time, it was not the proletarianized factory workers but those artisans threatened by modern industry or craft workers facing deskilling who turned out to be the backbone of the most militant and radical struggles in 19th-century Europe. Thus, in the Lancashire cotton industry—Marx's prototypical modern industry—first the handloom weavers and then the "aristocracy" of mule spinners were the most active in petitioning for parliamentary reform, in the cooperative movement, the 10-hour movement, the anti–Poor Law campaigns, and the Chartist movement. Not only the autonomy of craft workers, but preindustrial cultural tradition, provided resources for resistance. The "freeborn Englishman" provided the essential cement in the formation of the English working class (Thompson 1963). Artisans, outworkers, and factory operatives drew on community to buttress their struggles against the depredations of capitalism. The family, the friendly society, the cooperative, the pub, and the church were all arenas of resistance out of which was woven the social fabric of class. In other words, the popular class struggles of the 19th century sprang from the survival of community both within and outside the place of work, not where proletarianization and deskilling had advanced most but where they were being resisted.

Julia Wrigley's paper in this volume pursues these themes by drawing out some of the connections between resistance and domination at work and resistance and domination in the community. During the Industrial Revolution in England, manufacturers came to depend on systems of subcontracting and inside contracting, in which craft workers were responsible for the organization of production and the hiring and payment of helpers. These systems arose either as a result of entrepreneurs seeking to externalize risks or because skilled workers used their monopoly of knowledge to force their employers into a dependent relationship. In either case, factory owners had an interest in artisans acquiring scientific knowledge, and so they helped to found and sponsor Mechanics' Institutes. But these institutes subsequently became sources of resistance to capitalists' assertion of control over production through mechanization and the division of labor. The eventual separation of mental and manual labor in the second half of the 19th century therefore had to be closely linked to struggles over the dissolution of scientific education for the working class. Victory for capital in the workplace heralded the development of a dual system of education, aimed at "conceivers" on the one side and "executors" on the other.

Recent work on the English textile industry provides ample confirmation of Wrigley's implicit thesis—that the transformation of the labor process has political repercussions beyond the factory. Rejecting those explanations for the demise of radicalism in the heart of industrial England after 1850 which rely on the rise of a labor aristocracy, Gareth Stedman Jones (1975) focuses instead on the importance of the demolition of skill. New forms of politics emerge when workers are stripped of their control over production and work relations have been restabilized on the basis of modern machinery. Struggles over the appropriation of nature, over the control of production, give way to struggles over the appropriation of the product, over ownership and wages. Patrick Joyce (1980) explores Stedman Jones's argument in great detail, showing that, where labor is transformed from a subject guiding production into an object dominated by production, the formal subordination of labor to capital gives way to its real subordination, and community turns from an arena of resistance into an instrument of capitalist domination. In Yorkshire, where mechanization spread slowly and where mills were often small, workers were able to protect their autonomy and develop a more independent labor movement than in Lancashire, where modern industry advanced more rapidly. In Lancashire the new dependency of operatives on their employers gave rise to an overweening paternalism in the mill towns during the second half of the 19th century. Furthermore, in distinguishing between Tory and Liberal working-class communities in Lancashire, Joyce claims that the particular complexion of paternalism was decisively shaped by the political and cultural origins of the millowners.

In a similar way, Dwight Billings's essay in this volume highlights the importance of preexisting class relations in the development of the textile industry, this time in North Carolina. Contrary to conventional wisdom, but in line with Jonathan Wiener's recent work on Alabama (1978), Billings argues that the old planter class took a major part in creating the new industry. The world of the slaveholders colored the industrial relations of the mill towns, which in many ways came to resemble the earlier plantations. Different patterns of industrial relations emerged where the planter class was not involved, as in coal and tobacco in the South and textiles in New England.

We have argued so far that radical popular struggles of the 19th century arose in resistance to proletarianization and deskilling, often mobilizing preindustrial legacies and rooted in social spaces beyond the control of capital. Once the real subordination of labor to capital is accomplished, community is domesticated and struggles develop in response to new types of labor control. Marx envisaged only one form of labor control within modern industry—the despotic form—made necessary by the anarchy of the market among firms and made possible by the dependence of the laborer on the wage. While he did recognize that the dynamics of the capitalist mode of production ineluctably led to the concentration and centralization of capital, and thus to a lessening of competitive pressures, he saw this as capitalism's last gasp before its final dissolution. In reality, the rise of the large corporation laid the basis for a new and more stable form of capitalism, and with it appeared new forms of labor control.

Richard Edwards (1979) has provided a preliminary systematization of the link between changes in market structures, patterns of class struggles, and these new forms of labor control as they have evolved in the United States. He distinguishes three historically successive forms of control: simple, technical, and bureaucratic. In the 19th century, firms were generally small and markets competitive, so that management exercised arbitrary and personalistic domination over workers. With the 20th-century growth of large-scale industry, simple control gave way to new forms. After a series of unsuccessful experiments, capital sought to regulate work through such technological arrangements as the assembly line. This mode of control generated its own forms of struggle, and after World War Two it gave way to bureaucratic regulation, in which rules are used to define and evaluate work tasks and govern the application of sanctions. Bureaucratic regulation and the associated systems of collective bargaining, grievance machinery, and internal labor markets, usually found in the corporate sector, stabilize industrial relations in consonance with oligopolistic market structures. Although each period generates its own prototypical form of control, all nevertheless coexist within the contemporary U.S. economy as reflections of different market relations.

Robert Thomas's paper on the organization of work in the California lettuce harvest demonstrates the limits of Edwards's scheme. Here is an industry which by market criteria is clearly oligopolistic, yet which has a decidedly competitive-sector form of labor control. Thomas's participant-observation study of lettuce picking uncovers two forms of work organization. In the first, the lettuce is handpicked by crews consisting of both documented and undocumented workers. The position of undocumented workers is always precarious, and they attempt to earn as much as possible as quickly as possible—a tactic facilitated by a piece-rate system—thus setting the pace for the documented workers. A despotic regime of labor prevails. In the second labor process, the lettuce is machine wrapped; work pace and relations are governed by technology. Here we find women workers on low hourly wages. Without union protection and in transient employment, the work force is subject to arbitrary and personalistic domination by management.

In explaining these distinctive patterns of labor control, Thomas emphasizes the external "negative status" of the work force. Both gender and citizenship are manipulated by management to assert dictatorial power over the organization of work. Yet there is a further condition that fosters the binding of work and community to the advantage of management: the state's abstention from the regulation of industrial relations in agriculture. Agribusiness has been excluded from all the major labor legislation of this century, in particular the Wagner Act and its amendments. This has facilitated a despotic organization of work in the fields, deploying a succession of displaced minorities and migrants as pools of cheap labor. The 1975 California Agricultural Labor Relations Act and the partial unionization of farm workers resulted in mechanization, which in turn led to a weakening of the union.

One conclusion emerges clearly from Thomas's paper and, implicitly, from those of Billings and Wrigley: we cannot explain variations in capitalist relations of production without taking account of the state.[7] The organization of work in California agriculture depends on the state to generate supplies of cheap labor and to establish conditions for labor's subordination at the point of production. The persistence of coercive paternalistic industrial relations in the cotton mills of North Carolina depends not only on company control over the community but also on the exclusion of unions. Manufacturers exploit labor legislation which requires majority support for a union before its recognition, which outlaws union shops through right-to-work rules, which favors employer interference in organizing campaigns through free-speech amendments, and which disenfranchises strikers

[7] Larson (1977) makes the same point in her analysis of the rise of professions.

in union elections. The decline of craft control in British industry in the second half of the 19th century was assisted by official schooling policies and the dissolution of the Mechanics' Institutes, once centers of working-class power.

In short, we have come a long way from Marx's attempt to characterize England as the prototypical capitalist society. Its pioneer status in fact made it exceptional. In order to explain variations in capitalist relations of production, we have had to restore to the center of the stage what Marx either took for granted, deliberately ignored, or used as illustrative material: the historical legacies of the preindustrial period, the development of different market relations among firms, the linkages binding work and community, and the impact of the state on forms of labor control. Attending to these factors not only elucidates the decline of popular struggles in the first industrial nation but also, as Bonnell (in press), Johnson (1979), Koenker (1981), and others have recently shown, explains the revolutionary impulse behind sections of the Russian working class in 1905 and again in 1917.

THE CAPITALIST STATE

Although never theoretically developed, Marx's own account of the transformation of the labor process, in particular the substitution of machinery for labor power, also draws attention to the role of the state. In restricting the length of the working day, factory legislation forced manufacturers to seek new ways of intensifying production and thus maintaining rates of profit. Marx explains the Factory Acts as the result of working-class struggles against capital, parliamentary struggles between Whigs and Tories, and the autonomy of factory inspectors, who valiantly fought to enforce the new codes against resistance from employers, the judiciary, and even the operatives. Clearly the state is not "the executive committee of the bourgeoisie," a view which some mistakenly attribute to Marx (e.g., Parsons 1967, pp. 109, 114, 117). In the "Communist Manifesto" Marx and Engels actually write, "The executive of the modern State is but a committee for managing the *common* affairs of the *whole* bourgeoisie" (emphasis added). Factory legislation is just one example of the state acting against the economic interests of the dominant classes in order to protect their political interests in the reproduction of the capitalist order. But where Marx and Engels identified the political interests of the whole bourgeoisie as maintaining the "external" conditions of the capitalist economy, more recent analyses also focus on the regulation of its "internal" conditions. That is, in addition to its political role the state plays a crucial economic role in countering capitalism's tendency to destroy itself through ever more serious crises.

In this respect one of the most important pioneering analyses is Baran and Sweezy's *Monopoly Capital* (1966). Writing in the 1960s, they argued that the distinctive problem of the advanced capitalist economy was not the falling rate of profit, as Marx had argued in volume 3 of *Capital,* but the absorption of surplus. In the pursuit of profit, large corporations were now producing more than could be consumed. The ensuing crises of under-consumption could be temporarily muffled by the irrational utilization of surplus through waste—unnecessary consumption, built-in obsolescence, burgeoning sales and advertising expenditures, and, above all, military ex-penditures. The warfare state was not a political but an economic necessity, a response to an actual or anticipated recession, a means of boosting de-mand in Keynesian fashion.

In their paper, Larry Griffin, Joel Devine, and Michael Wallace set out to examine this theory for the period from 1949 to 1976. They discover that the state is responsive not so much to the needs of the economy as a whole as to the particular interests of "monopoly" capital and, to a lesser extent, organized labor. Their results offer more support for James O'Con-nor's analysis in *The Fiscal Crisis of the State* (1973) than for Baran and Sweezy's argument. In O'Connor's view, the state attempts to reconcile the contradictory pressures of capital accumulation by large corporations and the legitimation of the social order through concessions to the organized sectors of the labor force. Griffin, Devine, and Wallace argue that declining profits in the corporate sector and unemployment among unionized workers were among the forces prompting increases in military expenditures, where-as these expenditures fell when profits increased and unemployment dropped. Their paper immediately raises the question whether, as the war industry becomes increasingly research based and capital intensive, military expen-ditures can continue to be understood as a countercyclical fiscal policy. Can the development of the monstrous MX missile program or research into postnuclear laser technology supply the same new employment per dollar invested as the manufacture of tanks, helicopters, bombers, and rifles has in the past, or provide the same economic impulse to other corporate in-dustries outside production for "defense"? If military Keynesianism worked in the past this might also be attributed to the international economic dominance of the United States. In a situation of heightening competition from Europe and Japan—countries without such huge military budgets—expanding the production of the means of destruction is more likely to cripple than to stimulate the economy.

Griffin, Devine, and Wallace supply an empirically based corrective to the official account of escalating military expenditures—dubious claims about international parity which exaggerate the strength and aggressive-ness of the Soviet Union. To be sure, once established, such appeals to na-tional survival do develop into a self-fulfilling prophecy, generating a logic of deterrence which compels both sides to play a seemingly endless game of leapfrog. But proclaimed threats to national security benefit both the United States and the Soviet Union by justifying untold atrocities to keep their satellites in line, whether they be in Latin America, Eastern Europe, the Middle East, or Southeast Asia. Furthermore, with recent technological developments, commitment to this logic of deterrence has prompted some nuclear strategists to leap from the camp of the MAD (mutual assured destruction) to that of the NUTs (nuclear use theorists) who think the unthinkable—the possibility of a successful first strike (Joseph 1982). However, even if it assumes an autonomy of its own, the logic of state-to-state relations, as we will see again in Harriet Friedmann's paper, cannot be understood outside the relationship of the state to domestic class forces. We will now explore this further.

Baran and Sweezy (1966), O'Connor (1973), Holloway and Picciotto (1978), Offe and Ronge (1975), and Habermas (1975) all offer distinctive sets of theories of the capitalist state. They tend to rely on some logic of capital accumulation and pinpoint a "functional gap" that the state must fill if accumulation is to continue. Curiously, these theories, which highlight the economic rather than the political functions of the state, have received most attention in Germany and the United States, where popular struggles have been relatively weak. In countries such as France and Italy, where class struggles have been more expansive and the working class is informed by a radical tradition, different theories of the state have gained popularity. Against the orthodox notion of the French Communist party that the state is but an instrument of monopoly capital, new images of the state appeared in the 1970s. These stress the state's role in the regulation and containment of popular struggles, rather than its role in the management of the economy. Although produced at very different times, the theories of Poulantzas (1973) and Gramsci (1971) address similar questions: How is it that the working class and its allies have not captured state power, have been contained within a capitalist framework? The theories that emerge underline the importance of alliances among dominant classes: the formation of a "power bloc" under the leadership of a "hegemonic" fraction. The state presents the interest of that bloc as the universal interest, the interest of all, while dividing and atomizing the subordinate classes. Both Poulantzas and Gramsci stress the role of ideology in providing the terrain of struggle and the cement for the social order. In normal times the state appears to be autonomous; its apparatuses are constituted as formally neutral in relation to classes. In times of crisis this neutrality is suspended and the state comes to the defense of the capitalist order.

Eurocommunism provided the context for a new turn in Marxist theories of the state (see, e.g., Poulantzas 1978; Claudin 1978). The state is no longer seen in terms of the functions which it somehow "necessarily" performs; it is no longer a monolith which must be "smashed" before fundamental changes can occur. It is replete, instead, with internal contradictions which can be exploited by subordinate classes. It is neither an object to be manipulated nor a subject standing above society. Instead it is now seen as the condensation of class forces, so that reformist strategies which shift the balance of those forces can be considered. The state is viewed as a site of struggle, but for real change to take place, it is necessary for struggles outside the state to lend support to those within it, and vice versa. Social movements and parties now become interactive and interdependent. In this type of analysis, the limits of struggles within the state become less important than the struggles themselves; a peaceful transition to so- cialism is on the agenda.

In the light of these theoretical controversies, it is not surprising that the Chilean experience has become a battleground for alternative political perspectives. After it was voted into office in 1970, the Unidad Popular (UP) attempted to carry out a peaceful transition to socialism, based on Chile's legacy of parliamentary politics. The experiment ended three years later with a bloody military coup. What happened in the intervening years calls into question two perspectives on the transition to socialism—both of which underestimate the importance of divisions and struggles within the state. Against the social democratic perspective, which reduces the prob- lem of inaugurating socialism to the electoral victory of a socialist party, the Chilean defeat demonstrates that controlling the state involves much more than taking over the executive branch. Against the left-wing per- spective that anything short of smashing the state is cooptative, the ex- perience of the UP shows how assuming power through elections can pre- cipitate the intensification of socialist struggles. The outcome was by no means a foregone conclusion. Debates have raged over whether the UP moved too quickly or too slowly in consolidating its position. On the one side, a more gradualist program would have involved alliances with the Christian Democrats and certain middle strata, in particular small em- ployers and sections of the peasantry, and would have devoted more energy to the construction of an organizational basis of support. On the other side, it is claimed that the UP was naive in its commitment to constitutionalism and parliamentary democracy, was too cautious in neutralizing the military and arming the civilian population, and failed to exploit the momentum of popular mobilization at critical conjunctures. The debate inevitably re- volves around alternative conceptions of the ("dependent") capitalist state. Can shifts in the balance of forces, both within and outside the state, pave the way for a peaceful transition to socialism? Or does the capitalist state in the last instance always defend the capitalist order, in which case any transition to socialism requires the destruction of that state?

Two decades of debate have also posed the relevance of the Chilean experience for advanced capitalist countries. Would a peaceful road to socialism in Western Europe, with its very different class structures, political traditions, and international position, be less vulnerable to investment strikes, declining living standards, and military intervention? Is it possible, for example, that the Swedish social democrats could implement the gradual expropriation of capital without a counterrevolution (Stephens 1979)? If the Eurocommunist perspective is perhaps overly optimistic about the possibility of social democratic reforms, it nevertheless opens the black box of the state. It is now possible to address a problem unexamined by earlier functionalist accounts: how the state does what it is supposed to do.[8] Under what conditions might the state seriously fail in its "role" of "preserving the cohesion of the entire social formation"?

In explaining the particular procapital interventions of the state, both Block (1977*b*) and Lindblom (1977) have argued that state managers recognize their own interests as firmly tied to those of capital accumulation and therefore act in accord with the interests of the "capitalist class." In other words, a distinctive feature of capitalism is that the interests of capital—that is, profit—must be secured before any other class or group—including state functionaries—can realize its own interests. Yet, as Theda Skocpol (1980) has commented, it is not clear how state managers achieve that enlightened view of their own interests transcending the logic embedded in their own political apparatuses. The achievement of this Olympian perspective is rendered even more problematic by the constraints state managers face from struggles within the state. But breaking down the state into its constitutive elements and moving toward an organizational analysis of its apparatuses risks emphasizing its contradictory nature at the expense of its unity—a unity that becomes most clear in moments of crisis, when the capitalist order is threatened. Organizational analysis also highlights the autonomy of the state, leading one to wonder how capitalism continues to survive—precisely the point of departure of the earlier functionalist theories. It also encourages the neoconservative fallacy that restricting the size of the state will somehow "unstrangle" the economy.

Pat Shannon's article on accident compensation in New Zealand addresses this complex of problems around state autonomy. It is an attempt to understand the unity of the state in terms of the preservation of the conditions of capital accumulation, while focusing on the contradictory political pressures within the state which produce specific policies. Shannon distinguishes between the questions of "why" the state intervenes—to protect the profitability of monopoly capital—and "how" it intervenes—the legislative and

[8] Many Marxist theories have postulated an omnipotent, enlightened, and cohesive dominant class which manipulates the state for its own ends. Such crude "instrumentalist" perspectives were unable to explain the opposition of the dominant classes to state interventions or the virulent divisions within the dominant classes.

bureaucratic processes leading, in this case, to the Accident Compensation Act and its amendment. The legislation proposed by the state was tailored to the needs of one fraction of capital, monopoly capital. Shannon attributes that proposal to the form of the New Zealand state, in particular its powerful executive, and to New Zealand's location in the world economy, which makes it reliant on large-scale foreign investment. Following the initial proposals, the competing interests of various state apparatuses as well as anticipated and actual struggles outside the state reshaped the legislation's content. These internal and external limits to state policies account for the divergence between the interests of monopoly capital and the provisions of the act. The importance of Shannon's study lies in its attempt to go beyond "functionalist" conceptions, which define the state in terms of its "effects," to incorporate an understanding of how the "form of state" and struggles within as well as outside the state shape the production of those effects. He offers an institutional approach to distinguishing among different forms of states without losing sight of their capitalist nature.

CHANGES IN CLASS STRUCTURE

With this consideration of some recent developments in Marxist theories of the organization of work and the state, the groundwork is laid for examining the class structure of contemporary capitalist societies. Until recently, theories of stratification have tended to focus on patterns of social mobility, taking as given the structure of "empty places"—usually the occupational structure arranged on a linear continuum—through which individuals move. Marxists, on the other hand, derive the class structure and its dynamics from theories of the labor process and consider individual mobility patterns a secondary concern, related to class consciousness. Harry Braverman's (1974) derivation of changes in class structure has the virtue of being particularly simple. The transformation of work under advanced capitalism involves the expropriation of skill from the direct producer. Conception, having been separated from execution, is itself subject to fragmentation and deskilling, which result in the expansion of clerical and service occupations.

Following a similar analysis of fundamental economic changes, Daniel Bell's *The Coming of Post-industrial Society* (1973) has thrown out a major challenge to Marxists, forcing them to come to terms with their own understanding of the transformations of class structure under capitalism.[9] Put simply, Bell claims that the "axial principles" of contemporary U.S. society are shifting: from the production of goods to the pro-

[9] See Plotke (1980, 1981) for an explicit response to that challenge; see also Mandel (1975) and Castells (1979).

duction of services, from a society based on the coordination of people and machines to a society organized around theoretical knowledge, from the centrality of the market to the centrality of planning. The working class is being replaced by professional and technical classes. The emergent labor process, a "game among people" serving one another, is displacing a labor process in which the game is between people and machines. Bell argues that rising professional and technical classes cannot be seen as a "new working class"; instead, they spell the demise of the working class and, with it, any notion of a "proletarian revolution."

Erik Olin Wright and Joachim Singelmann take up Bell's challenge in their examination of changes in the class structure of the United States between 1960 and 1970. They pose the question in terms of Wright's class categories. Is the proletariat expanding or contracting? Are supervisory, professional, and technical workers—whom Wright and Singelmann subsume under the "contradictory class locations," between workers and capitalists on the one hand and workers and the self-employed on the other—increasing or declining in numbers? Whereas Bell would claim that the proletariat is shrinking, Braverman's analysis of the degradation of work through deskilling suggests the opposite.[10] Wright and Singelmann discover that the overall changes confirm Bell's thesis: over the years 1960–70, the importance of the proletariat declined relative to that of supervisory, technical, and professional employees. But they also demonstrate that the aggregate effect was due to the expansion of those sectors of the economy which are dominated by more "skilled" personnel. Within each sector, however, including services, they discover a tendency toward proletarianization.

The trajectory of the class structure depends, therefore, on the relative strengths of the two tendencies: the expansion of those sectors with relatively low levels of proletarianization (state and service sectors) and the development within each sector of a working class stripped of any significant skill or autonomy in the workplace. To understand the evolution of the class structure of advanced capitalist nations such as the United States, we must comprehend not only changes in the labor process and the expansion and contraction of the state, issues which we discussed earlier, but also the changing industrial structure. And this can be examined only in the context of a changing international division of labor.

THE NEW INTERNATIONAL DIVISION OF LABOR

As was remarked earlier, Marx conceived of the expansion of capitalism on a world scale, but as a unilinear process, in which noncapitalist modes

[10] Braverman, of course, recognized that new skilled workers are created with the introduction of new technology, but in ever smaller numbers. These skilled workers, moreover, are themselves subjected to the deskilling process. Thus, although there is reskilling, it is swamped by the countertendency toward deskilling.

of production would be destroyed through the forcible intervention of the market. Marx was little concerned about the implications of the world system of nations for an international division of labor. More attuned to the realities of imperialism and wars, Lenin, Kautsky, Luxemburg, and even Trotsky nevertheless also saw noncapitalist modes of production disintegrating in the face of capitalism's thirst for profits, markets, and raw materials—although each pictures this disintegration in a different way, with different political and economic consequences. Significantly, the "optimism" of Marxist orthodoxy has been shared by theories of modernization: both regarded the expansion of capitalism, along with its benefits and irrationalities, as relatively unproblematic.

This optimism turned sour after the Second World War, as liberated colonies found themselves saddled with escalating and apparently insurmountable economic problems. While modernization theory turned to the impediments of "traditional institutions" and "primordial loyalties," Marxists reconstructed their understanding of imperialism. They took as their basic premise the difference between the development of the first industrial nations and subsequent economic development, which took place in the context of already consolidated advanced capitalist nations. Paul Baran (1957), André Gunder Frank (1969), and Samir Amin (1976), to name but three, have argued that Third World nations could not recapitulate the development trajectory of Britain, which was able to exploit the international market for its own ends. Instead, they have argued, either we await the demise of capitalism as a world system or Third World nations must withdraw from the imperial order to pursue a strategy of self-reliance through socialist planning. Their analyses rest, in one way or another, on the conception of the international economic order as a chain of metropolises and satellites, with development at one end coming at the cost of underdevelopment at the other. In other words, between the center and the periphery there is "unequal exchange" due to transfers of surplus by multinational corporations, terms of trade advantageous to central countries, lower wages in the periphery, and so forth.

Crucial as these contributions have been, they nevertheless retain some of the defects of the modernization theory they attempt to refute. First, they tend to substitute one teleology for another: the development of underdevelopment is as inexorable as the advance of modernity. Second, they adopt an ideal type of analysis, in which underdevelopment in the periphery is compared to some unexamined model of "development" in the center. In the same way, modernization theory as it is applied to the Third World has worked with all sorts of implicit and questionable assumptions about the rise of capitalism in the West. Both underdevelopment theory and modernization theory homogenize "the periphery" and are therefore unable to interpret variations among countries and whatever development does take place. Finally, as a result of their reduction of politics to economics, early models of underdevelopment theory carry a certain determinism.

One of the most important attempts to rescue underdevelopment theory from some of these defects is Fernando Cardoso and Enzo Faletto's *Dependency and Development in Latin America* (1979). This comparative historical study underlines the diverse economic responses of Latin American societies to the development of international capitalism. In rejecting the teleologies of theories of underdevelopment and modernization, Cardoso and Faletto substitute an analysis of the way external linkages are mediated and carried by various classes and class fractions, acting at both the political and the economic levels. By endowing the political realm with a certain (unspecified) autonomy, Cardoso and Faletto are able to illuminate alternative patterns of development in Latin America, distinguishing three types of dependency: (1) enclave economies, in which capital originates from outside and products, usually raw materials, are sold in an external market; (2) economies controlled by a local bourgeoisie, in which there is national capital accumulation, but products are again sold on an international market; and (3) dependent industrializing economies controlled by multinational corporations, but with a substantial part of the product sold in the domestic market.

Peter Evans's study of economic development in Brazil, published in this volume, is in the tradition of Cardoso and Faletto. He starts from the view, widely held in such countries as Brazil, South Africa, and Nigeria, that import substitution can go only so far in promoting development and that a further stage requires active intervention by the state to bolster and protect an indigenous bourgeoisie. Although the local bourgeoisie cannot be the dynamic force that it was in the first industrial nations, neither is it reduced to a transmission belt of international capital, as it is often portrayed in underdevelopment theory. On the contrary, it can become an essential contributor to national economic development. Under what conditions and with what consequences, Evans asks, can the state facilitate such an expansion of indigenous capital? As the critical factor he highlights the restructuring of the market to facilitate collaborative ventures between state entrepreneurship and private capital. The consequence is a new form of capital, which joins state oligopolies and local capital into a single hybrid "oligopolistic community."

The examination of industrializing nations of the Third World highlights the changing international division of labor. Reservoirs of cheap labor power and particularly female labor, the technological explosion in communication and transportation systems, the international fragmentation of the labor process, repressive labor codes and fiscal policies favorable to international capital—all predispose manufacturing industry to move into industrializing nations of the Third World (Fröbel, Heinrichs, and Kreye

1980). In these countries we discover features reminiscent of the advanced capitalist nations at the same time that the economies of the latter experience "peripheralization": the development of informal sectors, increasing levels of unemployment, dual labor markets, and so on (Portes and Walton 1981). In short, just as theories of underdevelopment have always claimed that Third World nations could not be understood without reference to the rhythms of economic development in the metropolises, it is now impossible to examine the class structure of advanced capitalist nations without reference to economic changes in the periphery. The new international division of labor underlines the interdependence of the world capitalist system.

Changing patterns of international relations not only require the development of theory to fit the new realities but also lead to the reinterpretation of the past. Thus, in coming to terms with the changing international division of labor under "late capitalism," Ernest Mandel (1975) resurrects the idea of long waves, first analyzed by Kondratieff and Schumpeter, to periodize capitalist development according to cyclical changes in the rate of profit as determined by three technological revolutions, all of which took place in advanced capitalist countries. The first was based on the harnessing of steam power to industrial production in the second half of the 19th century. The second, beginning in the 1890s, led to the generalized application of electric and combustion engines to all branches of industry. The third involved the development of electronic apparatuses and the gradual introduction of nuclear energy beginning in the 1940s. Each technological revolution defined new needs for central capitalism and led to corresponding transformations in the international division of labor. In a similar way, Immanuel Wallerstein (1974) embarked on the study of the origins of capitalism after coming to the conclusion that underdevelopment in Africa had to be understood in terms of transnational transfers of surplus. Again, contemporary developments compel the continual reconstruction of history.

FROM MODES OF PRODUCTION TO INTERNATIONAL
POLITICAL RELATIONS

While Peter Evans raises important questions about the nature of the state in industrializing nations of the Third World, about the relations of dominant classes to the state, and more generally about the political conditions of dependent development, taking external linkages as a point of theoretical departure nevertheless tends to eclipse other equally important issues. First, the analysis is likely to dwell on the dominant classes and their relationship to one another and to the state, rather than on relations between dominant and subordinate classes. When these are considered they are usually examined in connection with, and as derivative of, external linkages. Second, dependency theory leaves unclear how international forces determine which countries will be export platforms, enclave economies, or industrializing nations. Endowing the political with an unspecified autonomy in no way explains the diverse consequences of the capitalist world economy for peripheral societies.

Alternative approaches take the class structure as the preeminent barrier to development and, therefore, as their point of theoretical departure. They study the patterns through which one class appropriates surplus from a class of direct producers, be they peasants, serfs, petty commodity producers, or wage laborers. A social formation is understood as the "articulation" of different modes of appropriating surplus—that is, the relations of interdependence and domination among different modes of production (Wolpe 1979; Taylor 1979; Foster-Carter 1978; Leys 1978). The state is seen in terms of regulating relations between and within modes of production, at the same time as it is a site and object of struggles. The character of the social formation—its class structure, if you will—fosters and permits certain types of penetration by external forces. The logic of these external forces is usually left unexamined.

To oversimplify, dependency theory sets out from the standpoint of the dominant classes of the Third World facing the daunting economic presence of metropolitan states, international financial agencies, and multinational corporations; it begins with the international economic order and external ties and proceeds to derive class structure. "Modes of production" analysis, on the other hand, begins with class structure and moves outward to the world economic system. Strategies for contesting underdevelopment suggested by the first framework involve the manipulation of external forces in the pursuit of nationalist goals, in particular capitalist growth (as in Brazil), whereas the second framework points toward the transformation of the class structure and the pursuit of socialist goals as a precondition for development (as in Cuba). Obviously neither perspective can ignore the other, but they do point to different priorities in development.

What role do political relations among states play in these two frameworks? While neither dependency theory nor modes of production analysis reduces the political to the economic, both implicitly claim that international economic forces are for the most part sufficient to guarantee capitalism's dominance in the periphery. This is not to say that political interventions do not take place or that they are unimportant, but that capitalism is increasingly able to reproduce itself without extraeconomic force, without forms of external and direct political domination, such as colonialism. This is the implication of Colin Leys's "neocolonialism" and Cardoso and Faletto's "internalization of external interests." It is as if imperialism had accomplished its task and we are now witnessing, for the first time, capitalism as a truly international phenomenon. Bill Warren's *Imperialism: Pioneer of Capitalism* (1980) captures and develops this inversion of

Burawoy

Lenin's *Imperialism: The Highest Stage of Capitalism*. But Warren's position is too extreme. We know that state-to-state relations are critical in maintaining and transforming the international economic system (Block 1977a). How does one examine these relations from a Marxist perspective?

In her paper on the international food order, Harriet Friedmann offers an original strategy for studying international relations from the standpoint of relations among modes of production (see also Friedmann 1978). Setting out from a discussion of the class forces within the United States, she highlights the significance of political relations among states for the reproduction of capitalism on a world scale and for class structure in Third World countries. Tracing the production and distribution of wheat surpluses, she shows how state-to-state relations have been critical in uprooting peasantries of the Third World and then allowing them to starve in the cities. The tragic story begins with farmers in the United States successfully campaigning for agricultural subsidies. This led to rising food surpluses which, in the 1950s and 1960s, were put to use in the form of "aid" to the Third World. Unable to compete with the importation of massive supplies of cheap wheat, peasants in the recipient countries were pushed out of basic food production, accelerating processes of proletarianization, overurbanization, unemployment, and the devastation of indigenous agriculture. When food aid diminished in the 1970s, due in part to geopolitical forces but also to the declining influence of the farmers' lobby in the United States, countries that had become dependent on cheap food found themselves increasingly impoverished. Friedmann underlines the continuing importance of political relations among states in generating, albeit unintentionally, reservoirs of cheap labor which were attractive to capital migrating from central countries. Just as the political realm cannot be reduced to economics at the level of the nation-state, political relations among states cannot be reduced to the international division of labor.

STATE SOCIALISM

Having reached the logic of world power, we can now retrace our steps. We began by restoring Marx's analysis of capitalism to the context of his times, highlighting those features of 19th-century Britain which differentiated it from other countries and contributed to its subsequent development. In remaining true to Marx's method, we have continued to take the relations of production, their conditions of existence, and their dynamics as our point of departure. In explaining variations in the form and regulation of the capitalist labor process we were led to the critical role of the state. We proceeded to examine the state itself as performing specific functions, on the one hand, and as a contradictory unity of specific institutions, on the other. Understanding the development of the labor process and of the state

S24

is still not a sufficient basis for the analysis of the dynamics of class structure. We must also grasp the changing international division of labor and the role of different peripheral societies in the global economic system. Finally, we suggested that, although international political relations could not be reduced to—indeed, often reshaped—economic relations within and between nations, nevertheless class factors remain an essential component of the explanation of the genesis and reproduction of state-to-state relations.

Throughout, I have emphasized the capitalist character of the labor process, the state, the class structure, and indeed the world system. There is a presumption, all too rarely confronted within Marxism, that somehow things are different (and "better") under socialism. Too easily Marxists compare the realities of capitalism with an unexamined and often unstated ideal notion of socialism. While such a "false" comparison provides a basis for critique, central to any Marxist analysis, it does not come to terms with the limits of the possible. Perhaps one of the greatest disservices to the Marxist tradition rendered by Marx and Engels was the disparagement of the construction and examination of "utopias," the study of the meaning and possibility of socialism as well as the variety of forms it could assume.[11]

Equally important, but almost as rare, is the examination of existing state-socialist societies as a basis for what could be and an illumination of what is capitalist about capitalism. Notwithstanding the debates among socialists in the 1930s, Marxism has been reluctant to confront what Alvin Gouldner calls its "nightmare": that the abolition of private property is not the "basis of a new emancipation but of a new, many times worse, domination" (1980, p. 382). When Marxists have examined such societies, they have too often been concerned with explaining them away as an aberration, a product of hostile international forces, the underdevelopment of the forces of production, the legacy of the Asiatic mode of production, or the megalomania of unscrupulous leaders. They have too easily presented the Soviet Union and Eastern Europe as an exception or deviation (e.g., a "deformed workers' state") from some unelaborated ideal, rather than examining their distinctive class structure, form of state, and so forth.

Exceptional in this regard is Ivan Szelenyi's paper, which approaches the study of class societies along two dimensions: the mode of appropriation of surplus and the mode through which that appropriation is legitimated. In capitalism, private property is the basis of both appropriation and legitimation. In state socialism, surplus is appropriated and distributed by central state apparatuses, acting in the name of a scientifically determined collective interest. Whereas in the one society capitalists, as expropriators of surplus, form the dominant class, in the other intellectuals emerge as a dominant class, based on their monopoly of scientific knowledge "neces-

[11] For a recent contribution to this issue, see the important article of Carmen Sirianni (1981).

sary" for the rational—that is, purposive—redistribution of goods and services. Intellectuals become the natural executors of a substantive rationality.

Szelenyi refers to intellectuals as being on the road to class power, since they are engaged in struggle against a "political elite" which captured state power in the period of socialist primitive accumulation, more commonly known as Stalinism. Although the dynamics of state-socialist societies can be seen in terms of the struggles between the political elite and the intelligentsia, these are shaped by the more fundamental struggles between the dominant class of planners and the subordinate class of direct producers. Here Braverman's analytical distinction between conception and execution is projected from the economic plane onto the political and ideological planes, where it expresses two opposed principles of legitimation and surplus appropriation. Direct producers claim control over what they produce, opposing the planners' logic of rational redistribution with the principle of workers' self-management. Szelenyi speculates about the institutionalization of the struggle between these two principles, about the possibility of a socialism with two antagonistic classes.

The contrast between advanced capitalist and state-socialist societies becomes clear. In the former, intellectuals are an intermediary class, holding one of Wright's contradictory class locations. They are divided in their allegiance between the dominant and subordinate classes, while at the same time advancing their own professional interests. Daniel Bell's claim that they are fast becoming a more significant group, as the axial principle of the postindustrial society moves from property to knowledge, is perhaps more descriptive of state socialism than of advanced capitalism. This is not to say that planning and technocrats are not becoming more important in capitalist societies, but that they emerge to fill "functional gaps" created by the irrationalities of the market—just as, in state-socialist societies, market institutions blossom to compensate for the irrationalities of planning.[12]

While the reexamination of 19th-century Britain illuminated the first paradox of Marxism—that revolutionary working classes emerged in backward rather than advanced societies—the delineation of the specificity of state-socialist societies sheds light on the second paradox of Marxism: that proletarian revolutions are likely to develop as anti-Marxist movements and in those societies whose leaders already claim to be socialist. Here a proletarian class consciousness develops, both from the dominant ideology, which distinguishes planners from direct producers, and as a result of the penetration of the state, in the form of the party, trade union, and state managers, into the place of production. Economic struggles, whatever their

[12] As recent events in Poland demonstrate, we still know very little about either the relations among the Soviet Union and East European countries or the relations among the military, the secret police, the party, and government bureaucracies.

intent, are immediately political and express demands for self-regulation by direct producers. Furthermore, as Szelenyi argues, the working class can begin to wage collective struggles with the emergence of civil society. And this, of course, happened in Poland, in part because of the institutional strength of the Church, which nurtured and protected socialist but nevertheless anti-Marxist nationalist movements.

But what does this mean for Marxism? Is it then the false consciousness of an intellectual class, a class that presents its own interest as a universal interest, that pursues its own interests in the name of the proletariat?[13] To be sure, Marxism has been appropriated by the dominant classes of the Soviet Union and Eastern Europe to justify a form of bureaucratic despotism. Insofar as the working class or intellectuals in those countries develop a class consciousness, it is more than likely to be anti-Marxist.[14] Can the same be said of other socialist countries? Does Marxism retain its critical function in Cuba, or in Yugoslavia? Does it provide a terrain upon which subordinate classes can effectively wage struggles on their own behalf? Clearly, Marxism has different political implications in different social and historical contexts. It is precisely because intellectuals in advanced capitalist countries are not on the road to class power that Marxism is able to retain its critical moment, posing alternatives to the existing order.

FOR AN AMERICAN MARXISM?

What are the prospects for an American Marxism? Is the current renewal just another flash in the pan which, as in the 1930s, will evoke only a transient commitment from intellectuals? At the beginning of this essay, I suggested that the recent surge of interest originated in the New Left, the internationalization of Marxism, and the development of an institutional basis, mainly around journals. None of these forces points to a sustained

[13] In calling for a general emancipation in which everyone becomes an intellectual, Rudolf Bahro, a dissident East German Marxist, writes: "The workers—individual exceptions apart—were never Marxist in the strict sense. Marxism is a theory based on the existence of the working class, but it is not the theory of the working class. It was always Left intellectuals who found themselves in a position to understand Marxism as a whole" (1978, p. 197). Szelenyi (1980) regards Bahro's call for the renewal of the party as another attempt by intellectuals to present their own particular interests as the interests of all. Where Bahro denies the existence of a "working class" in Eastern Europe, Szelenyi insists on its existence as a center of opposition.

[14] In the post-1956 thaw, dissenting Marxists in Eastern Europe appealed to the writings of the young Marx against the repressive practices of Stalinism. But it was not long before Communist parties had turned Marxist humanism into official slogans and undercut any oppositional potential. For both workers and intellectuals, Marxism is now too tainted and its dissemination too effectively controlled to be used as a basis for resistance or a call for emancipation.

commitment, as the New Left becomes a memory cut off from the present, as Marxism fragments internationally, collapsing in many Western European countries, and as journals face severe financial difficulties.

But there are countertendencies rooted in the very changes I have been describing: the transformation of the labor process, the changing functions of the state, the new international division of labor, a reorganization of international political relations, and the recomposition of the U.S. class structure—and (although this is not dealt with in this volume) changing relations between men and women, both within and outside the family. Moreover, the university lies at the intersection of many of these changes, making their analysis that much more urgent and immediate to the academic.

Just as sociology responded to the call of the immediate postwar era, Marxism has now taken the baton, trying to piece together a coherent analysis of these interconnected transitions. The optimistic sociology of the 1950s followed the defeat of fascism in a heroic if tragic war. It emerged together with the unquestioned supremacy of the United States in the international order, the Cold War, a period of economic growth and widespread confidence in the superiority of parliamentary democracy and "civic culture." Marxism is more consonant with the present climate of pessimism, following defeat in an ignominious war and the exposure of deceit and corruption in the highest circles of government. It is more consonant with the continuing economic decline and rising unemployment which have prompted the dismantling of what existed of the welfare state, with the continual challenges to the United States' international domination, which have prompted renewed aggression against foreign powers and the resurrection of the Communist scare, so that nuclear holocaust once more hangs over our heads. This scenario fits only too well Marxism's assessment of capitalism as beset with deep-seated tendencies toward economic crisis, political irrationality, and escalating global conflict.

In the final analysis, Marxism can never become anything more than a subordinate presence within the university if it is to retain its oppositional character. But that presence may not only push Marxism in new directions but may also be necessary for the vitality of sociology. At a time when the classical inspirations of sociology are beginning to wilt under technocratic impulses and pressure to be "useful," the renewal of an open, always provisional, empirically rooted Marxism could do much to animate debate over those basic issues at the heart of the sociological tradition. As Alvin Gouldner once wrote, Marxism and sociology are like Siamese twins: "The demise of the one presages the demise of the other. They have a common destiny not *despite* the fact that they have developed in dialectical opposition but precisely *because* of it" (1973, p. 401).

REFERENCES

Amin, Samir. 1976. *Unequal Development*. New York: Monthly Review Press.
Anderson, Perry. 1976. *Considerations on Western Marxism*. London: New Left Books.
Arato, Andrew, and Paul Breines. 1979. *The Young Lukács and the Origins of Western Marxism*. New York: Seabury.
Bahro, Rudolf. 1978. *The Alternative in Eastern Europe*. London: New Left Books.
Baran, Paul. 1957. *The Political Economy of Growth*. New York: Monthly Review Press.
Baran, Paul, and Paul Sweezy. 1966. *Monopoly Capital*. New York: Monthly Review Press.
Bell, Daniel. 1960. *The End of Ideology*. New York: Free Press.
———. 1973. *The Coming of Post-industrial Society*. New York: Basic.
———. 1981. "First Love and Early Sorrows." *Partisan Review* 48 (4): 532–51.
Block, Fred. 1977*a*. *The Origins of International Economic Disorder*. Berkeley and Los Angeles: University of California Press.
———. 1977*b*. "The Ruling Class Does Not Rule." *Socialist Review* 33:6–28.
Bonnell, Victoria. In press. *Roots of Rebellion: Workers' Politics and Organizations in St. Petersburg and Moscow, 1900–1914*. Berkeley and Los Angeles: University of California Press.
Braverman, Harry. 1974. *Labor and Monopoly Capital: The Degradation of Work in the Twentieth Century*. New York: Monthly Review Press.
Cardoso, Fernando, and Enzo Faletto. 1979. *Dependency and Development in Latin America,* translated by Marjory M. Urquidi. Berkeley and Los Angeles: University of California Press.
Castells, Manuel. 1979. *The Economic Crisis and American Society*. Princeton, N.J.: Princeton University Press.
Claudin, Fernando. 1978. *Eurocommunism and Socialism*. London: New Left Books.
Edwards, Richard C. 1979. *Contested Terrain*. New York: Basic.
Foster-Carter, Aidan. 1978. "The Modes of Production Controversy." *New Left Review* 107 (January–February): 47–78.
Frank, André Gunder. 1969. *Latin America: Underdevelopment or Revolution*. New York: Monthly Review Press.
Friedmann, Harriet. 1978. "World Market, State and Family Farm: Social Bases of Household Production in the Era of Wage Labor." *Comparative Studies in Society and History* 20 (4): 545–86.
Fröbel, Folker, Jürgen Heinrichs, and Otto Kreye. 1980. *The New International Division of Labour*. Cambridge: Cambridge University Press.
Gouldner, Alvin. 1973. *For Sociology*. New York: Basic.
———. 1980. *The Two Marxisms*. New York: Seabury.
Gramsci, Antonio. 1971. *Selections from the Prison Notebooks,* translated by Quintin Hoare and Geoffrey N. Smith. New York: International Publishers.
Habermas, Jürgen. 1975. *Legitimation Crisis,* translated by Thomas McCarthy. Boston: Beacon.
Holloway, John, and Sal Picciotto, eds. 1978. *State and Capital*. London: Arnold.
Jacoby, Russell. 1981. *The Dialectic of Defeat*. Cambridge: Cambridge University Press.
Johnson, Robert. 1979. *Peasant and Proletarian*. New Brunswick, N.J.: Rutgers University Press.
Joseph, Paul. 1982. "From MAD to NUTs: The Growing Danger of Nuclear War." *Socialist Review* 61 (January–February): 13–56.
Joyce, Patrick. 1980. *Work, Society and Politics*. New Brunswick, N.J.: Rutgers University Press.
Koenker, Diane. 1981. *Moscow Workers and the 1917 Revolution*. Princeton, N.J.: Princeton University Press.
Larson, Magali Sarfatti. 1977. *The Rise of Professionalism*. Berkeley and Los Angeles: University of California Press.

Leys, Colin. 1978. "Capital Accumulation, Class Formation and Dependency: The Significance of the Kenyan Case." Pp. 241–66 in *Socialist Register, 1978,* edited by Ralph Miliband and John Saville. London: Merlin.

Lindblom, Charles. 1977. *Politics and Markets.* New York: Basic.

Lipset, Seymour Martin. 1962. "Introduction." Pp. 15–39 in *Political Parties,* by Robert Michels. New York: Free Press.

————. 1981. "Whatever Happened to the Proletariat?" *Encounter* 65 (June): 18–34.

Mandel, Ernest. 1975. *Late Capitalism,* translated by Joris De Bres. London: New Left Books.

Marx, Karl. 1967. *Capital.* Vol. 1. New York: International Publishers.

Merleau-Ponty, Maurice. 1973. *Adventures of the Dialectic,* translated by Joseph J. Bien. Evanston, Ill.: Northwestern University Press.

Moore, Barrington, Jr. 1966. *Social Origins of Dictatorship and Democracy: Lord and Peasant in the Making of the Modern World.* Boston: Beacon.

O'Connor, James. 1973. *The Fiscal Crisis of the State.* New York: St. Martin's.

Offe, Claus, and Volke Ronge. 1975. "Theses on the Theory of the State." *New German Critique* 6 (Fall): 137–47.

Parsons, Talcott. 1937. *The Structure of Social Action.* New York: McGraw-Hill.

————. 1967. *Sociological Theory and Modern Society.* New York: Free Press.

Plotke, David. 1980. "The United States in Transition: Toward a New Order?" *Socialist Review* 54 (November–December): 71–124.

————. 1981. "The Politics of Transition." *Socialist Review* 55 (January–February): 21–72.

————. 1982. "Marxism, New Movements and Modernization in the United States, 1960–1980." Mimeographed. Berkeley: University of California, Berkeley, Department of Sociology.

Portes, Alejandro, and John Walton. 1981. *Labor, Class and the International System.* New York and London: Academic Press.

Poulantzas, Nicos. 1973. *Political Power and Social Classes,* translated by Timothy O'Hagan. London: New Left Books.

————. 1978. *State, Power, Socialism.* London: New Left Books.

Sirianni, Carmen. 1981. "Production and Power in a Classless Society: A Critical Analysis of the Utopian Dimension of Marxist Theory." *Socialist Review* 59:38–82.

Skocpol, Theda. 1980. "Political Response to Capitalist Crisis: Neo-Marxist Theories of the State and the Case of the New Deal." *Politics and Society* 10 (2): 155–202.

Stedman Jones, Gareth. 1975. "Class Struggle and the Industrial Revolution." *New Left Review* 90 (March–April): 35–70.

Stephens, John. 1979. *The Transition from Capitalism to Socialism.* London: Macmillan.

Szelenyi, Ivan. 1980. "Whose Alternative?" *New German Critique* 20:117–34.

Taylor, John. 1979. *From Modes of Production to Modernization.* London: Macmillan.

Thompson, E. P. 1963. *The Making of the English Working Class.* London: Gollancz.

————. 1978. *The Poverty of Theory and Other Essays.* London: Merlin.

Trotsky, Leon. 1969. *The Permanent Revolution and Results and Prospects.* New York: Pathfinder.

Wallerstein, Immanuel. 1974. *The Modern World-System: Capitalist Agriculture and the Origins of the European World-Economy in the Sixteenth Century.* London and New York: Academic Press.

Warren, Bill. 1980. *Imperialism: Pioneer of Capitalism.* London: New Left Books.

Wiener, Jonathan. 1978. *Social Origins of the New South.* Baton Rouge and London: Louisiana State University Press.

Wolpe, Harold, ed. 1979. *The Articulation of Modes of Production.* London: Routledge & Kegan Paul.

The Division between Mental and Manual Labor: Artisan Education in Science in Nineteenth-Century Britain[1]

Julia Wrigley
University of California, Los Angeles

Using historical data, this paper examines the relation between changes in production and changes in the forms and ideologies of education through specific analysis of the origin and decline of mechanics' institutes in Great Britain. Mechanics' institutes were founded by artisans and capitalists ca. 1820 with the aim of teaching artisans natural science. With the focus on skilled engineering workers in Manchester, the paper argues that, as the autonomy and work skills of these and other workers declined, the goal of a broad science education for artisans was replaced by that of a narrower technical education. The paper concludes with a discussion of contemporary implications.

In the last decade, sociologists and historians have focused attention on the way in which the work process has been shaped by the desire of corporate managers for control over both the intellectual and the practical aspects of production. Braverman (1974), Noble (1977), Aronowitz (1973), Kraft (1977), and Marglin (1974) in the United States and Cooley (n.d.) in Great Britain have analyzed the decline of skilled workers' control over production and their loss of unique work talents. Instead of skills inhering in the persons and abilities of individual workers, under developed capitalism control and intellectual direction shifted to the hands of managers and specially trained professional employees, in spite of occasionally successful efforts by skilled workers and by unions to retard the shift of control away from the shop floor (Burawoy 1978).

Educational systems in developed capitalist countries are so basically linked to class-sorting mechanisms and means of socialization that major shifts in the form of production are likely ultimately to find expression in changed forms of schooling. The links between the system of production

[1] I would like to thank Edna Bonacich, Eric Chester, Nora Hamilton, and Barbara Laslett for their comments on a previous draft of this article. I would also like to thank Lewis Coser, who commented on the paper when it was presented at the 1980 meetings of the Pacific Sociological Association. Requests for reprints should be sent to Julia Wrigley, School of Education, Moore Hall, University of California, Los Angeles, California 90024.

and the forms of education of a given society are not direct but are complex (Ben-David 1963). The unique history of each country, the pattern of religious controversy, the role of the state, the degree of working-class cohesion, all influence the shape of national educational systems and lead to variations among countries. It is fruitful, however, as Bowles and Gintis have argued (1976), to examine the ways in which changing forms of production have contributed to broad changes in the way in which people are prepared for jobs through schooling and in how education contributes to the stability or alteration of the class structure of the society.

I will suggest that examining the history of one set of working-class educational institutions in mid-19th-century Great Britain can contribute to our understanding of the way in which forms and ideologies of schooling are influenced by changes in the production process. In particular, few occupational groups suffered changes so radical as those experienced by skilled craft workers in the process of production. The mode of education that they received and the form of education considered appropriate for them therefore could be expected to have undergone some corresponding changes. In Britain in the early 1800s coalitions of artisans and capitalists established mechanics' institutes in hundreds of industrial cities and towns. These institutes were designed to teach artisans not specific skills but, rather, the sciences underlying their trades. The institutes faced a variety of obstacles in attempting to teach workers science and were in the main not very successful in reaching this goal, although some left lasting institutional legacies as they evolved into technical colleges. The striking aspect of their history, however, is the boldness of their initial aims as their founders proclaimed the intent to break down the barriers between mental and manual labor.

By the last third of the 19th century, government and private educational policymakers had largely abandoned the aim of teaching manual workers science. Instead, in both government forums and general writings, they urged that Britain concentrate on teaching managers and foremen scientific principles, while teaching manual workers only a limited range of technical skills. I will argue that, although later in British history access to schooling became less class stratified (Hurn 1978, p. 94), the sense of the class stratification of knowledge increased.

The decline of the mechanics' institutes, and, even more significantly, the failure in Britain to attempt again to educate manual workers in so sweeping a manner, must be understood in light of capitalists' efforts to undercut their reliance on craft skills through increased specialization and the introduction of new forms of self-acting machinery. By the time of the first major state intervention in education in Britain, in the 1870s, many types of craft workers had already suffered a radical diminution of their skills and independence (Yeo and Thompson 1971). The routinization of work at the bottom end of the scale made it less clear there was any economic point to workers' receiving scientific education; and, further, the development of science itself made it evident that intensive formal training was necessary in order for them fully to grasp scientific concepts. Even as levels of formal education rose, the ambition to teach workers intellectual principles relating to their work diminished.

It is impossible to convey a sense of the many and complex changes in occupational standing and skill that occurred during the Industrial Revolution. In order to be as historically specific as possible in examining changes in education in relation to changes in production, I will concentrate on examining the role of those craftsmen who worked on machinery, with particular emphasis on changes in the role of engineering workers in Manchester, England's major early center of industrial production (Vigier 1970, p. 92). The first section of the paper will review the national movement to establish mechanics' institutes; the second section will consider the founding of the Manchester Mechanics' Institution in the light of changes in the work situation of skilled craftsmen in that city; the third section will analyze political and economic reasons for the artisan interest in science; and the fourth section will examine the transformation in the educational mission of the Manchester Mechanics' Institution as a counterpart of reductions in the work autonomy of skilled machinery workers. The paper will conclude with a discussion of what the experience of the mechanics' institutes can tell us about the failure of schooling policies in contemporary capitalist countries.

THE FOUNDING OF THE MECHANICS' INSTITUTES

In England the state did not assume direct responsibility for education for more than 100 years after the onset of the Industrial Revolution. The absence of state responsibility for education until the passage of the Education Act of 1870, which provided for state aid to elementary education, stemmed from a powerful tradition of laissez-faire government, entrenched aristocratic fear of popular schooling, and controversies between religious groups (Musgrave 1968). In most other developed Western European nations, such as Germany, the state exhibited a more aggressive role in both the economic and educational spheres, and these countries moved earlier than England to establish centralized school systems.

In this political climate, more than half of the population was illiterate in 1841 (Musgrave 1968, pp. 8–9). Skilled workers usually had the money for school fees for their children, but unskilled laborers generally had to depend on charity schools. While at the national level middle-class advocates of expanded education, led by such figures as Jeremy Bentham and the Whig politician Henry Brougham, were failing to break the political control of the conservative bloc, in many of the industrial centers of Britain movements began in the early 1800s for education for adult workers (Simon 1960, pp. 151–52).

The specific impetus for the founding of the first mechanics' institute arose because of connections between experimental scientists and those artisans who worked as scientific instrument makers. In 1800 George Birkbeck, a professor of chemistry and natural philosophy at the Andersonian Institution in Glasgow, visited craftsmen in their workshops to explain what type of scientific apparatus he needed. He found that the workers were highly curious about the instruments they were making; during a visit to a tinworker's shop where a centrifugal pump was being built, Birkbeck was surrounded by men asking about the uses of the pump. Birkbeck later recalled that he asked himself, "Why are these minds left without the means of obtaining that knowledge which they so urgently desire; and why are the avenues of science barred against them because they are poor?" (quoted in Hudson 1851, p. 33). He decided to establish a series of lecture courses on science for artisans; he declared that his aim was to give lectures that would be "abounding with experiments, and conducted with the greatest simplicity and familiarity of illustration, solely for persons engaged in the practical exercise of the mechanic arts." The lectures quickly began drawing large and attentive crowds of more than 500 workmen, with others turned away at the door because of lack of space (p. 35).

After a lag, mechanics' institutes spread rapidly in the 1820s, particularly in the industrial areas of Lancashire and Yorkshire, where, in one year, more than 20 mechanics' institutes were founded (Kirby 1974, p. 87). Almost all of the manufacturing centers of Britain could claim an institute by the 1830s, and many of the smaller towns also competed to establish them (Dircks 1841, p. 3). By the 1850s a contemporary historian of the institutes, J. W. Hudson, reported that there were complete records of 677 institutes in Britain with 116,076 subscribing members. The institute libraries possessed roughly 758,016 books; in 1850, there were more than 2 million book issues to library subscribers (Hudson 1851, p. vii). Evening classes and lectures were the centerpiece of the program. By 1850 there were approximately 18,000 students enrolled in the classes, with many thousands more having attended lectures. The courses covered a range of topics, but the central purpose of the institutes was the teaching of science through lectures and courses on such topics as chemistry, natural philosophy, and the laws of motion.

SKILLED WORKERS IN MANCHESTER

The founding of the Manchester Mechanics' Institution took place as part of the national wave of interest in science education for artisans. In April 1824 a group of Manchester's leading capitalists met to lay plans for the founding of the Manchester institute. Most of the capitalists involved in its establishment came from Manchester's two leading industries, machine making and cotton. They included Sir Benjamin Heywood, a banker with strong ties to engineering firms; William Fairbairn, the founder of the famous machinery firm of Fairbairn and Lillie; Richard Roberts, noted for his invention of the self-acting mule, patented in 1825, and chief partner in the machinery firm of Sharp Roberts and Company; William Williams, of the large engineering firm of Peel and Williams; and cotton manufacturers George William Wood, George Philips, Joseph Brotherton, and H. H. Birley. The group also included members of the textile firms of McConnel and Kennedy and of Adam and George Murray, firms that were also important engineering companies (Tylecote 1974, p. 56; Kirby 1974, p. 87). These employers were primarily Dissenters (several were Unitarians), and politically most were Whigs (Kargon 1977, p. 20).

In other cities, conservative employers and religious leaders had sometimes denounced mechanics' institutes for giving workers ideas above their station (Grinfeld 1825), although in most places mechanics' institutes received some financial support from capitalists. Artisans themselves sometimes took the initiative in establishing institutes over conservative opposition. In early 19th-century Britain, working-class education remained controversial within the country's dominant classes. In Manchester, however, the pioneer city of the Industrial Revolution and a prime center of economic growth and technical progress, capitalists overrode ideological objections to the institutes from within their own class; the founders of the mechanics' institute told detractors that the institute would foster Manchester's technical growth and competitive position (Heywood 1843, pp. 32–33). While taking care to organize the mechanics' institute so as to keep control in their own hands (only financial donors could vote for the board of directors), they were sufficiently committed to the idea of artisan education in science to raise £7,000 for the erection of the largest institute building in Britain. The building contained a lecture hall seating 1,000, a chemical laboratory, classrooms, and a library (p. 23).

Manchester's capitalists cannot be said to have supported the mechanics' institute out of general social progressivism. One of its founders, for example, was H. H. Birley, a cotton manufacturer who had been captain of the yeomanry that had killed demonstrating workers at Peterloo in Manchester in 1819 (Tylecote 1974, p. 58); others, such as George William Wood, another cotton manufacturer, were instrumental in barring workers from suffrage in local elections and in bringing actions against local trade union leaders (Kirby 1974, p. 88). Rather, institute supporters such as Sir Benjamin Heywood, its president, emphasized that artisans could make economic contributions if they received science instruction to go along with the work skills which they learned through experience and apprenticeship.

Heywood (1825, p. 4) pointed out that cotton manufacture, still in its infancy, accounted for one-half of England's trade, but that for this industry to continue making rapid technical progress, it required that workmen be trained to understand the principles behind their work. If an artisan both observed carefully and understood some science, he would "be in the sure way of making improvements in the trade" (p. 5). Heywood declared that there was a strong connection between the principles of science and manual labor, but he warned that Manchester, with its workmen who were "unrivalled for their industry and skill" and its "unequalled machinery," could not hold foreign competitors at bay unless workmen were trained to unite their practical observation and experience with a developed scientific understanding. Or, as the vice-president of the institute, John Davies, argued, it was by "enlightening the mechanics" that Manchester would "keep in advance" of its competitors (quoted in Kargon 1977, p. 24).

The early support of Manchester's large employers for the mechanics' institute arose, I will argue, out of awareness of particular reliance on craft workers' skills in the city's major industries. It also reflected a sentiment held by some national political leaders, who at this stage of early capitalism stressed that Britain's economic well-being depended critically on the skills and the scientifically oriented education of its artisans. Henry Brougham, for example, lord chancellor under the Whigs, actively propagandized for artisan education with the claim that "those discoveries immediately connected with experiment and observation" were most likely to be made by artisans who were at the same time instructed in general principles. If artisans were well educated, "the chances of discovery, both in the arts and in science itself" were greatly multiplied (Brougham 1825, p. 10). Brougham's views were not peculiar to him but reflected a widespread conviction that artisans were central to economic progress (see Playfair 1870). One indicator of the importance that the government placed on the mechanical knowledge of the workmen is that until as late as 1825 it was illegal to enlist artisans for employment in other countries (Ashby 1959).[2] Britain's advanced technology was thought to inhere in the persons and knowledge of the artisans themselves, even as capitalists competed to develop new machinery that would reduce their reliance on artisan skills (Burgess 1969).

The founders of the Manchester Mechanics' Institution not surprisingly emphasized the contributions that could be made by workers in trades related to machine making and the production of cotton, the industries from which they themselves were largely drawn. John Davies explained in a fund-raising appeal to the public that artisans learned certain basic technical principles in the course of their work which could then be ex-

[2] In this connection, see Scoville (1952) for a discussion of the way in which Huguenot craftsmen diffused technical innovations throughout Europe by their migrations after they were evicted from France in 1685.

tended. The purpose of the institute was to "impart to the operative classes, upon easy terms and in a popular manner, a knowledge of the general principles which are illustrated in their daily occupations." In particular, the institute was intended to "give to the mechanic some knowledge of the laws which regulate the construction and motion of Machinery; and to the Dyer, Printer and Bleacher [of cloth], an acquaintance with those agencies and operations of Chemistry, which each of them witnesses . . . in the usual routine of his labour" (Davies 1831, p. 2). The "Preamble of the Manchester Mechanics' Institution" made it clear that the goal was not to teach specific trades or particular work skills, but as there was "no Art, which does not depend, more or less on scientific principles," that to "search what these are, and to point out their practical applications . . . will form the chief objects of this Institution" (quoted in Hudson 1851, p. 56).

The emphasis of the employers on skilled workers in the expanding textile and machine-making industries was practical. The Industrial Revolution had radically changed the character of Manchester's work force and had led to the creation of a stratum of highly skilled craftsmen who were experts in machine design and repair and who, along with the fine cotton spinners and machine printers in the cotton factories, were the elite of Manchester's working class (Cruikshank 1974, p. 135). The first cotton factory was not built in Manchester until 1789, but by 1821 there were 66 textile factories and the city had established its manufacturing dominance (Vigier 1970, p. 92). The development of factory production led to the creation of new engineering occupations. The Manchester and Salford directories for the latter part of the 19th century reveal a dramatic increase in the number of machine-making firms (Kargon 1977, p. 3). These firms made not only textile machinery, but also waterwheels, steam engines, boilers, locomotives, and machine tools (Musson and Robinson 1969, p. 475). From the ranks of clockmakers, millwrights, smiths, and woodworkers was emerging a more specialized group of workmen who, using such tools as lathes, wheel-cutting engines, chisels, files, and drills, were employed in the new iron-founding and machine-making firms (Cardwell 1974, p. 5).

These workers were able to demand and exercise a good deal of shop-floor autonomy due to their employers' dependence on their skills and mechanical aptitude. William Fairbairn, one of the founders of the Mechanics' Institution, said of the machine workers that "the men were Masters" because of the difficulty of standardizing their work (quoted in Burgess 1969, p. 219). Nearly all operations had to be conducted by hand, which placed a premium on workers' experience and dexterity. Even such essential items as screws were not standardized; each firm varied in the number of threads per inch, and workers made screws through a hand process of chipping and filing (Pole 1877, pp. 45–46). Manchester's industrialists competed for highly skilled workers such as fitters, moulders, patternmakers, and platers

(Cruikshank 1974, p. 135); Manchester's opportunities for these workers outstripped those available to them even in London.

The skills of these workmen went beyond those of mere dexterity. In designing and modifying equipment, they had to have a grasp of mechanical problems and possible solutions. "Fitters" were required to try to bring understandardized parts into smooth working relation with each other, and this was a task that called for years of experience and mechanical knowledge. Even in the 18th century, workers engaged in machine making were noted for the breadth of their abilities. Fairbairn wrote that the typical millwright in the 1700s was generally "a fair arithmetician, knew something of geometry, levelling, and mensuration, and in some cases possessed a very competent knowledge of practical mechanics" (quoted in Pole 1877, p. 27). Heywood, referring later to Manchester's engineering workers, declared that the construction and repair of machinery "was a trade peculiarly calculated to call into action intelligence and skill" (1843, p. 31). In the 19th century, when capitalists and workmen first recognized the growing importance of science in contributing to technical progress, the workers engaged in machine-making trades, long perceived as the carriers of technical skills, were considered natural candidates for scientific instruction. The mechanics' institutes were supported by forward-looking capitalists, in spite of intraclass opposition, on the grounds that they might hasten economic growth and that, if properly controlled, the institutes would not pose a political threat but might, in fact, draw workers away from more dangerous kinds of political study (see Heywood 1843, pp. 33, 121).

SCIENCE AND POLITICS IN THE ARTISAN MOVEMENT

Artisans had an interest in learning science that arose both from a widely held conviction that science would bolster their political and economic power (Simon 1960, p. 199) and from a history of overlap between the work of artisans and scientists that encouraged them to believe that they could learn scientific principles. The artisans' goals in learning science differed sufficiently from those of capitalist donors to mechanics' institutes that conflict was inevitable (Thompson 1963, p. 744). These conflicts in turn helped to bring about the decline of the institutes. Both artisans and capitalists wanted to *use* science, in a sharp break with past attitudes, when science was considered essentially irrelevant to either politics or production (Kargon 1977, p. 29). The development of inventions such as the steam engine, considered the consummate marriage between science and craft skills, made evident the enormous practical effect of scientific ideas (Bernal 1954, p. 416). This spurred artisan activists to argue that the transition between science and technical skills was bridgeable and that scientific knowledge would help maintain and safeguard their distinctive place in production. And, on an ideological level, artisan political leaders believed that scientific knowledge would help sweep away traditional and obscurantist ways of viewing the world. For this reason, science divorced from politics—in fact, counterposed to it, as the manufacturers who donated to the mechanics' institutes wished it to be—was unpalatable to the artisans who participated in the political movements of the early 19th century. To the more ideological artisan leaders, scientific and political knowledge appeared as two sides of the same coin (see Engels [1958, p. 272] for comments on the desire of Manchester's workers for an untrammeled scientific education).

Artisans had some grounds for believing that there was a connection between the way in which they worked and the way in which scientists operated experimentally. Science developed in part on the basis of craft knowledge (Bernal 1939, p. 20), particularly where advances came through a slow accretion of knowledge, as in chemistry. Some of Britain's preeminent early scientists, such as Robert Boyle, the chemist, and Sir Francis Bacon, argued that natural philosophers had much to learn from artisans. Bacon promoted the idea of writing a comprehensive "history of Trades" that would explore the "mysteries and seacrets [sic]" of each craft. This history would cover all of the trades in detail and would allow philosophers to reach conclusions based on a fund of knowledge. Bacon believed that the trades that were of the most relevance to natural philosophers were those in which the composition of materials was altered in the course of working them. He wrote that when nature "by the hand and art of man . . . is forced out of her natural state, and squeezed and moulded" (quoted in Houghton 1941, p. 36), scientists could gain the best idea of the fundamental properties of substances. Thus, chemistry, dyeing, agriculture, the manufacture of glass, enamel, sugar, gunpowder, paper, and the like were of the most relevance to philosophers, while the trades that consisted "principally in the subtle motion of the hands or instruments" (such as weaving or carpentry) were of less use, although, he emphasized, these too were "by no means to be neglected" (p. 38).

The Royal Society adopted the plan of writing the history of trades, and although the project eventually faltered, in the succeeding 200 years in which England was transformed into an industrial power, there were continuing links between scientists and artisans, of a sort that would later become very rare between intellectual and manual workers. Prominent scientists, for example, made an effort to write their works in language that would be comprehensible to craftsmen with little formal education. The Royal Society had early set a trend in this direction when it formally stated in the 1660s that it favored the use of "the Language of Artizans, Countrymen, and Merchants, before that of Wits, or Scholars" (quoted in Bernal 1954, p. 321). Joseph Black, the chemist whose researches into the quantitative science of heat helped to set off the pneumatic revolution in the late 18th century, deliberately wrote in a manner that would make his work understandable to artisans, according to his friend, the well-known Edinburgh professor of natural philosophy, John Robison. Robison declared that it was Dr. Black's "great aim to be understood completely by the most illiterate of his hearers" (Musson and Robinson 1969, p. 6).

Scientists also lectured directly to artisans. Gresham's College in London was noted in the 17th century for the number of well-known mathematicians on its faculty, whose instructions, according to John Woodward, professor of physic from 1693 to 1728, were "happily extended to mechanics, and even to the meanest artificers" (quoted in Musson and Robinson 1969, p. 14). In this light, it was not surprising that the great chemist, John Dalton, Manchester's premier scientific luminary, should have actively supported and lectured at the Manchester Mechanics' Institution (Dalton even contributed an article to the institute's publication, *Scientific Miscellany*) (Kargon 1977, p. 149). The integration of science into production helped to give a strong incentive to artisans to try to build up erratic and informal linkages between the technical and scientific worlds through a more systematic study of science. This was particularly the case because the rapid change of the Industrial Revolution rendered nearly all traditional work skills precarious (Thompson 1963, p. 244), even while their holders might enjoy accessions of prosperity and privilege, as did the Manchester machine workers.

England's radical artisan movement in the early 19th century adopted a view that emphasized the positive contributions that science could make in sweeping away prejudiced and outmoded religious beliefs. Robert Owen was particularly active in explaining the benefits that a scientific education could bring. Under his influence, artisans established "Halls of Science" in working-class districts of many towns. Other artisan political leaders, such as Richard Carlile, William Lovett, Henry Heatherington, and Thomas Paine, stressed that workers had to develop a rationalistic world view, and they polemicized for the teaching of science on the grounds that it would help to erode the power of repressive political systems (Simon 1960, p. 199). In "An Address to Men of Science," written while he was in the Dorchester jail for having printed Paine's *Age of Reason*, Carlile declared that "all tyranny, oppression and delusion have been founded upon the ignorance and credulity of mankind. Knowledge, scientific knowledge, is the power that must be opposed to these evils" (quoted in Simon 1960, p. 203).

Even those artisan activists who were passionately critical of the authoritarianism of the British government argued that increased knowledge would give workers greater political strength. In Manchester a self-educated fustian cutter named Rowland Detroisier became a leader of the city's artisans in the late 1820s. In urging the formation of worker-run mechanics' institutes, he wrote, "Unite—heart and hand unite—but let your union be to obtain that for yourselves and your children, the present want of which renders unions powerless—knowledge" (Detroisier 1831, p. 2).

The particular types of controversies that arose over the mechanics' institutes, given opposing views of science and its relation to politics, are best explored through an examination of the disputes that weakened the Manchester Mechanics' Institution.

SKILL DILUTION AND REDIRECTION OF SCIENTIFIC TRAINING

By the midpoint of the century, it was widely acknowledged that mechanics' institutes had generally failed in their major goal of teaching science to the working class (Hole 1853; Hudson 1851). The mechanics' institutes failed for political and organizational reasons. More fundamentally, however, the artisans' belief that knowledge of science would bolster their skill and power was being radically undercut by the continued development of industry and the narrowing of the artisan role. This helped lead to a lasting shift away from the idea of teaching workers scientific principles on any large scale. The conjunction of technical and ideological circumstances which had given rise to sweeping efforts to educate adult workers changed as the scientific enterprise, on the one hand, became far more highly structured and linked to the upper reaches of the academic world and as the role of craft workers in industry, on the other hand, became more restricted as power shifted within the workplace. The goal of making "the transition from manual to mental employment . . . easy, natural and healthy" (Dircks 1841, p. 4) ironically appeared more and not less visionary as the century proceeded and general levels of education rose.

The political and organizational difficulties of running mechanics' institutes were well illustrated in Manchester. Until about 1840, the institute's classes continued to deal primarily with scientific topics, including chemistry, mechanics, physics, astronomy, geology, and geography. Classes were also taught in mathematics and in mechanical and architectural drawing. One observer commented on his recollection of the institute's "large class-rooms crowded with silent and earnest pupils—so crowded indeed that the teachers had to refuse fresh admissions except as vacancies occurred" (Hole 1853, p. 33). Before 1833, there were usually roughly 500–600 subscribing members, each of whom paid a pound a year. Beginning in 1833, there were nearly always over 1,000 subscribing members each year (Hudson 1851, p. 129). In spite of these signs of progress, the institute's directors acknowledged that the body faced serious problems in holding the interest and loyalty of its working-class members.

In particular, the wealthy manufacturers who had founded the Manchester Mechanics' Institution refused during the first five years of its existence, in spite of strong pressure, to allow the subscribers any say in making policy. Their paternalistic control of every aspect of the institute's functioning was not viewed as simply an irritation, for it touched on basic political questions. The directors refused to allow any newspapers in the reading room on the grounds that party politics had no place in a mechanics' institute. A contemporary historian asserted that the controversy over the introduction of newspapers "tended, in no slight degree, to diminish the popularity and success of the Institution with that labouring class of the community they were so anxious to secure" (Hudson 1851, p. 130). John Davies, the vice-president of the institute, had said un-self-consciously that if the workers "came for instruction, they were, of course, incompetent to manage" (quoted in Tylecote 1957, p. 135).

Angered by this condescension, in 1829 a group of mechanics split off under the leadership of Rowland Detroisier to found the worker-controlled New Mechanics' Institution. Detroisier lectured on the need for artisans to control their own education, uniting scientific with political knowledge. "Numbers without union are powerless; union without knowledge is useless" (quoted in Kargon 1977, p. 23). The new institute succeeded in draining a considerable number of members from the old one; Benjamin Heywood referred to the old institute's "hopeless decline" in October 1830 (quoted in Kirby 1974, p. 95).

By 1835 the New Mechanics' Institution had itself gone into decline, caused by factional quarrels and Detroisier's departure for London. However, its founding had led to a democratization of the old Manchester Mechanics' Institution. Under the threat of competition, the board of directors voted in 1830 to allow five members chosen from the subscribers to join the board (Tylecote 1957, p. 137). This democratization led to increases in membership and a stabilization of the institute's fortunes. It did not stop the eventual founding of other competing bodies, though, including an Owenite "Temple of Science" in 1839 and several working-class "Lyceums" in 1838 (Hudson 1851, p. 136; Simon 1960, p. 236). The Manchester Mechanics' Institution remained the central educational body in spite of this competition, in part due to its greater resources.

The disputes over the control of the institute in Manchester were typical of those that occurred in other cities. In Glasgow, where the working class was particularly strong, the workers declared their intention to provide all of their own funding and thereby maintain full control; at Liverpool, this had been the practice from the beginning (Tylecote 1957, p. 17; Hudson 1851, p. 42). In other cities, such as London, long and hard-fought battles for the control of the institutes were one cause of their decline; in cases where artisans decisively lost control, this was likely to lead to an exodus from the institution.

The institutes also suffered, in Manchester and in other cities, from the fact that only a minority of workers had the educational background necessary to comprehend courses in science (Hole 1853). The lack of state-supported primary education meant that many workers were only minimally literate, and when these workers attended the institutes they could not follow the courses. As the need increasingly appeared to be not for a science-oriented education for a minority of skilled workers but for a broad floor of elementary education for the mass of the population, the curriculum of the institutes shifted in a more eclectic direction. Clerks who sought to fill gaps in their schooling enrolled in the institutes in increasing numbers, further encouraging the shift away from a scientific curriculum. In Manchester the institute introduced a greater range of courses in the early 1840s, and the shift coincided with a sharp drop in the enrollment of manual workers (Tylecote 1957, p. 149). The Manchester institute's directors also began belatedly to recognize the problems created by the long hours of even highly skilled workers (Heywood 1843, p. 56). In Manchester, for example, engineering workers generally worked at least $57\frac{1}{2}$ hours a week (Jefferys and Jefferys 1947, p. 34). Most other workers had hours that were considerably longer, which made it exceedingly difficult for them to remain alert for evening classes. This realization did not, however, lead employers who supported the institute to favor shorter hours (Tylecote 1957, pp. 253–54; see also Simon 1960, pp. 223–24).

More basic than the political and organizational problems that led to the decline of the mechanics' institutes was a change in the nature of artisans' work roles that led to an ideological shift away from the idea of instructing workers in science. The experience of skilled machinery workers in Manchester and its environs exhibits in a sharp form what was a more general process. During the period from 1830 to 1850 machinery workers suffered a major set of political and shop-floor defeats (Burgess 1969, p. 222; Foster 1974). The mechanization of weaving in the late 1820s led to a dramatic rise in textile output, which in turn meant that the demand for machine products for the textile industry increased. Large new engineering firms emerged that had the resources to develop standardized forms of machine production, whether the item produced was intended for the textile industry or for a locomotive. The industry became capital rather than labor intensive, a process which also involved a heightened division of labor.

Booms in demand for industrial machinery led employers to intensify efforts to replace independent and highly paid skilled workers with machinery. The railroad boom of the 1840s, in conjunction with expanded textile output, led employers to strike at the basis of craft workers' power and prerogatives by trying to hire laborers who would then be trained to perform semiskilled functions. Engineering workers' skills were also diluted

through the hiring of large numbers of apprentices, a practice which formerly workers had been able to limit. And, still more decisively, craft
workers' power was eroded through increased employment of the "piece-
master" system, a method of work control through which the skilled
workers were paid a lump sum for completing a job, and they then hired
unskilled laborers for subsidiary processes themselves. There was thus a
thin stratum of highly skilled workers who were pressed into becoming
pacemakers for industry, a practice antithetical to the earlier traditions of
more autonomous craft labor (Foster 1974, p. 228).

One prominent engineering entrepreneur whose Vulcan Foundry was in
the environs of Manchester, James Nasmyth, described the replacement of
men by machines in terms ironically consonant with those of Marx. The
rapid expansion of railways had led to an "increased demand for skilled
mechanical labour—a demand that was in excess of supply. Employers
began to outbid each other and wages rose rapidly. . . . The state of affairs
had its usual effect. It increased the demand for self-acting tools, by which
the employers might increase the productiveness of their factories without
having to resort to the costly and untrustworthy methods of meeting the
demand by increasing the number of their workmen" (quoted in Burgess
1969, p. 226). The effectiveness of the employer measures can be seen in
figures on the proportion of skilled workers in engineering firms in Oldham,
an industrial town not far from Manchester. Between 1841 and 1861,
skilled workers fell from roughly 70% to 40% of the engineering work
force, with semiskilled and juvenile workers making up the difference
(Foster 1974, p. 227).

In 1851 the employers struck a decisive blow against the engineering
workers, as they successfully organized a national lockout. The central
issue of the lockout was job control (Foster 1974, p. 226). Fifteen thou-
sand men were locked out, and the national union of engineering workers
was thoroughly defeated, with the returning men being forced to sign a
statement that they would not join a trade union that directly or indirectly
professed "to control or interfere with the arrangements or regulations of
this or any other manufacturing establishment" (p. 226).

Sir William Fairbairn summed up the changes in the occupational position of the engineering workers after the introduction of new types of machinery. He wrote that, in machine-making factories that relied on standardized machine-tool equipment, "the designing and direction of the work
passed away from the hands of the workman into those of the master and
his office assistants. This led also to a division of labour; men of general
knowledge were only exceptionally required as foremen or out-door super-
intendents: and the artificers became, in process of time, little more than
attendants on the machines" (quoted in Pole 1877, p. 47). These men were

the occupational descendants of the millwrights whose all-around skills Fairbairn had earlier described.

In Manchester the changing role of engineering workers, and of other skilled employees, led even those capitalists involved with the Manchester Mechanics' Institution to a declining emphasis on the importance of craft workers in production. Heywood, who in the 1820s had stressed that Britain would fall behind in international competition if her artisans were not educated in science, increasingly began to emphasize the moral and social, rather than the economic, advantages of instruction at the mechanics' institute (Heywood 1843). Entrepreneurs began to lag in their contributions to the institute, and the rhetoric of the institute's supporters shifted from the early statements of confidence in artisans' scientific potential.

By midcentury the institutes were also confronted with the fact that science was no longer an amateur enterprise whose boundaries blurred with those of craft production; instead, it was becoming an intellectual industry linked with the upper reaches of academic education (Roderick 1967). The separation between scientists and artisans was hastened by the development of official schooling policies that minimized the importance of scientific education for artisans as compared with scientific education of managers and foremen.

In Manchester, the founding of Owens College in 1851 meant that for the first time the sons of businessmen and managers could attend a college that offered a scientific orientation geared to the needs of industrial production. Growing concern over foreign competition (Manchester's textile manufacturers were importing German coal-tar dyes in large quantities by the 1860s) led employers to a belief that knowledge of science at the managerial level would be advisable (Kargon 1977, p. 197). Fairbairn remarked that, in the new era, "the age of the rule of thumb" was at an end (quoted in Kargon 1977, p. 187). The director of the college, Henry Roscoe, a chemistry professor, argued that Britain's great need was for scientifically educated managers rather than artisans. He told a parliamentary commission in 1868 that "I think that the attempt to teach science completely to the working class is a mistake, but I think we should give an opportunity for the best men in the working class to rise" (Select Committee 1868, p. 284).

During the period which witnessed the growth of Owens College, the Manchester Mechanics' Institution underwent a major transformation designed to shift the focus of its instruction away from educating workers in scientific principles. Instead, for the first time, the Manchester Mechanics' Institution developed the goal of instructing workers in practical technical matters. This occurred under the direction of a determined figure named John H. Reynolds, a self-educated bootmaker who became secretary of the institution in 1879 (Cruikshank 1974, pp. 144–45). Reynolds took note of industrial changes such as those that had occurred in the machine-making industry; he argued that increasing specialization in industry meant that most workers ended up doing only detail operations. This made it unnecessary and fruitless for such workers to learn science; they should, however, he argued, receive technical instruction, in part to train them as competent workmen and in part because technical education would play a valuable role in informing workers of parts of the production process beyond their immediate sphere. Under Reynolds's leadership, the Manchester Mechanics' Institution in 1883 formally converted to the Manchester Technical School and Mechanics' Institution (Cruikshank 1974, p. 146). In 1892 the city council took over the institute's management and it became the Municipal Technical School (still later it evolved into the University of Manchester Institute of Science and Technology).

Manchester's educational officials were explicit in recognizing the nature of the shift that they had put into effect in Manchester and that they advocated for other parts of Britain. In 1868 Alfred Neild, the chairman of the trustees of Owens College, wrote in a letter to the *Economist* that he differed with a previously published editorial on technical education, declaring that "I venture to think you have given a too exclusive prominence to the education of *artisans*." While not wishing to undervalue the importance of intelligence among workingmen, he continued, "the urgent need is for greater facilities for a thoroughly scientific education of those who have to direct them." This was particularly the case because of industrial developments that diminished the skill of artisans. "The effect of a large expansion and systematising of manufactures is, undoubtedly, to lessen more and more the sphere of ingenuity and responsibility of the worker, and to confine him to doing one or two things uniformly and accurately" (*Economist* [February 8, 1868], p. 153).

At the national level Neild's opinions resonated with those of other officials and politicians. After Britain fared badly at the 1861 Industrial Exhibition held in Paris, Parliament set up a Select Committee "to inquire into the Provision for giving Instruction in Theoretical and Applied Science to the Industrial Classes." The committee report broke with the long tradition in England by which artisans had been considered the appropriate bearers of technical skill and knowledge. The committee concluded that "as far as the workman, as distinguished from the managers are concerned [the acquisition of scientific knowledge] can be considered as an essential element only in certain trades, or generally, as enlarging the area from which foremen and managers may be drawn" (Select Committee 1868, p. vii). On the other hand, however, the committee stressed that all the witnesses were convinced that "a knowledge of the principles of science on the part of those who occupy the higher industrial ranks . . . would tend to promote industrial progress" (p. viii). Similarly, Lyon Playfair, secretary of the Department of Science and Art, established to foster technical progress, told the committee that "the crying want of this country is a higher class of education for the foremen and managers of industries" (Select Committee 1868, p. 62).

J. H. Reynolds, who had directed the conversion of the Manchester Mechanics' Institution into a technical school, had believed that workers would benefit more from a narrow than from a broad form of education. He accepted the view espoused by Thomas Twining, the vice-president of the Society of Arts, another agency set up (in 1870) to promote technical development, that industrial education for workers should be "strictly practical in all its bearings" (Twining 1851, p. 14). Just before his retirement in 1912, however, he questioned whether contemporary forms of industrial organization could give workers any degree of intellectual stimulation. He criticized aspects of scientific management because its advocates appeared to "look upon the human being as mere piece of mechanism, effective for a given period of life and then to be dismissed and replaced" (quoted in Marshall 1964, p. 193). The transformation from craft to a highly specialized division of labor, however, had already exerted a powerful effect in leading to changed definitions of what workers could reasonably expect from their jobs and how they could best be educated for them.

CONCLUSIONS

Adam Smith believed that the increased division of labor would bring great benefits in terms of more efficient production. He had warned in *The Wealth of Nations*, however, that it could also lead to intellectual stultification for those employed in manual tasks. Smith in fact declared bluntly that workers who labored without needing to think would lose "the habit of such exertion and generally [become] as stupid and ignorant as it is possible for a human creature to become" (1822, 2:182).[3] He argued that education would become a necessary corrective, in effect replacing work stimulation with formal academic stimulation.

The governing idea of the mechanics' institutes had been a very different one. Those artisans who wanted to learn science argued that scientific knowledge would increase their ability and ingenuity and that scientific knowledge would represent a natural extension of their work knowl-

[3] As Karl Marx dryly remarked, "For preventing the complete deterioration of the great mass of the people by the division of labor, A. Smith recommends education of the people by the State, but prudently and in homeopathic doses" (1967, 1:326).

edge. It could also, if coupled with political ideas, represent a challenge to orthodox beliefs. Some capitalists, such as those in Manchester, operating in a political climate in which state-supported primary education was still unacceptable, supported mechanics' institutes, in spite of opposition from within their own class. Whatever risks mechanics' institutes might be thought to pose by those still wedded to the most conservative views of working-class education, Manchester's most prominent industrial employers believed that they potentially could gain economically if artisans increased their level of scientific knowledge. This cross-class conviction that artisans were legitimate bearers of technical and also, desirably, scientific knowledge stemmed from the reality of employer dependence on artisan skills. As pointed out in matter-of-fact language by James Nasmyth, one of Manchester's leading engineering employers, and in far grander theoretical language by Marx, employers were not long to rest content with such a situation. Even while some continued to support mechanics' institutes, industrialists were working energetically to undercut their dependence on craft skills by means of technical innovations, tighter forms of supervision, and political defeats of union efforts to maintain high levels of workplace control.

As production methods were transformed under these pressures, formal education became an increasingly important route to jobs, while many industrial jobs were sufficiently drained of their content that they provided little stimulation for further learning. In Britain, and in the United States, there developed over the late 19th and early 20th centuries an almost complete divorce between working-class life and the main currents of science (Bernal 1939). The mechanics' institutes faded into the background as artifacts of an earlier period when some artisans had exercised a higher level of workplace control and had had aspirations toward full participation in the intellectual life of the society.

What are the implications for contemporary industrial societies? In the United States, while there has been a shift toward white-collar as opposed to manual work, many jobs require little exercise of judgment or skill (Braverman 1974). For the workers who fill these jobs, formal education beyond minimal literacy is without occupational relevance. Under these conditions, formal education assumes the role that Adam Smith suggested, that of bringing intellectual stimulation from the outside. Studies of informal learning have shown that there are significant cognitive challenges involved in mastering such crafts as weaving or tailoring; tailors and weavers are called on to judge proportions, to make decisions about the appropriate use of materials and techniques, and to coordinate hand and eye motions (Greenfield and Lave 1981). This was still more the case with the very complex crafts that held pride of place in the early stages

cation." Pp. 45–54 in *Thirty-second Annual Proceedings*. Springfield: Illinois State Federation of Labor.

Jefferys, M., and J. B. Jefferys. 1947. "The Wages, Hours and Trade Customs of the Skilled Engineer in 1861." *Economic History Review* 17:27–44.

Kargon, R. H. 1977. *Science in Victorian Manchester: Enterprise and Expertise*. Baltimore: Johns Hopkins University Press.

Kirby, R. G. 1974. "An Early Experiment in Workers' Self-Education: The Manchester New Mechanics' Institution, 1829–35." Pp. 87–98 in *Artisan to Graduate*, edited by D. S. L. Cardwell. Manchester: Manchester University Press.

Kraft, P. 1977. *Programmers and Managers: The Routinization of Computer Programming in the United States*. New York: Springer.

Marglin, S. A. 1974. "What Do Bosses Do? The Origins and Functions of Hierarchy in Capitalist Production." *Review of Radical Political Economics* 6:33–60.

Marshall, J. D. 1964. "John Henry Reynolds: Pioneer of Technical Education in Manchester." *Vocational Aspect of Secondary and Further Education* 16:176–96.

Marx, K. 1967. *Capital*. Vol. 1. New York: International Publishers.

Musgrave, P. W. 1968. *Society and Education in England since 1800*. London: Methuen.

Musson, A. E., and E. Robinson. 1969. *Science and Technology in the Industrial Revolution*. Manchester: Manchester University Press.

Noble, D. 1977. *America by Design: Science, Technology, and the Rise of Corporate Capitalism*. New York: Knopf.

Ogbu, J. 1978. *Minority Education and Caste: The American System in Cross-cultural Perspective*. New York: Academic Press.

Playfair, L. 1870. "Address on Education." (September.) London.

Pole, W. 1877. *The Life of Sir William Fairbairn*. London: Longmans, Green.

Roderick, G. W. 1967. *The Emergence of a Scientific Society*. London: Macmillan.

Scoville, W. 1952. "The Huguenots and the Diffusion of Technology." *Journal of Political Economy* 60:294–311.

Select Committee on the Provisions for Giving Instruction in Theoretical and Applied Science to the Industrial Classes. 1868. *Report*. Irish University Press Series on British Parliamentary Papers, vol. 1. Shannon: Irish University Press.

Simon, B. 1960. *The Two Nations and the Educational Structure, 1780–1870*. London: Lawrence & Wishart.

Smith, A. 1822. *The Wealth of Nations*. 3 vols. London: G. Walker.

Thompson, E. P. 1963. *The Making of the English Working Class*. New York: Vintage.

Twining, T. 1851. *Notes on the Organization of an Industrial College for Artisans*.

Tylecote, M. 1957. *The Mechanics' Institutes of Lancashire and Yorkshire before 1851*. Manchester: Manchester University Press.

———. 1974. "The Manchester Mechanics' Institution, 1824–50." Pp. 55–86 in *Artisan to Graduate*, edited by D. S. L. Cardwell. Manchester: Manchester University Press.

Vigier, F. 1970. *Change and Apathy: Liverpool and Manchester during the Industrial Revolution*. Cambridge, Mass.: MIT Press.

Yeo, E., and E. P. Thompson. 1971. *The Unknown Mayhew*. New York: Random House.

Class Origins of the "New South": Planter Persistence and Industry in North Carolina[1]

Dwight B. Billings
University of Kentucky

A conventional view shared by sociologists and historians asserts that an ascendant middle class led the American South along a new path of capitalist industrial development in the early decades following the Civil War. This paper challenges this class interpretation of southern postbellum modernization, asserting instead the centrality of cotton planters in building key sectors of southern industry. A comparison of class relations in the textile, coal mining, and tobacco industries reveals the historical patterns which shaped industrial relations and ideology in planter-dominated southern industries.

An extensive sociological literature asks why economic growth in the American South has lagged behind the rest of the nation's economy. This literature addresses the region as a whole as well as its unevenly developed subregions. Cultural modernization theorists stress a "stubborn adherence" in some sections of the South "to a set of values inconsistent with a high rate of industrialization" (Nicholls 1960, p. 15). This approach ignores the social basis for both the persistence and the displacement of such traditions. Other regional sociologists use the imprecise metaphor of colonialism to explain the South's relatively "backward" economic performance, pointing to the dependent character of its growth and to alleged effects of northern "imperialism" (Odum 1936; Vance 1935). Both models divert attention from the region's class structure and the role of that class structure in shaping southern development.

From a class-analytic perspective, the South's regional distinctiveness can be traced to the social relations of its plantation mode of agricultural production. Southern plantations developed as part of the modern world market system, but slaveholding produced an aristocratic society with class interests at odds with the dynamic, expansionist industrial capitalism of the North and with industrialization within the South (Genovese 1967,

---

[1] Numerous people contributed to this research, including Alan Banks, Dan Chirot, Robert Goldman, Gerhard Lenski, and Lester Salamon. I am especially grateful to Karen Tice for her insights into the New England textile industry. Requests for reprints should be addressed to Dwight B. Billings, Department of Sociology, University of Kentucky, Lexington, Kentucky 40506.

pp. 13–39). The Civil War determined which system of class relations—servile labor or free-wage capitalism—would be dominant on the North American continent (Moore 1966); according to historians of the South, the war fundamentally altered the region's social structure as well. In his *Origins of the New South*, C. Vann Woodward (1951, p. 29) advanced the interpretation that no other class in our history ever fell so rapidly or so completely as the South's planter class after the war. According to the conventional view among historians, this set the region on a new route of capitalist industrial development, led by an ascendant middle class. This paper challenges this class interpretation of postbellum southern development, asserting instead the centrality of planters in building southern industry.

In order to assess the relative contributions of planters and middle-class businessmen to southern development, I will examine the social origins of industry in postbellum North Carolina. North Carolina was an unlikely candidate for the industrial leader of the New South. The poorest southern state in 1860, it had fewer slaves and fewer big plantations than any other state in the South but Tennessee. In 1880 North Carolina was still relatively backward, ranking near the bottom among southern states in per capita agricultural productivity and lowest in capital assets; only Mississippi and Alabama were more rural. Nonetheless, from 1880 to 1900 its textile manufacturing increased 1,100%, at a rate of six new cotton mills per year. Along with these, new railroads, banks, tobacco factories, highways, and schools began to dot the rural landscape, signaling a new era. North Carolina's reputation for progress began to set it apart from the rest of the South. V. O. Key referred to the education, transportation, and public health improvements that occurred in North Carolina at the turn of the century as a "political and educational renaissance" that "set in motion the progressive, productive forces that today distinguish the state" (1949, p. 206).

This paper questions the conventional interpretation that North Carolina's rapid postbellum industrial development resulted from the state having been relatively unhindered by plantation agriculture and having lacked a planter class with enough power to resist progressive change. This common interpretation accords with the state's popular image. In comparison with Virginia and South Carolina, its aristocratic, planter-dominated neighbor-states, North Carolina has been called a "vale of humility between two peaks of pride." A prominent North Carolinian, writing in the *Nation* in 1921, called North Carolina a "militant mediocracy," claiming that its development represented "the triumph of a vigorous middle class" (Winston 1921, p. 731). Despite the plausibility of this interpretation, I will argue instead that planters spearheaded North Carolina's industrial transformation.

The first part of this paper examines the role of planters in the early history of the North Carolina textile industry. For it was here, in the relationship between cotton manufacturing and the agrarian order during the first decades after the Civil War, that the modern configuration of class, culture, and economics that we call the "New South" was constructed. Furthermore, the fact that industrialization in the Carolina Piedmont was more rapid and extensive than in other sections of the South raises the question of how and to what extent variations in planters' opportunities and constraints influenced subregional development patterns. Finally, by comparing class relations in textiles, coal mining, and tobacco manufacturing, the second part of the paper examines factors which shaped industrial relations in planter-dominated industry.

1. SOCIAL ORIGINS OF SOUTHERN INDUSTRY

Economic development theory, Marxian analysis of the dynamics of slaveholding, and traditional historical accounts of the New South movement all lend plausibility to the conventional belief that an ascendant entrepreneurial class led the southern states toward capitalist industrialism after the Civil War. Development theory asserts that historical patterns of class struggle open up or foreclose different courses of economic development or underdevelopment in response to market opportunities. As a "peripheral" region within an emerging "core" society of the capitalist world system, the political economy of the antebellum South, with its pattern of class relations and its trade dependency, faced the same limits on development as do many primary producers in the Third World today. At least in principle, primary producers can break out of dependency. They can at least partially "close off" from the world market, substitute domestic products for imports, and aim for economic diversification. A few dissident North Carolina leaders unsuccessfully urged this path of development for the state as early as 1828 in a report to the state legislature entitled "On the Establishment of Cotton and Woolen Manufactures" (Lefler 1955, pp. 251–55). Such development policies rarely emerge in plantation societies, however, because of limits imposed by their class relations. Efforts to reallocate productive resources and to change the demand structures of plantation societies are tantamount to social revolution. Typically, in such societies, "the keepers of the past cannot be the builders of the future" (Baran 1970, p. 300).

Eugene Genovese has shown why class interests in the antebellum South prohibited capitalist industrial development. Slaveholding produced a civilization at odds with the rest of the bourgeois world. "The planters," he says, "were not mere capitalists; they were pre-capitalistic, quasi-aristocratic landowners who had to adjust their economy and ways of thinking to a capitalistic world market. Their society, in its spirit and fundamental direction, represented the antithesis of capitalism, however many compromises it had to make" (1967, p. 23). Far more than a purely economic arrangement, the master-slave relationship was a class relationship that implied distinct politics, ideology, and social behavior for the plantation region. The whole social order presumed this relationship; its preservation was more important than short-run profits. According to Genovese, plantation cultivation was pursued even when it was economically irrational.[2] Changes that threatened it were opposed; industrialization, which threatened planters' control of labor, was resisted. While they needed some industrial products and supported limited manufacturing for plantation markets, southern planters "could not sustain economically or tolerate politically a general industrialization" (Genovese 1967, p. 181).

If the landlord classes in plantation societies refuse to carry out modernizing reforms, other classes lack the power to do so. Since servile labor systems limit the buying power of the home market, the commercial middle classes are too dependent on the planters, their best customers, to risk opposing their interests. Genovese's analysis of the Old South and the economic development literature together suggest the following hypothesis: southern economic development has best flourished in those subregions (and during those historical periods) where an independent, industrial capitalist class has countered the negative power of the planter classes to promote industrial development.

This hypothesis is compatible with mainstream interpretations of postbellum southern history. C. Vann Woodward (1951) has most forcefully endorsed this thesis to explain the dramatic rise of the New South. As one reviewer summarized it, Woodward's classic account "is the story of the decay and decline of the aristocracy, the suffering and betrayal of the poor whites, and the rise and transformation of a middle class" (Hackney 1972, p. 191). According to Woodward, the Civil War destroyed planter dominance. "Involved in the downfall of the old planter class were the leading financial, commercial, and industrial families of the region" (Woodward 1951, p. 29). This made room for the rise of a new class of capitalist entrepreneurs, freed from agriculture and with a vision of a new industrial South. These leaders are said to have carried out an industrial revolution comparable to England's, only in less time. "The 'vic-

[2] Genovese's assumption of low returns on cotton sales has been challenged by Fogel and Engerman (1974), who demonstrate that slaveholding was highly profitable and that southern agriculture was highly productive. The fact that planters realized greater average profits in the circulation sphere than Genovese assumed, however, does not contradict his fundamental premise that the production relations of slaveholding resulted in a noncapitalist social order. On the persistence of noncapitalist social relations in a capitalist world system, see Brenner (1977); also, see Wiener (1979) for a critique of neoclassical accounts of the economics of postbellum tenancy which also neglect the production side of plantation agriculture.

tory of the middle classes' and the 'passing of power from the hands of landowners to manufacturers and merchants,' which required two generations in England, were substantially achieved in a much shorter period in the South" (1951, p. 140).

Woodward's interpretation of the class origins of the New South is widely accepted.[3] It is consistent with mainstream sociological accounts of southern development which implicitly identify modernization with the rise of a southern middle class (Reissman 1966). After reviewing the vast research Woodward's study has generated, Sheldon Hackney concluded that "the remarkable thing is that there has been so little fundamental challenge to the outlines of the story established by Woodward twenty years ago" (1972, p. 191). I believe, however, that a close reading reveals that empirical evidence for Woodward's interpretation was skimpy. He relied heavily on a historical sketch of the southern textile industry which claimed that small-town businessmen and professionals built the mills of the New South (Mitchell 1921), even though the same author claimed contradictorily in a subsequent work that the mills were largely established by cotton planters (Mitchell and Mitchell 1930).

Because of the apparent ease and rapidity of its postbellum industrial development and because of its reputation for having had a relatively small planter class during the antebellum period, North Carolina provides an excellent test of the theory of middle-class leadership in southern industrialization. Prior research has established that North Carolina's early postbellum mill builders were indigenous to the state, but their class positions have not been probed. It is commonly assumed that capital for postbellum factories came from the North, but the South's industrial thrust actually grew from local initiative. Northern capital was available to finance cotton crops which New England mills needed, not for building an industrial competitor in the newly subjugated region. Industrial capital and textile firms migrated from New England only in the 20th century, after the South had established an industrial base and won its production competition with the North. According to Herring, "the industrial development of the South has been, in a measure, the result of conscious efforts by Southerners to build an industrial empire" (1931, p. 1). Studies of North Carolina business leaders show that "not a single person from the Northeast played a decisive role in the building of North Carolina industry in the years 1865–1900" (Sitterson 1957, p. 114; see also Lacy 1935). Although pioneer industrialists are known to have been native to North Carolina, their class status has not been closely examined

---

[3] For example, see Buck 1937, p. 145; Gilman 1956, pp. 69–70; McLaurin 1971*b*, pp. 42–43; Odum 1947; Pope 1942, p. 15; Thompson 1931, pp. 11–20. The principal challenge to this view is W. J. Cash, *The Mind of the South* (1941); for a critique of Cash, see Woodward (1971, pp. 261–83).

because of insufficient social-historical research on the development of the Carolina textile industry.

Textile Mills and Cotton Planters

Early historians of the New South dated the textile industry from 1880, minimizing its antebellum foundations. They claimed that "cotton mills were set down suddenly in cotton fields" (Mitchell 1931, p. 24) when "new men came to the front as the fortunes of the planters declined" (Thompson 1931, p. 17). Actually, southern textile production dates back to the 17th century, when a vigorous domestic manufacturing system thrived in opposition to the mercantilist policies of the British empire. During the antebellum phase of factory development, beginning in North Carolina in 1818, both planters and merchants built mills in the state. This was true especially during periods of agricultural price declines. For instance, the plantation-based Battle family of eastern North Carolina raised a half million dollars to enlarge its cotton mills during a severe agricultural recession in the 1840s but reinvested the capital in land and slaves after a sudden recovery of cotton prices (Standard and Griffin 1957). The continuity between North Carolina's antebellum industrial development—which had slowed by 1853, "but not until considerable advance had been made" (Herring 1931, p. 8)—and its rapid postbellum growth was important. In the early 1870s North Carolina newspapers campaigned for industrial reconstruction in response to the ruin of war.

In order to discover the social origins of postbellum North Carolina mills, I compared a complete list of millowners (Griffin 1964) operating from 1865 to 1884—crucial years when the modern industry emerged—with state business directories (Branson 1869, 1872, 1877–78, 1884) which identified prominent planters in many North Carolina counties. These data do not support the hypothesis that early cotton mills were built by a new capitalist middle class. After eliminating 10 mills because of insufficient ownership information, I found that 18 of the remaining 78 mills (23%) were owned by men identified in Branson's *Directory* in 1869 as planters. In addition, 26 other mills (an additional 34%) were owned or co-owned by men who were identified as "prominent agrarians" by the less restrictive criteria of subsequent volumes of the directory.[4] That is, over half (57%) of the mills operating in North Carolina in this early postbellum period were fully or partly owned by agrarians. This is a conservative test, for additional millowners also may have been mem-

[4] Editions of Branson's *Directory* published after 1872 did not report the number of acres owned by each individual. Consequently, I do not know whether the criteria for determining agricultural prominence remained constant. This is doubtful, since later editions typically listed more "prominent agrarians" in each county than did the 1869 edition.

bers of the landholding class but not included in the brief *Directory* listings. Still others were undoubtedly sons of planters. Eight of the remaining mills were owned by men who shared the same family names as prominent farm operators in their counties. (This possible family linkage would increase the estimate of the number of mills connected with landholding families to 68%.) The Appendix shows how data for one county were coded and indicates that these percentages probably *underestimate* the connection between early industrialists and the landed upper class.

Given the conventional wisdom and the literature cited above, it is surprising to find that planters and prominent agriculturalists laid the foundation in the first two decades after the Civil War for North Carolina's revolution in textile manufacturing. These men combined interests in textile manufacturing with large-scale agriculture; they were important political leaders as well. Some served in the United States Congress. One planter-industrialist, Walter Steele (described in the Appendix), served in the state legislature as early as 1846, was secretary of the state convention that passed the ordinance for secession, and was elected to Congress after Reconstruction in 1876. This fact suggests that these planters were not only builders of the New South—some were power holders in the old order as well. The tendency to identify modernization with the rise of a middle class has caused historians and sociologists to overlook the facts of industrial sponsorship, just as the "romantic" accounts of the sudden rise of the New South have blinded others to the actual roots of the industrial revolution there. Consequently, important links have been obscured between southern agriculture and industry, between the planter class and southern industrialists, and between the world antebellum slaveholders built and the social order ex-slaveholders reestablished after the Civil War.

Superficially, aggregate census data support the apparent disappearance of planters and the common contention that postbellum North Carolina was "a state of small farmers" (Lefler and Newsome 1973, p. 576). A more careful examination of the data,[5] however, reveals the dual structure of rural North Carolina society, which consisted of two sectors, plantations and independent family farms. The postbellum break-up of plantations is indicated by an increase in the total number of farms from just over 75,000 in 1860 to 225,000 in 1900. Much of this increase, however, merely reflects a shift from the plantation mode of supervision to the tenancy system of small holdings from which former slaveholders continued to extract surplus labor. By 1900 41% of the state's farmers were tenants. Another 33% were small farmers who owned less than 100 acres of land. While 72.2% of all tenant holders in North Carolina controlled

[5] Calculations are based on the *Twelfth Census of the United States: Agriculture* (U.S. Census Office 1900, pp. 12–13, 108–11, and 308–17).

only one tenant-operated farm each, the small number of landowners who controlled five or more tenant-operated farms each (3.9% of North Carolina tenant holders) controlled one-fifth of all the tenants (19.8%) and one-fifth (20.5%) of the total value of farm property in the state. When this ownership concentration is seen in conjunction with the fact that nearly half (48%) of the state's cotton crop in 1899 was produced by tenant labor, one appreciates the wealth and power of North Carolina's small landed upper class.

The continuing hegemony of planters in North Carolina can be seen clearly in the histories of the state's landed families. Murchisons, Moreheads, Pattersons, Battles, and Camerons dominated North Carolina social and economic life for generations. In some cases their prominence extended from the colonial period into the 20th century. These were not isolated individuals but members of a social class bound together by common interests in plantation agriculture and by an extensive web of social relationships. Landed families were interconnected by marriage and united by business interests. They worked jointly on the same development projects and they served together as directors of the same railroads, banks, textile mills, and business firms. A brief glimpse at one of the most prosperous of such families, the Camerons, illustrates this pattern of agricultural and industrial dominance.

The Cameron family of the North Carolina Piedmont was probably the wealthiest family in North Carolina during the decades surrounding the Civil War. The story of the Cameron family "is the story of two families, the Bennehans and the Camerons, joining in the early 19th century and making one family so strong that neither the Civil War nor Reconstruction could shake it loose from its foundations or damage it in any serious way" (Sanders 1974, p. 1). Richard Bennehan moved to North Carolina from Virginia in 1768. He became a business associate of a wealthy and influential planter from Scotland, a nephew of the colonial governor. In 1776 Bennehan purchased an 893-acre plantation; soon he married into one of the leading planter families in the state. By 1790 he was the largest slaveholder in Orange County and the second largest landowner (2,355 acres); in 1802 he owned 4,803 acres.

Duncan Cameron (1776–1853) was the son of the Reverend John Cameron, who came to Virginia from Scotland in 1770 and married Annie Nash, niece of Abner Nash, a colonial governor of North Carolina, and of Gen. Francis Nash, a Revolutionary War hero. In 1797, Duncan Cameron settled in Hillsborough in Orange County, where he began to practice law. He married Richard Bennehan's daughter, Rebecca, in 1803 and was deeded a plantation by his father-in-law. Cameron became a superior court judge in 1814. He was president of the State Bank of North Carolina, a University of North Carolina trustee, clerk of the state supreme court, and a member of the State Board of Internal Improvements. He devoted the last 20 years of his life to his enormous plantation, Fairntosh, which is said to have "contributed to a way of life and an economy as well balanced and complete as that of a medieval lord" (Ashe 1905a, p. 45).

Duncan Cameron had eight children, but only two survived to inherit his wealth. Only one of his daughters married. She wed George Mordecai, a wealthy planter who succeeded Duncan Cameron as president of the State Bank of North Carolina. (Mordecai's plantation was valued at $85,000 in 1869). Duncan Cameron's son, Paul Carrington Cameron, who was born in 1808, inherited an "immense fortune" in 1853. He attended the University of North Carolina and Washington College in Connecticut. In 1832 he married Anne Ruffin, daughter of the chief justice of the North Carolina Supreme Court. Owning at least 30,000 acres by the time of the Civil War, Paul Cameron was "unquestionably the richest man in North Carolina" (Sanders 1974, p. 6). His four plantations, along with adjoining smaller farms, extended over what are today Durham, Granville, and Wake Counties. His more than 1,900 slaves qualified him as one of the largest, if not the very largest, slaveholders in the entire South.[6] "The wealthiest man in the State at the beginning of the War, he was still the wealthiest, despite the loss of his slaves, at the end of it" (1974, p. 6).

Biographical accounts of individuals such as Paul Cameron give insight into the interests and consciousness of Carolina planters. Cameron was said to have been "conservative in his attitude toward social change but progressive in terms of whatever had to do with improving the material accommodation of life—land, livestock, rivers, canals, railroads, forests, building, and industrial processes." He was "perhaps the supreme example of the benign enlightened Southern planter, citizen, and builder of institutions of his day, who was guided, not by the principles of equality but by the kind of humanized paternalism that Carlyle advocated" (Sanders 1974, pp. 6, 7). Paul Cameron's chief interest was agriculture. "He saw in agriculture the great mainspring of commerce, of prosperity and social happiness, and the foundation upon which was laid the great superstructure of human advancement and enlightenment" (Ashe 1905b, p. 49). Cameron, however, was also a banker and an industrialist. He promoted the building of the North Carolina Railroad and served as a director of the Raleigh and Gaston Raleigh and Augusta Air Line. He owned stock in two Raleigh banks and in textile mills in Rockingham, Rocky Mount, and Augusta, Georgia. Cameron was moderately active in politics.

[6] Herbert Gutman (1976, pp. 169–80) used the Cameron plantation records in his analysis of the black family in slavery. Thomas Dixon drew on his knowledge of and friendship with the Camerons for his popular novel, *The Clansmen*. The movie version of this story, *Birth of a Nation*, was partially filmed on the Cameron plantation.

He served in the state senate in 1856, and he chaired the North Carolina delegation to the 1876 Democratic National Convention.

Paul Cameron's personal papers reveal his attitude toward postbellum industrial development. In 1868, after touring Virginia with his friend Gen. Wade Hampton and visiting Robert E. Lee on the occasion of Hampton's commencement address at Washington College, Cameron wrote a 26-page open letter to friends entitled "A Peep into the Old Dominion."[7] In this long letter—written when Atlanta journalist Henry Grady, the New South movement's most familiar spokesman, was only 18 years old and still two decades away from his famed "New South Speech" of 1886 to the New England Society—North Carolina's largest planter described his dream of an autonomous, industrial South.

> Everywhere in Virginia the farmers are providing themselves with species of labor saving machinery, especially the Reaper-Mower and Storage [illegible word]. Many of the Railroad warehouses were crowded with every tool that a farmer needs. Much of the larger part had been manufactured in Baltimore. It will not be long before the city of Richmand will take the lead not only in this but as the great Manufacturing City of the South. From its forges and furnaces came the Crimson and Shell of four long years of strife—and it can soon provide us with all that we need from a horseshoe to a reaper or from a fishhook to an ocean of iron clad steamers. Not until the South shall hammer and plane, stitch and grind and bring the plow, loom, and anvil close to each other will it become self-dependent and *independent*. This is our road to wealth and consequence.

Here, in Cameron's image of the future, uniting loom and plow, one finds a vital link between the Old South and the New South.

When Paul Cameron died, properties in his estate included a 10-acre family home in Raleigh; an additional 300 acres in Raleigh; four city lots and assorted properties in Graham County, Person County, and Charlotte; 100,000 acres of land in the North Carolina mountains which were later sold to the Vanderbilts for the Biltmore Estate; 2,240 acres near Memphis, Tennessee; 1,500 acres in a Florida phosphate belt; 100 shares of a Florida orange grove; and, finally, Fairntosh, which by then had come to comprise 13 contiguous plantations (Sanders 1974, p. 8).

Paul Cameron had only one son to survive to adulthood; he inherited the bulk of the Cameron estate. Bennehan Cameron (1854–1925) continued the work of his father, grandfather, and great-grandfather. He married the daughter of Peter Mayo, a large planter and industrialist in Richmond, Virginia. He studied law but devoted his life to agriculture. He served many terms as director and president of the State Agricultural Society, as vice-president of the Southern Cotton Growers' Protective As-

---

[7] This letter is available in the Cameron Family Papers (Box no. 133) in the Southern Historical Collection of the Wilson Library at the University of North Carolina at Chapel Hill.

sociation, and as president of the Farmers' Congress of America. At the same time, like his father, Bennehan Cameron was greatly interested in finance and industry. He was a director of the Morehead Banking Company and helped to organize the First National Bank of Durham along with Eugene Morehead, son of the antebellum governor and planter-industrialist, John Motley Morehead. He served as a director and president of the Rocky Mount Cotton Mills, which the powerful Battle family had established. Other investments in textile manufacturing included mills in Richmond and Nash Counties, the Great Falls Manufacturing Company, and a mill in Georgia.

As a planter-industrialist, Cameron was particularly concerned with the South's transportation deficiencies. He was involved in building the Caraleigh Railroad Branch, the Union Depot in Raleigh, the Oxford and Clarksville Railroad, the Lynchburg and Durham Railroad, the Durham and Northern Railroad, the Oxford and Dickerson Railroad, and the Oxford and Coast Line Railroad. He served as a director of the partially state-owned North Carolina Railroad for 35 years. As a representative of its private stockholders, he played a leading part in leasing it to the Southern Railroad for 99 years in 1895, an act of cooperation with the Morgan financial empire that outraged North Carolina Populists. Finally, according to biographers, his "greatest work" was his role in the creation of the vast Seaboard Air Line System, one of the South's three principal railroads. He served as president of the railroad from 1911 to 1913.

Cameron's interest in transportation was not confined to railroads. He was an organizer and director of the Quebec-Miami International plan, the head of the Bankhead Highway Association, which sought to connect the southern states with better roads, and a director of the American Automobile Association. In 1915, as a member of the state legislature, he introduced a bill to create the North Carolina Highway Commission and another to issue $50 million in bonds to pay for highway improvements in the state.

The history of the Cameron family, along with the histories of other landed families, contradicts the middle-class development thesis. "Conspicuous in the story of the Camerons and their progenitors is a pattern which has persisted for at least five generations. It is a striking fact that neither the institution of slavery nor the abolition of it was able to destroy or even seriously change this pattern" (Sanders 1974, p. 11). Agriculture produced wealth in North Carolina that was used in diverse ways, including industrialization; former slaveholders built a New South. Sometimes individuals such as Paul and Bennehan Cameron actively pursued both agricultural and industrial interests. In other instances a division of activities occurred within landed families. Among the Pattersons, for instance—another prominent planter-industrialist family I have described elsewhere (Billings 1979)—Rufus Patterson managed the family's cotton mills, while his brother Samuel ran the family plantation and served as State Commissioner of Agriculture in the 1890s before he became more directly involved in the mills later in his career. As we shall see, this situation produced a complex yet durable system of class relations in North Carolina.

Agricultural Class Relations and Industrialization in the Plantation South

Despite stress on the demise of planters and the plantation system that characterized New South promotional literature, new evidence is accumulating to suggest that planters remained economically and politically dominant in many southern states at the end of the 19th century.[8] How, then, can we account for variations in the development of industry among southern states?

After the Civil War, former slaveholders retained their land but temporarily lost control of the black labor force; they faced new obstacles to their formerly unchallenged hegemony, yet, in the Upper South, they enjoyed new opportunities. Recent Marxist research on postbellum agriculture (Mandle 1978; Wiener 1979) shows that planters continued to extract surplus labor from black workers, but their methods were conditioned by new forms of class conflict. Initially planters had hoped to force former slaves to work for low wages as gang laborers on plantations, but the freedmen resisted, holding out for land redistribution. Jonathan Wiener (1979, pp. 973–76) has shown that southern landlords cooperated to limit competition among themselves for labor, backed this resolve with antienticement laws, as well as antivagrancy and contract enforcement statutes to secure workers, and used terror to intimidate blacks. Despite such measures, "by creating a 'shortage of labor,' the freedmen defeated the planters' efforts to preserve the plantation as a single, large-scale unit worked by gangs" (Wiener 1979, p. 976). Consequently, planters were forced to subdivide their plantations and organize production by family sharecropping, which in the course of agricultural disorganization and depression came to include many white farmers as well as former slaves. Labor mobility was restricted by the system of "debt peonage," which bound tenants to the soil through the planter-controlled credit system just as surely as slavery had done. The culture of paternalism persisted into the 20th century (Mandle 1978, pp. 28–52).

Rural class relations were largely unchanged until the Great Depression, when the collapse of the southern cotton-growing economy forced

[8] Evidence of the continuance of planter hegemony in the postbellum South can be found in Wiener (1978) for Mississippi, Salamon (in press) for Alabama, Hunter (1980) for Georgia, Cooper (1968) for South Carolina, and Pulley (1968) for Virginia.

agricultural reorganization. Jay Mandle and Jonathan Wiener agree that New Deal agricultural policies, which paid planters not to grow, and welfare programs, which sustained a reserve labor supply at no cost to landlords, encouraged a shift to wage labor. Only then did exploitation begin to shift to the ensemble of "modern" capitalist relations of agricultural production common to other American farm regions. Manpower requirements on capital-intensive southern farms shifted to demand for skilled labor for about half of the work force after the Depression. "By and large, by the early or mid-1960s sharecropping as a form of labor force control had passed into insignificance and so too had the southern plantation economy" (Mandle 1978, p. 95). Prior to this, however, the southern plantation system profoundly shaped southern industrial development.

Many historical conditions—demographic factors, structural locations in trade markets, capital availability, international conflict and state traditions, political resources of leadership classes and the power of lower classes to resist, rudimentary manufacturing bases, etc.—interact to influence whether and how agrarian societies modernize (Skocpol 1976). Among these, class relations are the most important. Postbellum tenancy, no less than slaveholding, potentially inhibited industrial development. Demographic and economic conditions in the Upper South, however, distinguished the Piedmont states from the Deep South, where planters continued to oppose all but limited industries which manufactured goods such as fertilizer, agricultural tools, and cheap clothing for plantation markets (Wiener 1978; see also Salamon, in press).

Demographically, with its small core of plantation counties in the east and its larger population of yeoman and subsistence farmers in central and western counties, North Carolina was the reverse of the Deep South. Well before 1900, white tenant farmers had begun to outnumber blacks in the sharecropping system. Vast numbers of uprooted white farmers were a political threat to upper-class privilege, especially when they moved to unite with the black underclass during the Populist revolt of the 1890s (Billings 1981). The economics of agriculture and especially cotton production helped tip the balance of these forces in favor of further industrialization. North Carolina had a limited but significant antebellum industrial base. Cotton manufacturing once again became attractive, just as it had been during antebellum periods of recession. North Carolina planter-industrialists sustained a local market for cotton and profited from its heightened value as a manufactured product. At the same time, industrialization promised new hope for many bankrupt white farmers, thus helping to prevent rural revolution as thousands of displaced farmers and their families were absorbed into rapidly expanding rural textile mills.

The more vulnerable a state was to drops in the price of cotton (as compared with other products), the greater was its manufacturing activity. According to DeCanio (1974), North Carolina ranked as the second most vulnerable southern state to drops in cotton prices from the mid-1880s until World War I. In contrast, Mississippi and Alabama, with the second and third lowest price elasticities, could better weather price declines. In fact, Stephen DeCanio concludes that, despite myths of cotton overproduction, the Deep South's comparative advantage in cotton, relative to other crops, was so great that it would have been economically irrational for planters there to have done otherwise than plant cotton.

Although econometric analyses of southern agriculture ignore this factor,[9] it was primarily the labor needs of cotton production that disinclined Deep South planters to sponsor industry in their states. Unlike planters in the Upper South, their resistance was enhanced by their comparative advantage in cotton growing and by the relatively small proportion of independent white farmers in the Deep South. By contrast, in North Carolina, developments in the technology of cotton spinning permitted the use of surplus unskilled white labor at low wages; investment returns were initially as high as 22%. For Carolina planters wealthy enough to take advantage of these opportunities, cotton manufacturing appeared to be the answer to the economic plight of their class and region. By 1895 half of North Carolina's cotton crop was consumed in the state's textile industry.

Planter-industrialists thus created a dual labor system in North Carolina: cotton was grown with forced labor and manufactured with all-white, free-wage labor. Mill operators manipulated traditional racial antipathies to segment these work forces, and a culture of paternalism in mills and fields alike reinforced their domination.[10] In the following sections I will suggest how this pattern of development shaped industrial relations in planter-dominated industry.

2. INDUSTRIAL LABOR RELATIONS AND IDEOLOGY IN THE NEW SOUTH

In the New South, under planter leadership, textile manufacturing was accommodated to paternalistic class relations as the ethos of the cotton plantation was extended into mill villages. Whether apologetic or critical, descriptions of labor relations in the Carolina textile industry all suggest an industrial pattern distinctive to southern cotton manufacturing. (See

[9] For critiques, see Wiener (1979) and Woodman (1977).

[10] Elsewhere, in an analysis of the role of planters in state modernization and their use of government for social control and for developing an industrial infrastructure, I have compared this pattern of development to what Barrington Moore (1966, pp. 433–52) calls "conservative modernization" through "revolution from above" (Billings 1979). I am indebted to Lester Salamon for pointing out this similarity; Jonathan Wiener (1978) makes use of the same analogy to explain an alternative route to modernization taken by Deep South planters.

Mitchell and Mitchell 1930; Cash 1941; Pope 1942; Gilman 1956; Roy 1965; McLaurin 1971*b;* Boyte 1972; Newman 1978.) The incorporation of mill villages into postbellum rural social structure resulted in industrial communities with strong social cohesion but a work force with blunted class consciousness.[11] Single-factor explanations, stressing the isolation of mill villages or the dependency of the workers, do not adequately account for this development.

In the following sections I will argue that the ownership structure of the textile mills and the political-economy formation within which the mills developed shaped this industrial pattern and influenced the consciousness of mill workers. Planter ownership of the mills was important for reasons other than any psychological characteristics which may have distinguished planters from capitalist entrepreneurs. Rather, the planters' class position placed them under certain constraints, such as the necessity for maintaining and controlling an adequate agricultural labor supply, as well as offering certain opportunities. These opportunities included antebellum factory experience, traditional social authority which extended to yeoman farmers in the plantation counties, political resources, and control over the black population which planters repeatedly used as a threat to insure white labor discipline.

Following a brief discussion of southern industrial ideology, I will compare class relations in southern textile mills with those of other industries. A comparison with production relations in northern textile firms which controls for the effects of machine-governed aspects of the labor process reveals the impact of variant political-economic contexts on the development of a textile work force. A second comparison contrasts the quiescence of southern textile workers with the class consciousness and militancy of southern coal miners. Coal camps in the Appalachian South were also isolated and paternalistic, but absentee ownership, craft skills, and a tradition of autonomous social relations in the nonplantation, mountain South produced a pattern of industrial relations in the southern coalfields which was very different from that characterizing the planter-dominated textile industry. Finally, the growth of the North Carolina tobacco industry further illustrates the course of southern industries that developed independently from plantation culture.

Southern Industrial Ideology

During the antebellum period, the paternalistic master-slave relationship had "permeated Southern life and influenced relationships among free

[11] Robert Blauner (1964, pp. 58–88) found that, in comparison with other American workers, southern textile workers were far less psychologically "alienated" than would be predicted on the basis of their job tasks. He attributed this to the unusually strong social cohesion of southern mill villages.

men," including planters' interactions with yeoman farmers (Genovese 1967, p. 13). These class relations persisted after the Civil War in the tenancy system and in southern textile factories as poor white farmers became millhands. Mill village paternalism first developed "naturally" from planters' traditional social obligations; their dealings with white mill operatives were guided by the old grammar of master-slave relations. Out of necessity, as well, millowners built villages and provided services for their geographically isolated workers, since early mills were typically located in remote areas where waterpower could be harnessed. Along with jobs, industrialists provided housing, stores, churches and clergy, schools and teachers, and recreational and social services. Workers' loyalty to planter-industrialists was heightened by the racial exclusivity of the mill villages; although antebellum industrialists had experimented with slave labor in the mills (Lander 1969), after emancipation factory jobs were for whites only.

Gradually, paternalistic relations became an institutionalized dimension of life in southern mills. "What at first had been a necessity of mill building, and a perfectly natural expression of traditional responsibility of the master for his dependents . . . became, on the part of many, a studied, tactical pose" (Mitchell and Mitchell 1930, p. 11). Eventually, a system of professional welfare work (Herring 1929), which routinized the charisma of pioneer planter-industrialists, aided in the social control of the work force and the rationalization of production, all the while grounded in agrarian tradition.

The myth that accompanied the spectacular growth of isolated mills in the South was that these were families—"white families"—separated from the rest of the world. The millowner was the model of "adulthood"; millhands were the dependents for whom he assumed full responsibility (Boyte 1972, p. 5). The mill movement itself was legitimated by the claim that it was motivated by a concern for the poor honest farmers and laborers of North Carolina who desperately needed employment. In the words of one early Carolina mill builder, "This was not a business, but a social enterprise. Any profit that might accrue to the originators of the mill was but incidental; the main thing was the salvation of the decaying community, and especially the poor whites, who were in danger of being submerged altogether. The record of those days is filled with a moral fervor that is astounding. People were urged to take stock in the mills for the town's sake, for the South's sake, literally for God's sake" (quoted in Gilman 1956, pp. 81–82).

Conflicts of interest between owners and workers were obscured by appeals to regional and racial solidarity as the myth of the "Lost Cause" and the myth that the wealth of the aristocracy was depleted by Reconstruction were advanced (Gaston 1973). According to Mitchell and Mitchell, "The employers, certainly in the cotton manufacturing business, have tried to make their private interests appear as synonymous with the well-being of society, and have largely succeeded" (1930, p. 34). Manufacturers had effective ideological allies in the southern clergy, as Liston Pope's account in *Millhands and Preachers* (1942) ably demonstrates. Most observers agree that profit alone "cannot account for the public zeal that . . . converted an economic development into a civic crusade inspired with a vision of social salvation" (Woodward 1951, p. 133).

Ideological efforts to assure subordinate classes that their rulers act in their best interests are, of course, hardly unique to the South. In terms of American cultural experience, however, southern ideology was unusually effective. The hegemony of southern paternalism must not, however, be interpreted simply as a continuity in southern ideology; it was also a consequence of continuities in southern class relations. Mill towns were not simply cloaked by a canopy of paternalist values; their paternalism was more than a legitimating idiom.

Industrial paternalism had its grounding in the social relations of the servile mode of agricultural production. The organization of textile mills and villages reproduced rural class relations, though they did so contradictorily with wage labor. Melton McLaurin (1971*b*) stressed this continuity by referring to Carolina mill villages as "industrial plantations," and W. J. Cash claimed that the southern cotton factory was "a plantation, essentially indistinguishable in organization from the familiar plantation of the cotton fields" (1941, p. 205). McLaurin and Cash err in too closely assimilating free–wage labor mobility and industrial capitalism to the system of forced plantation labor, yet it is true that historically emergent patterns in postbellum textile relations were conditioned by the surrounding plantation milieu. Two distinct and otherwise incompatible modes of production coexisted symbiotically in rural North Carolina. Textile manufacturing developed as an adjunct to cotton growing but was separated from agriculture by racial caste barriers. Both sectors, however, were dominated by the same ruling class, the planter-industrialists and their lesser allies in industry and farming. Brief comparisons with class conflict in the northeastern textile industry and with class struggles in the southern coalfields demonstrate how this situation influenced work relations in southern mills.

Class Struggles in the Northeastern and Southern Textile Industries

Industrial paternalism is not unique to the South. Many large capitalist firms experimented with efforts to secure workers' loyalty with after-work "benefits"—"welfare capitalism"—prior to the Great Depression (Brandes 1970). Generally, these efforts at social control were ineffective, as strikes

in paternalistic company towns such as Homestead and Pullman drama-
tized (Edwards 1979, pp. 91–98). American welfare capitalism (as distinct from southern paternalism) originated in the antebellum textile industry of New England. Here industrialists provided many services for
their workers since, just as their southern counterparts, they initially built
mills in rural areas (Copeland 1923, pp. 1–16). However, industrial relations in the two regions soon diverged. Millowners in New England were
far more distant, socially and geographically, from their workers than
were the planter-industrialists of the South. Cochran and Miller describe
an important group of antebellum merchant-capitalists, the Boston Associates, who controlled 20% of the nation's cotton spindles by 1850:
"Living sumptuously on Beacon Hill, admired by their neighbors for
their philanthropy and their patronage of art and culture, these men
traded in State Street while overseers ran their factories, managers directed their railroads, agents sold their water power and real estate. They
were absentee landlords in the most complete sense. Uncontaminated by
the disease of the factory town, they were also protected from hearing the
complaints of their workers of suffering mental depression from dismal and
squalid surroundings" (1961, p. 72). Recent social-historical research
shows how the paternalistic practices imposed by these absentee owners
backfired (Dublin 1979).

Unlike in the postbellum Upper South, unskilled labor was scarce in
New England in the 1830s. The English invention of the power loom
enabled Boston capitalists to tap one of the few relatively abundant supplies of unskilled labor, farm daughters (Jeremy 1973, p. 47). The vast
majority of textile workers in Lowell, Massachusetts, in the 1830s and
1840s were unmarried women who lived in closely supervised, company-
owned boardinghouses. Corporate paternalism, which promised to protect
the "morals" of young, single women, was developed to legitimate factory
work and to secure a tractable, disciplined labor force (Dublin 1979, p.
77). Despite the intent of the Boston owners, factory women developed
strong social solidarity by living and working together 24 hours a day.
They struck in the 1830s to oppose wage reductions and again in the
1840s for a 10-hour day, signing their written protests "Daughters of
Freemen." Corporate paternalism did not mesh with the economic independence of Yankee yeoman farmers and their "revolutionary republican
traditions" (Dublin 1979, pp. 93, 103). Women established patterns of
class struggle in northeastern factory towns that continued throughout
the 19th century.

Beginning with the Irish in the late 1840s (Gitelman 1967), immigrants
augmented the New England labor supply, and paternalism began to diminish in the 1850s. In 1860, when roughly 60% of the textile labor force
was nonnative, a majority of workers lived in private housing (Dublin

1979, p. 143). By 1900, only 28% of the New England textile families lived in company housing, and there are said to have been "few traces" of industrial welfare work left in the industry (Lahne 1944, p. 29).

Social historians agree that new immigrant populations entering New England mills each needed a decade of industrial experience before renewing the class struggles of earlier groups (Dublin 1979, pp. 145–64; Walkowitz 1978, pp. 158–77). First, they had to create networks of voluntary associations, churches, and community ties (Walkowitz 1978, p. 3)—organizational prerequisities for labor militance (Shorter and Tilly 1974). Autonomous working-class institutions were far more free to develop in New England, where diversification and urbanism paralleled the growth of the textile industry, than in the South. Mill workers contributed to working-class struggles in New England (Lahne 1944, pp. 175–202), and, at least in urban settings, they benefited from the experience and organization of militant skilled workers in surrounding craft industries (Walkowitz 1978).

As I will describe more fully below, similar traditions did not emerge in the southern textile industry. In the South, millowners' control "functioned effectively to destroy any autonomous social space and institutions which the working class could claim as their own—in which independent leadership could emerge and develop, in which popular traditions could be sustained, or in which workers could compare and analyze their experience as working people" (Boyte 1972, p. 23). Cross-sectional studies of strike activity suggest that labor militance is most likely to occur in large communities and in large plants with absentee owners (Stern 1976). In North Carolina, textile factories were typically small, isolated, and personalistic. In 1919, when 53% of New England's textile workers were employed in factories with more than 1,000 workers, only 18% of southern millhands worked in factories this size (Lahne 1944, p. 14). (North Carolina factories averaged 18,000 spindles in 1900, while many New England mills had 50,000–100,000 spindles by then.) As late as 1929, 70% of North Carolina's textile workers were still employed in mills with fewer than 200 workers, where owners or officials could know all the operatives personally (Herring 1929, p. 387).

Factory size alone, however, does not account for the lack of workers' autonomy in southern mills. In the first decades after the Civil War, North Carolina's rural factories were built primarily by planter-industrialists who drew on local labor supplies. Traditional rural class relations were upheld as planter-industrialists and farmer-millhands alike fluctuated between cotton growing and cotton manufacturing activities. Unlike the situation in New England, industrial paternalism resonated with the authoritarian dimensions of southern class relations. Personalistic recruitment and paternalist favors were exchanged for workers' loyalty. This pattern is illustrated in the following description of labor recruitment reported in a 1905 biographical sketch of Mark Morgan, a North Carolina cotton manufacturer, banker, legislator, and cotton planter:

> Mr. Morgan walked through the surrounding country personally soliciting the services of such laborers as were properly open to such proposals, and by his *personal contact* with prospective laborers protecting the character of the mill settlement by not taking people whose appearance seemed to indicate criminal tendencies. In truth . . . *he has always endeavored to protect the character of his people* by excluding the vicious, so much so that it was a matter of pride often referred to by his more experienced hands that they were with Mr. Morgan so long. *Nor is this confined to his mill operatives, but applied to his farm laborers and tenants as well.* Often they state that they intend to remain with Mr. Morgan so long as they live, if he will keep them so long. [John 1905, p. 287, italics added]

Local labor recruitment and homogeneity of the work force remain characteristic of southern mills. A survey of 500 mill families in Gaston County, North Carolina, in 1926 found that 94% of the workers were born in nearby counties. Of these, 71% were born in North Carolina, half of them in the immediate county (Rhyne 1930, p. 70). Millowners recruited whole families—as is reflected in the familistic imagery of textile ideology—which tended to remain in the industry for generations, so that the southern "mill people" became almost a closed group. Rhyne (1930, p. 77) found that lifelong mill careers had increased from 18% to 71% for the three generations represented in his sample; by 1930, given the absence of diversification, mill village populations were becoming increasingly self-sustaining. This contrasts with the situation in New England, where most workers spent only a few years in the mills before going on to better-paying, more permanent industrial jobs or marriage (Walkowitz 1978, p. 60). Since the self-sufficiency of antebellum plantations had retarded community and urban development in the South, southern millhands remained far more dependent on mill village services than were textile workers in New England. Lahne (1944, p. 35) estimated that, in 1900, 87% of the southern cotton mill labor force lived in company housing, and Rhyne (1930, p. 123) found that 70% of the Gaston County workers still lived in company houses in 1926. Over half of the 322 Carolina mills surveyed in 1929 still provided a wide range of paternalistic services (Herring 1929).

Workers' dependence on millowners, which mirrored planters' rural dominance, and the closed, almost "caste-like" character of the mill villages (Lahne 1944, p. 65) contributed to workers' blunted class consciousness. The southern textile industry exanded at a propitious time in the late 19th century, when raw cotton prices were low and prices for manufactured cotton goods were high (Lemert 1933, p. 27). Economists disagree about whether access to cotton fields, which presumably lowered transportation costs, was a significant factor in the profitability of the cotton manufacturing industry (Copeland 1923, p. 36), but all agree that lower wage costs in the South primarily accounted for the higher profit margins of southern textile manufacturing compared with the returns in New England (Lemert 1933, pp. 59–81).[12] Average wages were 40% lower in the South than in the Northeast; work days were 24% longer (Vance 1935, pp. 291–328). Success presumed control of the work force.

In addition to the style of production relations in southern mills and the paternalism of the mill villages, the large white labor reserve produced by agricultural depression in the Upper South also inhibited labor militancy. Since average monthly wages in 1899 for male farm laborers in North Carolina were only $8.91, even the average daily wage (in 1893) of 69 cents for unskilled labor in cotton mills was attractive to financially desperate farmworkers. This was especially true since wives and children could also work, though at lower wages than adult males, and since mill-owners provided many desirable services. For the most part, grievances were privatized. Harry Douty (1936, p. 81) argues that, from 1880 to 1930, labor turnover within the textile industry, rather than strikes, was an index of protest at wages, hours, and working conditions. He describes some mill families as industrial nomads "wandering from mill to mill in search of something better than they had known." This form of private protest, the search for a more beneficent patron, reinforced the personalistic style of labor relations in the industry.

The introduction of industrial wage labor on a large scale in the South, however, was not entirely smooth. Two phases of industrial conflict occurred in North Carolina. Skilled craft workers struggled sporadically at the turn of the century, and unskilled workers resisted rationalization and labor-process intensification during the Depression. Whenever textile workers did protest collectively, however, millowners invoked the black labor force as a threat to keep wages and hours unchanged. This was an effective weapon. A Greensboro newspaper, for instance, warned operatives in the 1890s that "the colored man is now knocking at the door of the cotton mill asking for work at lower wages than white men could think of" (quoted in McLaurin 1971b, p. 63).

In addition to racial threats, millowners' control was augmented by technological innovations in textile manufacturing. The ring spindle, which was invented around 1870 and installed in all the new southern factories after the Civil War, eliminated the mule spindle, which had required great

[12] In 1900 average yearly earnings in the Massachusetts textile industry for males, aged 16 and older, were $405.69; the comparable rate in North Carolina was $216.39. In North Carolina, where 25% of the work force was under age 16, children earned only $102.79 per year—half the wage level of New England youth.

skill and strength to operate. Male "mule spinners" were among the most militant and well-organized craft workers in the New England industry in the 1880s (Lahne 1944, pp. 180–81; see also Copeland 1923, pp. 123–24). Because southern factories typically produced coarser grades of cloth than rival firms in the North, they made earlier and more extensive use of the ring spindle. With it, they relied more heavily on unskilled labor than did the northern factories (Copeland 1923, p. 73). Millowners' control, however, was still limited by their dependence on other craft occupations such as loom fixers, carders, and skilled weavers. Although this has not received the scholarly attention it deserves, these skilled workers organized a number of local craft unions in the South and led several localized strikes against wage reductions and to demand shorter work weeks around the turn of the century. These strikes occurred primarily in the older mills of the Carolinas and Georgia where skilled workers had developed traditions of industrial justice which in some cases dated back to antebellum times (McLaurin 1971a, 1971b; Reid 1973). These occupations were largely eliminated from southern factories by mechanization before World War I (Stern 1937; Copeland 1923, pp. 54–100). "These inventions brought the coarse and medium cotton-goods industry to the point where the foreman and a few machinery repairmen were the only skilled employees necessary to a cotton-goods mill" (Lemert 1933, p. 33). Because of mechanization, children made up 25% of the southern textile labor force but only 7% of the labor force in the North in 1900.

Following the elimination of craft occupations from southern factories, a period of industrial calm lasted until the Depression. Beginning in the 1920s, however, southern manufacturers started to respond to post–World War I price declines for cotton products with consolidation and rationalization. Horizontal mergers and vertical integration intensified throughout the decade (Lemert 1933, pp. 120–99), although typically individual plant units remained small (Herring 1929, p. 19). Managerial strategies combined the professionalization of welfare programs (Herring 1929) with Taylorist techniques, such as the "stretch-out," which reduced employment levels and intensified the labor process. Describing the outlook of this generation of southern manufacturers, Mitchell and Mitchell wrote: "In fact, they are industrialists, businessmen, capitalists, and congratulate themselves upon supporting these characters. They are not subject to the restraints of their fathers. They do not have an emotional attitude toward their workers. They are not burdened with a sense of noblesse oblige. They are not aristocrats, but bourgeois. They are class-conscious and money-wise" (1930, p. 33). By the time of the Great Depression, the logic of industrial, wage-labor capitalism had begun to contradict the old style of paternalistic class relations institutionalized by pioneer planter-industrialists just as agricultural relations, too, were soon to give way.

The most extensive strikes which ever occurred in North Carolina, such as the one in Gastonia in 1929 at the Rhode Island–owned Loray Mills, were in response to these developments. Class struggle centered in the large, absentee-owned factories where labor relations had become impersonal and overtly conflictual (Bernstein 1960, pp. 1–45; Marshall 1967, pp. 166–81). "When southern labor stirs," to borrow a phrase from Tippett (1931), most often, in the early textile industry at least, it was in part to restore the balance of rights and duties and to defend the style of personal relations in the mills which southern workers had come to expect since the early postbellum years. This interpretation is consistent with Liston Pope's observation that "lower wages appear not to have been crucial" in the Gastonia strike, "nor was the fact of a stretch-out of itself of supreme importance." Rather, he says, "so far as internal mill policies were concerned, the impersonal and arbitrary methods of the superintendent appear to have been the most significant factors underlying the strike" (1942, p. 231). Even today, some textile workers react with hostility to the replacement of paternalism by bureaucratic modes of industrial control. Union organizers at the mills in Roanoke Rapids, North Carolina, for instance, have found that older, white mill workers disparage the current J. P. Stevens management for neglecting to carry on the personalistic treatment they had come to expect from "old Mr. Sam" Patterson, a planter-industrialist mentioned above, who sold out to the New England firm (Conway 1979, pp. 16, 25, 35–36). This attitude toward authority contrasts sharply with the attitudes of at least some southern workers outside planter-dominated industry.

Contrasts in the Southern Coalfields

Too readily, scholars attribute the repeated failures of unionization efforts in Carolina cotton factories simply to the geographical isolation of mill villages, to worker dependence on owners, or to the homogeneity of the work force (Boyte 1972; Roy 1965). These factors were significant, as I have shown, but it is crucial to see that their causal impacts were mediated by the class relations of the plantation social order. This can be demonstrated by a brief look at industrial relations in the southern coal mining industry. Coal camps in the mountains of the South, like mill villages, were isolated; their populations were relatively homogeneous and utterly dependent. Ironically, these same characteristics are frequently invoked to explain the strength of occupational community and labor militancy among miners (Kerr and Siegel 1954). In contrast to the relative quiescence of Carolina mill villages, southern coalfields were hotbeds of industrial conflict. Only 32 strikes involving 9,274 workers occurred in the southern textile industry from 1887 to 1905. In the same years, 519 strikes involving 205,156 workers occurred in southern coal mines. One third of all southern strikers in those years were coal miners (Marshall 1967, pp. 30–33).

The loss of land to absentee railroad, mineral, and timber companies in the southern mountains produced levels of tenancy comparable to those in other southern regions in the late 19th century; significantly, though, there was no landlord class to organize and appropriate agricultural production (Caudill 1963; Banks 1980a). Land shortages, along with natural population increases, insured a large labor reserve. Appalachian coal counties were typically nondiversified. Many coal camps, especially those built by sons of southern planters and by large corporations such as U.S. Steel, which practiced "welfare capitalism," were just as paternalistic as the mill villages of the Carolina Piedmont (Eller 1979, pp. 251–311). As in the textile industry, hours were longer and wage levels were much lower than in the north-central coal fields (Hevener 1978, p. 5). Unlike the planter-industrialists, however, who were generally able to secure workers' loyalty, southern coal operators were forced to hire private mine guards and Chicago gun thugs, and occasionally to request federal troops to police dissident mining camps. Some of the nation's most violent labor struggles took place in southern mountain communities such as Cabin Creek, Paint Creek, and Logan in West Virginia and "Bloody Harlan" in eastern Kentucky (Dreiser 1932; Williams 1976; Hevener 1978; Green 1972).

In a study of differential levels of contemporary miners' militancy, Nelson and Grams (1978) found that structural blame must intervene between workers' access to occupational community and militancy. The authors err in psychologizing this factor of structural blame. A sociological basis for differences in occupational consciousness and protest actions between workers in southern mines and mills can be found in variant production relations between the two industries and in the class relations of the two distinct social structures of the mountain and plantation South.

In large, mechanized factories managerial power is partially concealed in the technological organization of production since owners or managers need not directly intervene in the labor process to exert power over workers (Edwards 1979). Machines appeared to direct the labor process in textile mills, except when owners or managers interfered with routine production processes to impose speed-ups or stretch-outs. Since most southern firms were small and personalistic, however, millowners in North Carolina also exercised direct personal power over their workers in their roles as benevolent patrons caring for the mill families in their villages. This relative invisibility of millowners in the production process and their prominence in mill village affairs helps to explain the tendency for southern textile workers to "absolve top management of responsibility for the out-of-line activities of supervisors and to consider the latter as indicative of personality quirks of individuals rather than as representative of company policy" (Gilman 1956, p. 144).

Coal mining, in contrast, was a craft occupation prior to the period of mechanization (roughly 1930–60). Mine operators exerted direct control through foremen, but miners had an unusual degree of labor autonomy (Dix 1977). Work teams developed strong social solidarity because of the shared danger and interdependence underground. Miners' independence at work was reinforced by preindustrial social experience in the southern mountains. Social structure in the Appalachian South combined two modes of production—independent commodity production on the family farms and free-wage capitalist labor in the mines. Coal camp paternalism, imposed by entrepreneurs foreign to the region, had no grounding in the prior experience of autonomous mountain farmers as did the mill village paternalism in the cotton South which, as I have argued, reproduced the servile labor mode of cotton fields. Consequently, in the coalfields, industrial conflict was not restricted to workplace issues: miners opposed various forms of company paternalism including company store profits, owners' control of housing and evictions, script payments, and the civil control exercised by private mine deputies (Marshall 1967, pp. 71–86). Recent research suggests that coalfield struggles were as much political as economic (Hevener 1978, p. 40; Banks 1980b). There is no historical evidence of similar opposition to paternalism by southern mill workers. On the contrary, abrogations of personalistic treatment often appear to have violated mill workers' traditional sense of justice in the not too distant past.

A Different Ethos along Tobacco Road

Social consequences of the continuity between textile manufacturing and agrarian social patterns can be seen, finally, in contrasts provided by North Carolina's tobacco industry. Tobacco manufacturing was an important exception in North Carolina to the pattern of planter dominance. Its leaders were indeed "new men." Washington Duke owned 300 acres of land, two mules, and 50 cents in cash at the end of the Civil War. He farmed and manufactured tobacco with his sons on his small farm. At one point, out of financial desperation, he had to sell his farm to a neighbor and work on it for wages. The other early manufacturers in Durham who merged with the Dukes to establish the American Tobacco Company—W. T. Blackwell, Julian S. Carr, Richard Wright, and George Watts—were also upwardly mobile "new men." Only R. J. Reynolds, whose father was a Virginia planter, merchant, and tobacco manufacturer, was an exception, developing a business independently at Salem.

The absence of large landowners from the development of the tobacco industry is explained by planters' lack of experience with growing tobacco, as well as their inexperience with its preparation and manufacture. In 19th-century North Carolina, tobacco was a cash crop grown primarily by small farmers. Since the production of plug and smoking tobacco initially required only simple equipment, tobacco manufacturing developed as a craft industry among yeoman farmers and artisans. Prior to mass-production techniques, its manufacture required little capital (Tilley 1948, pp. 489–544). Tobacco processing was an important investment opportunity for small businessmen, unlike textile manufacturing, a much greater undertaking which attracted only wealthy individuals. Washington Duke's first tobacco "factory" was a small log house where he prepared leaf tobacco during the winter. With his two sons, he expanded this domestic craft into one of the largest industrial enterprises in the world at the time.

The invention of cigarette-making machinery in the 1880s provided new technology for mass production which radically changed the tobacco industry. Among the first to take advantage of this technology, the Dukes and their associates in Durham built the largest business organization in the South, capitalized at $300 million in 1904 (Ezell 1963, pp. 144–48). In distinct contrast to the highly competitive textile industry, the American Tobacco Company grew to exemplify the bureaucratically organized monopolies which came to dominate American business in the period from 1870 to 1900. As did other "big businesses" of the period which manufactured consumer goods from farm products for sale nationally in urban markets, the Dukes combined and centralized raw material purchase, mass production, distribution, and finance functions in a single, vertically integrated business structure (Chandler 1966, pp. 79–101). Since supply soon overran demand, the Dukes developed modern marketing techniques, such as mass advertising. They created a national and then a worldwide selling organization, capturing 95% of the American cigarette market in the 1890s. Cigarettes manufactured in North Carolina soon became one of the nation's first name-brand products. Unlike the planter-industrialists in the textile sector who manufactured a partially finished product, cloth, tobacco manufacturers broke out of North Carolina's otherwise dependent economy by manufacturing a complete product.

Tobacco manufacturing conflicted in many ways with the rest of North Carolina's political economy. Tobacco manufacturers were new men with a new product. They were industrial capitalists with no class interest in preserving the agrarian social order. Unlike the early textile manufacturers, they were not landowners.[13] Social relations in the tobacco in-

[13] Benjamin Duke owned a farm in North Carolina, along with his mansions in Durham and New York City, but it was not the source of his wealth and power. When Duke sold his North Carolina farm in 1919 he noted, "I am glad it is off our hands" (quoted in Durden 1975, p. 127).

dustry deviated from the traditional pattern of southern labor relations. Tobacco manufacturers paid relatively high wages and employed blacks, two violations of usual industrial practices within the state. In contrast with mill village paternalism, they built no industrial communities or housing. They accepted unionization when it came. A different ethos came to characterize the towns along tobacco road.

Initially wages in the tobacco industry were lower than textile wages. By 1900, however, wages in the two industries were equivalent. Mechanization and marketing success in tobacco eventually permitted substantial wage increases. By 1929 the work day in cigarette factories was shorter and wages were much higher than in cotton manufacturing (Rice 1941, p. 128). Wage disparities between tobacco and textile manufacturing can be traced to differences in industrial structure. In contrast to the competition between southern and northern textile firms in which southern manufacturers benefited from lower wage costs, the American Tobacco Company competed through advertising wars rather than price wars. Tobacco manufacturers "aimed at increasing the volume exchanged not by reducing the price for a given product but by inducing consumers to take more of the product at a given price" (Cox 1933, p. 113). This strategy, plus the high monetary value of workers' productivity in the industry, permitted high wages.

Industrial organization and profit structures account for wage disparities between tobacco and textile jobs but not for the industries' comparative racial practices. Southern textile manufacturers kept the cotton industry "lily-white." In 1930 there were only 477 black textile operatives in North Carolina out of a work force of 100,000 employees; southern mill towns were strictly segregated (Pope 1942, p. 12; Lewis 1955, p. 114). In sharp contrast, the tobacco industry always employed a high proportion of black workers. In 1930 almost 2,500 of the 3,865 male tobacco operatives in North Carolina were black, as were 4,166 of the 4,966 male laborers. Black women comprised an even higher proportion of the female work force. Of 9,904 female tobacco operatives, 7,143 were black, as were 1,292 of the 1,831 female laborers. This cannot be explained simply as the exploitation of black labor in disagreeable, low-income jobs, since "the tobacco worker, both white and colored, in general [was] envied by fellow workers in other southern industries, and the wages far exceed[ed] those of many white-collar workers, teachers, and professionals" (Rice 1941, p. 62).

Durham tobacco manufacturers employed blacks in their factories and broke the South's racial code even more significantly by employing blacks in textile mills. Unlike the planter-industrialists, they had little directly at stake in preserving the racial caste system on which the plantation order was based. Julian Carr, though a white supremacist, encouraged black economic participation in cotton manufacturing in accord with the philosophy of Booker T. Washington. "Inviting Negroes to help the South overtake the economy of the North, he established a 'Jim Crow' cotton mill to provide employment for blacks outside the established lily-white mills. Carr's Negro mill could be seen entirely as a tactic to exploit cheap Negro labor, but he just as eagerly lent his support to a Negro-owned cotton mill begun in 1898 by W. C. Coleman, a black businessman in Concord, North Carolina (Weare 1976, pp. 40–41). The Dukes also loaned money to this black-owned mill, although it failed in 1904. Their involvement in black businesses was "both incidental and, in the last analysis, kept on a cool, businesslike basis" but, of course, as Robert Durden stresses, "even that kind of relationship was in stark contrast to the harshly discriminatory policies of disfranchisement and segregation of blacks that the Southern Democrats championed so successfully in those same early years of the twentieth century" (1975, p. 147).

The existence of a landless black working class in tobacco cities such as Durham created a market for black businesses and sustained a black middle class. With the financial support of the Dukes, the North Carolina Mutual Insurance Company, for instance, grew to become the world's largest black-owned business (Weare 1976, p. 20). Black businesses did so well in the relatively permissive atmosphere of Durham that the new city acquired a special reputation in the South. Booker T. Washington reported finding in Durham "the sanest attitude of white people toward the blacks" in the South (Rice 1941, p. 34), and black sociologist E. Franklin Frazier described Durham in the 1920s as the "capital of the black middle class in America" (1925, p. 333). Durham also permitted space for the development of a relatively autonomous black working-class culture.[14] The point is not to celebrate Durham but, rather, to suggest that the class relations of tobacco manufacturing generated a social structure that was quite distinct from that of the planter-dominated textile villages. The latter permitted the development of far less cultural autonomy for its working classes than did the tobacco centers. These cities saw the emergence of solidary ethnic and class communities unlikely elsewhere in the Carolinas.

3. CONCLUSION

I have provided evidence against the commonplace belief that after the Civil War "when the planters went down, their way of life went down also"

[14] One can sense something of the vitality and independence of this urban black culture in the upbeat music performed in Durham. Blues performers such as Blind Boy Fuller created a musical style in the 1930s, known as "Bull Durham Blues," which reflected the hopes and disappointments of the urban black working class. Its ragtime sound was a departure from the usual melancholy of rural southern blues (Bastin 1971).

Billings

(Genovese 1971, p. 230). Emancipation altered planters' tactics for expropriating surplus labor from former slaves; nonetheless, the political economy of the plantation South persisted well into the 20th century through the class relations of tenancy and sharecropping. This interpretation of southern development challenges the liberal contention that social relations in the postbellum South, with the important exception of psychological attitudes of racial prejudice, were essentially similar to those elsewhere in the United States. The liberal remedy for overcoming southern economic "backwardness" has been simply more of what—as mainstream modernization theory asserts—all developing societies need: more capital investments, better roads, better education, etc. Such accounts divert attention from the effects of class exploitation in the South and elsewhere.

The structure of southern class relations accounts for the region's distinctiveness in American society. From the Civil War to the Depression, the New South was a hybrid social form combining two predominant modes of production under the leadership of planter-industrialists. The uneasy accommodation of all-white wage labor in the expanding industrial-capitalist sector to the servile labor system of plantation agriculture produced great strain and required intense measures of social control in the Upper South. The old grammar of paternalism and the new logic of capitalist industrialism were tensely interwoven. By the time of the New Deal the system was giving way in southern cotton fields to subsidies, mechanization, and federal welfare payments just meager enough to keep a reserve labor force on the land; in North Carolina cotton mills, institutionalized paternalism lingered but consolidation, rationalization, and, occasionally, industrial conflict became the rule. Today, North Carolina ranks second among the 50 states in the percentage of the nonagricultural work force employed in industry. At the same time, however, North Carolina ranks fiftieth in level of industrial wages and fiftieth in level of unionization. These are legacies of planter dominance that remain.

APPENDIX

An example of how I coded the data for one county illustrates why these percentages probably underestimate the connection between early industrialists and the landed upper class in North Carolina.

Seven cotton mills operated from 1865 to 1884 in Richmond County, a cotton-producing county in the Piedmont section of North Carolina. One factory operated less than one year with a very small capital investment; its owners were not identified. Of the remaining mills, two were definitely owned by cotton planters, Col. Charles Malloy and John Leake, each of whom, according to Branson (1869), operated 3,000-acre plantations in 1869. Their mills dated from 1867 and 1879, respectively. Col. Walter

Leake Steele, who was perhaps a relative of R. J. Steele, a wealthy Richmond County planter, and of John Leake, also owned two mills. Another mill was owned by T. B. and J. S. Ledbetter. Although neither was identified as a planter in the 1869 directory, several Ledbetters in Richmond County were large landowners. Finally, Midway Mills, chartered in 1881, was identified simply as owned by "Leake, Wall, and McRae." The Leake referred to is probably planter-industrialist John Leake, but I eliminated this mill from the total since no first names were available. Although I cannot establish conclusively that its owners were landowners, these three families were prominent in the county. Among the 16 planters listed in the 1869 directory, five were Leakes, one was a Wall, and one was a McRae. These three families owned at least 31,000 acres of land. Steele and Ledbetter account for three more names—a total of 10 out of 16 prominent agricultural landowners. These five families owned at least 40,000 acres of land in 1869. Following my conservative method, however, I counted only two Richmond County mills as having been owned by members of the landed upper class.

From this type of historical data, one can discern three types of mill-owners: (1) planters, (2) members of planter families, and (3) upwardly mobile businessmen.[15] Many North Carolina millowners operating from 1865 to 1884 were prominent planters (type 1), such as Col. Thomas M. Holt of Alamance County. Born in 1831, Holt was the grandson of Edwin M. Holt, one of the earliest southern industrialists. He expanded his father's textile factory at a cost of nearly one-half million dollars after the war. He lived on the Haw River across from his mills in a princely mansion, described by biographers as the largest, most elegantly furnished country dwelling in North Carolina. He also operated the famous Linwood plantation. Holt served 12 years as president of the North Carolina Railroad and was a member of the State Board of Agriculture. He served three terms in the U.S. Congress and was governor of North Carolina from 1891 to 1893. Other industrialists, such as William Holt Williamson, were members of prominent landed families, although I have no evidence as to whether these men personally operated plantations (type 2). Williamson, who established his first factory in 1884, was the grandson of an extensive planter and merchant. His father, also a planter, married one of Edwin Holt's daughters and began to manufacture cotton as well as grow it. Williamson built mills in Raleigh, Burlington, and Henderson and also invested in banking. Finally, other industrialists, though a minority, were upwardly mobile (type 3). Some, such as John Ferree, began careers in textile manufacturing as employees of pioneer-industrialists and eventually were able to invest in the postbellum expansion.

[15] Unless otherwise indicated, biographical data are compiled from scores of sources indexed in the North Carolina Historical Collection of the Wilson Library at the University of North Carolina at Chapel Hill.

Billings

REFERENCES

Ashe, Samuel. 1905a. "Duncan Cameron." Pp. 43–47 in *Biographical History of North Carolina,* edited by Samuel Ashe. Vol. 3. Greensboro, N.C.: Van Noppen.
———. 1905b. "Paul Carrington Cameron." Pp. 48–55 in *Biographical History of North Carolina,* edited by Samuel Ashe. Vol. 3. Greensboro, N.C.: Van Noppen.
Banks, Alan. 1980a. "The Emergence of a Capitalistic Labor Market in Eastern Kentucky." *Appalachian Journal* 7:188–200.
———. 1980b. "Labor and the Development of Industrial Capitalism in Eastern Kentucky, 1870–1930." Ph.D. dissertation, McMaster University.
Baran, Paul. 1970. "On the Political Economy of Backwardness." Pp. 285–301 in *Imperialism and Underdevelopment,* edited by Robert Rhodes. New York: Monthly Review Press.
Bastin, Bruce. 1971. *Crying for the Carolines.* London: Studio Vista.
Bernstein, Irving. 1960. *The Lean Years.* Boston: Houghton Mifflin.
Billings, Dwight. 1979. *Planters and the Making of a "New South."* Chapel Hill: University of North Carolina Press.
———. 1981. "Class and Class Politics in the Southern Populist Movement of the 1890's." *Sociological Spectrum* 1:259–92.
Blauner, Robert. 1964. *Alienation and Freedom.* Chicago: University of Chicago Press.
Boyte, Harry. 1972. "The Textile Industry: Keel of Southern Industrialization." *Radical America* 6:4–49.
Brandes, Stuart. 1970. *American Welfare Capitalism, 1880–1940.* Chicago: University of Chicago Press.
Branson, Levi. 1869, 1872, 1877–78, 1884. *Branson's North Carolina Business Directory.* Raleigh, N.C.: Branson.
Brenner, Robert. 1977. "The Origins of Capitalist Development: A Critique of Neo-Smithian Marxism." *New Left Review* 104:25–92.
Buck, Paul. 1937. *The Road to Reunion, 1865–1900.* Boston: Little, Brown.
Cash, W. J. 1941. *The Mind of the South.* New York: Vintage.
Caudill, Harry. 1963. *Night Comes to the Cumberlands.* Boston: Little, Brown.
Chandler, Alfred. 1966. "The Beginnings of 'Big Business' in American Industry." Pp. 79–101 in *Views of American Economic Growth,* edited by Thomas Cochran and Thomas Brewer. New York: McGraw-Hill.
Cochran, Thomas, and William Miller. 1961. *The Age of Enterprise.* New York: Harper & Row.
Conway, Mimi. 1979. *Rise Gonna Rise.* Garden City, N.Y.: Anchor.
Cooper, William J. 1968. *The Conservative Regime: South Carolina, 1877–1890.* Baltimore: Johns Hopkins University Press.
Copeland, Melvin. 1923. *The Cotton Manufacturing Industry of the United States.* Cambridge, Mass.: Harvard University Press.
Cox, Reavis. 1933. *Competition in the American Tobacco Industry.* New York: Columbia University Press.
DeCanio, Stephen. 1974. *Agriculture in the Postbellum South.* Cambridge, Mass.: MIT Press.
Dix, Keith. 1977. *Work Relations in the Coal Industry, 1880–1930.* Morgantown: West Virginia University Press.
Douty, Harry. 1936. "The North Carolina Industrial Worker, 1880–1930." Ph.D. dissertation, University of North Carolina.
Dreiser, Theodore, ed. 1932. *Harlan Miners Speak.* New York: Harcourt, Brace.
Dublin, Thomas. 1979. *Women at Work.* New York: Columbia University Press.
Durden, Robert. 1975. *The Dukes of Durham, 1865–1929.* Durham, N.C.: Duke University Press.
Edwards, Richard C. 1979. *Contested Terrain.* New York: Basic.
Eller, Ronald D. 1979. "Miners, Millhands, and Mountaineers." Ph.D. dissertation, University of North Carolina.
Ezell, John Samuel. 1963. *The South since 1865.* New York: Macmillan.

Fogel, Robert, and Stanley Engerman. 1974. *Time on the Cross.* New York: Little, Brown.

Frazier, E. Franklin. 1925. "Durham: Capital of the Black Middle Class." Pp. 333–40 in *The New Negro,* edited by Alain Locke. New York: Boni.

Gaston, Paul. 1973. *The New South Creed.* New York: Vintage.

Genovese, Eugene. 1967. *The Political Economy of Slavery.* New York: Vintage.

———. 1971. *The World the Slaveholders Made.* New York: Vintage.

Gilman, Glenn. 1956. *Human Relations in the Industrial Southeast.* Chapel Hill: University of North Carolina Press.

Gitelman, Howard. 1967. "The Waltham System and the Coming of the Irish." *Labor History* 8:227–53.

Green, Archie. 1972. *Only a Miner.* Urbana: University of Illinois Press.

Griffin, Richard. 1964. "Reconstruction of the North Carolina Textile Industry, 1865–1885." *North Carolina Historical Review* 41:34–53.

Gutman, Herbert. 1976. *The Black Family in Slavery and Freedom, 1750–1925.* New York: Pantheon.

Hackney, Sheldon. 1972. "Origins of the New South in Retrospect." *Journal of Southern History* 38:191–216.

Herring, Harriet. 1929. *Welfare Work in Mill Villages.* Chapel Hill: University of North Carolina Press.

———. 1931. "Early Industrial Development in the South." *Annals of the American Academy* 153:1–10.

Hevener, John W. 1978. *Which Side Are You On?* Urbana: University of Illinois Press.

Hunter, Floyd. 1980. *Community Power Succession.* Chapel Hill: University of North Carolina Press.

Jeremy, David. 1973. "Innovation in American Textile Technology during the Early Nineteenth Century." *Technology and Culture* 14:40–76.

John, Maxcy. 1905. "Mark Morgan." Pp. 258–88 in *Biographical History of North Carolina,* edited by Samuel Ashe. Vol. 2. Greensboro, N.C.: Van Noppen.

Kerr, Clark, and Abraham Siegel. 1954. "The Interindustry Propensity to Strike—an International Comparison." Pp. 189–212 in *Industrial Conflict,* edited by Arthur Kornhauser, Robert Dunn, and Arthur Ross. New York: McGraw-Hill.

Key, V. O. 1949. *Southern Politics.* New York: Random House.

Lacy, Dan. 1935. "The Beginnings of Industrialism in North Carolina." Ph.D. dissertation, University of North Carolina.

Lahne, Herbert. 1944. *The Cotton Mill Worker.* New York: Farrar & Rinehart.

Lander, Ernest. 1969. *The Textile Industry in Antebellum South Carolina.* Baton Rouge: Louisiana State University Press.

Lefler, Hugh. 1955. *North Carolina History Told by Contemporaries.* Chapel Hill: University of North Carolina Press.

Lefler, Hugh, and Albert Newsome. 1973. *North Carolina: The History of a Southern State.* Chapel Hill: University of North Carolina Press.

Lemert, Ben. 1933. *The Cotton Textile Industry of the Southern Appalachian Piedmont.* Chapel Hill: University of North Carolina Press.

Lewis, Hylan. 1955. *Blackways of Kent.* Chapel Hill: University of North Carolina Press.

McLaurin, Melton. 1971a. "Early Labor Union Organizational Efforts in South Carolina Cotton Mills, 1880–1905." *South Carolina Historical Magazine* 72 (1): 44–59.

———. 1971b. *Paternalism and Protest.* Westport, Conn.: Greenwood.

Mandle, Jay. 1978. *The Roots of Black Poverty.* Durham, N.C.: Duke University Press.

Marshall, F. Ray. 1967. *Labor in the South.* Cambridge, Mass.: Harvard University Press.

Mitchell, Broadus. 1921. *The Rise of Cotton Mills in the South.* Baltimore: Johns Hopkins University Press.

———. 1931. "Growth of Manufactures in the South." *Annals of the American Academy* 153:21–29.

Mitchell, Broadus, and George Mitchell. 1930. *The Industrial Revolution in the South.* Baltimore: Johns Hopkins University Press.

Moore, Barrington. 1966. *Social Origins of Dictatorship and Democracy.* Boston: Beacon.

Nelson, Joel, and Robert Grams. 1978. "Union Militancy and Occupational Community." *Industrial Relations* 17:342–46.

Newman, Dale. 1978. "Work and Community Life in a Southern Textile Town." *Labor History* 19:204–25.

Nicholls, William. 1960. *Southern Tradition and Regional Progress.* Chapel Hill: University of North Carolina Press.

Odum, Howard. 1936. *Southern Regions of the United States.* Chapel Hill: University of North Carolina Press.

———. 1947. *The Way of the South.* New York: Macmillan.

Pope, Liston. 1942. *Millhands and Preachers.* New Haven, Conn.: Yale University Press.

Pulley, Raymond. 1968. *Old Virginia Restored, 1870–1930.* Charlottesville: University of Virginia Press.

Reid, Merl. 1973. "The Augusta Textile Mills and the Strike of 1886." *Labor History* 13 (1): 41–59.

Reissman, Leonard. 1966. "Social Development and the American South." *Journal of Social Issues* 22:101–16.

Rhyne, Jennings. 1930. *Some Southern Cotton Mill Workers and Their Villages.* Chapel Hill: University of North Carolina Press.

Rice, John David. 1941. "The Negro Tobacco Worker and His Union." M.A. thesis, University of North Carolina.

Roy, Donald. 1965. "Change and Resistance to Change in the Southern Labor Movement." Pp. 225–47 in *The South in Continuity and Change,* edited by J. C. McKinney and E. T. Thompson. Durham, N.C.: Duke University Press.

Salamon, Lester. In press. *The Social Origins of Mississippi Backwardness.* Bloomington: Indiana University Press.

Sanders, Charles R. 1974. *The Cameron Plantation of Central North Carolina.* Durham, N.C.: Seeman.

Shorter, Edward, and Charles Tilly. 1974. *Strikes in France, 1830–1968.* Cambridge: Cambridge University Press.

Sitterson, J. Carlyle. 1957. "Business Leaders in Post–Civil War North Carolina, 1865–1900." *James Sprunt Studies in History and Political Science* 39:111–21.

Skocpol, Theda. 1976. "Old Regime Legacies and Communist Revolution in Russia and China." *Social Forces* 55:284–315.

Standard, Diffee, and Richard Griffin. 1957. "The Cotton Textile Industry in Antebellum North Carolina." *North Carolina Historical Review* 34:131–64.

Stern, Boris. 1937. "Mechanical Changes in the Cotton-Textile Industry, 1910 to 1936." *Monthly Labor Review* 45 (August): 316–43.

Stern, Robert. 1976. "Intermetropolitan Patterns of Strike Frequency." *Industrial and Labor Relations Review* 29:218–35.

Thompson, Holland. 1931. "The Civil War and Social and Economic Changes." *Annals of the American Academy* 153:11–20.

Tilley, Nannie May. 1948. *The Bright-Tobacco Industry, 1860–1929.* Chapel Hill: University of North Carolina Press.

Tippett, Tom. 1931. *When Southern Labor Stirs.* New York: Cape & Smith.

U.S. Census Office. 1900. *Twelfth Census of the United States: Agriculture.* Vol. 5. Washington, D.C.: Government Printing Office.

Vance, Rupert. 1935. *Human Geography of the South.* Chapel Hill: University of North Carolina Press.

Walkowitz, Daniel. 1978. *Worker City, Company Town.* Urbana: University of Illinois Press.

Weare, Walter. 1976. *Black Business in the New South.* Urbana: University of Illinois Press.

Wiener, Jonathan. 1978. *Social Origins of the New South: Alabama, 1860–1885.* Baton Rouge: Louisiana State University Press.
———. 1979. "Class Structure and Economic Development in the American South." *American Historical Review* 84:970–1006.
Williams, John A. 1976. *West Virginia and the Captains of Industry.* Morgantown: West Virginia University Press.
Winston, Robert. 1921. "North Carolina: A Militant Mediocracy." *Nation* 112:731.
Woodman, Harold. 1977. "Sequel to Slavery: The New History Views the Postbellum South." *Journal of Southern History* 43:523–54.
Woodward, C. Vann. 1951. *Origins of the New South, 1877–1913.* Baton Rouge: Louisiana State University Press.
———. 1971. *American Counterpoint.* Boston: Little, Brown.

Citizenship and Gender in Work Organization: Some Considerations for Theories of the Labor Process[1]

Robert J. Thomas
University of Michigan

Recent analyses of changes in the organization of work and authority relations have stimulated a concern for extending and elaborating a theory of the labor process under capitalism. Works by Braverman, Edwards, and Burawoy, in particular, have made significant, though divergent, steps in that direction. It is argued in this paper, however, that their works do not go far enough in connecting issues of race, gender, and citizenship (political inequality) with structures of control over the labor process. An analysis of data from a case study of the labor process in an agribusiness (lettuce) industry is employed to highlight the importance of citizenship and gender as statuses constructed external to economic organizations but applied internal to them. Three principal arguments are derived from that case study: (1) that differences in citizenship status and gender serve to distinguish among labor market participants; (2) that nonmarket processes affect not only the distribution of individuals into positions in the labor process but also provide distinct advantages to employers in the creation and maintenance of different labor processes; and (3) that citizenship and gender have a material basis external to the labor process, that is, they are not simply labels attached to workers. The findings from the case study are then used to suggest alternative directions for labor process theory and research.

A critical reexamination of the organization of production and trends in the development of new productive forms has emerged in the wake of Harry Braverman's masterful *Labor and Monopoly Capital* (1974). Studies of the capitalist labor process by Edwards (1979) and Burawoy (1979), in particular, have occasioned a new direction in the sociology of work, organizations, and stratification.[2] Sweeping assumptions about the nature

[1] Portions of this research were supported by grants from the National Science Foundation (SOC 78-25914) and the Graduate School of Northwestern University. Special thanks go to Arnold Feldman, Whit Soule, Michael Reich, William J. Wilson, and James Baron for their comments on an earlier draft of this paper.

[2] Although Braverman, Edwards, and Burawoy represent only three of a growing number of people with work on the labor process, I have chosen to concentrate on them because they provide the most thoroughgoing analyses published recently and because they offer distinct theoretical contrasts within the literature on the labor process.

of industrial and "postindustrial" systems of production have been subjected to intense scrutiny and reformulation as sociologists and political economists seek a better understanding of technological change and its relationship to conflict, negotiation, and consent among owners, managers, and workers. Shortcomings in industrial sociology have been recognized through attempts to link the social organization of work with the world outside the factory, the office, and the field. Furthermore, case studies in specific production settings (e.g., machine shops, longshore gangs, computer centers, and corporate offices) offer significant empirical insights for research on stratification and income determination, especially the work based on dual economy and segmented labor market models. By going back to the material roots of capitalist society, one might argue, sociologists are rediscovering the vitality of Marxian theory.

There is, however, a catch to contemporary labor process research and theory. While analysts such as Braverman, Edwards, and Burawoy have been quick to point out that the labor process in late-20th-century capitalism differs significantly from that described in Marx's 19th-century observations, their theories have by and large sought to squeeze 20th-century observations into a 19th-century model. More precisely, Braverman, Edwards, and Burawoy focus on the transformation of the labor process coincident with the transformation of the capitalist economy and enterprise. Each offers a distinct approach to the context and consequences of the rise of large-scale, monopolistic organizations. Yet all three largely adhere to a model of society which emphasizes class as the fundamental category of social life and social action and which locates the origin of inequality in the labor process. Nonclass categories and relations, such as race, gender, and citizenship, are viewed as appendages to, or functional aspects of, class inequality. Even in the face of historically persistent social, political, and economic inequality between and among racial groups, sexes, and nationalities, Braverman, Edwards, and Burawoy insist on a "class-first" (Hartmann and Markusen 1980, p. 87) theory of the labor process in contemporary capitalist society. Are these merely ideological distinctions used to fragment politically an otherwise homogeneous working class? Or, can nonclass categories have an impact on the organization of the labor process? In other words, can we develop an understanding of race, gender, or citizenship as products of systems of inequality without rejecting Marx's theory of the labor process?

In this article, I will address those questions through data collected in a case study of the labor process in industrial agriculture. The empirical object of the study—the harvest process in the southwestern U.S. lettuce industry—offers a unique opportunity to assess the relationship between citizenship, gender, and work organization. Three basic arguments will be presented with interview, participant-observer, and survey data. First, I will argue that differences in citizenship and gender serve to distinguish among labor market participants. That is, differences in citizenship status and gender do not necessarily reflect market-based characteristics of workers (e.g., skill, education, experience, or seniority) but do reflect statuses produced external to participation in economic organizations. Thus, I will suggest, citizenship status and gender are not indicators of an individual's or a group's ability to work or acquire skills; rather, they pertain to the social and political status of the individual or group in the larger community of which the labor market is a part.

Second, I will argue that nonmarket statuses affect not only the distribution of individuals into positions in the labor process, but that they also provide distinct advantages to employers in the creation and maintenance of different labor processes. Through a comparison of two separate harvest processes I will demonstrate how citizenship and gender are manipulated to enhance managerial control over the organization and pace of work.

Finally, I will argue that citizenship and gender have a material basis external to the labor process, that is, they are not simply labels attached to workers. In order to understand the origin of those statuses it is necessary to step outside the confines of the labor process. In particular, I will argue that it is crucial to develop theories of citizenship inequality and of patriarchal authority in the family in order to understand the roles of citizenship and gender in the organization of the labor process.

Before proceeding to the case study, I will elaborate briefly what I see to be shortcomings or ambiguities in the analyses offered by Braverman, Edwards, and Burawoy.

BRAVERMAN, EDWARDS, AND BURAWOY

Braverman's (1974) contribution to the study of work organization and technological change has been a mighty one. By drawing attention to the social and organizational forces which mediate technological change, he managed to sweep aside a number of sociological cobwebs and to make problematic once again the mechanisms of capitalist control over production. By emphasizing that control is made possible through the separation of conception and execution, Braverman shows how the labor process in the era of monopoly capitalism acquires the nature of an "expressive force" (Burawoy 1978): a linear model of capitalist development and change working its way through all sectors of society and social relationships.

Though his argument seems to capture the historical sweep of capitalist development, a major theoretical problem remains: Braverman fails to provide an adequate explanation for the continuing division of the population along the lines of race, gender, and, increasingly, citizenship status. The specific issues of race and gender inequality are subsumed under the more general, but less useful, rubric of the industrial reserve army of labor

(1974, pp. 377–401). For Braverman, the industrial reserve army of labor is a segment of the working class created and sustained as a buffer for the oscillating and uneven development of capitalism. This "relative surplus population" (p. 386) is composed, in part, of those people unemployed as a result of business cycles, technological change, and uneven regional or sectoral development. However, a significant segment of that labor pool is made up of those for whom steady employment is rare or unattainable or who are crowded into relatively limited niches in the economy (e.g., service, agricultural, or domestic employment). It is in this portion of the industrial reserve army that one finds a disproportionate share of blacks, Hispanics, women, and immigrant workers.

It is, however, precisely this coincidence between nonmarket status and real or potential market position which constitutes the major problem for the reserve army formulation. Why should blacks, women, or other groups be concentrated in the industrial reserve army? Moreover, how do we account for the historical persistence of that concentration? Braverman provides few clues to these questions. In large part, his conceptualization of capitalism as a system of inequality presumes that the categories of actors in that system are determined entirely by their positions in the labor process. Thus, all other categories and organizations are determined entirely by, or are a function of, that fundamental relationship. Yet what is often critical for the part of the industrial reserve army composed of blacks and women is that these people are full- or part-time participants in something other than a capitalist labor process—for example, housework or welfare transfer programs. In other words, participation in those other organizations provides the means for material existence when an individual is not engaged in value-producing activities; and, at the same time, participation in those organizations confers a status separate from class position.

Unfortunately, Braverman's use of the concept of the industrial reserve army does not provide sufficient clarity as to how or why certain groups should show up in its ranks consistently or of what distinct status is attached as a result. Thus, the reserve army comes to represent a residual category. I would argue, by contrast, that it is necessary to develop a better understanding of the distinctive processes responsible for constructing the category and for maintaining its important social and political consequences.

Edwards (1979), in contrast to Braverman, recognizes that race and gender are important considerations in the analysis of work organization and stratification. For example, he writes: "For members of both groups [blacks and women], their daily existence as workers is always conditioned by their special status" (p. 197). Yet Edwards is only slightly more helpful when it comes to identifying the basis of that special status or demonstrating how it is reproduced over time. Despite passing reference to the "special dialectics of race and gender" (pp. 194, 196) and to a cultural legacy of slavery and women's subordination to patriarchal authority (p. 197), the analysis focuses on the labor market positions of blacks, women, and, to some extent, alien workers.

While it might be unfair to criticize Edwards for not having broadened his analysis to account for parallel systems of inequality, the "special status" of blacks, women, and other identifiable groups plays an important role in his research on the labor process. In particular, his concept of "simple control" (pp. 34–36) in peripheral enterprises is built around the additional (nonmarket) leverage exercised by employers over workers. Simple control encompasses paternalistic authority, lack of formal job rights, and arbitrary employment practices. This form of control, according to Edwards, is rooted in both the personal qualities of the employer and in the vulnerable position of employees. What accounts for their vulnerability?

The answer provided by Edwards is a partial one: vulnerability derives from the concentration of workers into specific (segmented) labor markets. That is, when there exists an overabundance of people to fill a limited number of positions and when those positions require little personal or organizational investment in training, then the specter of replacement by a labor market competitor creates vulnerability among employees and, therefore, leverage for employers. However, that explanation is incomplete in two senses: (1) it fails to account for the mechanisms which produce the vulnerability of secondary workers external to the labor process, and (2) it displaces to the level of the labor market the explanation of why some markets are crowded (and competitive) and others are not.

Again, let me suggest that for Edwards, as for Braverman, the inability or unwillingness to allow for the existence of a system of inequality not directly determined by the structure of the labor process leads to a rather incomplete explanation. Although Edwards concludes that racism and sexism have "become real material forces in society" (p. 195), we are directed neither to a material base nor to a set of organizational practices which might serve as their foundation.

Finally, there is the recent work by Michael Burawoy (1979). While Burawoy offers an important theoretical contribution to labor process research, he also creates an obstacle to explaining the relationship between race, gender, and citizenship and the organization of work. In the introduction to his case study of a modern machine shop, Burawoy warns (p. 25): "The political, legal and ideological institutions of capitalism guarantee the external conditions of production. . . . [U]nder capitalism, these institutions mystify the productive status of workers, capitalists, managers, etc. Thus, the political, legal and ideological apparatuses of the capitalist state transform relations among agents of production into relations among citizens, sexes, races and so on." In other words, the explanation for the continued participation of workers in the capitalist inequality relationship lies squarely in the labor process. For Burawoy, the organization of the labor process simultaneously obscures the capitalists' appropriation of surplus and secures workers' participation in the wage labor contract (pp. 23–30). Therefore, workers' interests cannot simply be taken as given, nor can opposition (or cooperation) between workers and managers be assumed as an invariant characteristic of industrial organization. Rather, interests, opposition, and consent are manufactured through the activities of the labor process.

Although Burawoy's argument presents a formidable challenge to under-lying (but generally unsubstantiated) assumptions about conflict or har-mony, his theory of the structural determination of interests and attitudes tends to overlook the ways in which the status of workers external to work organizations can be manipulated internally. This is evident in two ways. First, the theory is heavily weighted in the direction of work structures and practices found in monopoly or core industries. The insulation of the machine shop labor process from the vagaries of market fluctuations made possible the development of bureaucratically administered job structures and increased the importance of seniority and job rights over other worker characteristics, such as race and gender. However, outside of such enter-prises, Burawoy's theory lends little insight. How, for example, do we account for the manipulation of women or minorities in settings which do not provide job rights equivalent to those in internal labor markets?

Second, even in those enterprises or industries ostensibly employing internal labor markets, job segregation by race and gender have not been eliminated. As Doeringer and Piore (1975) point out, internal labor markets can operate quite effectively to produce segregated job ladders in which the recruitment of women and minorities facilitates the separation of labor processes. Equally important, supposedly objective testing criteria within internal labor markets are often suborned by subjective assessments made about workers by supervisory personnel.[3]

In this light, Burawoy's assertions about the primacy of activities in the labor process must be questioned. If statuses created external to the organi-zation do indeed have consequences internally, then how are those statuses produced and what impact do they have on work organization? Similarly, if those statuses are manipulated to the advantage of employers, ought we not expect them to have a direct bearing on relationships between workers as well?

CITIZENSHIP, GENDER, AND THE HARVEST LABOR PROCESS

In order to shed some light on these issues, I will now move to an analysis of data collected in a year-long (1978–79) study of the social organization

[3] Whit Soule pointed this out to me in conjunction with his survey of job-related dis-crimination cases.

Thomas

of lettuce production in the southwestern United States.[4] The analysis will focus most directly on the organizational and economic effects of citizenship status and gender on the harvest labor process. I will begin by comparing the two predominant labor processes in harvesting and demonstrate how citizenship and gender inequality are related to the form of the labor process. The concluding section will concentrate on developing the outlines of an amended theory of the labor process.

The Industrial Setting

The lettuce industry provides a useful focus for the analysis of work organization in modern agriculture for several reasons. First, the lettuce industry is an integral part of the agricultural economy of the Southwest: 85% of the nearly $1 billion national crop comes from California and Arizona (California Crop and Livestock Reporting Service 1979). Second, lettuce production is highly concentrated organizationally. Nearly 50% of southwestern lettuce is produced by the three largest firms (see Thomas [1980, p. 53] and Friedland, Barton, and Thomas [1981] for two different calculations of market share). A single firm can account for up to 40% of the lettuce shipped during certain seasons (Federal Trade Commission 1976, p. 1675). The three giants of lettuce production are examples of complex, diversified corporate organizations: they harvest and ship lettuce (and a variety of other crops) on a year-round basis. Entire harvest operations are shifted with the season in a loop stretching from central to southern California and then east to Arizona.

Third, lettuce production is organized around a labor-intensive production process. Wages average close to 60% of direct production costs (Monterey County 1979). Despite more intensive use of chemical herbicides and pesticides over the past two decades, hand labor remains the overwhelming force in cultivation and harvest operations. Approximately 12,000–15,000 workers weed and harvest the crop each year (Farm Labor 1979). Fourth and finally, the lettuce industry is the most highly unionized of the major

[4] Data collection was organized into three main activities: in-depth interviews, fieldwork in the lettuce harvest, and survey interviews with a sample of harvest workers. In-depth interviews were conducted with individuals from the following groups: growers, managers, and industry representatives; organizers and officials of the United Farm Workers union (UFW) and Teamsters; and present and retired lettuce workers. These interviews and the survey instrument were broadened by over four months of fieldwork. I worked in two different harvest crews, one organized around piece-rate production and the other paid on an hourly basis. A quota sample of 152 workers was selected for the survey interviews. The survey (written and administered in Spanish) focused on three major areas: work histories, patterns of migrancy, and workers' economic and political status. Contacts made during the fieldwork enabled me to include undocumented workers in the survey sample. This provided the opportunity for comparing undocumented workers with others in the lettuce harvest along dimensions of work history, migrancy, and earnings. For a more detailed discussion of the methodology, see Thomas (1980, pp. 20–24).

fruit and vegetable crops in the Southwest. Approximately 70% of lettuce companies are covered by a contract administered either by the United Farm Workers (UFW) or the Teamsters union.[5]

Lettuce harvesting is carried out in two organizational forms: the ground or piece-rate crew and the wrap-machine crew. Close to 80% of the lettuce shipped from California and Arizona is harvested by ground crews; the remainder is wrapped in the field on machines prior to shipping (Drossler Associates 1976). I will briefly describe the labor process in each.

Ground Crews

The average ground or piece-rate crew (the names are used interchangeably) consists of 36 workers. The major subunit of the crew is the three-person team or *trio;* an average crew will contain nine trios and nine auxiliary workers. Each trio is a team of two lettuce cutters and one packer. The auxiliary workers assemble and distribute cartons for the packers, seal the filled cartons, and load them onto trucks for transport out of the field. The largest companies often have more than 20 crews working during the peak of harvest in any single production area.

The cutters lead off the crew and walk stooped through the rows of mature lettuce, cutting and trimming the heads. Packers follow behind, squeezing the lettuce into empty cartons (24 heads per carton). The cartons are then glued, stapled shut, and loaded for transport to the cooling facilities, where they will be loaded on pallets and forklifted onto trucks or railroad cars headed for market. In the field, all the work is done by hand. With the exception of a few mechanical aids (e.g., knives and a staple gun), no form of machine is used in the harvest process. Although the length of the work day may vary according to weather, field, or market conditions, the physical exertion required is tremendous. One need only imagine walking stooped for 10 hours a day or completing 2,500 toe-touches to get a sense of the endurance needed in the cutting and packing of lettuce. The labor process takes its toll: "careers" in the industry are generally short. Older and retired workers reported that a long career ranges in the neighborhood of 10–18 years.

The harvest labor process of the ground crew may be quite demanding and physically destructive, but it is also remarkably productive, efficient, and adaptable. The division of labor among crew members is precise and controlled: workers interact with one another so as to minimize extraneous movement and to establish a routine. A crew of 36 workers can, under normal conditions, cut, pack, and load 3,500 cartons of lettuce per day— enough to fill three and one-half railroad cars.

[5] Space does not permit an adequate consideration of the role of union organization, differences in union structure, and jurisdictional conflicts in this article. See Thomas (1981) for a more thorough analysis.

Trios, the central workers in the crew, are paid on a per carton piece-rate basis. Cutters and packers divide among themselves the total earnings of the trio for production during a given period, usually a week. The auxiliary workers are most often paid on an hourly basis. However, efficiency and productivity depend much more on crew coordination than on individual or trio ability. While individuals and trios may be particularly adept at the activities they perform (e.g., cutting and packing), wages are ultimately determined by the overall speed and, therefore, coordination of activities within the crew. Workers reported that the time required for acquiring individual proficiency is relatively short, as little as a day or two. Crew coordination and articulation, on the other hand, are much more difficult to attain. The crew in which I worked only began to develop a high degree of teamwork after the fifth week together.

Since the coordination of all crew members is quite important in determining work pace and earnings, cutters, in particular, may push fellow members to coordinate their activities and to maintain the crew's pace. For example, one of the veteran cutters gave the following pep talk to the crew in which I worked during one of the infrequent rest breaks: "You guys aren't making our job easy. You have to keep up or you mess up the rhythm. My money depends on you getting the boxes closed good. And your money depends on me cutting a lot of these heads. If you start falling behind, then you screw everything up. . . . " The collective dimension of skill in the harvest is, therefore, embodied in the high degree of mutual coordination and experience which shows up among crew members.

In this regard, the ground crews bear clear similarities to other work groups which rely on immediate and mutual coordination of group members in the labor process. Gouldner's description of the contrast in interaction between surface (factory) and mining workers highlights the common features of mining and harvesting crews: "Unlike most workers in the board plant, members of the mining teams worked together in closest association. The size of their work group was larger, their rate of interaction more intensive, and their expectations of informal work reciprocities were more pronounced. . . . The nature of their work permitted a greater degree of discretion" (1954, p. 133). Whyte notes a similar combination of individual and collective skill in the administration and performance of glass-making (1961, p. 220). In his analysis of longshoring gangs, Finlay concludes: "The gang is an amalgamation of different activities, and the element of skill derives from the coordination of these activities—it has no single occupational base" (1980, p. 7). In harvest crews, as among the miners, glassblowers, and longshoring gangs, the administration and performance of the activities of production are united.

In addition, most harvest crews are characterized by social interaction beyond the workplace itself. That is, they also exist as relatively cohesive social units external to the labor process. This shows up in two ways: in recruitment of new members and in the ways in which they deal with the exigencies of migration. In the first instance, many crews recruit and help train their own members. Kinship often serves as an important avenue of entry into the crew. In addition, overlapping ties, such as distant family relations or common village origin in Mexico, serve to bind the crew and to facilitate entry. The second form of social cohesion involves the migrancy of the crew. Since most crews migrate as a group with their employer or between employers, the crew represents a fairly closely knit collection of married men and bachelors.

Finally, the adaptability of the ground crew is an important aspect of work organization in the lettuce harvest. Weather, field, and market conditions render work schedules uneven. Even in the largest firms, where stable marketing and sales arrangements have been negotiated with large buyers, fluctuation exists in the amount of work available in any given period. Skilled harvest crews, in contrast to capital intensive machinery, can be activated for varying periods of time, adapted to a wide range of field conditions, and easily transported between fields at a moment's notice.

Taken in combination, these attributes—productivity, efficiency, and adaptability—underscore the critical role played by the ground crews in the harvest labor process. It would not be an exaggeration to argue that they constitute formidable *social* harvesting machines.

Wrap Crews

Approximately one-fifth of the lettuce shipped from California and Arizona is sent out enveloped in plastic film (Drossler Associates 1976). Known as "wrapped" or "source-wrapped" lettuce, it is the product of a labor process which differs in several important respects from that of the ground crew. The wrap machine[6] and its auxiliary equipment mark a significant increase in the capital intensification of lettuce harvesting. Individual machines cost in the neighborhood of $75,000–$125,000—about the price of the largest and most powerful generation of farm tractors. Given the fact that two machines are necessary to match the output of one ground crew (Zahara, Johnson, and Garrett 1974), investments approach nearly a quarter of a million dollars per ground crew equivalent. Thus, in contrast to the minimal hand tools necessary to outfit the ground crews, wrap machines represent a sizable increase in fixed costs. Although the total volume of wrapped lettuce is low in comparison to that of conventional

[6] The machine consists of a steel frame with hinged wings which fold back for highway transport. Electrically powered conveyor belts are mounted on the wings and center section of the machine for moving lettuce between fixed work stations. For a schematic diagram, see Thomas (1980, p. 79).

Thomas

(unwrapped) lettuce, the three largest firms in the industry wrap nearly half their production and may have as many as 20 machines in the field at one time.

The second major difference between the ground crew and wrap crew is that, in the latter, the critical element of mutual coordination and collective skill has been eliminated. In effect, the machine appropriates the mutual coordination of ground crew members while leaving in place many of the activities they previously performed: workers still cut, pack, and load lettuce, but now a machine regulates the pace and coordinates the performance of those activities.

Like the rationalization of the automobile industry some 60 years earlier, wrap-machine technology has important consequences for the social organization of production (see Chinoy 1955; Braverman 1974). First, the elimination of the coordination and skill of the ground crew cutter has transformed the cutter into a sort of detail worker. That is, cutters are trained to perform a single task. Individuals in the wrap crew need not have even a passing acquaintance with fellow workers or their work to perform adequately. This orientation to the parts but not the whole of the labor process contrasts sharply with the social cohesion and group experience of the ground crew. Second, the pace of work has been subordinated to mechanical control, like an assembly line. The volume of lettuce arriving at any one work station is manipulated externally by supervisors. Finally, the pay rate for wrap crews has been converted from a piece rate to a lower hourly rate. Thus, the variability and the relatively high level of wages which had characterized different crew positions and different crews in the ground method have been replaced by a flat hourly wage structure.

The harvest labor process in the lettuce industry thus poses two sets of problems. First, in contrast to an "unstructured" labor market (Fisher 1953) created by a highly variable demand for unskilled workers, the labor process in the ground crews calls for the development of well-organized and skilled work teams. Yet, as I will show in the next section, the ground crews are largely unable to extract compensation or status commensurate with their labor market position or to exercise control over the content of their work. How can such valuable labor be had at so low a price? Second, the wrap machine, with the changes it has made in work organization, wage rates, and capital intensity, has undercut the basis for worker commitment to crew and company. How, then, do lettuce firms resolve this problem? How is sufficient labor found and work-force stability induced?

Using data collected in the three-part research design, the remainder of this article will be devoted to demonstrating that there exists a strong relationship between citizenship, gender, and work organization in the lettuce industry. Furthermore, I will argue that the relationship can be explained in terms of the relative advantages to employers of distributing workers of varying degrees of social and political vulnerability to different positions in the labor process. That is, the concentration of undocumented workers in the ground crews has two important effects: (a) the subordination of productivity levels to manipulation on the basis of workers' external political status, and (b) the denial to both undocumented and documented workers of the capacity to claim higher status or reward for their skills or to mount a sustained challenge to control over the labor process. On the other hand, the concentration of documented and citizen workers, especially women, in the wrap crews has the effects of (a) ensuring the availability of low-skilled, low-status workers, and (b) transforming the social and economic restrictions associated with gender and alien status into the means for increasing work-force stability.

LABOR SUPPLY AND CONTROL OVER PRODUCTION

Data collected in a survey of lettuce workers and in semistructured interviews demonstrate that citizenship and gender are critical factors in both the construction of the labor market and the organization of harvest crews. Results depicted in table 1 show that for the survey sample there is a strong relationship between citizenship status and an individual's crew location (harvest occupation): undocumented workers are concentrated (83.4%) in the ground crews and citizens (94.7%) show up largely in the wrap crews.

The importance of citizenship status is also reflected in the distribution of weekly earnings. While the amount one can potentially earn is most strongly affected by crew type, table 2 presents a finding which tends to run counter to most expectations. That is, on average, undocumented workers tend to earn more than either documented or citizen workers:

TABLE 1

PERCENTAGE DISTRIBUTION OF HARVEST OCCUPATIONS BY
CITIZENSHIP STATUS

	CITIZENSHIP STATUS (%)			
HARVEST OCCUPATION	U.S. Citizen	Documented Immigrant	Undocumented Immigrant	TOTAL
Ground crew (skilled)..........	5.3	34.1	83.4	42.1
Wrap crew (unskilled)..........	94.7	65.9	16.6	57.9
Total.....................	100.0	100.0	100.0	100.0
	(19)	(97)	(36)	(152)

NOTE.—Numbers in parentheses are N's.

27.8% of undocumented workers reported making $251 or more per week, compared with 5.3% of citizens and 8.5% of documented immigrants.[7]

Finally, the division of employment by gender is reflected in the concentration of women in the categories of documented immigrant or citizen and in the complete segregation of women into the wrap crews. As demonstrated in table 3, there were no undocumented women found working in the harvest, and those women employed in the harvest worked exclusively in the wrap crews (see table 4).

Citizenship and Ground Crew Organization

The high degree of mutual coordination and the potential for internal regulation in the ground crews create the basis for the crew to emerge as

TABLE 2

PERCENTAGE DISTRIBUTION OF AVERAGE WEEKLY EARNINGS
BY CITIZENSHIP STATUS OF RESPONDENT

| AVERAGE WEEKLY INCOME ($) | CITIZENSHIP STATUS (%) | | | |
	U.S. Citizen	Documented Immigrant	Undocumented Immigrant	TOTAL
101–150	47.4	48.9	.0	36.9
151–200	47.4	22.3	13.9	23.5
201–250	.0	21.3	58.3	27.5
251–300	5.3	8.5	25.0	11.4
301–350	.0	.0	2.8	.7
Total	100.0 (19)	100.0 (94)	100.0 (36)	100.0 (149)

NOTE.—Missing = 3. Numbers in parentheses are N's.

TABLE 3

PERCENTAGE DISTRIBUTION OF CITIZENSHIP STATUS BY GENDER

| CITIZENSHIP STATUS | GENDER (%) | | % DIFFERENCE |
	Men	Women	
U.S. citizen	2.2	28.4	−26.2
Documented immigrant	58.7	71.6	−12.9
Undocumented immigrant	39.1	.0	39.1
Total	100.0 (92)	100.0 (60)	... (152)

NOTE.—Numbers in parentheses are N's.

[7] The figures for average weekly earnings represent estimates for periods when there is work to be had. Because of shifts in production areas, inclement weather, and breaks from employment due to injury or need for rest, the average work year for most lettuce harvesters comprises less than nine months. For a more detailed discussion, see Thomas (1980, chaps. 4 and 5).

TABLE 4

PERCENTAGE DISTRIBUTION OF CREW TYPE BY GENDER

CREW TYPE	GENDER (%)		% DIFFERENCE
	Men	Women	
Ground..........	69.6	.0	69.6
Wrap............	30.3	100.0	69.6
Cutter.........	(17.4)	(1.7)	(15.7)
Packer.........	(13.0)	(25.0)	(12.0)
Wrapper.......	(.0)	(73.3)	(73.3)
Total........	100.0	100.0	...
	(92)	(60)	(152)

NOTE.—Numbers in parentheses are N's.

an alternative locus of control. What distinguishes the organizational potential of the ground crew from the more influential miners, glassmakers, or longshore workers described earlier, however, is the general inability of lettuce workers to use their skill effectively as a negotiating device. Even with the implementation of favorable labor legislation in California[8] and the aggressive unionization drives spearheaded by Cesar Chavez and the United Farm Workers union, work in the lettuce harvest remains poorly paid, physically destructive, and largely unchanged in its organization.

The most common explanation for this state of affairs (see, e.g., Fisher [1953] for a widely cited argument) is the competitive nature of the labor market. And, indeed, competition is a powerful force: having achieved a berth in a crew is no guarantee than an individual (or an entire crew, for that matter) can retain his or her position indefinitely. Moreover, the availability of potential replacement workers makes it possible for employers to exercise considerable leverage over individual and crew performance. Within the crew, as well, competition is translated into efforts to sustain high levels of productivity. At the extreme, crews have been known to "burn out" (fatigue to the point of exhaustion and embarrassment) members who are either unpopular or incapable of maintaining an accustomed pace.

However, competition is a factor which must itself be explained; as Edwards (1979, pp. 164–65) points out, competition exists to some degree in all labor markets. Furthermore, real job insecurity (i.e., the constant removal of crew members) would operate against the maintenance of mutually experienced and skilled crews. Rather, let me suggest, competition must be *constructed*. In the case of the ground crews, that competition is a product of the construction of a labor system around the political inequalities

[8] Fuller and Mamer (1978) provide a useful description and analysis of the potential implications of the California law (the California Agricultural Labor Relations Act of 1975).

associated with differences in citizenship status. The systematic recruitment of undocumented and noncitizen labor not only creates a basis for engendering competition among workers in the same labor market, but it also acts to enhance managerial control over skilled crews. Let me begin by considering the effects of citizenship status on workers' employment strategies.

Significant differences in the employment strategies of documented and undocumented workers emerged from the in-depth interviews and fieldwork. Undocumented workers expressed a sense of urgency in describing their work experiences and plans. Documented workers, on the other hand, focused on the monetary and organizational advantages of work in the lettuce harvest. These different orientations appear quite openly in terms of categories of citizenship status, as the comments below demonstrate. Typical of many of the undocumented workers, a young cutter summarized his position this way: "Anywhere I work I take chances of being picked up and sent home. Sure, it's easy to get work in the strawberries or with the [lettuce] machines, but you don't make much money. . . . So, if you have to take so many chances, you better make as much money as you can." Another *lechugero* (lettuce worker) explained: "If I was 10 years younger and had papers, I might look at things differently. But I am 30 years old and I've been working in the lettuce for eight years. . . . If I could get papers, maybe I'd work as a tractor-driver or something and make less money. Then I could work more years. I was arrested once and besides it takes so long to get papers. . . . So, I stay cutting lettuce until I can't do it anymore. Then I go home."

Documented workers, on the other hand, tended to concentrate on achieving a balance between maximum earnings and the physical demands of working. A "green-card" (permanent immigrant) who began working in the fields without papers offered an insightful comparison of the difference between his past and present orientations: "Before, I wanted to make as much money as I could when I got work. It was a struggle all the time. If I found a job, I had to lay low and keep out of trouble. . . . I worried all the time about getting picked up by *la migra* [Border Patrol]. Now it's different. I can walk the streets and not worry. For me it means that I can get a job and make money when I want. If I get tired of this, I can maybe try to get a job driving a truck. I won't make as much, but at least I'll still be able to work."

While citizenship limits the occupational opportunities of all immigrants, the range of choices appears wider for legal immigrants than for undocumented ones. Documented workers at least can choose between higher-paying, physically destructive work and lower-paying, less demanding work. Undocumented workers, on the other hand, are susceptible to apprehension and deportation wherever they work; thus, many attempt to maximize earnings when and where possible. Nonetheless, the potential for higher wages and steadier work in lettuce draws both groups to seek employment in the crews. Jobs in the lettuce harvest are, therefore, the object of intense and sometimes bitter competition between documented and undocumented workers. The nature of that competition is, however, profoundly affected by the differential statuses of the competitors. That is, precisely because documented workers and citizens have neither the legal nor the organizational means to close off the flow of undocumented aliens or to sanction employers for hiring undocumented aliens, they are forced to compete on the same terrain with that most vulnerable category of labor. Thus, the perpetuation of competition turns on the ability of employers to manipulate citizenship status to their advantage—that is, to, in effect, convert the vulnerability of undocumented workers into a device for control over a labor process which engages both undocumented and documented workers. An important element of that control is the conflict it engenders between workers who share the same national and ethnic heritage but who have a different status in the labor market.

In a fashion very similar to what Bonacich (1976) describes as a split labor market, undocumented workers pose a significant dilemma for documented immigrants, particularly union members and supporters. On one hand, they are countrymen and countrywomen who share a common background as Mexicans; on the other hand, however, they belong to a segment of the labor force which, because of its vulnerability, has historically acted to undercut both formal and informal worker organization against management.[9]

For example, when looking for work in the fields, I often talked with farm workers in local gathering places—in bars, grocery stores, and friends' houses.[10] In most cases, I tried to tap into the grapevine for jobs by asking for an assessment of particular companies: How were they to work for? Was it a good place to learn to cut lettuce? On several occasions, I was told that crews at certain companies were inordinately hard working and that the reason was their high percentage of undocumented workers. On one occasion, I was warned: "You don't want to work at Salad Giant! They're real fast. You wouldn't be able to keep up because all those guys are illegals . . . every one of them. That's all Salad Giant hires. They bring those guys up and work them till they drop. . . . " Efforts to sample comparisons by other workers more systematically bore similar results: most

[9] I examine this situation much more closely in a part of the larger study devoted to relations among workers in a large unionized lettuce firm; see Thomas (1980, chap. 5).

[10] Two important issues being explored in this connection are the role of informational networks in maintaining migrant flows and the manipulation of those networks by lower levels of management. In many respects, the job networks described by lettuce workers paralleled those charted by Granovetter (1974). I am indebted to James Baron for pointing this out.

documented workers and citizens argued that undocumented workers did indeed work harder. Those employers who would respond to questions about undocumented workers agreed as well. An undocumented worker, in response to my query about relations with documented *lechugeros*, remarked quietly: "A lot of those guys think we're just *zopilotes* [buzzards]. You know, men who go around stealing other men's work. It's not that way . . . we all have to eat and we have families who need to eat. When you have no papers and you have a chance to work, you take it. It's not stealing. . . . Me and my friends have to work harder or the ranchers take away our jobs. We all support Chavez and his union, but our stomachs and our children's stomachs are more important right now."

The remarks of workers with regard to both their job strategies and their assessments of performance reflect consciousness of the effects of citizenship status. For undocumented workers, vulnerability is a fact of life. Potential political sanctions get translated into strategies of work and performance which are designed to acquire and maintain employment. In other words, the accessibility of work and the ever-present threat of deportation are viewed not so much as contradictory elements of a larger labor system, but as invariant conditions of employment. For documented workers and citizens, job strategies are constructed within limits imposed by constrained job opportunities. However, the presence of undocumented workers acts to constrain further their degrees of freedom both in job choice and in performance on the job. The differential effort displayed by undocumented workers and the greater desirability of those workers in the eyes of employers are translated into competition for work and, ultimately, into competing norms of performance.

Finally, the presence of undocumented workers has a direct effect on the organization and conditions of work for all lettuce workers in the ground crews. More than simply being vulnerable labor, undocumented workers represent an identifiable category of "rate-busters." Rather than being randomly distributed across a labor pool, these rate-busters can be identified and actively recruited by lettuce firms. Thus, for industry managers, they serve to maintain high levels of productivity and to undermine the organizational potential of the ground crews. Unlike the classic rate-busters depicted in the literature on output restriction (see, e.g., Roy 1952; Collins, Dalton, and Roy 1946), undocumented workers are not one or two deviants within an informal network of workers. On the contrary, the location of undocumented workers in the most influential positions in the crews—cutting and packing—tends to shift the balance in the opposite direction, that is, toward the imposition of sanctions against those who cannot make the rate.

Limitations on the availability of productivity figures make this argument difficult to support statistically.[11] In a separate analysis of the survey data, I used earnings as a rough surrogate for productivity (calculating output as a function of wages divided by piece rates) and found that among ground crew workers in the sample there was no substantive relationship between citizenship status and earnings.[12] This lends some support to the conclusion that crews constitute a "community of fate" (Stinchcombe 1965) determined by the status of the most vulnerable members.

Fieldwork and interviews produced more supportive findings. In particular, interviews with workers from a cross-section of crews revealed that few crews are composed entirely of documented or undocumented workers; most contain a mix. According to several workers (whose reports were corroborated by interviews with a company foreman), mixed crews are brought about by crew members bringing in friends and relatives (who may be documented or undocumented). Alternatively, foremen may use their leverage to intervene in the recruitment process. Often they will do so in order to inject undocumented workers. In either case, the undocumented workers are especially vulnerable to manipulation because of their citizenship status. When they are kin or friends of other crew members or when they are put into leading positions in the crew, the effect is the same: the fact of illegality becomes a lever with which the entire crew is moved in the direction of higher productivity.

Gender and Wrap Crew Organization

In the wrap-machine labor process, the shared experience, commitment, and coordination of the ground crew are replaced by a system which minimizes group interaction, individualizes skill acquisition, reduces skill requirements, and enhances managerial control over the pace and organization of work. It represents a shift to what Edwards (1979, pp. 110–30) refers to as "technical control." For workers, wages are much less a function of crew skill than they are of the total number of hours worked in any given period. The reorganization of harvesting has recreated the traditional conditions of agricultural employment: a high demand for low-skilled labor, low (hourly) pay, restricted occupational mobility, and little or no incentive for employment stability. Yet the change has been accomplished by means of a substantial increase in fixed capital investment. In other words, the replacement of crew skill by technical control devices has not made the economics of production impervious to the potential effects of low worker commitment and high employee turnover. Therefore, labor force stability remains a critical issue.

[11] Industry representatives and employers would not provide such information. The Teamsters union representatives also refused to make the data available. Finally, staff of the UFW reported that the union did not collect productivity figures.

[12] For a more detailed discussion of the procedures and findings of this analysis, see Thomas (1980, pp. 118–24).

Thomas

In this section, I will argue that firms have been able to increase capital intensity and labor demand simultaneously through recruitment from another low-status labor pool: women. While the costs associated with worker turnover have not been eliminated, they have been reduced by means of recruitment from large local and stable supplies of women workers. The effectiveness of this system results from the disadvantaged social, political, and economic status of women, especially noncitizen and Mexican-American women. In the ground crew, manipulation of the political vulnerability of noncitizen (especially undocumented) workers enhanced managerial control over productivity. In the wrap crew, I will argue, manipulation of women's disadvantaged position in the labor market and subordinate position in the family enhances work-force stability.

Data collected in the survey and through in-depth interviews demonstrate that, on the whole, women wrap crew workers differ from their male counterparts in several important respects. Among the most relevant of these to this discussion are the following: (1) Women workers tend to be more evenly distributed by age than men. Men tend to be either relatively young (aged 17–23) or relatively old (aged 52 and above). (2) A much higher proportion of women are married (75%) than men (33%). (3) Nearly twice as many women as men have dependent children who need some daily care (66.7% vs. 34.6%). (4) Women were six times more likely to have a working spouse than men. (5) Fewer than one-fifth of the women worked away from their home, while over 90% of the men migrated. These findings tend to substantiate the argument that women are drawn from a much more localized, geographically stable labor pool.

Equally important, women also tend to be much more stable than men in terms of their employment. As table 5 points out, women in the survey sample reported working much more consistently with the same company than male wrap crew workers. Similar findings were revealed for job and crew tenure (see Thomas 1980, pp. 190, 192).

TABLE 5

YEARS OF EMPLOYMENT WITH PRESENT COMPANY
BY GENDER ($N = 82$)

Years with Present Company	Men (%)	Women (%)	% Difference (Women—Men)
< 1 year	50.0	15.0	−35.0
1 ≤ 3 years	13.6	25.0	11.4
3 ≤ 5 years	27.2	35.0	7.8
≥ 5 years	9.2	25.0	15.8
Total	100.0 (22)	100.0 (60)	...

NOTE.—Numbers in parentheses are N's.

S104

The greater overall stability of women in terms of work, company, and crew is itself a product of the factors which serve to segregate women into a separate labor market. Two major constraints operate on women's labor market chances: those imposed by women's status vis-à-vis all other labor market participants and those imposed by women's traditional family roles. Together these constraints reduce the range of job opportunities for women and, in turn, make women highly accessible as a pool for low-paid, low-status employment. While it is not possible here to discuss gender segregation in employment in great detail,[13] it is important to show how women come to constitute the primary source of labor for wrap crew production and how those jobs come to be defined as "women's work."

Many of the women I interviewed in the course of this study were acutely aware of the range of jobs open to them. When asked why she did not seek work in some other job in town, a 19-year-old wrapper replied: "You mean like at Penney's or Mervyn's [department stores]? I make better money out here a lot of the time! Anyway, those jobs are no better. All the men have the good jobs. . . . If you're a woman, nobody wants to hire you. Everybody says that they don't want to train you to do a job because you'll just run off and get married. If you're a woman, that's one strike against you. If you're a woman and Mexican, forget it." Even when women seek to work outside the fields, they are often steered back there. In an interview with a male counselor at a state employment office in Salinas (California), I was told: "Most Mexican-American women who come in here are given the names of employers who need field help. We have one woman who all she does is handle those calls. When a Mexican woman comes in, we just send her right over to talk to Dolores. It saves a lot of time . . . especially if they don't speak English." The barriers to nonfarm employment are real ones for women, and, moreover, within agriculture work opportunities are restricted. In a study of women farm workers in California, Barton (1978) found that, even when women workers seek to acquire skills, they are often met by hostile employers and insufficient training programs.

Women's traditional role in the family acts as the other major constraint on employment opportunities and also serves to influence job tenure. The division of labor in the family is often cited as a major obstacle to the working careers of married women (see Gubbels 1977; Jones 1970; Oppenheimer 1970; Bell 1977; Stromberg and Harkess 1978). The obligation to perform household labor and child rearing has traditionally fallen on women farm workers, even those who migrate (Barton 1978). Nearly all the married women I interviewed reported that they performed the major household chores on a regular basis. The remainder said they divided that labor between themselves and older children (in most cases, older daughters).

[13] See, e.g., Tepperman (1970), Blau and Jusenius (1976), U.S. Department of Labor (1975), Gubbels (1977), Glazer and Waehrer (1977), Hartmann (1976), Hartmann and Markusen (1980), and Sen (1980).

All of this work is carried out in addition to working in the fields during the harvest season. As one of the women with whom I worked explained methodically: "Every morning in the summer I get up at 4:00 to make my lunch, his lunch and the children's breakfast. At 5:00 I take the kids to my mother's house down the street. At 6:00 I leave for work. Then, at 3:00 in the afternoon he gets home and takes a nap . . . he works real hard. I am usually home by 4:00. I start dinner and then get the girls [daughters]. After dinner I do the dishes and maybe some cleaning. . . . If I'm lucky I get to bed around 8:00 or 8:30." While many of the women complained about the tremendous amount of work to be done each day and on week-ends, the dual roles of housewife and wage earner are most often accepted as a condition of their employment and the family's well-being.

The subordinate position of women in the family is also reflected in the practice of determining whether a wife will work. In almost all instances, women reported having to secure their husbands' permission prior to taking a job; 93% of the women lettuce workers surveyed said that their husbands held veto power over their employment. A woman's wage may represent an integral part of the family budget (particularly in the case of families living in the United States and border areas), but the range of work opportunities and the duration of her employment are limited by her status as wife, mother, and domestic laborer. The availability of work in low-skilled, seasonal production allows women to carry out these roles. At the same time, however, the availability of this attractive labor pool facilitates expansion of those jobs.

Furthermore, the forces which restrict the employment opportunities of women also act to stabilize that labor pool residentially. The role of wife and mother, the subordinate status of a woman's work to that of her husband, and the various earnings strategies families develop severely limit the geographic mobility of married women. In some instances, migrancy is a feature of the work career, but only under the condition that the family migrate as a unit. In the majority of cases, married women remain in one location whether or not their husbands have jobs which require seasonal relocation.

Making It "Women's Work"

The ratio of women to men in the wrap crews differs from company to company and sometimes from crew to crew. However, the numerical predominance of women in that segment of the harvest labor process is clear. Evidence collected in this study showed that, with the exception of jobs which require considerable physical strength, women were represented in all occupational categories (see table 4). However, a search for the origins of the concentration of women on machines yields little illumination of the present situation. More important are the processes by which certain jobs become "women's work." I will argue that there are three related processes taking place: (1) employers actively recruiting women, (2) men reacting to the negative status attached to the work, and (3) efforts on the part of women to monopolize access to the work.

For most employers, the actual recruitment of women is taken more as a matter of standard procedure than as an innovative technique. That is, the fact that in certain situations women are more attractive labor is not constantly rediscovered. Rather, employers simply look around and see that women have been continuously employed in canneries, packing sheds, and harvesting in other industries (e.g., the mechanical harvest of canning tomatoes) and follow suit. Said one grower: "So far we haven't found anything better or faster than women doing the wrapping. They're fast and efficient" (*Packer* [May 1977], p. 16C).

The recruitment and job allocation process, however, is an active part of making and perpetuating women's work. Employers intervene directly in an attempt to ensure that the same category of labor continues to show up where it is most advantageous. This takes two forms in the wrap crews. First, wage reductions eliminate the basis for men working in those jobs because earnings are neither sufficient to encourage migration nor high enough to support the single-paycheck family. Second, women are actively recruited through a variety of networks to occupy positions on the machines. The utilization of foremen's networks and those of women crew members enables firms to perpetuate identification of gender with occupation.

The successful construction of enclaves of production as women's work also acts to discourage the voluntary entry of men into those positions. As in most organizations where women are concentrated into an occupational category (e.g., secretarial and clerical work), the occupation comes to reflect the status of the occupants, not the skills or aptitudes requisite for the work they perform (for a broader discussion of this process, see Kanter [1977]). There is nothing feminine about the job of wrapping, for example, though most employers assert that women are better suited to do the work (e.g., women are "more patient" or are capable of doing "mindless chores"). Nonetheless, workers and managers both respond to the status associated with the occupants and internalize it as a condition of employment. Even on those occasions when one or more women workers were absent from the crew in which I worked, the foreman took women from other jobs and made them wrap. When I asked the foreman why he did not use male cutters (which would have balanced the crew) as replacements, he replied simply: "It's a woman's work." The brevity of the explanation assumed that enough was said.[14]

[14] The foreman's remark proved an understatement in comparison to the view held by many male workers. After the incident described above, several workers told me straightforwardly that men who wrap are usually suspected of being homosexual.

Finally, the construction of women's work is a process in which women themselves take a hand. Though certainly not intending to further management's purpose, women may organize around their communal status for the purpose of monopolizing access to jobs defined as women's work. For example, one wrapper in her thirties explained that her crew was entirely female with the exception of the closers and loaders. That situation, she argued, " . . . is much better than having some men and some women. The women all get together and talk. We all get along and we don't have to worry what the men think." Any time an opening occurs in cutting, wrapping, or packing, kinship networks are used to fill it: "We don't have any agreements . . . that men shouldn't be hired. It's just that we like having all women together. . . . Nobody's ever tried to bring a man in."

Thus, on the one hand, the making of women's work involves the purposive activity of management and, to some extent, women; on the other hand, it involves the reaction of men to the gender identification of the occupations. The net result is the perpetuation of an enclave of occupations in which women are concentrated.

Gender differences are thus used to create and enforce the distinction between crews. Like citizenship, gender is a communal status which, while socially constructed external to the labor process, has considerable consequences for the organization of work and wages. The status of women external to economic organizations like the lettuce firms described in this article enables employers to use their labor in particular ways. The severe restriction of women's labor market opportunities is seized on by employers as a means for recruiting large quantities of low-skilled labor. But, additionally, the enforced geographic stability of farm-worker wives and children increases the availability of women's labor on a regular, seasonal basis. Employers can avail themselves of this element of an internal labor market without having to pay wages sufficiently high to encourage labor migration with the firm. Put slightly differently, women's geographic stability, a product of their subordinate family and economic position, makes their labor available on a regular seasonal basis. Employers, therefore, are ensured that at least a portion of the labor they trained at an earlier juncture will be available in local labor pools in each production area. As a result, the high costs of regularly training new workers are reduced through the attachment of local women to the firm.

CONCLUSION

This case study of the labor process in the lettuce industry has attempted to show that a system of labor recruitment and utilization built around citizenship and gender inequalities has provided considerable advantages for employers. The principal dimensions of advantage are found in control over the productivity of the labor process and in the enhancement of work-force stability.

In the ground crew harvest, in particular, the recruitment of noncitizen workers enhances managerial control over skilled production teams. Furthermore, the recruitment of undocumented workers serves as a form of insurance for the organization's investment in training individual workers and crews. The nonmarket control exercised by employers over workers virtually prevents skills acquired within the organization from being appropriated by labor and withheld from the firm for the purpose of wage negotiation or negotiation over the content of the work itself. In other words, the political vulnerability of undocumented labor prevents skills from showing up as the property of the worker independent of the organization. Even when skills are acquired external to the organization which purchases their use (i.e., in the event that individuals or crews are trained in another firm), workers cannot use those skills as the basis of wage negotiation. In the wrap crews, by contrast, the pace of work is much less influenced by the skills or coordination of workers than by the technology of the machine. Thus, the value of undocumented workers in the ground crews—that is, their vulnerability to political manipulation—is less important in the wrap crew. However, recruitment of women (both citizen and noncitizen) enables firms to reorganize production without having to make concessions or compensation to the work force. At the same time, the concentration of women in the crews creates a gender identification with key positions in the crews, especially in wrapping, and acts to enhance external control over production.

In both the ground and the wrap crew harvests, the recruitment of non-citizens and women enhances the stability of the labor force. That stability translates into savings in production costs; it reduces the number of workers who have to be trained to carry out tasks associated with the harvest. In the wrap crews, in particular, the recruitment of women and older workers enables firms to turn labor's vulnerability to the organization's advantage.

Overall, these findings suggest quite strongly that it is necessary to connect status inequalities external to the labor process more directly with the way in which activities and positions are structured internal to economic organizations. In this examination of the roles of citizenship and gender in the harvest labor process, I have attempted to show that statuses produced outside the lettuce industry are seized on by employers to facilitate the organization of highly productive labor processes. The utilization of labor in particular ways may succeed in reproducing segmentation in the labor force and citizenship and gender identification with certain occupations; however, the political and economic vulnerability of undocumented workers and women is itself the product of their participation in another set of processes.

The nature of those processes and their relationship to class inequality remain to be more fully developed. Burawoy, in his comparative analysis of migrant labor systems in U.S. agriculture and South African mining (1976), provides one starting point for a theory of citizenship inequality. The separation of the productive activities of the migrant worker in one economy from the reproductive activities of the worker and his family in another, according to Burawoy (1976, pp. 1056–67), enables employers to enjoy certain economic and political advantages. In particular, it is suggested, the separation of production and reproduction results in lower labor costs. Though that point is debatable, a more general implication is important. The denial to foreign workers of the rights and entitlements of citizenship in the host economy (e.g., the United States for Mexican workers) creates a form of political stratification divorced from, but consequential for, the organization of the labor process.[15] In this context, I would argue, citizenship is not limited to an ideological phenomenon, but is instead associated with participation in a concrete political unit, a nation-state. To the extent that claims to certain rights and entitlements (e.g., negotiation of legally enforceable work contracts or non-work-related subsistence when unemployed) can be accepted or denied, citizenship represents a structure of inequality parallel to, but not directly determined by, the labor process.

With regard to gender inequality, another set of processes may be identified. As Hartmann and Markusen (1980) and others have argued, the structure of relations between men and women cannot be immediately deduced from theories of class inequality under capitalism. Rather, the nature and functioning of patriarchal authority and the sexual division of labor in the family provide a material basis for understanding how gender roles are produced external to the labor process. That gender inequality may be seized on by employers is not disputed. However, the analytic separation of family and economy makes it possible to see how those two organizations structure one another.

These comments can but indicate a future direction for theory and research on the labor process. Perhaps the case-study analysis presented in this article can contribute to that pursuit.

REFERENCES

Barton, Amy. 1978. "Campesinas: Women Farmworkers in the California Agricultural Labor Force." Sacramento: California Commission on the Status of Women.
Bell, Carolyn. 1977. "Economics, Sex and Gender." Pp. 30–38 in Glazer and Waehrer, eds., 1977.

[15] The concept of inequality based on citizenship has been raised elsewhere (e.g., Castells 1975; Castles and Kosack 1975) but within the context of working-class politics, not the organization of the labor process.

Blau, Francine, and Carol Jusenius. 1976. "Economists' Approaches to Sex Segregation in the Labor Market." *Signs: Journal of Women in Culture and Society* 1 (Spring): 181–99.

Bonacich, Edna. 1976. "Advanced Capitalism and Black-White Relations in the United States: A Split Labor Market Interpretation." *American Sociological Review* 41 (February): 34–51.

Braverman, Harry. 1974. *Labor and Monopoly Capital: The Degradation of Work in the Twentieth Century.* New York: Monthly Review Press.

Burawoy, Michael. 1976. "The Functions and Reproduction of Migrant Labor: Comparative Material from Southern Africa and the United States." *American Journal of Sociology* 81 (5): 1050–77.

———. 1978. "Contemporary Currents in Marxist Theory." *American Sociologist* 13 (February): 50–64.

——— 1979. *Manufacturing Consent: Changes in the Labor Process under Monopoly Capital.* Chicago: University of Chicago Press.

California Crop and Livestock Reporting Service. 1979. *Annual Report (1978).* Sacramento: Calif.: Department of Agriculture.

Castells, Manuel. 1975. "Immigrant Workers and Class Struggles in Advanced Capitalism: The Western European Experience." *Politics and Society* 5 (1): 33–66.

Castles, Steven, and G. Kosack. 1975. *Immigrant Workers and Class Structure in Western Europe.* London: Oxford University Press.

Chinoy, Eli. 1955. *Automobile Workers and the American Dream.* Boston: Beacon.

Collins, Orvis, Melville Dalton, and Donald Roy. 1946. "Restrictions of Output and Social Cleavage in Industry." *Applied Anthropology* 5:1–14.

Doeringer, Peter, and Michael Piore. 1975. *Internal Labor Markets and Manpower Analysis.* Lexington, Mass.: Heath.

Drossler Associates. 1976. *Results of the Distribution Research Study Conducted for California Iceberg Lettuce Advisory Board.* San Francisco: Drossler Research.

Edwards, Richard C. 1979. *Contested Terrain.* New York: Basic.

Farm Labor. 1979. "Report of California Department of Employment." Sacramento, Calif.: Department of Employment.

Federal Trade Commission. 1976. "In the Matter of United Brands Company." Pp. 1614–76 in *Decisions, Findings, Opinions and Orders.* Vol. 83. Washington, D.C.: Government Printing Office.

Finlay, William. 1980. "The Occupational Community as a Labor System: The Case of Pacific Coast Longshoremen." Mimeographed. Evanston, Ill.: Northwestern University, Department of Sociology.

Fisher, Lloyd H. 1953. *The Harvest Labor Market in California.* Cambridge, Mass.: Harvard University Press.

Friedland, William H., Amy Barton, and Robert J. Thomas. 1981. *Manufacturing Green Gold: Capital, Labor and Technology in the Lettuce Industry.* New York: Cambridge University Press.

Fuller, Varden, and John Mamer. 1978. "Constraints on California Farm Worker Organization." *Industrial Relations* 17 (May): 143–55.

Glazer, Nona, and Helen Y. Waehrer, eds. 1977. *Woman in a Man-made World.* Chicago: Rand McNally.

Gouldner, Alvin. 1954. *Patterns of Industrial Bureaucracy.* New York: Free Press.

Granovetter, Mark. 1974. *Getting a Job.* Cambridge, Mass.: Harvard University Press.

Gubbels, Robert. 1977. "The Supply and Demand for Women Workers." Pp. 320–31 in Glazer and Waehrer, eds., 1977.

Hartmann, Heidi. 1976. "Capitalism, Patriarchy, and Job Segregation by Sex." *Signs: Journal of Women in Culture and Society* 1 (Spring): 137–69.

Hartmann, Heidi, and Ann Markusen. 1980. "Contemporary Marxist Theory and Practice: A Feminist Critique." *Review of Radical Political Economics* 12 (Summer): 87–94.

Jones, Beverly. 1970. "The Dynamics of Marriage and Motherhood." Pp. 46–61 in *Sisterhood Is Powerful*, edited by Robin Morgan. New York: Random House.

Kanter, Rosabeth Moss. 1977. *Men and Women of the Corporation.* New York: Basic.

Thomas

Monterey County. 1979. *Annual Crop and Livestock Report—1979*. Salinas, Calif.: Monterey County Agricultural Commissioner's Office.
Oppenheimer, Valerie K. 1970. *The Female Labor Force in the United States*. Berkeley, Calif.: Institute of International Studies.
Packer: Newspaper of the United Fresh Fruit and Vegetable Association (May 1977).
Roy, Don. 1952. "Quota Restriction and Goldbricking in a Machine Shop." *American Journal of Sociology* 57:427–42.
Sen, Gita. 1980. "The Sexual Division of Labor and the Working Class Family." *Review of Radical Political Economics* 12 (Summer): 76–86.
Stinchcombe, Arthur. 1965. "Social Structure and Organizations." Pp. 142–93 in *Handbook of Organizations*, edited by James G. March. New York: Rand McNally.
Stromberg, Ann, and Shirley Harkness. 1978. *Women Working*. Palo Alto, Calif.: Mayfield.
Tepperman, Jean. 1970. "Two Jobs: Women Who Work in Factories." Pp. 115–24 in *Sisterhood Is Powerful*, edited by Robin Morgan. New York: Random House.
Thomas, Robert J. 1980. "Citizenship and Labor Supply: The Social Organization of Industrial Agriculture." Ph.D. dissertation, Northwestern University.
———. 1981. "The Social Organization of Industrial Agriculture." *Insurgent Sociologist* 10 (Winter): 5–20.
U.S. Department of Labor. 1975. *1975 Handbook on Women Workers*. Washington, D.C.: Government Printing Office.
Whyte, William F. 1961. *Men at Work*. Homewood, Ill.: Dorsey.
Zahara, M., Stan Johnson, and Roger Garrett. 1974. "Labor Requirements, Harvest Costs and the Potential for Mechanical Harvest of Lettuce." *Horticultural Science* 99 (6): 535–37.

Monopoly Capital, Organized Labor, and Military Expenditures in the United States, 1949–1976[1]

Larry J. Griffin
Indiana University

Joel A. Devine
Tulane University

Michael Wallace
Yale University

In this paper we systematically assess the neo-Marxian view that military expenditures are used by the state as a countercyclical fiscal policy either to forestall a serious recession or to facilitate economic recovery. In particular, we examine the post–World War II political-economic experience of the United States, because the military expenditures thesis was most fully developed initially in an attempt to explain postwar American prosperity. We evaluate what we term the "naive" model of Baran and Sweezy, which suggests that the degree to which national output is absorbed by military spending should be dependent on aggregate economic conditions such as unemployment. Finding only inconsistent evidence to support the naive view, we incorporate the insights of recent neo-Marxists (especially O'Connor) on the linkages among the monopoly corporate sector, the unionized sector of labor, and the state. The empirical evidence appears consistent with this "modified" view, with unemployment in the unionized sector and rate of growth of monopoly profits significantly affecting variation in military expenditures as a percentage of GNP during the postwar period. We then introduce a variety of controls in an attempt to determine if our results are simply statistical artifacts of equation specification, of time dependence, of estimation procedures, or of measurement strategy. Despite a multitude of such checks, we find

[1] We are greatly appreciative of the following people for their reading and thoughtful criticisms of previous versions of this paper: H. Aldrich, E. Amenta, P. Burke, M. Cook, P. Cutright, N. Davis, T. Gieryn, L. Hazelrigg, A. Hicks, R. Hodson, L. Isaac, E. Jackson, A. Kalleberg, D. Knoke, J. Lincoln, W. Pope, B. Rubin, D. Snyder, S. Stryker, D Zaret, and several anonymous reviewers. We are also grateful to B. Rubin for her contribution in gathering the data for this analysis. Portions of this paper were presented at the 1980 American Sociological Association meetings, to the New York State School of Industrial and Labor Relations at Cornell University, to the National Opinion Research Center at the University of Chicago, and to the Indiana University Research Group on the Military and the Draft. Requests for reprints should be sent to Larry J. Griffin, Department of Sociology, Ballantine Hall, Indiana University, Bloomington, Indiana 47405.

that our results remain statistically significant and in the predicted direction. We do find, however, that additional economic (i.e., concentration) and political (i.e., the electoral cycle) variables also affect military spending.

INTRODUCTION

One of the fundamental tenets of Marxian political economy is that the processes of capital accumulation produce periodic economic crises which generate a tendency for the ultimate "breakdown" of the system (see Sweezy [1942] 1970, pp. 133–236; Wright 1978, pp. 111–80; Mandel 1975, pp. 438–73). Most neo-Keynesian economists (see Keynes 1936) argue, however, that (a) Marxian breakdown hypotheses are simply vestiges of an antiquated theory applicable, if at all, only to 19th-century capitalism, and (b) the judicious use of macroeconomic fiscal policy by an activist state can permanently forestall the collapse of the economy (e.g., see the optimistic statements of Heller [1967] and Okun [1970]).

The neo-Keynesian perspective has received considerable support due, in part, to the post–World War II prosperity and the (until quite recently) apparent success of "managed growth" in the international capitalist economy (cf. Wright 1978; Mandel 1975). Keynesian economists have singled out active state intervention in the economy as a critical factor in this latest expansionary phase of capitalist development (see Okun 1970; Heller 1967). Empirical data, of course, are often open to alternative interpretations, and Baran and Sweezy (1966), in their influential book *Monopoly Capital*, offer a neo-Marxian explanation of the postwar American prosperity. Since their theory is rather complex and diffuse (see Zeitlin's [1974] succinct summary), we highlight only those aspects of their thought most salient for the purposes of this paper.

The Baran and Sweezy Hypothesis

American capitalism, at least since the beginning of the 20th century and especially since 1945, is "monopolistic" in character; that is, it is dominated by giant profit-maximizing corporations operating in imperfectly (or non-) competitive industries. These industries are characterized by a high degree of capital centralization and concentration (see O'Connor 1973; Hodson 1978), and the monopolistic structure of markets in these industries allows these huge firms to control crucial clearing mechanisms (prices, wages, etc.) and to reap the productivity and financial advantages resulting from technological innovation. Given that the basic drive of a capitalist economy is long-run profit maximization and capital accumulation, monopoly corporate power, therefore, must generate an economic surplus (i.e., the difference between output and the costs of production) that "tends to rise both absolutely and relatively [to national product] as the system develops" (Baran and Sweezy 1966, p. 72).

This is argued to be a fundamental law of monopoly capitalism. For several reasons, however, monopoly capitalism "fails to provide the necessary consumption and investment outlets required for the absorption of rising surplus" (p. 108) and constrains capitalists either to reduce their level of production or to reduce commodity prices so as to bolster sagging demand. But given the institutional structure of monopoly capitalism, the usual strategy pursued by monopoly capital is to maintain price levels, so as to avoid an unsettling "price war" among giant rivals, and to reduce production levels (Galbraith [1973]; for suggestive evidence on this point see Sherman [1977]). The consequence of reducing production is that the profit which would have been embedded in the now unproduced goods is not realized. In Baran and Sweezy's terms, "since surplus which cannot be absorbed will not be produced, it follows that the normal state of the monopoly capitalist economy is stagnation" (p. 108).

Through a variety of mechanisms—improved sales and marketing techniques, epoch-making inventions, imperialism, and civilian and military expenditures by the state—monopoly capitalism, however, stimulates effective demand and thereby produces counteracting forces which temporarily avert underconsumptionist stagnation tendencies. While all such mechanisms are thought to be important in maintaining and expanding markets, Baran and Sweezy attribute to military spending a unique role in spurring economic prosperity (see esp. pp. 76, 153).[2]

The presumed importance of military expenditures in the age of monopoly capitalism ultimately rests on Baran and Sweezy's view of the state. In contradiction to the pluralist Keynesian view (cf. Okun 1970; Heller 1967; Hartley and McLean 1978), which conceives of the state as an institution standing above classes and representing general societal interests, Baran and Sweezy argue that state intervention in the economy necessarily is in the long-term interest of capital. Since capital dominates the state, macro-economic policy must perform certain critical functions to insure the viability of the capitalist order (see also Sweezy [1942] 1970, p. 243).[3]

[2] Baran and Sweezy, of course, were neither the first nor the last Marxists to stress the critical importance of military expenditures for capital accumulation and reproduction. The basic idea can be traced as far back as Luxemburg ([1913] 1951), and an important early statement, containing many of the ideas elaborated by Baran and Sweezy, may be found in Oakes (1944). Two economists writing in the early 1950s, Kalecki ([1956] 1972) and Steindl ([1952] 1972), are also acknowledged by Baran and Sweezy to have stimulated their thinking.

[3] See Dobb (1950) for an insightful discussion of the pluralist roots of the Keynesian perspective on state structure and functioning. We should note that Baran and Sweezy's view of the state is not shared by all Marxists. A discussion of the controversies about the state is beyond the scope of this paper, and the interested reader is directed to Esping-Andersen, Friedland, and Wright (1976) and Crouch (1979) for discussions of Marxist perspectives on the state.

Rather than civilian government expenditures, military expenditures are thought by Baran and Sweezy and other Marxists (see esp. Reich 1978) to perform the above functions most effectively because (a) military expenditures are easily manipulated by the state; (b) armaments are quickly consumed or become obsolete, ensuring a never-ceasing demand for weapons; (c) powerful ideological rationales, centering on the Cold War and global insurgency, exist to reinforce a high level of such expenditures; (d) the threat or use of U.S. military power functions to maintain American political and economic hegemony in the capitalist world system; and (e) large-scale social service expenditures by the state are not a desired alternative because the expansion of the civilian state sector may compete with private enterprise and profit making, redistribute income in favor of labor, or weaken the disciplinary or control functions exerted by the labor market over the working class (on this last point, see esp. Kalecki [1943]).

The constellation of political forces in the United States throughout the post–World War II period reflected and reinforced the above structural constraints and, hence, is also presumed to be responsible for the use of military rather than civilian expenditures as a vehicle for state intervention in the economy. According to Gold's (1977) analysis of the development of Keynesian macroeconomic policy in the United States, three broad coalitions were vying for control over state economic policy after World War II. The group which emerged victorious was what Gold has labeled the "Keynesian coalition" (1977, p. 143). Located both in the Truman administration and in key sectors of organized labor and monopoly capital, its members included New Deal social spending advocates dedicated to Keynesian-style intervention, Cold War protagonists interested in the containment of the Soviet Union, and elite business people committed to the expansion of monopoly capital. A compromise was reached within this "center" coalition during the late 1940s based on the agreement that military expenditures—not civilian spending—could best address the goals of big business, organized labor, and political strategists. "Military Keynesianism"—that is, the policy of using the defense budget as a countercyclical and economic growth device—then, was the chosen mechanism through which economic stabilization and stimulation and the protection of the capitalist world economy were to be insured. Importantly, this aspect of state policy tended to reinforce, not undermine, both organized labor's commitment to the business elite and private market relations in general. The strength of the Keynesian coalition varied over time—it was much stronger during the Truman, Kennedy, and Johnson administrations than during the Eisenhower years—but the use of military Keynesianism remained unchecked throughout the entire postwar period (Gold 1977). For these structural and instrumental reasons, then, Baran and Sweezy (and other Marxists) single out military expenditures as playing an essential, if not exclusive, role in averting economic crises in postwar American capitalism.

Baran and Sweezy's stimulating and controversial thesis has generated extensive debate (see, e.g., Mandel 1975; Gough 1975; Lubitz 1970) but, unfortunately, much less systematic empirical investigation. Only one investigation (Smith 1977) and a series of comments and replies (Chester 1978; Hartley and McLean 1978; Smith 1978) have attempted to test the proposition that military spending is affected by aggregate economic conditions. Smith (1977, 1978), using cross-national data on the 15 wealthiest capitalist nations, found that military spending was not dependent on an indirect measure of the need for surplus absorption (the nation's per capita income) or on a more direct indicator of economic downturn, percentage of the labor force unemployed. Smith's analyses, however, have several major weaknesses, the most telling of which is his use of cross-sectional data to test an essentially dynamic and historical argument pertaining to the political-economic experience of the United States. We provide a detailed critique of Smith's research elsewhere (Griffin, Wallace, and Devine 1982). Our point here is simply that, in an area such as this, where the theory is not precisely specified and where cross-national meaning and measurement of key concepts are not standardized, the most judicious approach is to examine the hypothesized processes for the nation serving as the model for the development of the theory—the United States. This is the approach we take in this paper.

THE PRESENT RESEARCH

Our analysis is limited to the post–World War II United States; specifically, we examine the period from 1949 to 1976, though we also report selected results for the years 1949–77 as a check on the stability of our parameter estimates. There is no reason to expect military Keynesianism to have been used before the war. Keynes's (1936) theory justifying massive state intervention in the economy to promote full employment or to stabilize the economy was only five years old when the United States entered the war, and it had yet to be adopted as an official policy by any capitalist nation (Kindleberger 1973). Roosevelt, in 1938, flirted with Keynesianism, but America's commitment was, as Kindleberger notes, "both belated and faint-hearted" (1973, p. 275; see also Brown 1956). It was only because of the full-employment prosperity accompanying the war, during which the state necessarily had to assume almost total control of the economy, that the possibilities of Keynesian intervention were fully appreciated (Lekachman 1966; Gold 1977). We present some evidence bearing on this periodization argument later in the paper.

Our choice of 1949 for the initial observation stems from both theoretical and pragmatic concerns. Theoretically, it appears that around 1949, and certainly by 1950, the United States adopted the policy of military Keynesianism (Block 1977a, pp. 103–8; Gold 1977). The United States experienced its first postwar recession in 1948–49, and Truman's advisors realized that some fiscal stimulant was necessary to increase effective demand. An increase in defense spending was the chosen stimulus (Block 1977a). That the use of military expenditures represented a conscious countercyclical policy by state managers now seems likely. Block (1977a, pp. 242–43, nn. 90, 91) excerpts official State Department reports, as well as memoranda from Secretary of State Dean Acheson, indicating precisely that intent. Fortuitously for state managers, this period coincided with the expansion of Soviet militarism and, later, the Korean War, thus insuring "a political context in which the administration gained a free hand for the pursuit of its rearmament plans" (Block 1977a, p. 108). Hence, we can date the initiation of the policy of military Keynesianism as 1949–50 (see DuBoff [1977] and Gold [1977] for a similar dating). Pragmatically, time-series data on one crucial variable—unemployment rates by major industry groups—do not begin until 1948, and, with a one-year lag, the first usable year is 1949.

We begin our analysis with a "naive" model specifying the relationships among a number of economic variables and military spending. The first equation we consider is as follows:

$$\text{Mil Exp/GNP} = B_1 \text{ Civ Exp/GNP}_{(t)} + B_2 \text{ Inflation}_{(t)} \tag{1}$$
$$+ B_3 \text{ Revenue/GNP}_{(t)} + B_4 \text{ Unemp}_{(t-1)} + e,$$

where Mil Exp/GNP is military expenditures as a percentage of gross national product (GNP)—the conventional measure of military burden (Smith 1977); Civ Exp/GNP is current civilian state expenditures as a percentage of GNP; Inflation is the current inflation rate; Revenue/GNP is federal revenue as a percentage of GNP; and Unemp is the aggregate unemployment rate, lagged one period.[4] The data sources of all variables appear in the Appendix. Our use of military expenditures standardized by the GNP is based on more than simple convention. For the problem at hand, such an index is more appropriate substantively than is a measure of the absolute amount of expenditures. Baran and Sweezy (1966, p. 72) ex-

[4] Several readers have noted, in opposition to our specification, that economic conditions may depend on (and not only affect) state fiscal policy. We agree but also argue (a) that lagging our economic variables removes the possibility of simultaneous determination between economic conditions at time $t - 1$ and state expenditures at time t (Heise [1975]: we lag all of our economic variables so as to not confuse "cause" and "consequence") and (b) that these equations should be considered part of a larger econometric model where economic conditions at time $t + 1$ are specified to depend on state policy at time t. These considerations do not obviate all concern about possible simultaneity, an issue to which we return later (see table 6 and n. 18).

plicitly argue that the rising surplus must be viewed relative to the actual national output (i.e., GNP); the "absorption" or "realization" problem, then, is how monopoly capital can "absorb" a significant portion of this output and, hence, "realize" the profit embodied within it (see also Mandel 1975, p. 275). Military expenditures expressed as a percentage of GNP measure precisely the degree to which national output is absorbed by military spending.

Civilian expenditures (as a percentage of GNP), the inflation rate, and federal revenue represent either political or budgetary constraints on military expenditures. Both civilian expenditures and the inflation rate should reduce military expenditures, the former due to the well-known trade-off between the two types of state expenditures (Griffin, Devine, and Wallace 1981; Wilensky 1975; Hartley and McLean 1978) and the latter due to the relative difficulty of following expansionary fiscal policies of any sort during inflationary periods (Keohane 1978). Revenue should positively affect military expenditures since increased state spending depends in part on increased revenue (Frey and Schneider 1978). These three variables are included in the equation primarily as controls. The variable most pertinent to the hypothesis, of course, is the unemployment rate. Our interpretation of the naive hypothesis is that state managers should increase the share of the national product devoted to military expenditures in an attempt to offset further stagnation or to reverse the downswing phase of the business cycle; that is, aggregate unemployment should positively affect military spending. We lag the unemployment variable (Unemp) one year, so as to allow time for policy adjustments (i.e., increased defense spending) to respond to changes in employment conditions. Ordinary least squares (OLS) estimates of equation (1) are presented in column 1 of table 1. We see that all of our control variables have the expected signs and are statistically significant. That is, the rate of inflation and civilian expenditures depress military spending, while revenue increases these expenditures. We do not, however, find a significant policy response to fluctuations in aggregate un-employment, perhaps the key variable in Baran and Sweezy's analysis of American monopoly capitalist stagnation, though the coefficient is positive (as expected) and its associated t-ratio is greater than one. This empirical ambiguity is further reflected by the changing levels of significance of the unemployment variable across equations and time periods: when we control for a number of additional variables to be introduced later in the paper, the impact of aggregate unemployment increases and ultimately obtains statistical significance. The adult male unemployment rate, possibly a more sensitive barometer of economic hardship (Wachter 1976), behaves identi-cally (data not shown). This tendency is particularly pronounced for the period 1949–77. Thus, the hypothesis receives some empirical support, but the instability of the unemployment coefficient across equation specifications

TABLE 1

DETERMINANTS OF MILITARY EXPENDITURES AS A PERCENTAGE OF GNP:
VARIOUS INDICATORS OF ECONOMIC STAGNATION (OLS Estimates)

INDEPENDENT VARIABLES	EQUATION (1)						
	1	2	3	4	5	6	7
Inflation (t)	-.233[a] (3.24)*	-.182 (1.87)*	-.238 (3.18)*	-.226 (2.66)*	-.234 (3.17)*	-.227 (3.27)*	-.133 (1.76)*
Civ Exp/GNP (t)	-.452 (4.31)*	-.383 (3.25)*	-.389 (4.22)*	-.433 (4.51)*	-.403 (4.40)*	-.423 (4.91)*	-.376 (4.61)*
Revenue/GNP (t)	1.18 (6.80)*	.469 (2.27)*	1.07 (7.34)*	1.13 (7.45)*	1.10 (7.33)*	1.10 (8.25)*	.852 (5.26)*
Unemp (t-1)	.210 (1.13)	…	…	…	…	…	…
Predict Un (t-1)	…	.050 (.426)	…	…	…	…	…
Duration (t-1)	…	…	.002 (.281)	…	…	…	…
Empunemp 15 (t-1)	…	…	…	.393 (1.14)	…	…	…
Punemp 15 (t-1)	…	…	…	…	.211 (.694)	…	…
Recession (t-1)	…	…	…	…	…	.595 (1.76)*	.302 (.905)
Mil Exp/GNP (t-1)	…	…	…	…	…	…	.274 (2.35)*
Adjusted R^2	.799	.738	.788	.799	.792	.813	.843
D-W	1.88	1.43	1.77	1.89	1.83	1.82	.476[b]
ρ	-.012	.286	.011	-.019	-.005	.002	.071
Years	1949-76	1955-76	1949-76	1949-76	1949-76	1949-76	1949-76

NOTE.—D-W = Durbin-Watson statistic.

[a] Metric coefficient (t-statistic).

[b] Durbin's H (used with lagged dependent variable).

* $P < .05$ (one-tailed test).

and time periods differing only by the addition of one year (1977) is troublesome and possibly suggestive of some statistical artifact.

Nonetheless, these initial results encourage us to continue our search for a robust unemployment indicator which serves to trigger a reaction by state managers. In column 2 of table 1, we estimate the sensitivity of defense spending to predicted unemployment rates (Predict Un). Our reasoning was that state managers might initiate a countercyclical expenditure policy if they *thought* unemployment would rise in any given year. The operational measure of this concept is the Council of Economic Advisors' predictions of the next year's average aggregate unemployment level. However, we see that predicted unemployment, lagged one year, has no effect on military expenditures (see col. 2), and alternative specifications of this variable did not change this conclusion.

We also reasoned that perhaps only "severe" economic conditions— rather than simple annual unemployment fluctuations—would trigger a countercyclical response by the state. Three indicators of the severity of economic downturns are based on aggregate unemployment statistics: average duration of unemployment in weeks (Duration), percentage of the civilian labor force unemployed 15 weeks or longer (Empunemp 15), and percentage of the unemployed who were out of work 15 weeks or longer (Punemp 15). As we can see from columns 3–5, these indicators of unemployment severity register insignificant, though positive, influences on military spending in the naive equations. Estimates of the impact of these variables are unstable, however; they increase, as did the adult male unemployment rate, with the addition of other variables to the defense equation (data not presented).

An additional measure of severe economic conditions is the National Bureau of Economic Research's index of "official" recession, which is defined as two or more consecutive quarters in which real GNP fails to grow. Operationally, we created a dummy variable that takes a value of 1 when a calendar year, or a portion thereof, is part of an official recession (Recession). The results using this variable, lagged one year, and presented in column 6, are consistent with the predictions of the naive model. That is, we find that military expenditures as a percentage of GNP do increase significantly a year after a "recessionary" year. The remaining coefficients in column 6 are of plausible sign and magnitude, and there is no evidence of autocorrelation. Baran and Sweezy's (1966) thesis, then, seems to receive support. Unfortunately, this result disappears when controls are introduced for the lagged value of the dependent variable (Mil Exp/GNP $[t-1]$; see col. 7). Such a control is necessary to account for what political scientists have termed "bureaucratic momentum," whereby "the budget administered by a government in any given year is expected to amount to an approximately fixed percentage higher than the one the previous year" (Rattinger

1975, p. 575; see also Ostrom [1978] for an analysis of the defense budgetary process and the coordination among defense and other executive and legislative bureaucracies). Similar insignificant results, however, are obtained if controls are introduced for a variety of variables used later in the analysis (see table 4).

We then assessed the possibility that a more direct measure of Baran and Sweezy's notion of "unrealized surplus" might yield more stable estimates of the influence of economic variables on military expenditures. While it is impossible to operationalize precisely this concept with conventional data, we were able to find data on two indicators of unrealized output or underutilized productive capacity. These are (a) the GNP Gap, which is defined as the difference between potential GNP (i.e., national product that would have been produced if the economy were operating at "full employment") and actual GNP; and (b) manufacturing output gap (Manuf Gap), which is the actual output of manufacturing firms measured as a percentage of potential manufacturing output. The latter measure is identified by Weisskopf (1979) as central to the "realization failure" hypothesis. If the military Keynesianism hypothesis is correct, we would expect to find that these indicators positively influence defense spending. As we can see from columns 1 and 2 of table 2, however, these variables (and additional specifications not presented here) produce insignificant results. We also examined the

TABLE 2

DETERMINANTS OF MILITARY EXPENDITURES AS A PERCENTAGE OF GNP:
ADDITIONAL INDICATORS OF AGGREGATE ECONOMIC STAGNATION
(OLS Estimates)

Independent Variables	1	2	3	4
Inflation	$-.217$[a]	$-.167$	$-.237$	$-.176$
(t)	(2.94)**	(1.48)*	(3.39)**	(2.63)**
Civ Exp/GNP	$-.489$	$-.392$	$-.412$	$-.535$
(t)	(4.11)**	(2.91)**	(4.76)**	(5.80)**
Revenue/GNP	1.12	4.86	1.06	1.16
(t)	(7.77)**	(2.08)**	(7.94)**	(9.28)**
GNP Gap	.009	...	...	...
$(t-1)$	(1.26)			
Manuf Gap	...	$-.013$	...	...
$(t-1)$		$(.421)$		
Pct Ch Cons	...	...	$-.085$	...
$(t-1)$			(1.52)*	
Pct Ch GNP	...	...	...	$-.185$
$(t-1)$				(2.88)**
Adjusted R^2	.801	.723	.807	.844
D-W	1.88	1.37	1.62	1.60
ρ	$-.036$	.291	.031	.113
Years	1949–76	1956–76	1949–76	1949–76

NOTE.—D-W = Durbin-Watson statistic.
[a] Metric coefficient (t-statistic).
* $P < .10$ (one-tailed test).
** $P < .05$ (one-tailed test).

influence of a third indicator of underutilization, the gap between actual and potential industrial capacity, and found it to be nonsignificant as well (data not presented).

Other implications of the naive view are that military expenditures should increase if the rate of real (i.e., deflated) growth of consumption (Pct Ch Cons) and/or rate of real economic growth (Pct Ch GNP) is declining; that is, underconsumptionist and stagnation tendencies should lead to a countercyclical fiscal response. The net negative relationship between these indicators and defense spending (see cols. 3 and 4) appears to support this hypothesis. That is, military expenditures appear to rise after years in which the rate of real personal consumption or real GNP declines. These results, moreover, remain significant after controlling for the lagged value of military spending as a percentage of GNP (data not shown). Again, we find support for Baran and Sweezy's hypothesis, but, as we show below, the influences of both variables are reduced to nonsignificance when sector-specific unemployment and profits are introduced into the equation (see table 4).

What should we make of all these results? Is the neo-Marxist hypothesis that military expenditures are employed countercyclically to offset actual or expected aggregate stagnation correct? The evidence we have generated on this issue is simply unclear. The performances of the aggregate indicators of economic downturns are inconsistent among themselves and unstable across model specifications and time periods. No measure yielded consistently robust estimates supporting the hypothesis. While we tend to reject the "strict" interpretation of military Keynesianism as a countercyclical fiscal policy, we are unwilling as yet to dismiss the general neo-Marxist interpretation of military expenditures, because several of our stagnation indicators approach significance or are significant when only the budgetary constraints are controlled. We believe that many of these associations are quite important—indicative of, but only imperfectly capturing, more deeply rooted structural phenomena. Below we attempt to draw some implications from these unstable results by using O'Connor's (1973) notion of "industrial dualism" as the interpretational vehicle. In the next section, then, we develop and test a modified version of the countercyclical military Keynesianism hypothesis.

O'Connor's Theory of State Monopoly Capitalism and Fiscal Crisis

O'Connor's (1973) most general tenet (p. 6) is that the capitalist state must involve itself in two basic, but often contradictory, functions: accumulation (i.e., the production or reproduction of conditions necessary for profitable private accumulation of capital) and legitimation (i.e., the maintenance or recreation of conditions of social harmony, which often requires the concealment and/or justification of the accumulation functions of state policy).

Griffin, Devine, and Wallace

In carrying out its accumulation functions, however, the state is not equally sensitive to all sectors of capital because, among other reasons, the state is not equally dependent on the two sectors of capital—monopoly and competitive. The state's ability to finance accumulation and/or legitimation policies and programs depends disproportionately on tax revenue from the monopoly sector and on favorable business conditions, which are increasingly affected by patterns of private investment in the monopoly sector in particular. In short, firms in the monopoly sector are the "engine" (p. 23) of the capital accumulation and economic growth necessary for general prosperity and social harmony.

To fulfill the state's basic functions, state managers must ensure unimpeded accumulation in the "key" monopoly sector. However, the relationship between monopoly capital and the state is not asymmetrical. The monopoly sector actively courts state intervention of certain types because monopoly sector accumulation and growth depend on the continued expansion of state expenditures to socialize investment and consumption. The increasingly social character of monopoly production requires investments which are financially prohibitive or entail too much risk even for the monopoly sector to undertake. Only the state has the necessary economic resources and political entitlement to ignore short-run profitability criteria for such massive investments. Hence, continued monopoly sector productivity and accumulation depend on the socialization of such production costs—that is, on the assumption of these expenses by the state (some non-Marxists present similar arguments, e.g., Galbraith [1973]). The growth of the state, then, is both a cause and a consequence of accumulation in the monopoly sector.

O'Connor further argues that a tacit "pact" has existed between monopoly capital and organized labor since, at least, the end of the Second World War (see esp. O'Connor 1973, pp. 40–42). Economic prosperity during the postwar period has depended, in O'Connor's view (p. 43), on the maintenance of harmonious production relations in the monopoly sector. This has been accomplished by a rapidly growing national output, some portion of which could and, given its power, must be redistributed to organized labor. Effectively, this was accomplished by indexing the wage gains of unionized workers (and only of this sector of labor) to productivity gains in the monopoly sector (see also Hibbs 1978). In return for wage indexing, unions have become "guarantors of managerial prerogatives" (O'Connor 1973, p. 23). Union leaders attempt to inhibit spontaneous rank-and-file activity, maintain labor discipline, and regulate the supply of labor to monopoly firms: "Hence unions are one agent of technical progress and rational (in terms of profit) labor power planning by monopoly capital" (p. 23). Rather than challenge monopoly capital, then, organized labor has become an integral component of (and integrated into) state monopoly capitalism.

How has the coalition of organized labor and monopoly capital affected the growth of military expenditures? Like Baran and Sweezy, O'Connor argues that monopoly sector productive capacity tends to rise more rapidly than either the demand for labor or the demand for monopoly products, creating political pressures for "aggressive foreign economic expansion" (1973, p. 150). Maintaining aggregate demand, then, is a problem of expanding markets and investment abroad. Additionally, monopoly sector productivity is assumed to depend heavily on technological innovation, much of which is rooted in the production of armaments (Kidron 1968). O'Connor further argues that, toward these ends, monopoly capital has been abetted by organized labor in a variety of ways. First, organized labor has supported corporate and state programs that promote commodity exports and the control of foreign sources of raw materials (1973, p. 152). Second, monopoly capital and organized labor have advocated increased military outlays and the development of new military programs and hardware (p. 41). (Organized labor's involvement in and ideological support of U.S. militarism has been documented by Radosh [1969].) Moreover, as an important agent within the politically dominant Keynesian coalition (see the discussion above), organized labor is an important source of monopoly capital's political power in determining state expenditure policy (Galbraith 1973). In O'Connor's words (p. 153), "These considerations strongly support the conclusion that organized labor and capital in the monopoly sector have had an important common interest—namely, foreign expansion and control of overseas markets. [Thus], . . . military spending [is] determined by the needs of monopoly capital *and the relations of production in the monopoly sector* [p. 150] [and] the warfare system not only keeps foreign rivals at bay and inhibits the development of world revolution (thus keeping labor power, raw materials, and markets in the capitalist orbit) but also helps stave off domestic economic stagnation" (p. 151) (emphasis added). O'Connor thus identifies the accumulation and employment needs of particular sectors—monopoly capital and organized labor—as the forces underlying the policy of military Keynesianism.

Before formalizing and testing a model based on O'Connor's insights, we first want to discuss briefly the empirical basis of O'Connor's assumptions about the relative importance of both the unionized[5] sector and the monop-

[5] Following Lewis (1963), we define as the "unionized" sector the following industry groups: mining, manufacturing, construction, transportation, and public utilities. The remaining industry groups constitute the nonunionized sector. Precise estimates of the degree of unionization within each of the unionized industry groups are difficult to ascertain, but Lewis (1963, p. 192) reports that since the war more than half of the wage and salary workers in these groups were unionized, compared with less than 10% in the nonunionized sector. Constituting only 30%–40% of the nonagricultural work force during the period 1920–58, these industry groups nonetheless represented more than 85% of all unionized workers. Lewis based his categorization of industries on research conducted by the U.S. Department of Commerce in the mid-1950s, and the practice has since be-

oly[6] sector of labor and capital, respectively. In table 3, panel A, we present some suggestive descriptive data which compare the relative economic power and vitality of the sectors. We see, first, that the average annual level of monopoly profits is roughly 3.5 times greater than the comparable statistic for the competitive sector. Based on these data we can conclude that, on the average, about 78% of all profit emanating from the corporate sector has been generated by monopoly capital. Moreover, since 1949 the monopoly sector has held, on the average, over 90% of all corporate assets.[7] In terms of pure financial power, then, monopoly capital overwhelms competitive capital, despite the fact that the monopoly sector includes but a small minority of business firms in the United States today (O'Connor 1973; Galbraith 1973). This sectoral imbalance does not extend to employment—roughly half of the employees in the private sector have been employed in each segment of capital since 1949—but the imbalance is quite dramatic as we observe sector-specific contributions to total (federal, state, and local) tax revenue. Fully 80% of the total corporate revenue available to political authorities in the post-World War II period has flowed from

come standard usage in labor economics (see, e.g., Ashenfelter, Johnson, and Pencavel 1972). Unemployment in each sector of labor is defined as the weighted average of unemployment in the major industry groups defining each sector. We realize that our proxy for unionized unemployment rates contains some error. To the extent that we have included relatively nonunionized detailed industries in the unionized sector (as defined by major industry groups), as we undoubtedly have (see Freeman and Medoff 1979), we underestimate the true level of unionized unemployment and, possibly, the effect of this variable on military spending.

[6] Throughout most of the paper, the "monopoly" sector is defined as the following industries: mining, construction, transportation, communications, public utilities, finance, insurance, real estate, and all durable and nondurable manufacturing except lumber, leather, furniture, textiles, and apparel. All other industries constitute the competitive sector. Our operationalization of the monopoly sector follows as closely as possible the categorization developed by Hodson (1978). Hodson's definition seems preferable to alternative definitions developed by others (e.g., Beck, Horan, and Tolbert 1978; Bibb and Form 1977) for two reasons: (a) Hodson explicitly rooted his operational measures in O'Connor's conceptualization of capital sectors; and (b) Wallace and Kalleberg (1981) compared the empirical utility of Hodson's, Bibb and Form's, and Beck et al.'s measures and concluded that Hodson's was statistically superior. Monopoly and competitive profits and employees are simply the summation of the profits and employees of the industries in each sector. We include construction in the index because this operational measure yields more conservative regression estimates of the influence of monopoly profits and is more consistent with O'Connor's assessment (1973, p. 25) of the importance of the construction industry.

[7] We were unable to obtain information on corporate assets using the categorization scheme described in n. 6. Assets are reported by major industry titles only, hence, we were forced to aggregate some specific industries into broad industry groups (e.g., all manufacturing industries are included in the monopoly sector). Our estimate of monopoly sector assets, therefore, is overstated, and our estimate of competitive sector assets is understated. This more inclusive, and less precise, categorization is also employed in the operationalization of the return on assets (i.e., the "rate of profit"). Here, monopoly profits include profits from all manufacturing industries.

monopoly capital. O'Connor thus far appears correct in his reasoning: monopoly capital is the economically more powerful of the sectors, and the state's ability to finance accumulation and/or legitimation programs depends disproportionately on revenue from monopoly sector profits.

In panel B of table 3, we present zero-order correlations between sector-specific unemployment and profit rates and the three indicators of aggregate economic vitality which generated suggestive confirmatory evidence for the military Keynesianism hypothesis (see tables 1 and 2): recessionary year, growth of real consumption, and growth of real GNP. The general pattern of relationships is quite clear: economic fluctuations in the key monopoly

TABLE 3

DESCRIPTIVE STATISTICS BY SECTOR, 1949–76
A. MEANS OF KEY VARIABLES BY SECTOR

	SECTOR	
VARIABLE	Monopoly	Competitive
Average level of sectoral profits.....................	50,913*	14,289*
% change in profits............................	6.3	7.1
% change in return on assets......................	−3.0	−1.6
% of total corporate assets.......................	90.2	9.8
% of private employees..........................	48.9	50.1
% of total corporate revenue......................	79.8	20.2
	Unionized	Nonunionized
% of private employees...........................	44.0	56.0
Average level of unemployment (% of work force)......	5.94	4.26

B. CORRELATIONS BETWEEN SECTOR-SPECIFIC ECONOMIC CONDITIONS
AND INDICATORS OF AGGREGATE PROSPERITY

Sector	Recessionary Year (Recession)†	Consumption (Pct Ch Cons)‡	Economic Growth (Pct Ch GNP)‡
Monopoly/unionized:			
% change in profits................	−.580	.569	.754
(Pct Ch Mon Prof)			
Unionized unemployment...........	.294	−.107	−.424
(Union Unemp)			
Adjusted R^2......................	.356	.275	.688
Competitive/nonunionized:			
% change in profits................	−.581	.492	.585
(Pct Ch Comp Prof)			
Nonunionized unemployment........	.079	.029	−.207
(Nonunion Unemp)			
Adjusted R^2......................	.326	.186	.407

* In millions of dollars.
† Variable from table 1.
‡ Variable from table 2.

capital and unionized labor sectors are more highly related to general economic prosperity than are competitive and nonunionized sector conditions. Real economic growth, in particular, seems susceptible to these divergent influences. We can, for example, explain over 68% of the variation in postwar growth with only two variables, growth of monopoly profits and unionized unemployment. The comparable competitive sector equation explains only 40% of the variance. Again, O'Connor's argument is supported: the economic health of, especially, big business (note in particular the correlations among the indicators of prosperity and monopoly profits) and, less dramatically, big labor exerts profound influence on the overall economic vitality of the nation. This is, perhaps, the clearest expression of the structural power of monopoly capital.

Economic power does not necessarily imply invulnerability, however, and in panel A we see that the average annual percentage change in the rate of monopoly sector profits (i.e., profits/assets) has actually declined since 1949. This falling rate of profit, also noted by Weisskopf (1979) and Nordhaus (1974), suggests some form of "crisis" tendency and may also imply the necessity of state intervention to relieve or moderate such tendencies. An examination of employment and unemployment data for the unionized and nonunionized sectors of labor is also instructive on this point: the unionized sector has been subject to greater unemployment than has the nonunionized sector (and greater variation in unemployment as well; the respective standard deviations are 1.97 and 1.0). Unemployment in the unionized sector is more subject to pronounced cyclical fluctuations, increasing markedly in recession periods and decreasing in periods of boom (Hodson 1978). Hence, the unionized sector's relatively high unemployment and cyclical variation should make that politically important segment of labor particularly desirous of state intervention designed to promote growth or stabilize downswings.

If our (and O'Connor's) reasoning is correct, then we should expect military spending to be conditioned primarily by the economic vitality of these key sectors—monopoly capital and organized labor—rather than by competitive sector fluctuations. These data and the implications we have drawn from them may also suggest why the measures of aggregate stagnation (recession, consumption, growth, unemployment, GNP gap, etc.) employed earlier as regressors yielded such mixed and unstable results. If, in fact, military expenditures are subject primarily to fluctuations in key sectors, as we hypothesize, then indicators of aggregate prosperity, which are also modestly affected by movements in the other sectors (see table 3), should be considered imperfect and statistically inferior proxies for the variables of true interest—unionized unemployment and monopoly profits.

We now develop and estimate a model linking military expenditures and economic processes in the monopoly capital sector and the unionized sector of labor. Equation (2) represents an initial formulation:

$$\text{Mil Exp/GNP} = B_1 \text{ Civ Exp/GNP}_{(t)} + B_2 \text{ Inflation}_{(t)}$$
$$+ B_3 \text{ Revenue/GNP}_{(t)} + B_4 \text{ Union Unemp}_{(t-1)} \quad (2)$$
$$+ B_5 \text{ Pct Ch Mon Prof}_{(t-1)} + e,$$

where Union Unemp is the unemployment level of unionized labor lagged one year and Pct Ch Mon Prof is the growth rate of monopoly sector profits lagged one year. All other variables are as defined above. Again, we lag the unemployment and profits variables one period to allow a countercyclical policy response (i.e., increased military expenditures) to fluctuations in the unionized and monopoly sectors. We use the rate of growth in monopoly profits because it is a more appropriate indicator of "accumulation" than are simple level or change measures.

The rationales for the expected patterns of the control variables are discussed above. We expect the impact of unemployment in the unionized sector to be positive because stagnation in that sector should provoke state managers to increase military expenditures in an attempt to stimulate employment of organized labor. We expect the monopoly profits coefficient to be negative because a decreasing rate of growth of profits in monopolized industries should stimulate defense spending as state managers attempt to create or recreate an economic climate conducive to further business investment (see Kidron [1968] for a discussion of the linkage between military spending and declining rates of profit). Once again, therefore, we are attempting to ascertain if military expenditures are employed by the state as a countercyclical policy. The OLS estimates of equation (2) for 1949–76 are presented in column 1 of table 4, those for 1949–77 in column 2.

The control variables again operate as expected. More important, and as expected, unionized unemployment (Union Unemp) significantly[8] increases defense spending, while changes in monopoly profits (Pct Ch Mon Prof) significantly decrease such expenditures. In all ways the equation is well behaved. Explained variance is high, there is no indication of autocorrelation or, based on the Haitovsky test of the singularity of the variance-co-variance matrix (Rockwell 1975), of severe multicollinearity, and the results are quite stable across the two periods. These results lend considerable support to the empirical validity of the modified neo-Marxist interpretation of the relationship between military expenditures and economic prosperity: military expenditures do appear to be employed as a countercyclical fiscal policy tool by the state, and their use appears to be affected significantly by economic fluctuations in politically and economically important sectors of the economy.

[8] We use an "unconventional" significance level here because we have so few cases ($N = 28$), a condition which inflates the standard error of the regression coefficient. Heise (1975) argues that in such situations a more "generous" significance level is justified.

TABLE 4

SECTOR-SPECIFIC ECONOMIC DETERMINANTS OF MILITARY EXPENDITURES AS A PERCENTAGE OF GNP (OLS Estimates)

INDEPENDENT VARIABLES	Equation (2)						
	1	2	3	4	5	6	7
Inflation (l)	−.137[a] (2.12)***	−.138 (2.23)***	−.159 (1.86)***	−.156 (1.80)***	−.133 (1.98)***	−.137 (2.04)***	−.137 (2.08)***
Civ Exp/GNP (l)	−.526 (6.53)***	−.525 (7.03)***	−.475 (4.51)***	−.476 (4.47)***	−.527 (6.37)***	−.526 (6.36)***	−.534 (5.93)***
Revenue/GNP (l)	1.18 (8.07)***	1.16 (8.60)***	1.15 (6.13)***	1.06 (6.12)***	1.15 (7.82)***	1.16 (7.89)***	1.17 (7.65)***
Union Unemp ($t-1$)	.138 (1.45)**	.139 (1.56)*	…	…	.143 (1.46)**	.138 (1.42)**	.132 (1.31)*
Pct Ch Mon Prof ($t-1$)	−.036[b] (3.29)***	−.035[c] (3.79)***	…	…	−.038 (2.79)***	−.035 (2.77)***	−.033 (1.86)***
Pct Ch Comp Prof ($t-1$)	…	…	−.017[b] (1.74)***	−.016[c] (1.63)**	…	…	…
Nonunion Unemp ($t-1$)	…	…	.250 (.881)	.080 (.321)	…	…	…
Recession ($t-1$)	…	…	…	…	.102 (.277)	…	…
Pct Ch Cons ($t-1$)	…	…	…	…	…	.002 (.037)	…
Pct Ch GNP ($t-1$)	…	…	…	…	…	…	.021 (.210)
Adjusted R^2	.866	.877	.806	.809	.860	.860	.860
D-W	1.82	1.82	1.64	1.58	1.83	1.82	1.80
ρ	.065	.064	.085	.088	.058	.065	.073
Years	1949-76	1949-77	1949-76	1949-77	1949-76	1949-76	1949-76

NOTE.—D-W = Durbin-Watson statistic.

[a] Metric coefficient (t-statistic).

[b] Coefficients differ significantly.

[c] Coefficients differ significantly.

* $P < .15$ (one-tailed test).

** $P < .10$ (one-tailed test).

*** $P < .05$ (one-tailed test).

That economic conditions in these particular sectors—organized and monopolized industries—and not aggregate or unorganized and competitive sector fluctuations are the prime determinants of the policy of military Keynesianism is further supported by other evidence. Unemployment in the unorganized sectors of labor (Nonunion Unemp) has no significant impact on defense spending in either period, affirming the commonly held view that nonunionized labor has little influence on at least this dimension of state expenditure policy (see cols. 3 and 4). Moreover, the apparent "largeness" of the 1949–76 Nonunion Unemp coefficient appears quite unstable, since the introduction of 1977 into the series reduces the size of that effect by two-thirds. Competitive profits, however, do significantly affect military expenditures, a finding consistent with the traditional Marxist view that state managers are sensitive to the accumulation needs of all sectors of capital. Whatever the accuracy of this proposition, the effect of the growth of monopoly profits is significantly larger than that registered by the competitive sector (see table 4, nn. *b* and *c*).[9] Finally, we see in table 4 that even controlling, alternatively, for recession (col. 5), the rate of consumption (col. 6) and the rate of economic growth (col. 7) do not materially affect our estimates of the impact of either unionized unemployment or monopoly profits. And, as the last three columns of table 4 indicate, no measure of aggregate prosperity or general economic vitality remains significant once we control for economic conditions in these sectors. (Compare these estimates of the efficacy of these aggregate prosperity indicators with those presented in tables 1 and 2.)

We tentatively argue, then, that military Keynesianism is employed in the interests of organized labor and particularly monopoly capital and not to offset stagnation or cyclical downturns in the less influential sectors of capital or labor. Insofar as the aggregate economy affects defense spending, moreover, it is derivative of and based on the accumulation and employment situations of the monopoly and unionized sectors. Before we can accept this argument, however, we need to determine if the results pertaining to organized labor and monopoly profits are simply spurious artifacts of equation specification (including the omission of the lagged dependent variable), of time dependence, of estimation procedures, or of measurement strategies.

A. Equation specification.—Consider first the impact of additional economic influences on military spending. We examined the influence on defense spending of the U.S. dependence on the world economy by in-

[9] We cannot include the economic conditions of both sectors (or sector-specific and aggregate fluctuations) in the same equation due to collinearity. The remainder of the paper, therefore, considers only the consequences of monopoly growth rates, but we should note that several of our general findings may pertain both to monopoly and, though less dramatically so, to competitive capital.

cluding imports, exports, total trade, and balance of payments in equation (2). These variables had no effect on military expenditures (data not presented).

Following Zeitlin's (1974) suggestion, we then ascertained the influence of economic concentration on military expenditures. Industrial concentration, as a defining characteristic of "monopoly," has obvious and profound consequences for O'Connor's (and Baran and Sweezy's) theory of military spending in the United States. Increasing concentration should be linked both to a rise in the potential surplus and to a curtailment of output, generating what O'Connor (1973, p. 150) calls "surplus capital." These processes establish the need for fiscal stimulation and, coupled with Marfels's (1978) finding that the military-industrial complex involves markets with high and still increasing concentration, lead us to expect that increasing concentration should increase military spending. Our measure of industrial concentration is the annual average percentage change in the percentage share of manufacturing assets held by the 200 largest corporations (Pct Ch Con 200). The results, presented in column 1 of table 5, suggest that changes in industrial concentration, lagged one year, significantly increase military expenditures. Hence, our expectations are supported; as industrial wealth becomes more concentrated, state managers respond by increasing the proportion of national output devoted to defense spending. We tentatively conclude, then, that, in addition to other budgetary and political determinants, military spending is affected by both increasing industrial concentration and economic fluctuations in the key monopoly capital and organized labor sectors.[10]

We have thus far controlled only additional economic determinants of military expenditures, ignoring altogether political factors which also affect defense spending. Two obvious external political forces which plausibly affect U.S. military expenditures are wars and the military expenditures of the Soviet Union (Ostrom 1978). Waryear is a dummy variable coded 1 if the United States is engaged in a war (i.e., the Korean or Vietnam conflicts). Soviet Union expenditures are measured as a growth rate (Pct Ch USSR Mil). We see that, net of the economic variables (which now include concentration) in our modified model, these two geopolitical forces have no impact on U.S. military expenditures (see table 5, cols. 2 and 3). Neither alternative operationalizations of these variables nor altering the specification of equation (2) changes these essentially null results. Thus, we can conclude that the omission of these external political factors from our

---

[10] We do not control for investment in this analysis because rate of growth of investment and rate of growth of profits are highly collinear ($r = .93$). We suspect that both variables are observable indicators of an unobservable concept—capital accumulation—and to include both observables in the same equation would be tantamount to controlling a variable against itself. If we substitute the rate of investment for the rate of profit growth and reestimate eq. (2), we obtain results almost identical with those reported in this paper.

TABLE 5

DETERMINANTS OF MILITARY EXPENDITURES AS A PERCENTAGE OF GNP: OLS ESTIMATES OF THE "MODIFIED" MODEL WITH ADDITIONAL ECONOMIC AND POLITICAL VARIABLES, 1949–76

INDEPENDENT VARIABLES	EQUATION (2)					
	1	2	3	4	5	6
Inflation	−.079[a]	−.079	−.078	−.065	−.097	−.150[b]
(t)	(1.11)	(1.09)	(1.06)	(.835)	(1.43)*	
Civ Exp/GNP	−.536	−.537	−.524	−.538	−.523	−.647
(t)	(6.84)**	(6.68)**	(6.65)**	(6.75)**	(7.07)**	
Revenue/GNP	1.19	1.19	1.19	1.22	1.23	.812
(t)	(8.30)**	(8.10)**	(8.32)**	(7.90)**	(9.24)**	
Union Unemp	.179	.178	.180	.197	.165	.168
$(t-1)$	(1.88)**	(1.67)**	(1.85)**	(1.97)**	(1.84)**	
Pct Ch Mon Prof	−.028	−.028	−.028	−.028	−.025	−.184
$(t-1)$	(2.39)**	(2.30)**	(2.37)**	(2.37)**	(2.30)**	
Pct Ch Con 200	.148	.148	.149	.165	.163	.174
$(t-1)$	(1.61)*	(1.57)*	(1.59)*	(1.68)**	(1.89)**	
Waryear	…	−.009	…	…	…	…
(t)		(.029)				
Pct Ch USSR Mil	…	…	.062	…	…	…
$(t-1)$			(.380)			
Demo Party	…	…	…	.176	…	…
(t)				(.560)		
Election	…	…	…	…	.563	.132
$(t-1)$					(1.95)**	
Adjusted R^2	.875	.869	.870	.871	.890	…
D-W	1.72	1.71	1.70	1.77	1.93	…
ρ	.105	.105	.106	.109	.004	…

NOTE.—D-W = Durbin-Watson statistic.

[a] Metric coefficient (t-statistic).

[b] Standardized estimates of variables in col. 5.

* $P < .10$ (one-tailed test).

** $P < .05$ (one-tailed test).

modified model does not bias our estimates of the influence of economic fluctuations in key sectors.[11]

We now turn to an examination of the influences of two internal political processes, political party representation in the executive branch of the state and presidential elections. Parties in the United States differ in both their economic ideology (Ginsberg 1976) and in their actual impact on the economy (Hibbs 1977). Compared with the Republican party, the Democratic party has shown greater sensitivity to the desires of organized labor (Greenstone 1977; Reich and Edwards 1978) and greater readiness to use fiscal policy to reduce unemployment (Tufte 1978). Additionally, U.S. involvement in the Korean and Vietnam wars was initiated under Democratic administrations. Because of all these linkages, then, it is plausible to assume that our results are simply artifacts of the omission of political party representation from our equations. We tested this hypothesis by including a dummy variable, with a score of 1 if the Democrats controlled the executive branch of government, as a regressor (Demo Party—see table 5, col. 4), but we find no evidence that political party affects either military expenditures or (upon its insertion in the equation) the coefficients of the other variables.

We have assessed only the additive effect of political party, implicitly assuming that there is no interaction between economic conditions and the governing party. One implication of the interdependence of the Democratic party and organized labor (Greenstone 1977) is that the policy of using military expenditures to ameliorate unionized unemployment might be

[11] Again, we tried a variety of alternative specifications of our "external threat" variables. We computed two separate Waryear dummies—i.e., Korean War and Vietnam War— but this did not alter significantly the conclusions presented in table 5. During the Vietnam War, military expenditures as a proportion of GNP did not exhibit any detectable trend. Defense spending as a percentage of GNP did rise during the Korean War, but such increases can be fully accounted for by the variables thus far included in the model and, therefore, we do not need to employ a dummy representing the Korean War as an additional regressor. Additionally, we specified the war variable for only "peak" war years, but, again, the results were insignificant. Moreover, substitution of annual casualties for the dichotomous Waryear variable did not alter our general conclusions. We did find some suggestive evidence that the number of incidents in which the United States displayed the potential for military force did stimulate defense spending, but inclusion of this variable does not reduce the significance of indicators thus far discussed. We present these findings and discuss more generally non-Marxist theories of defense spending (i.e., "arms race" and "bureaucratic politics") in Griffin et al. (1982). For reasons of space, we do not present these coefficients here. We also evaluated the significance of interactions between the Waryear variable and monopoly profits and unionized unemployment but found little evidence to support their importance. Alternative measures of Soviet Union expenditures included (a) the actual level, (b) changes in the level, (c) as a percentage of U.S. GNP, and (d) changes in that percentage. We also experimented with a variety of lag structures on these measures. Finally, we assessed whether Soviet expenditures interacted with profits or unemployment. None of these alternative specifications or interactions yielded evidence that U.S. defense spending as a proportion of GNP is dependent on Soviet military expenditures. Hartley and McLean (1978) report similar null results.

invoked more frequently or with greater intensity when the Democrats are in power. A test of this hypothesis is straightforward. We computed two unionized unemployment variables: (a) unemployment during years when the Democrats controlled the executive branch of government (and 0 in the other years) and (b) unemployment during years when the Republicans controlled the executive (and 0 in other years). Our expectation was that unionized unemployment would have a greater impact on defense spending during Democratic years, but the data (not presented here) did not support that hypothesis. The two unemployment coefficients did not differ significantly. Given depressed employment conditions in unionized industries, both Democratic and Republican administrations increase military expenditures, and apparently equally so. We offer an interpretation of this finding below, but first we need to discuss another nondifference.

Using procedures identical with those employed to compute the two party-specific unemployment variables, we calculated the growth of monopoly profits during Democratic years and Republican years. We had no expectation as to the direction of differences in these two profit variables. On the one hand, the Republican party is assumed to be the "party of business" and, therefore, may be more sensitive to the desires of the corporate sector than the Democratic party. On the other hand, the Democratic party is occasionally identified as the party which is both perceptive enough to discern the need for structural economic reforms in order to insure unimpeded accumulation and willing to pursue interventionist strategies to accomplish this end, even over the objections of capital (see Gold 1977; Reich and Edwards 1978). This line of reasoning would lead us to expect that the rate of growth of monopoly profits should have a more pronounced impact during Democratic administrations. Whatever the accuracy of these competing views, there is no significant difference in the impact of monopoly profit rates on military expenditures (data not presented here). Republican and Democratic administrations respond in roughly the same way to fluctuations in monopoly profits. We should also note that we found no interaction between political party and concentration.

We interpret these results as reflecting the structural constraints limiting the use or nonuse of state policy. The accumulation needs of the monopoly sector, which depend on the growth of profits and on the maintenance of harmonious production relations (O'Connor 1973), override differences in ideology and political coalitions. With respect to the policy of military Keynesianism, Republican and Democratic administrations behave similarly for structural economic reasons.[12]

[12] Because economic policy is generally formulated in the executive branch, we believe that partisan control of the executive is the appropriate variable to use for our purpose here. Indicators incorporating both elected branches of government, the executive and legislative, did not alter our conclusions about either the main or the interactive influence of political parties.

The ideologies, structures, and policies of political parties, of course, do not exhaust the political dimensions of state policy. In the competitive political environment of the United States, political parties vie for votes every two or four years, and the rhythms of these electoral cycles can cause substantial macroeconomic fluctuations (Tufte 1978; Frey and Schneider 1978). Briefly, an incumbent government's popularity declines when unemployment and/or inflation rises. State managers react to changes in popularity because this is taken to be indicative of future electoral success or failure. By means of fiscal and/or monetary policy, state managers then attempt to steer the economy so as to increase their reelection chances (Griffin et al. 1981). This notion implicitly assumes that the state is relatively autonomous from capital and that the objective class interests of state managers and capitalists may not be identical (see Block 1977b). The obvious implication of this hypothesis is that the use of any economic policy, but especially stimulative policies such as military Keynesianism, is determined not only by economic fluctuations and structural instability but also by the rhythms of electoral politics.

The United States has experienced two types of political business cycles: a two-year cycle of acceleration and deceleration in real personal income and a four-year presidential cycle of unemployment fluctuations (Tufte 1978). Typically, unemployment is relatively high in the year preceding an election, begins to decline as the election approaches due to the expansionary fiscal policy, and is relatively low at election time (Tufte 1978). The reason for the timing of the unemployment cycle, of course, is to improve the reelection chances of the incumbent president. This theory has been used to explain fluctuating civilian expenditures (Frey and Schneider 1978; Griffin et al. 1981), and we argue that it may be applicable to military expenditures as well. By expanding defense spending a year or so before an election, state managers can attempt to handle both monopoly capital's accumulation requirements and the exigencies of their own political careers. If this speculation is accurate, then we should see a rise in defense spending in the year immediately preceding an election year (Election). The data presented in column 5 of table 5 support the hypothesis. (We will return to col. 6 later in the paper.) Net of the economic determinants of military expenditures, the electoral cycle does generate increased defense spending, implying that state managers use expansionary fiscal policy to serve their own ends and not only because of economic structural determinants.[13]

We are not suggesting, of course, that electoral politics somehow destroy the structural linkage between the state and the economy; however, the precise impact of capital or labor sector fluctuations may be conditioned by the political business cycle. The degree to which unemployment in the

[13] We have shown elsewhere (Griffin et al. 1981) that an alternative indicator of electoral influence, presidential popularity, stimulates welfare spending. It does not appear to affect defense spending, however.

unionized sector, in particular, affects military expenditures plausibly depends on whether there is a presidential election. Continued incumbency in political office probably depends on (at least) minimal appeasement of the demands of the politically influential sectors of organized labor. This effectively means the pursuit of full employment programs in years immediately preceding an election. The actual data on this point are somewhat ambiguous: defense spending appears substantially more sensitive to unemployment in years preceding a presidential election ($B = 0.286$) than in nonelection periods ($B = 0.116$—compare these estimates to the "pooled" estimate in table 5, col. 1), but the coefficients do not differ significantly ($t = 0.813$, $P > .10$).[14] Hence, these processes appear to be invariant across the electoral cycle, again suggesting their basis in economic structure. In the remaining sections of this paper, therefore, we will use the pooled unionization variable, acknowledging, however, that we may be masking some important differences in the operation of this indicator. Fortunately, no other coefficient in our equation is affected by the specification of unionized unemployment.

Our results do not appear to be spurious associations resulting from the omission of additional explanatory variables (though, of course, we can never definitively exclude such a possibility), but they could be a consequence of an incorrect functional form of one or more of our regressors (Draper and Smith 1966). Accordingly, we evaluated the linearity assumption for all of the variables retained in the model (i.e., those contained in col. 5 of table 5). Only revenue significantly departed from linearity; the degree to which revenue financed military spending decreased as revenue increased. And while the inclusion of a squared revenue term in our equation also reduced the size and significance of the unionized unemployment coefficient, unemployment nonetheless remained significant and substantively important ($B = 0.121$, $P < .10$). No other coefficient was affected by the nonlinear specification of revenue. Because the basic pattern of estimated effects remained unchanged and because the decreasing marginal importance of revenue is of peripheral interest to us here, we have chosen to continue our analysis with the more parsimonious linear specification of revenue.

Finally, we examined the possibility that the regressors interacted with one another. As we have noted in several footnotes, we found no evidence of significant interactions among theoretically pertinent variables. Importantly, we were also unable to detect a significant interaction between profits and unemployment, suggesting that state managers do not provide additional "boosts" of military expenditures if organized unemployment and monopoly profits are simultaneously depressed, over and above what we

[14] The rate of growth of monopoly profits did not interact with election year, nor did unemployment rates specific for Republican or Democratic administrations. Finally, we found no evidence of an effect of the two-year electoral cycle on military expenditures.

would predict from the additive specification of these two variables. Hence, stagnation in either sector is sufficient to trigger a countercyclical response by the state. In sum, the linear and additive specification of the model appears consistent with the observed data. We do not, however, want to exaggerate the relative importance of these political-economic variables. An examination of the standardized regression coefficients presented in column 6 of table 5 reveals that defense spending is structurally limited by the state's ability to finance expenditures of any sort (i.e., revenue) and then by the constraints established by nondefense, civilian state expenditures. Compared with these influences, which we have labeled "budgetary constraints," the effects of economic fluctuations in key monopoly and unionized sectors, of the presidential electoral cycle, and of industrial concentration are relatively small. A consideration of "relative effects," however, in no way contradicts any of our previous inferences: the standardized coefficients assessing the impact of the political-economic variables are of modest magnitude and show that a nontrivial proportion of the variation in military spending as a proportion of GNP is due to fluctuations in unemployment, profits, concentration, and electoral politics (about 8% of the variation in the dependent variable can be "uniquely" attributed to these four variables).

B. *Time dependence.*—We performed several checks on the stability of our estimates across time; for example, we estimated the model for the periods 1949–77, 1950–77, and 1949–65 (the last period being the "age of Keynes," according to Lekachman [1966]). The first two estimation procedures yielded essentially the same results as those presented in table 5, column 5[15] (though for 1950–77 the unemployment coefficient failed to reach conventional levels of statistical significance). The 1949–65 results differed somewhat (see table 6, col. 1) from the 1949–76 results. Considerably more of the variance is explained, and the slope of the unionized unemployment variable is significantly larger for the 1949–65 period (see table 6, n. *b*). This is consistent with the notion that Keynesian-type interventions and military Keynesianism in particular (Gold 1977) were more heavily utilized before the current economic crisis (see Gold 1977). Nonetheless, our earlier analyses have demonstrated that even as late as 1976 military Keynesianism was employed as a countercyclical fiscal policy.

Earlier we argued that the reorganization of the American political economy induced by the Great Depression and the Second World War both necessitated the use of military Keynesianism and provided state managers

[15] In order to control for possible idiosyncratic influences induced by the inclusion of any given year in the series, we computed a dummy variable for each year and reestimated our equation 28 times, including each annual dummy as a control. While there was some variation in the magnitude of the coefficients, the basic pattern of effects remained, and no systematic changes in the coefficients were attributed to the introduction of these annual dummies.

with the opportunity for "demand management." There is a consensus among neo-Marxists that the use of the defense budget as an instrument of economic stabilization, crisis management, or surplus absorption is a peculiarly postwar phenomenon (Baran and Sweezy 1966; O'Connor 1973; Gold 1977; Lo 1975). Thus, if analyses suggested that military spending in the interwar period was subject to the sectoral and political influences we have identified as driving post–World War II defense expenditures, then either the theory is wrong or the supporting data we have thus far accumulated are suspect, evidence not of structural processes but of statistical artifact.

The data presented in column 2 of table 6 bear on this speculation. There we present generalized least squares (GLS) estimates of the influence of

TABLE 6

DETERMINANTS OF MILITARY EXPENDITURES AS A PERCENTAGE OF GNP:
ALTERNATIVE PERIODS AND ESTIMATION TECHNIQUES

	DEPENDENT VARIABLES			
INDEPENDENT VARIABLES	Mil 1 Exp/GNP OLS (1949–65) (1)	Mil 1 Exp/GNP GLS (1921–40) (2)	Mil 1 Exp/GNP 3SLS (1949–76) (3)	Civ Exp/GNP 3SLS (1949–76) (4)
Inflation	−.089[a]	−.047	−.073	−.136
(t)	(1.01)	(8.18)**	(1.23)	(1.75)**
Civ Exp/GNP	−.541	.058	−.505	...
(t)	(4.20)**	(1.23)	(7.17)**	
Revenue/GNP	1.49	.213	1.13	1.33
(t)	(12.8)**	(8.40)**	(7.96)**	(2.42)**
Union Unemp	.291[b]	.000	.151	.117
(t−1)	(2.39)**	(.538)	(1.97)**	(.833)
Pct Ch Mon Prof	−.024[c]	.000	−.022	−.033
(t−1)	(2.05)**	(.323)	(2.38)**	(2.44)**
Pct Ch Con 200	.197[c]	...	.140	.188
(t−1)	(1.41)*		(1.89)**	(1.74)**
Election	.666[c]	−.017	.503	.673
(t−1)	(2.18)**	(2.50)**	(2.08)**	(1.89)**
Mil Exp/GNP	...	...	...	−1.03
(t)				(2.24)**
Civ Exp/GNP	...	...	...	.531
(t−1)				(1.80)**
Mil Exp/GNP	...	...	.104	...
(t−1)			(1.17)	
System R²	...	...	.998	
Adjusted R²	.954	.944	.901	.906
D-W	1.92	1.83	1.93	2.02
ρ	.012	−.079	.020	−.014

NOTE.—D-W = Durbin-Watson statistic.
[a] Metric coefficients (t-statistic).
[b] Ho: B = 0.165 (1949–76 value); t = 1.40 (P < .10).
[c] Coefficients do not differ from their 1949–76 values.
* P < .10 (one-tailed test).
** P < .05 (one-tailed test).

most of the variables thus far discussed for the period 1921–40.[16] (Concentration is omitted from this table since we have data for this variable only since 1927.) We see that the coefficients most important to our argument—those associated with unionized unemployment, presidential election year, and monopoly profits—are not only generally insignificant but, additionally, the signs of the last two are opposite those predicted and estimated for the postwar period. (We also estimated the "full" model for the period 1927–40 and found no influence of concentration.) Elections, moreover, significantly depress military expenditures. We also note, in passing, the radically reduced size of the influence of revenue and the significant near-positive effect of civilian expenditures on defense spending. While in no way purporting to represent a comprehensive examination of the "periodization" argument, the results presented in column 2 strikingly demonstrate that American military expenditures during the interwar period simply were not subject to the same political-economic forces as were postwar defense outlays and suggest, once again, that our findings are not artifactual.

C. *Estimation procedure.*—All equations thus far discussed were estimated with OLS (though GLS produced almost identical results), which can yield biased and inconsistent estimates of the parameter values if the equation contains nonrecursivity (Johnston 1972). Our model does contain one nonrecursive relationship—that between civilian expenditures and military expenditures. We argued earlier that a trade-off exists between the proportion of national output devoted to civilian expenditures and the proportion devoted to military expenditures. Simply put, the state can only do so much—especially if it is already absorbing a large proportion of national output—and each percentage of output allocated to civilian programs reduces the percentage of output allocated to defense.[17] Of course,

[16] We present GLS estimates since a preliminary OLS estimation suggested that the disturbances were autocorrelated. Because of data limitations, we were forced to estimate unionized unemployment for the entire period 1921–40 and monopoly profits for the years 1921–28. Our estimate of unionized unemployment is based on a regression equation which employed blue-collar occupational unemployment rates as the criterion (see text below, n. 19, and table 7 for the justification of this measure) and aggregate unemployment rates as the predictor. The two variables correlate at .94 for the years (1948–77) for which we have data for both series. A similar regression formula was employed to estimate monopoly profits for the years 1921–28; there aggregate corporate profits before taxes constituted the predictor variable. The two variables, monopoly profits and aggregate profits, correlate at .98 for the years (1929–77) for which we have data on both series. We recomputed the regression coefficients for the period 1949–76 using the estimated unionized unemployment and monopoly profit series discussed here, with results almost identical with those presented in table 5, thus insuring that the essentially null results presented in table 6 are not due simply to the measurement error necessarily induced by the use of the two estimated series. Our analysis of the interwar period begins in 1921 because the use of the lagged percentage change in (estimated) monopoly profits requires the loss of the first two years in the series (1919 and 1920).

[17] This trade-off exists for the substantive reasons discussed above and not because of any methodological dependency between the two types of expenditures. Even expressed as percentages of GNP, both military and civilian expenditures can rise at the expense

the converse is true: military expenditures (as a percentage of GNP) should reduce civilian expenditures (also as a percentage of GNP—see Griffin et al. [1981]). Therein lies the model's nonrecursivity and the potential source of bias. Military expenditures and civilian expenditures should properly be considered joint endogenous variables, each simultaneously determining the other. This small system can be represented by the following equations:[18]

$$
\begin{aligned}
\text{Mil Exp/GNP} = {} & B_1 \text{ Civ Exp/GNP}_{(t)} + B_2 \text{ Inflation}_{(t)} \\
& + B_3 \text{ Revenue/GNP}_{(t)} + B_4 \text{ Union Unemp}_{(t-1)} \\
& + B_5 \text{ Pct Ch Mon Prof}_{(t-1)} + B_6 \text{ Election}_{(t-1)} \qquad (3) \\
& + B_7 \text{ Pct Ch Con 200}_{(t-1)} \\
& + B_8 \text{ Mil Exp/GNP}_{(t-1)} + e,
\end{aligned}
$$

and

$$
\begin{aligned}
\text{Civ Exp/GNP} = {} & B_8 \text{ Mil Exp/GNP}_{(t)} + B_9 \text{ Inflation}_{(t)} \\
& + B_{10} \text{ Revenue/GNP}_{(t)} + B_{11} \text{ Union Unemp}_{(t-1)} \\
& + B_{12} \text{ Pct Ch Mon Prof}_{(t-1)} + B_{13} \text{ Election}_{(t-1)} \qquad (4) \\
& + B_{14} \text{ Pct Ch Con 200}_{(t-1)} \\
& + B_{15} \text{ Civ Exp/GNP}_{(t-1)} + e,
\end{aligned}
$$

where Election is the election year variable and Pct Ch Con 200 is aggregate concentration. We include the lagged value of the endogenous expenditures (Mil Exp/GNP [$t - 1$] and Civ Exp/GNP [$t - 1$]) as additional regressors. This is necessary to identify the system and, additionally, serves to introduce still another determinant of state expenditures, bureaucratic momentum (Rattinger 1975).

Johnston (1972) argues that, when the structural disturbances of a simultaneous equation system are contemporaneously correlated, and ours are likely to be, the appropriate estimation technique is three-stage least squares (3SLS). We present 3SLS estimates of equations (3) and (4) in

---

of consumption and investment, both expressed as percentages of GNP (as has actually happened during this century—see the 1921–40 results in table 6 indicating that the two types of expenditures positively covaried). The modest size of the correlation between civilian spending and defense spending (both expressed as percentages of GNP, $r = -.59$) attest to lack of definitional dependency. Additionally, the use of specific types of civilian spending—e.g., welfare expenditures—yields results quite similar to those presented here (see Griffin et al. 1981).

[18] It could be argued that since both the inflation rate and federal revenue are measured in the current period, as is military expenditure, a simultaneity bias exists with these variables also. We reject that view since these variables would adjust to military expenditures only after some time lag, not instantaneously as such a proposition would assume. See, e.g., the specification of the equations and lag structures of Niskanen (1978), Stein (1978), and Frey and Schneider (1978), all of whom assume lags of one year or longer, and our discussion in n. 4.

columns 3 and 4 in table 6. Our main concern, of course, is with the military expenditures equation, and we see that our previous findings are confirmed by the 3SLS estimation. The coefficients of most variables in that equation are statistically significant and in the expected direction. Autocorrelation does not appear to be a problem. Hence, the conclusions we reached earlier about unemployment in the unionized sector, the growth of monopoly profits, electoral politics, and increasing concentration do not appear to be artifacts of the simultaneity problem or of the omission of the statistically insignificant lagged military expenditures variable.

   D. *Prediction.*—Land and Felson (1976) suggest that one method of evaluating the adequacy of macro over-time models of the sort developed here is to see how well they forecast the values of the endogenous variables for time points in advance of those on which the model was estimated, conditioned on observed values of the predetermined variables. Our model was estimated for the period 1949–76, and forecast values were obtained for military expenditures in 1977. The estimated structure of the model is presented in table 5, column 5. The results of the forecast for 1977 are as follows: the observed value of military expenditures as a percentage of GNP in 1977 was 5.17. Our forecast is 5.63, yielding an absolute error of 0.46. This represents only 9% error (0.46/5.17) and is less than three-fourths the size of the standard error of estimate of the observed percentage. The error in the 1978 prediction using the 1949–76 estimated structure was greater, about 20%, but the 1977 and 1978 predictions are accurate enough to suggest that both of those observed values plausibly are generated by the same causal structure as the 1949–76 observed defense scores.

   Finally, an extensive examination of the residuals, including plotting them against time, against the predicted values of military expenditure, and against each of the explanatory variables in the model (see Draper and Smith 1966, pp. 86–103), suggested that the disturbances (or "errors") were purely random. And, net of the variables included in the model, we found no evidence of a significant linear or nonlinear time trend. This gives us even greater confidence in the adequacy of the model's specification.

   E. *Measurement.*—If the hypothesized links between key sector fluctuations and concentration, on the one hand, and military spending as a percentage of GNP, on the other, are "real," we should find that alternative indices of these variables should behave similarly to those already discussed. Fortunately, we could find and/or construct alternative measures of our key concepts. We substitute unemployment in relatively unionized occupations (Union Occ Unemp) for our industry-based unionized unemployment;[19] the average annual percentage change in the monopoly profit rate

[19] Time-series data on the unemployment levels of detailed occupations are not published, but such data are available for major occupational groups. The most heavily unionized occupational groups are "craftsmen and kindred workers" and transport and nontransport "operatives" (Freeman and Medoff 1979), where the levels of unionization approached

(i.e., Profits/Assets) and the rate of growth of *nondefense* related monopoloy industry profits (Nondef Mon Prof) for the rate of growth of total monopoly profits (see n. 7 for details on the construction of rate of profit); and the average annual percentage change in share of manufacturing assets held by the largest 100 firms (Pct Ch Con 100) for a similar measure based on the 200 largest firms. The remaining variables are identical with those used earlier. In table 7, columns 1 and 2, we present the OLS estimates obtained

TABLE 7

DETERMINANTS OF MILITARY EXPENDITURES AS A PERCENTAGE OF GNP: ALTERNATIVE MEASURES OF SECTOR-SPECIFIC FLUCTUATIONS AND OF MILITARY EXPENDITURES

INDEPENDENT VARIABLES	DEPENDENT VARIABLES				
	Mil 1 Exp/GNP (1)	Mil 1 Exp/GNP (2)	Mil 2 Exp/GNP (3)	In Level Mil 1 (4)	In Level Mil 1 (5)
Inflation..........	$-.100$[a]	$-.105$	.076	$-.031$	$-.033$
(t)	(1.40)*	(1.54)*	(1.11)	(3.66)**	(3.97)**
Civ Exp/GNP.....	$-.556$	$-.522$	$-.765$[b]	-1.09	-1.16
(t)	(7.01)**	(7.01)**	(15.5)**	(9.06)**	(9.49)**
Revenue/GNP.....	1.22	1.25	1.20	2.33	2.36
(t)	(9.52)**	(9.49)**	(7.40)**	(14.7)**	(15.4)**
Union Unemp.....	...	.209	.246	.008	.014
$(t-1)$		(2.37)**	(2.36)**	$(.888)$	(1.52)*
Pct Ch Mon Prof...	...	...	$-.020$	$-.003$	...
$(t-1)$			(1.44)*	(2.45)**	
Pct Ch Con 200....	...	.186	.172	.017	.018
$(t-1)$		(2.23)**	(1.66)**	(1.58)*	(1.90)**
Election..........	...	.499	.487	.617	.077	.065
$(t-1)$		(1.71)**	(1.64)**	(1.77)**	(2.22)**	(1.88)**
Union Occ Unemp..	.185	...	...	...	...
$(t-1)$	(2.06)**				
Profits/Assets......	$-.027$	...	...	...	...
$(t-1)$	(2.34)**				
Pct Ch Con 100....	.137	...	...	...	...
$(t-1)$	(1.67)**				
Nondef Mon Prof...	...	$-.022$	...	...	$-.003$
$(t-1)$		(2.23)**			(2.75)**
Adjusted R^2.......	.887	.887	.918	.955	.978
D-W..............	1.98	1.89	1.68	1.91	1.95
ρ................	$-.021$	.019	.161	.013	.020
Years.............	1949–76	1949–76	1949–76	1949–76	1949–76

NOTE.—D-W = Durbin-Watson statistic.
[a] Metric coefficient (t-statistic).
[b] Civilian expenditures equal total federal expenditures minus Mil 2 (see text).
* $P < .10$ (one-tailed test).
** $P < .05$ (one-tailed test).

50% in the early 1970s. Representing about 35% of all workers in the private sector, these occupational groups accounted for more than 68% of unionized workers. Unionization in the remaining occupational groups ranged from 5% ("sales workers") to 33% ("nonfarm laborers"). Unemployment in the unionized occupations is a weighted average of unemployment in major occupational groups comprising the unionized sector.

with these alternative indicators. These results are virtually identical with those presented in table 5, column 5, and strongly suggest that our results are not dependent on the precise measurement of important independent variables.

The dependent variable we have thus far employed is the actual Department of Defense (DOD) expenditures as a proportion of GNP. These expenditures exclude veterans' benefits, even though the latter expenditure is obviously related to U.S. militarism. We added veterans' benefits to DOD expenditures and reestimated our equations with almost identical results (data not presented). The inclusion of only veterans' benefits, however, may still be insufficient to measure adequately the full impact of the defense burden. Cypher (1974), for example, argues that DOD expenditure patterns underestimate "true" military spending in a variety of ways, and he constructs a more inclusive index of defense spending. Cypher considers military expenditures to include DOD obligations incurred (N.B.: *not* actual expenditures), the budget of the Atomic Energy Commission, veterans' benefits, the budget of the National Aeronautics and Space Administration, 50% of the International Affairs and Finance budget, and 75% of the interest on the public debt. Cypher's (1974, pp. 16–19) justification for this elaborate conception of military expenditures is not an issue here. We simply want to see if this highly expanded operationalization of military spending is subject to the same processes we have documented above. The results using Cypher's measure (Mil 2 Exp/GNP) are presented in column 3 of table 7. (We employ the original specification of our independent variables in this equation.) We see that some differences exist when we employ this measure (e.g., the coefficient associated with inflation is positive but nonsignificant), but, once again, the same basic patterns emerge: military expenditure as a proportion of GNP is positively affected by unemployment in the organized labor sector, increasing industrial concentration, and the electoral cycle and negatively influenced by the rate of growth of monopoly profits.[20]

The use of Cypher's measure as a percentage of GNP does not, however, obviate the potential problems associated with ratio variables (Schuessler 1974; but see Long 1980). In columns 4 and 5 of table 7, we address the possibility that our results are artifacts of GNP-based military expenditures measures by examining the performance of an operationalization of defense spending which is quite different from those discussed thus far: logged level of expenditures. The specification of the equation presented in column

---

[20] For the period 1949–72, we used the data on military spending reported by Cypher (1974, p. 3). Since his series stopped in 1972, we computed a prediction formula, using DOD expenditures plus veterans' benefits as the predictor and Cypher's measure as the criterion, in order to estimate expenditures for the years 1973–76.

4 is identical with that of the estimated equation in column 5 of table 5, except that all variables in dollars/GNP metrics (defense spending, civilian outlays, and revenue) were converted into appropriate log-level metrics. We see that with both specifications all coefficients are in the same direction as those discussed above, and, with the exception of unionized sector unemployment, all are significant. Substitution of nondefense monopoly profits for total monopoly profits, moreover, renders even that coefficient statistically significant (col. 5), suggesting that modest alterations in the specification of the independent variables produce results virtually indistinguishable from those presented in table 5. It is unrealistic to expect quite different dependent variables to be driven by exactly identical specifications of the hypothesized causal processes, and, therefore, the essential similarity in substantive conclusions reached by an examination of the political and economic determinants of two distinct measures of military spending (as a percentage of GNP and logged level) is impressive indeed. Finally, we estimated our equations using "real" (i.e., deflated) profits, expenditures, GNP, and revenue rather than, as above, the nominal dollar values of the variables. These estimates were almost identical with those presented and discussed in this paper.

All of these checks point to the same conclusion: our results appear robust across a variety of equation specifications allowing for numerous additional controls and theoretically pertinent interactions, time periods, estimation procedures, and measurement strategies. This is not to imply that the evidence we have presented cannot be dented statistically. It can. The unemployment coefficient, in particular, is sensitive to the inclusion of both civilian expenditures and revenue in the regression equation (i.e., without both controls, unemployment among the ranks of organized labor does not significantly stimulate defense spending) and, in general, is more unstable than estimates of other influences in the analysis (note our 1950–77 results and the data presented in col. 4 of table 7). We believe, however, that the specification of our defense spending equations is empirically viable and theoretically sound: the state must, at least in part, finance expenditures via tax revenues and, simultaneously, strike a compromise among competing interest groups and bureaucracies by trading off military for civilian outlays and vice versa.[21] We have attempted to model these "structural constraints" on state expenditure policy. Given this specification, our results do not appear to be methodological artifacts, and, importantly, our model has predictive power.

[21] We write this just as the incoming Reagan administration has vowed to increase military spending and, at the same time, to reduce taxes. The solution to this economic paradox? A slashing of civilian—especially welfare—outlays.

Griffin, Devine, and Wallace

SUMMARY AND DISCUSSION

Military expenditures are used as a countercyclical fiscal tool to regulate unemployment within organized labor and the rate of growth of monopoly profits and not directly to offset aggregate economic stagnation. Contemporary American capitalism is dualistic; monopoly capital unequally competes alongside competitive capital. The social and technical organization of production, the economic health, and the linkages and interdependencies with the state differ substantially between these two sectors. Monopoly capital does appear to be the engine of U.S. prosperity, and, as such, this sector is of unparalleled importance to the national economy. If monopoly profits decline, economic growth is stymied. If the decline is precipitous enough or prolonged enough, the consequence is recession or depression. The state loses legitimacy, society loses the fragile cohesion based, in part, on material progress, and the social fabric begins to unravel. The interests of the capitalist state and of monopoly capital, then, are isomorphic: the state must underwrite the financial security of monopoly capital in an attempt to maintain the social order. Hence, if the profit rate of monopoly capital falls, the state responds by increasing military expenditures in an attempt to absorb surplus (and hence allow monopoly capital to realize the profit embedded in that surplus), stimulate research and development and technological innovation (thus socializing part of this sector's production costs), and secure monopoly capital's foreign markets against military adversaries and ideological or nationalistic opponents.

Monopoly accumulation depends not only on state intervention, of course, but also on a productive, disciplined labor force. A chaotic labor market cannot guarantee a regular supply of competent labor. Unions can, however; and in return for doing so, organized labor has become an essential component of state monopoly capitalism. Compared to the unorganized segments of the working class, unionized labor is better paid and exercises greater political influence. When necessary, then, the state responds to stagnant or stagnating employment in the unionized sector by boosting military expenditures. That defense industries are heavily unionized (Freeman and Medoff 1979) simply facilitates this policy response. The state, then, appears sensitive not only to monopoly capital (and possibly to capital-in-general, though less dramatically so) but also to the organized working class, a previously powerless group (see Hicks, Friedland, and Johnson [1978] for results which suggest that organized labor also influences the redistributive policies of state governments within the United States). We do not wish to exaggerate the influence of unionized labor per se, and, given the instability of the effect of unemployment in that sector, we cannot do so. The economic and political impact of organized labor is essentially (though not completely) derived from its close ties with monopoly capital. Our results, nonetheless, indicate that unemployment among the ranks of unionized labor independently stimulates defense spending.

Structural influences must be interpreted and acted on by real men and women, however, and we attempted, in our discussion of the Keynesian coalition, to show how this was accomplished in the years immediately following World War II. The formulation and implementation of military Keynesianism was (and remains) the result of a complex series of political events coupled with the structural limits on state policy created by the engine of postwar American prosperity—monopoly accumulation and production relations. A simple economistic interpretation, therefore, seems inappropriate.

Increasing levels of aggregate concentration increase military expenditures. A characteristic feature of monopoly capitalism is its long-term trend toward the concentration and centralization of capital. This process occurs at the aggregate economic level, but it is an especially prominent feature of firms in defense and defense-related industries. Marfels (1978) suggests that, due to unique "nonmarket" aspects of the transactions between the state and military contractors, increasing industrial concentration is both a cause and a consequence of higher levels of military procurement, and, hence, of the defense budget. Most of the largest manufacturing corporations are tied, directly and/or indirectly, to lucrative military contracts (Marfels 1978), and this nonmarket relationship between these top firms and the Pentagon (also noted by Galbraith [1973]) represents another mechanism used by some segments of monopoly capital to shape state expenditure policy. We should emphasize, however, that our results with nondefense monopoly industry profits demonstrate that this linkage does not "explain" the relationship between monopoly profits and defense spending: military expenditures appear sensitive to the accumulation requirements of monopoly capital in general and not simply to that portion of the monopoly sector engaged directly in military production.

State managers use the defense budget in an attempt to insure their incumbency in positions of power in state apparatuses. In years preceding presidential elections, military expenditures increase over and above what we would predict from a knowledge of economic conditions. Our interpretation is that state managers manipulate defense expenditures in preelection years so as to stimulate the economy, increase investment, and reduce unemployment, thus increasing their popularity and likelihood of reelection. To the extent that such behavior is a consequence of the structural interdependency of the state and monopoly capital, then, the political business cycle is one of the mechanisms linking the accumulation needs of monopoly capital to specific state policies (Block 1977b). However, to the extent that state managers opportunistically pursue a particular policy so as to further entrench themselves within the state, then we are not sure that even sophisticated structural Marxism can account for this phenomenon. Weber or Michels, not Marx, may be the intellectual father of a theory to explain an autonomous state bureaucracy manipulating organizational policy for its own class interests. The capitalist state may possess more autonomy than even current structural Marxism allows, and state managers may represent a "class-for-itself" in various ways. Our data do not permit us to adjudicate between these competing explanations, but our findings once again underscore the role of political determinants of state fiscal policy. Strictly economistic explanations of defense spending are inadequate.

The state's response is countercyclical, not ever-upward. We have stressed throughout this paper that defense spending rises as profits fall or as unemployment and concentration increase. Our emphasis, we believe, is in keeping with the spirit of the arguments discussed above. But our data indicate that the state responds to changes in the economic conditions of key sectors by both increasing and decreasing military expenditures. Hence, if monopoly profits are rising or unemployment falling, our data would lead us to conclude that military expenditures will fall. The state's response is essentially countercyclical and is geared toward stabilization. This may seem counterintuitive; why should the state decrease military expenditures to "cool" the economy and possibly engender a recession with all of its attendant political and economic disruptions? One interpretation may be found in Kalecki's (1943) discussion of the "political aspects of full employment." In times of economic expansion, production increases and unemployment—especially among the ranks of organized labor—falls. Two consequences of full employment are particularly pertinent here. First, low unemployment and, correlatively, high inflation rates lead to a more equitable distribution of income (Blinder and Esaki 1978), eroding the financial advantages of capital. Second, falling unemployment improves the bargaining position of (especially) organized labor and increases working-class strike activity (Hibbs 1976), which generates continued upward pressure on wages. Labor discipline degenerates, costs rise, and, if unabetted, profit margins are squeezed as the boom continues (Boddy and Crotty 1974). Sustained economic expansion, then, can be objectively harmful to capital: the balance of power may shift toward labor (Weisskopf 1979). Military expenditures thus may be decreased in order to dampen the economy as full employment approaches. It is impossible to test this view directly with the available data, but we did attempt to explain rising military expenditures (the variable was scored 0 if fluctuations were constant or fell) with falling profits and rising unemployment (where both variables were scored 0 if fluctuations were contrary to the direction intended by the concept). The results using this perspective were generally insignificant and exhibited extremely low explanatory power, implying that a theory positing a unidirectional movement of the variables is simply wrong. The equation which best fit the observed data suggested the countercyclical response. One implication of this finding is that the state intervenes in the economy to protect the long-term interests of the capitalist system as a whole (but perhaps especially of monopoly capital) if and when (as in a period of sustained boom) the interests of monopoly capital and organized labor diverge. These dynamic processes may explain (a) the United States' rather weak commitment to genuine full employment and (b) the cyclical fluctuations in aggregate demand, unemployment, prices, and so on which have characterized the postwar American economy. Together with rhythms of the electoral cycle (Tufte 1978), this economic dimension of class struggle helps explain the "stop-and-go" economic policies of all administrations since the war. Obviously, more research is necessary before this can be characterized as anything more than informed opinion, but our interpretation does suggest how class struggle affects particular state policies and how these policies, in turn, feed back to determine partially economic conditions and to reproduce or transform existing class relations.

APPENDIX

Unless otherwise indicated, all variables pertain to the United States, are annual observations, and, when dollar amounts, are measured in current dollars. Federal budgetary items are for fiscal rather than calendar years. The following abbreviations are used in this appendix: HS, *The Historical Statistics of the United States: Colonial Times to 1970* (1975); SA, *The Statistical Abstract of the United States* (annual); ERP, *The Economic Report of the President, 1978* (1978); NIPA, *The National Income and Product Accounts of the United States, 1929–1974* (1977); BEA, U.S. Department of Commerce, Bureau of Economic Analysis, "Survey of Current Business" (monthly); BLS, U.S. Department of Labor, Bureau of Labor Statistics, *Handbook of Labor Statistics* (1977). All of the above sources are published by the Government Printing Office, Washington, D.C.

1. Gross National Product (GNP): NIPA; BEA (July 1977, July 1978).
2. GNP Gap: BEA (June 1973); ERP.
3. Defense Spending: HS; SA (1971–77).
4. Veterans' Spending: HS; SA (1971–77).
5. Civilian Spending (total federal expenditures less defense spending): HS; SA (1971–77).
6. Revenue: HS; SA (1978).
7. Consumption: NIPA; BEA (June 1977, June 1978).
8. Inflation (the annual percentage change in the consumer price index): HS; SA (1977).

9. Balance of Payments: ERP.
10. Industrial Unemployment: BLS; HS; SA (1978).
11. Adult Male Unemployment: ERP.
12. Predicted Aggregate Unemployment: SA (annual).
13. Occupational Unemployment: "Manpower Report of the President" (1965); "Employment and Training Report of the President" (1978).
14. Recession: NIPA; BEA (June 1975, June 1978).
15. Manufacturing Gap: Artus 1977.
16. Industrial Underutilization: Board of Governors, Federal Reserve System, "Federal Reserve Bulletin" (January 1972, January 1976, January 1979).
17. Profits: NIPA; BEA (June 1976, June 1978).
18. Assets: NIPA; BEA (June 1976, June 1978).
19. Employment: NIPA; BEA (June 1976, June 1978).
20. Corporate Tax Revenue: NIPA; BEA (June 1976, June 1978).
21. Concentration: Federal Trade Commission, *Economic Report on Corporate Mergers*, Washington, D.C. (Part 8a of the Economic Concentration Hearings of the Senate Subcommittee on Anti-Trust and Monopoly) (1969); SA (1970–77).
22. Democratic Party: HS.
23. Soviet Military Expenditures (as measured in current U.S. dollars at the Benoit-Lubell exchange rate): Stockholm International Peace Research Institute (1968/1969, 1977).
24. Nondefense Monopoly Profits (total monopoly profits minus profits of those industries defined as "defense oriented"): SA (1977, p. 365).

REFERENCES

Artus, J. R. 1977. "Measures of Potential Output in Manufacturing for Eight Industrial Countries, 1955–1978." *International Monetary Fund Staff Papers* 24:1–35.
Ashenfelter, O., G. E. Johnson, and J. H. Pencavel. 1972. "Trade Unions and the Rate of Change of Money Wages in United States Manufacturing Industry." *Review of Economic Studies* 39:27–54.
Baran, P., and P. Sweezy. 1966. *Monopoly Capital*. New York: Monthly Review Press.
Beck, E. M., P. M. Horan, and C. M. Tolbert. 1978. "Stratification in a Dual Economy: A Sectoral Model of Earnings Determination." *American Sociological Review* 43:704–20.
Bibb, R., and W. H. Form. 1977. "The Effects of Industrial, Occupational, and Sex Stratification on Wages in Blue-Collar Markets." *Social Forces* 55:974–96.
Blinder, A., and H. Y. Esaki. 1978. "Macroeconomic Activity and Income Distribution in the Post-war United States." *Review of Economics and Statistics* 60:604–8.
Block, F. 1977a. *The Origins of International Economic Disorder*. Berkeley and Los Angeles: University of California Press.
———. 1977b. The Ruling Class Does Not Rule: Notes on the Marxist Theory of the State." *Socialist Revolution* 7:6–28.
Boddy, R., and J. Crotty. 1974. "Class Conflict and Macro-Policy: The Political Business Cycle." *Review of Radical Political Economics* 7:1–19.
Brown, E. C. 1956. "Fiscal Policies in the Thirties, a Reappraisal." *American Economic Review* 66:857–79.

Chester, E. 1978. "Military Spending and Capitalist Stability." *Cambridge Journal of Economics* 2:293–98.

Crouch, C. 1979. "The State, Capital, and Liberal Democracy." Pp. 13–54 in *State and Economy in Contemporary Capitalism*, edited by C. Crouch. New York: St. Martin's.

Cypher, J. 1974. "Capitalist Planning and Military Expenditures." *Review of Radical Political Economics* 6:1–20.

Dobb, M. 1950. "Full Employment and Capitalism." *Modern Quarterly* 5:125–35.

Draper, N. R., and H. Smith. 1966. *Applied Regression Analysis*. New York: Wiley.

DuBoff, R. 1977. "Full Employment: The History of a Receding Target." *Politics and Society* 7:1–25.

Esping-Andersen, G., R. Friedland, and E. O. Wright. 1976. "Modes of Class Struggle and the Capitalist State." *Kapitalistate* 4/5:186–220.

Freeman, R., and J. Medoff. 1979. "New Estimates of Private Sector Unionism in the United States." *Industrial and Labor Relations Review* 32:143–74.

Frey, B. S., and F. Schneider. 1978. "An Empirical Study of Politico-economic Inter-action in the United States." *Review of Economics and Statistics* 60:174–83.

Galbraith, J. K. 1973. *Economics and the Public Purpose*. New York: Houghton Mifflin.

Ginsberg, B. 1976. "Elections and Public Policy." *American Political Science Review* 70:41–49.

Gold, D. 1977. "The Rise and Fall of the Keynesian Coalition." *Kapitalistate* 6:129–61.

Gough, I. 1975. "State Expenditure in Advanced Capitalism." *New Left Review* 92:53–91.

Greenstone, J. D. 1977. *Labor in American Politics*. Chicago: University of Chicago Press.

Griffin, L. J., J. A. Devine, and M. Wallace. 1981. "Accumulation, Legitimation, and Politics: Neo-Marxist Explanations of the Growth of Welfare Expenditures in the United States since the Second World War." Paper presented at the 76th Annual Meeting of the American Sociological Association, Toronto.

Griffin, L. J., M. Wallace, and J. A. Devine. 1982. "The Political Economy of Military Spending: Evidence from the United States." *Cambridge Journal of Economics* 6:1–14.

Hartley, K., and P. McLean. 1978. "Military Expenditure and Capitalism: A Comment." *Cambridge Journal of Economics* 2:287–92.

Heise, D. 1975. *Causal Analysis*. New York: Wiley.

Heller, W. 1967. *New Dimensions of Political Economy*. Cambridge, Mass.: Harvard University Press.

Hibbs, D. 1976. "Industrial Conflict in Advanced Industrial Societies." *American Political Science Review* 70:1033–58.

———. 1977. "Political Parties and Macroeconomic Policy." *American Political Science Review* 71:1467–87.

———. 1978. "Trade Union Power, Labor Militancy and Wage Inflation: A Comparative Analysis." Mimeographed. Cambridge, Mass.: Harvard University, Department of Government.

Hicks, A., R. Friedland, and E. Johnson. 1978. "Class Power and State Policy: The Case of Large Business Corporations, Labor Unions and Governmental Redistribution in the American States." *American Sociological Review* 43:302–15.

Hodson, R. 1978. "Labor in the Monopoly, Competitive, and State Sectors of Production." *Politics and Society* 8:429–80.

Johnston, J. 1972. *Econometric Methods*. New York: McGraw-Hill.

Kalecki, M. 1943. "Political Aspects of Full Employment." *Political Quarterly* 14:322–31.

———. (1956) 1972. "The Economic Stagnation in the United States as Compared with the Pre-War Period." Pp. 85–97 in *The Last Phase in the Transformation of Capitalism*. New York: Monthly Review Press.

Keohane, R. 1978. "Economics, Inflation, and the Role of the State: Political Implications of the McCracken Report." *World Politics* 31:108–28.

Keynes, J. M. 1936. *The General Theory of Employment, Interest, and Money*. London: Macmillan.

Kidron, M. 1968. *Western Capitalism since the War*. London: Weidenfeld & Nicolson.

Kindleberger, C. 1973. *The World in Depression: 1929–1939*. Berkeley and Los Angeles: University of California Press.

Land, K., and M. Felson. 1976. "A General Framework for Building Dynamic Macro Social Indicator Models: Including an Analysis of Changes in Crime Rates and Police Expenditures." *American Journal of Sociology* 82:565–604.

Lekachman, R. 1966. *The Age of Keynes.* New York: Random House.

Lewis, H. G. 1963. *Unionism and the Relative Wage in the United States.* Chicago: University of Chicago Press.

Lo, C. 1975. "The Conflicting Functions of U.S. Military Spending after World War II." *Kapitalistate* 3:26–44.

Long, S. 1980. "The Continuing Debate over the Use of Ratio Variables: Facts and Fiction." Pp. 37–67 in *Sociological Methodology, 1980,* edited by K. Schuessler. San Francisco: Jossey-Bass.

Lubitz, R. 1970. "Monoploy Capitalism and Neo-marxism." *Public Interest* 21:167–78.

Luxemburg, R. (1913) 1951. *The Accumulation of Capital.* New Haven, Conn.: Yale University Press.

Mandel, E. 1975. *Late Capitalism,* translated by J. De Bres. London: New Left Books.

Marfels, C. 1978. "The Structure of the Military Industrial Complex in the United States and Its Impact on Industrial Concentration." *Kyklos* 31:409–23.

Niskanen, W. 1978. "Deficits, Government Spending, and Inflation: What is the Evidence?" *Journal of Monetary Economics* 4:591–602.

Nordhaus, W. 1974. "The Falling Share of Profits." *Brookings Papers on Economic Activity,* no. 1, pp. 169–208.

Oakes, W. 1944. "Toward a Permanent War Economy?" *Politics* 1:11–17.

O'Connor, J. 1973. *The Fiscal Crisis of the State.* New York: St. Martin's.

Okun, A. 1970. *The Political Economy of Prosperity.* Washington, D.C.: Brookings Institution.

Ostrom, C. 1978. "A Reactive Linkage Model of the U.S. Defense Expenditure Policymaking Process." *American Political Science Review* 72:941–57.

Radosh, R. 1969. *American Labor and United States Foreign Policy.* New York: Random House.

Rattinger, H. 1975. "Armaments, Detente, and Bureaucracy." *Journal of Conflict Resolution* 19:571–95.

Reich, M. 1978. "Military Spending and Production for Profit." Pp. 410–17 in *The Capitalist System,* edited by R. C. Edwards, M. Reich, and T. Weisskopf. Englewood Cliffs, N.J.: Prentice-Hall.

Reich, M., and R. Edwards. 1978. "Political Parties and Class Conflict in the United States." *Socialist Review* 8:37–57.

Rockwell, R. 1975. "Assessment of Multicollinearity: The Haitovsky Test of the Determinant." *Sociological Methods and Research* 3:308–20.

Schuessler, K. 1974. "Analysis of Ratio Variables: Opportunities and Pitfalls." *American Journal of Sociology* 80:379–96.

Sherman, H. 1977. "Monopoly Power and Stagflation." *Journal of Economic Issues* 11:269–84.

Smith, R. 1977. "Military Expenditure and Capitalism." *Cambridge Journal of Economics* 1:61–76.

———. 1978. "Military Expenditure and Capitalism: A Reply." *Cambridge Journal of Economics* 2:299–304.

Stein, J. 1978. "Inflation, Employment, and Stagflation." *Journal of Monetary Economics* 4:193–228.

Steindl, J. (1952) 1972. *Maturity and Stagnation in American Capitalism.* New York: Monthly Review Press.

Sweezy, P. (1942) 1970. *The Theory of Capitalist Development.* New York: Monthly Review Press.

Tufte, E. 1978. *Political Control over the Economy.* Princeton, N.J.: Princeton University Press.

Wachter, M. 1976. "The Changing Cyclical Responsiveness of Wage Inflation." *Brookings Papers on Economic Activity,* no. 1, pp. 115–67.

Wallace, M., and A. L. Kalleberg. 1981. "Economic Organization of Firms and Labor Force Consequences: Towards a Specification of Dual Economy Theory." Pp. 77–117 in *Sociological Perspectives on Labor Markets*, edited by I. Berg. New York: Academic Press.

Weisskopf, T. 1979. "Marxian Crisis Theory and the Rate of Profit in the Postwar U.S. Economy." *Cambridge Journal of Economics* 3:341–78.

Wilensky, H. 1975. *The Welfare State and Equality*. Berkeley and Los Angeles: University of California Press.

Wright, E. O. 1978. *Class, Crisis, and the State*. London: New Left Books.

Zeitlin, M. 1974. "On 'Military Spending and Economic Stagnation.' " *American Journal of Sociology* 79:1452–56.

Bureaucratic Initiative in Capitalist New Zealand: A Case Study of the Accident Compensation Act of 1972[1]

Pat Shannon
University of Otago, New Zealand

New Zealand's position in the world economic order and the form of its state determine the limits and possibilities of state initiative. One such initiative—the Accident Compensation Act of 1972—has been something of a revolution in social policy, as it abolished the whole field of tort law with respect to accident injury, covers all accident-related costs for all citizens, and provides earnings-related compensation for all earnings lost. The paper analyzes how the act, first framed in the interests of monopoly capital, was reshaped through struggles both outside and within the state.

In 1972, the New Zealand government passed the Accident Compensation Act—the first truly comprehensive no-fault accident compensation system in the world, which completely abolished legal action at tort for personal injury and workers' compensation insurance arrangements. As amended in 1973, the scheme operates through an automatic system of coverage and payment for all costs associated with accidental injury, 24 hours a day, for all citizens. The payments extend for the length of any disablement, and there are special lump-sum payments for permanent disability and death. Finance is provided through levies on motor vehicle owners, employers, and the self-employed and through a direct grant from taxation funds for nonearner costs. The scheme is administered by the Accident Compensation Commission, a government department. While there is some provision for appealing the commission's eligibility decisions, in every other respect the courts have been eliminated from the compensation process.

As the first example of such legislation in the Western world, this system has been seen by many commentators as a major breakthrough in the area of community responsibility (Szakats 1973), one which might "point the way in which social policy in the developed countries will advance"

---

[1] I am indebted to Geoff Neill, Peter Wilson, and many of my New Zealand colleagues for assistance in revising and refining the arguments presented here. A grant from the University of Otago assisted with research costs for this paper. Requests for reprints should be sent to Pat Shannon, Community Studies Centre, Otago University Extension, Dunedin, New Zealand.

(Kaim-Caudle 1973, p. 97). It has also received considerable attention from researchers and has been the focus of at least two major studies (Palmer 1979; Kronick et al. 1978). Both of these conclude that the legislation sprang from some special value of altruism. Thus, Kronick et al. speak of a "value response to technological change" (p. i), and Palmer speaks of the "special" nature of New Zealand society and its welfare concerns (p. 55 ff.).

That explanation is hardly satisfactory. If a "special" value of altruism exists in New Zealand (which is certainly debatable), why does it exist? Where did it come from? Why did it take this particular form? Why are other nations lacking in this value? In the face of these questions, a far more conclusive and satisfactory account of the genesis of the accident compensation system can be provided by adopting the perspective of historical materialism to examine the requirements of state policy and continued capital accumulation within the context of the capitalist mode of production in New Zealand.

From a Marxist perspective, the key to state intervention and the growth of "public law" is not the normally cited process of industrialization but the necessity of providing conditions of profitability for capital. Because the state does not need to make a profit, shifting the burden of nonproductive investment onto it is cheaper for capital (Rowthorn 1974; Gough 1979). State intervention will therefore occur first and most substantially in peripheral and dependent social formations to the degree that indigenous capital is lacking and continued accumulation is dependent on providing a clear profit for international capital.

Thus, the Accident Compensation Act is linked with the historical process in New Zealand, where the early development of a highly centralized and interventionist state apparatus is connected with features such as the very early introduction of universal suffrage, state control of trade unions, and, indeed, the earliest introduction of a comprehensive welfare state. Instead of a circular argument postulating the (unexplained) existence of a nation of altruists, all such development can therefore be more plausibly related to New Zealand's "dominion capitalism" (Armstrong 1978; Ehrensaft and Armstrong 1978) and the requirements of capital accumulation in a dependent and semiperipheral social formation.[2]

The accident compensation legislation is less surprising when viewed in this light, and recent developments in Marxist theories of the state further clarify its role. Until recently, such theories had oscillated between a crude

2 "Dominion capitalism" is a term devised by Ehrensaft and Armstrong to refer to "19th century 'regions of recent settlement' supplying temperate foodstuffs and other staple products to the imperial centre of the world system, Britain" (Armstrong 1978, p. 303). These countries (New Zealand, Argentina, Canada, Australia, and Uruguay) are seen as occupying an "intermediate position between the world centres and peripheries" and "exhibiting characteristics of both."

economism, in which the state as "superstructure" is a mere reflection of the economic "base," and the critical theory position, which turns the Marxist architectural metaphor on its head: the "legitimation" function of the political superstructure defines the economic base.

Discussion has now moved beyond a mechanical application of the super-structure/base metaphor and is searching for a middle position where the requirements of the capitalist mode of production are given priority, yet adequate attention is given to intentional human action, particularly working-class struggle. The two main positions here are Miliband's (1969) "instrumentalism," in which the state is staffed and controlled by the ruling class, and Poulantzas's (1973, 1976) neoorthodoxy, in which the state is "relatively autonomous" of the economic base but is determined by it in "the last instance."

Making the nature of the relation between economic base and human initiative within the state contingent on the specific state personnel, as Miliband does, is hardly satisfactory: it is implausible that the replacement of those officials by persons of working-class sympathies would change very much. On the other hand, the "relative autonomy" position, while theoretically more coherent, is similarly inadequate. How relative is the autonomy? When is the last instance reached, and how do we know this? There is no specification, no enumeration of the mechanisms and criteria involved. Thus, anything and everything can be explained by saying that the state has become more or less autonomous. We have no way of knowing how, or why, that degree of autonomy has been reached.

Marxist theory can plausibly explain why the state intervenes when and where it does. But on the issue of how it intervenes—its relationship to democratic forms, working-class action, and so on—Marxist theory is currently less than satisfactory.

This case study addresses these issues. The history of the Accident Compensation Act in New Zealand demonstrates the importance of examining in detail how the state intervenes and how the process of change itself, shaped as it is by structural features of the state in a situation of class struggle, determines policy outcomes. An important feature of this process is how the results themselves, the actual legislative outcomes, then become issues which require more state intervention.

This paper will first outline the "why" of state intervention with respect to the accident compensation legislation by examining the conditions required for capital accumulation in New Zealand and how the Accident Compensation Act partially fulfilled these conditions. This argument has been advanced in detail elsewhere (Shannon 1980) and will be covered only briefly here. The paper will then demonstrate the extent to which the act did not fulfill these conditions and discuss how and why it failed in many significant respects. I will conclude with an assessment of the implications of this case study for Marxist approaches to the state.

THE LOGIC OF CAPITAL ACCUMULATION IN NEW ZEALAND

It was suggested earlier that New Zealand's dependent dominion capitalism demanded the development of a strong, highly interventionist state. Indeed, this was a key feature of New Zealand's short European history. Prior to the 1930s, New Zealand conformed to the traditional patterns of colonial societies, importing most manufactured products and exporting agricultural produce. It was a boom-and-bust economy almost completely dependent on agricultural prices. Manufacturing consisted only of rural service industries and the processing of agricultural goods. During this period, there was a high degree of state intervention in the provision of infrastructural support for agriculture and the regulation of industrial relations.

The depression of the 1930s saw the election of the worker-oriented Labour party and the introduction of comprehensive welfare measures (to ensure a more equitable distribution of the products of a staples-oriented economy). From 1935 to 1950, the Labour government attempted to insulate the economy through import controls, in order to offset dependency on agricultural prices and to hasten the development of indigenous industry.

However, since 1950 (with a total of only six years of Labour party rule, in two separate terms), the country has been ruled by the National party, which represents above all the mercantile-financial and farming groups. The state has gradually dismantled import controls and has encouraged overseas investment capital. This has resulted in the gradual development of a small number of firms in large-scale production with high capital intensity, developed technology, and high rates of productivity. New Zealand has a higher degree of market concentration than either the United States or Britain (Ellis 1976), with one or two firms dominating important sectors of the economy. These companies are often surrounded by a large number of smaller companies with greater labor intensity and lower productivity.

These large-scale units have grown due to economies of scale, high capital requirements, a rapidly increasing rate of merger activity, and protection against external competition provided by the state (Ellis 1976, p. 25). They have been the locus of foreign investment, which increased by 80% from 1955 to 1965 (Rosenberg 1975, p. 47), so that during the 1960s New Zealand became a "mature debtor," with foreign investors' income exceeding their investment (Lane 1973, p. 7). It is this group of companies which has been defined here as "monopoly capital" and which, from the standpoint of capital accumulation, dominates other classes and fractions of capital.

From the point of view of a structural analysis, therefore, the weakest form of the hypothesis to explain the conditions for the appearance of the Accident Compensation Act is that the change involved in the accident compensation (or any other) legislation must not worsen monopoly capital's situation; a stronger version would be that the change must improve that situation. This structural requirement can be further specified with respect to the use of labor. First, the type of labor required by monopoly industry is likely to be skilled (professional/technical or manual) or semi-skilled (process workers, machine operators) rather than unskilled. Any action which assists in the supply (or oversupply) of such labor is to the advantage of the monopoly sector. Second, the cost of an accident to monopoly capital is greater than its cost to smaller, less capital-intensive industry, as the marginal productivity of each worker in a capital-intensive situation is higher and the use of expensive machinery is disrupted (especially since training a replacement worker is likely to be required). Finally, any reduction of the costs of accidents to capital in general is, of course, a reduction to monopoly capital.

The Accident Compensation Act fulfilled these "conditions of possibility" with respect to monopoly capital. First, skilled workers were more advantaged than were the unskilled, as accident payments became earnings related (unlike the previous flat rate of compensation). Second, there was some reduction in the cost of accident compensation to industrial employers compared with costs to the professional and self-employed groups, as the risk scale according to which employer levies were paid was changed to the advantage of the former group. And, finally, the shift from a private insurance scheme to a state monopoly involved savings to all capital (except the small insurance industry), since the state did not need to make a profit.

The conclusions of an investigation of the structural conditions of possibility of the Accident Compensation Act therefore go a considerable distance toward explaining some features of the legislative change (state monopoly and earnings-related compensation). However, such an analysis can account for neither the specific area of change nor for features such as absolute liability (the abolition of the "fault" provisions of common law). For this we must turn to a specific causal account of why accident compensation became an issue.

CAUSES OF THE ACCIDENT COMPENSATION CHANGE

Accidents are important to capital because they involve costs, in terms of lost production, compensation payments, and the loss of labor power. These issues were of major concern during the period leading up to the initial promotion of the issue of accident compensation. The director of the New Zealand National Safety Association claimed that more work time had been lost through accidents in one year than through all strikes since 1924 (*Evening Post* [Wellington], August 24, 1966). The official government publication *Labour and Employment Gazette* claimed that the cost of work accidents had reached $24 million every year and that employers bore the whole burden: both the "direct" cost (premiums, etc.) and the "indirect," hidden cost of loss of production (December 1966).

Another major feature of the New Zealand economy during the early 1960s was a chronic shortage of labor, especially skilled labor. This was the subject of numerous inquiries, reports, and state initiatives, including vigorous promotion of immigration and greater overall intervention in labor-force regulation and control. It had been realized by 1966 that most of the initiatives to solve the shortage of labor had been ineffective due to New Zealand's inability to compete for and retain skilled labor (Shannon 1980).

In summary, then, a Marxist approach to why a change in the system of accident compensation came about would stress the concern about accident costs (both financial and in terms of available labor) in a situation of a chronic shortage of skilled labor. The structural requirements of a society increasingly dominated by monopoly capital required a change which at least did not increase, and preferably would reduce, accident costs for that group. The new system of accident compensation which featured state monopoly and earnings-related compensation fulfilled this condition.

We must stress the two levels on which this explanation has been conducted—the structural requirements of the dominance of monopoly capital, and the specific historical situation of a peripheral country with a labor shortage. The logic of capital accumulation alone did not specify this particular accident compensation measure, but it did set the terms and conditions under which such a measure could be introduced.

In many respects this explanation accounts for the "why" of state intervention and action for this case. It is deficient, however, in advancing the Marxist understanding of the relative autonomy of the state and in explaining how the state intervenes. For one thing, it completely ignores the role of class struggle. Furthermore, the demand for reform seems to be due solely to the initiative of the state bureaucracy. Finally, close analysis of the actual process of negotiation and compromise leading to the final legislation reveals that the actual outcome was far less advantageous to monopoly capital than had been the original proposals. These features constitute objections to any crude functionalism and help elucidate the vexatious problem of relative autonomy. To clarify this, it is necessary to look briefly at the whole legislative process from the first raising of the issue to the actual legislation.

THE LEGISLATIVE PROCESS

Although the reform of workers' compensation had been a matter of concern at least to the Labour Department for some time, the occasion for explicitly suggesting the reform was the 1965 government adoption of a convention by the International Labour Organisation (ILO) calling for higher standards in workers' compensation schemes.[3] This led to a November 1965 Labour Department memorandum advocating a state monopoly in workers' compensation and appointment of a Royal Commission, because "the changes required were so substantial and perhaps controversial" (Palmer 1979, p. 119).

The cabinet's original decision in favor of a "permanent pensions scheme" had been changed by the time the terms of reference for the Royal Commission appeared, on September 14, 1966. The commission was to "receive representations upon, inquire into, investigate and report upon the law relating to compensation and claims for damages and incapacity or death arising out of accidents (including diseases) suffered by persons in employment and the medical care, retraining and rehabilitation of persons so incapacitated and the administration of said law, and to recommend such changes therein as the Commission considers desirable" (Woodhouse Report 1967, p. 11).

The Labour Department carefully arranged the commission so as to ensure that its members leaned in the desired direction.[4] The exercise of bias and bureaucratic initiative seemed to be openly known. As the Storemen and Packers' Union representative put it, "Where, then, has the desire for change come from? It has not come from the people concerned. They do not want it. It has obviously come from a small group of civil servants" (Transcript of Royal Commission Hearings 1967, 1:3). Similarly, from

---

[3] This account is heavily dependent on Palmer's meticulous study of the change process (1979). This work is notable not only for its exhaustive consultation of primary sources but as a primary source itself. Palmer's personal involvement in the process enables him to provide a view based on "insiders' knowledge" unique in accounts of the New Zealand bureaucracy.

[4] Palmer notes how the Labour Department advised against representativeness of the Royal Commission. The membership was made up of Woodhouse (chairman), a Supreme Court judge known to be in favor of the reform of tort law; Bockett, a former Labour Department head who had openly advocated the state monopoly of Workmen's Compensation; and Parsons, an accountant. Palmer goes on to comment, "New Zealand is a very small country and the men of affairs who would have the qualifications and experience to be appointed to a Royal Commission would often be known to one another. But the composition of this Royal Commission indicated closer ties than usual" (1979, p. 120). Certainly the exercise of bias was openly known; because of his well-known views, Bockett's appointment was challenged at the first session of commission hearings by the representative of the New Zealand Labourers' Union (Transcript of Royal Commission Hearings 1967, 1:3). Following accepted practice, the Royal Commission and its report will be referred to by the name of its chairman, the Hon. Justice Woodhouse.

the other side of the industrial fence, the Employers' Federation representative remarked that the ILO recommendation was not sufficient reason for the change, as the New Zealand government was quite accustomed to ignoring such recommendations (Transcript of Royal Commission Hearings 1967, 1:17–18).

THE WOODHOUSE REPORT

The Woodhouse Royal Commission acted quickly: within one year, it held two stages of hearings, visited overseas to investigate other compensation schemes, and presented its report. The report went much further than the commission's own terms of reference, advocating complete abolition of all common-law claims at tort, state monopoly of an automatic compensation system, and earnings-related compensation for earners. Compensation for earners was to be financed by a flat 1% levy on employers and compensation for automobile accident victims by levies on owners and drivers, the balance of the cost being met by the state.

The report was more than the ruling National party wanted. The commission had ignored almost all the submissions made to it—from employers, trade unions, the insurance industry, and a wide range of smaller groups—with the exception of those by government departments and the Public Service Association (the public servants' union) and some "arranged" presentations by legal academics (Palmer 1979, p. 123). The report then went through a five-year process of reviews, caucus committees,[5] and two Parliamentary Select Committees (the Gair Committee in 1970 and the McLachlan Committee in 1971) before its enactment in 1972 and major amendment by the new Labour government in 1973. Throughout this process, the state bureaucracy, particularly the Labour Department, played a major role.

The Gair Committee recommended major changes to the Woodhouse proposals. In the first of these, bowing to trade union pressure over the low level of initial payments, it suggested that employers pay 100% of employees' earnings for the first week after injury, the state then taking over at the rate of 80%. Other changes excluded nonearners injured in accidents other than automobile accidents and replaced the flat levy on employers with a graduated "risk" scale. In the event, the fury of employers over the 100% payment rate resulted in such pressure on the McLachlan Committee that this provision was reduced to require payment for work-related injuries only (Palmer 1979, p. 174). In the 1972 election campaign, the Labour party took advantage of the developing feminist political move-

5 "Caucus" refers to the regular (usually weekly) meetings of all the members of a political party in Parliament.

Shannon

ment to highlight the exclusion of "housewives" from the program. In line with their election promises, their 1973 amendment reintroduced coverage for all citizens.

As will be indicated below, the overall result is potentially contradictory to the needs of monopoly capitalist accumulation. However, the initial proposals of the Woodhouse Report would have markedly improved monopoly capital's position relative to other classes and fractions of capital.

First, the scheme was to be financed by a flat 1% levy on all employers. This would have markedly disadvantaged the self-employed, small business, and the service sector, areas of low accident costs, while advantaging large-scale, capital-intensive, and extractive industries.[6] Second, compensation was to be earnings related, thus reinforcing margins for skilled labor. Third, the costs of accident compensation would be reduced. It was projected that a state monopoly would spend only 10% of total costs on administration; the corresponding figure for the private insurance industry was 42% (Woodhouse Report 1967, pp. 163–69). Fourth, workers were to receive only a very low flat rate of compensation for the first four weeks of their disability. Since most accidents resulted in less than four weeks' absence, this would reduce employer costs. And, finally, automobile accidents were to be covered. In this respect, the extra cost of accidents to capital-intensive monopoly industry, due to idle machinery, must be borne in mind.

If implemented, these provisions would almost have justified a crudely functionalist understanding of the state as the "executive committee of the bourgeoisie." The actual legislative result, however, was a far cry from the Woodhouse proposals and demands a different type of explanation of the formation of state policies. First, the initiative in raising the issue in the first place seems to have come from within the bureaucracy. At no stage did the representatives of monopoly capital call openly for a change. Second, the revision of the original Woodhouse proposals marked a retreat from the best possible results for monopoly capital. The extension of accident coverage to all citizens greatly increased the cost of the scheme overall, and with respect to employed workers there was a reduction of gains to both capital in general and monopoly capital in particular. The proposal of a low rate of payment for the first four weeks of disability was dropped in favor of full payment by the employer for the first week after a work-related accident, followed by 80% payment by the accident compensation scheme. Further, the flat 1% levy on all employers was changed

[6] The issue of costs is somewhat complex, as a distinction must be drawn between accident *rates* and accident *costs*. By examining the statistical evidence of accident rates, Kronick et al. (1978, pp. 167 ff.) determine that the rates for high technology, "machine-paced" industry are in fact lower than those for labor-intensive, "operator-paced" industry. The higher marginal productivity of workers in the monopoly capitalist sector, however, means that a lower rate of accidents may result in a higher cost.

to a risk-related scale (an improvement for service industries and the professional sectors).

THE SOURCES OF BUREAUCRATIC INITIATIVE

Many proponents and critics of the cruder forms of Marxist analysis have regarded bureaucratic initiative as running contrary to Marxist theory. From this perspective, such initiative is impossible; there must be a group of clear-sighted Machiavellian capitalists, greedily thirsting for profit, behind every change. Recent developments have rendered this thesis untenable, yet bureaucratic initiative still awaits theoretical explanation.

In this case, the issue of legislative change was originally raised by one government department (Labour) in the context of an earlier, unsuccessful attempt at a similar change by another department (Justice)[7] and calls for the reform of tort law by some legal academics. All government departments which made submissions were in favor of legal reform.

Throughout the process of proposing and evaluating changes in accident compensation legislation, almost all the interest groups involved, employers and unions alike, expressed a constant, if gradually muted, opposition. The state was alone in favoring the proposed changes. The explanation for this lies in the nature of interest-group representation and in the structural features of social democracy under dominion capitalism in New Zealand.

The earlier discussion suggests that the groups which became involved were not necessarily the most significant from a theoretical point of view. Basic to the theoretical explanation are New Zealand's dependent dominion capitalism and the distinction between different fractions of capital. It can be argued that monopoly capital was not represented by the overt interest groups because it was at least partly foreign and numerically weak vis-à-vis other fractions of capital in those groups. Given a conflict of interest between fractions of capital, then, interest groups are unlikely to represent monopoly concerns. The power of the monopoly fraction, almost by definition, is economic rather than numerical. Its power lies in its ability to structure the requirements of continued capital accumulation. The only group in the current case which could be expected to represent such interests is therefore the state bureaucracy.

It must be stressed, however, that one cannot take a simple instrumentalist view of the state bureaucracy. The argument merely suggests that the bureaucracy is the interest group which acts "in the national interest" within the confines of a monopoly-dominated economy. Here it is essential to note a point made by Perez-Diaz in his analysis of Marx's discussion of the Paris Commune (1978, p. 64): the state takes action on its own terms

[7] This was the 1962 Committee on Absolute Liability (the Wild Committee), set up by the minister of justice (Szakats 1968, p. 80).

in the sense that it supports capital unambiguously only as long as its own existence depends on capital accumulation.

Structurally, the centralized political system in New Zealand aids monopoly capital representation. Although the political system is based on the Westminster model, there is only one elected house of representatives; a party which has a majority in that house has no upper chamber to block or delay legislation. There is no written constitution limiting the exercise of legislative power, and thus Parliament, as the collection of elected representatives of all parties, is formally in control. Rigid party discipline (it is extremely rare for a representative to vote against his or her party's policy) means that Parliament is largely a debating chamber. Policy and legislation are usually decided by the majority party through regular caucuses of its elected members or through the cabinet. Cabinet ministers have major formal power.

The public service is relatively large (almost 25% of the total work force) and contains no elected representatives. Theoretically, the civil service only advises the cabinet ministers, who make the political decisions. But the centralized unitary system, the lack of any federal or regional political units, and the strong tradition of cabinet government give considerable scope to the state bureaucracy to at least "set the agenda" for political decisions.[8] The only structural constraint on such power and influence is the caucus of the ruling party and, ultimately, public opinion. The power of the bureaucracy is therefore even further enhanced if both the caucus and the public are as uninformed as possible. The process of change demonstrates that the state bureaucracy consciously used these structural features of power to bring about the accident compensation reforms.

Secrecy of the operation was undoubtedly a major tactic used by the state in this particular legislative change. Palmer argues that the fact that government departments made their suggestions "in secret is unfortunate because the Departmental submissions tend to be most influential with Select Committees, and the Departments were able to analyse and comment upon the merits of other submissions made to the Committee" (1979, p. 162). Perhaps the clearest exposition of the way these tactics are used is the manner in which the insurance industry, which was totally opposed to the Woodhouse Report at all stages, was completely neutralized. The industry initially responded to the report with a publicity campaign. The government countered by persuading the industry to agree to a policy of

[8] This has been the focus for considerable comment by political scientists in New Zealand, although it has rarely been analyzed in depth; e.g.: "ministers are not so much 'policy initiators' in New Zealand as 'policy legitimators.' The Public Service tends to monopolise the crucial stages of the policy-making process by identifying and defining policy problems, stipulating objectives, priorities and criteria for discussion, formulating the alternative proposals and arriving at a set of recommendations which the minister then endorses" (Jackson 1978, p. 69).

confidential consultation and negotiation, thus leading it onto the bureaucracy's own terrain of secrecy and ultimately into a position where its views were ignored. Palmer's meticulous account, which is obviously designed to sidestep neatly the extensive Official Secrets Act, points in detail to the influence of public servants in this process.

Secrecy, however, while enabling change to take place without public debate when politicians can be influenced, does not necessarily guarantee such influence. The use of a Royal Commission indicates the other major tactic of the bureaucracy: judicious publicity to put politicians in embarrassing positions. Royal Commissions have considerable prestige in New Zealand and are often called into being to inquire into controversial matters on which the government does not wish to make a decision. Their aura is one of impartiality and consultation with interested parties. A Royal Commission report is therefore difficult to ignore, especially by the government which has called the commission into being (Simpson 1978, pp. 22 ff.; Palmer 1979, p. 129).

In summary, then, the structural features of the government have led to a significant degree of power for the state bureaucracy, and the historical process of this legislative change indicates the ability and willingness of that bureaucracy to act consciously on the basis of that power. This is not to suggest that social democratic forms are meaningless. There are clearly limits on the bureaucratic power to act. The first of these is the bureaucracy's degree of dependence on, or independence from, the legislature. That the new accident compensation scheme was introduced through a Royal Commission indicates that the bureaucracy was (or saw itself as being) unable to put enough pressure on the legislature without opening the issue to public participation.

The legislature was dominated by the National party, whose traditional base was one of "free enterprise" and resistance to state growth, especially "welfare"-oriented intervention. The proposed reform therefore faced National party resistance; the executive could not depend on legislative acquiescence. Thus is revealed the legislature's main counterweight to bureaucratic control: control by the constituency. From the present case, it could be argued that bureaucratic ability to act will be constrained on issues of major concern to the constituency, when the legislature is likely to be under pressure. The discussion of bureaucratic initiative has therefore indicated that the development of state provision of accident compensation in New Zealand is not only compatible with a Marxist explanation but may even fill lacunae in Marxist treatments of the capitalist state by suggesting when state initiative is likely and the salience of specific features of social democratic forms for such initiative.

We can now consider the other features of the legislation and the change process which shed further light on the state action. There are two main aspects to this and to the way the resultant legislation failed to meet the needs of capital accumulation: divergences among various government departments (the "internal limits" on state action), which led to the extension of coverage to all citizens, and divergences between the state apparatus as a whole and capital (the "external limits" on state action), which are relevant to the legal changes, workers' benefits, and employer levies.

INTERNAL LIMITS: DIFFERENCES AMONG
GOVERNMENT DEPARTMENTS

There were substantial differences among the approaches of various government departments to the proposed changes. The Health, Transport, and Inland Revenue Departments' submissions were tightly tied to each department's own area of interest (rehabilitation, traffic accidents, and levy collection, respectively) and did not conflict with the approaches of other departments. The other submissions, however, addressed identical issues, but with varying foci. The Social Security Department stressed the necessity of total coverage for the whole population and the parallel treatment of all financial need. The Justice Department was concerned with the inequity and inefficiency of the tort system for injury compensation, the need for legal reform in the area of accidents, and the pressure on the court system. The Labour Department made noncommittal submissions which focused on the ILO resolution and the need to reform workers' compensation.

Three factors need discussion here: the submissions of each department being tied to its own substantive task, the direct conflict which arose over the differences displayed, and the ability of any one department to have its perspective put into practice.

While it could be argued that each department's focus on its own task and responsibility was to be expected, the implication of the expectation and the effects of the division of labor within the state are important. The evidence suggests that each department is primarily concerned with the efficient and rational fulfillment of its own substantive task. Senior management's concern with its department's growth in power and importance as well as career patterns in the civil service contribute to the development of sectional interests (Smith 1974, pp. 95 ff.).

The Social Security Department is likely to make submissions leading toward a viable income-maintenance system; the Justice Department will want a coherent, easily administered court system; and the Labour Department will try to promote an efficient workers' compensation system, in tune with a "rational" view of industrial relations and the pressure put on the labor supply by the industrial accident rate.

The differences among the "rationalities" displayed in each department's submissions had a major effect on the outcome. Their conflict played a major role in enabling the exclusion of nonearners injured in accidents other than automobile accidents to become an issue.

This brings us to the second point of the conflictual process. The open and public nature of the Royal Commission allowed the introduction of the "antitort" legal ideology, which coincided with differences and conflicts within the state bureaucracy. The orientations of the various departments were the cause of some friction between the legal representative on the commission and the representative of the Labour Department (Palmer 1979, p. 128). The Justice Department's "law reform" orientation was really nothing of the sort. The suggestion that the reform be limited to industrial and auto accidents meant retaining a dual system of tort law for some and not for others, which in purely legal terms was little better than the previous dual system. But this suggestion was consistent with the Labour Department's position, since it more or less fitted in with the workers' compensation approach.

The later stages of the process, however, saw a gradual but marked attenuation of both the legal ideology and the income-maintenance perspective, with the original focus on workers' compensation brought back in and nonearners injured in accidents other than auto accidents excluded from the scheme. This exclusion was largely due to the vigorous trade union reaction produced by the low level of initial payment suggested in the Woodhouse Report. Public debate ensued over the exclusion of nonearners (and thus housewives). In the context of the developing feminist input into the political arena, the opposition Labour party promised to extend coverage to all citizens once again.

The compromise and negotiation process would have been far less problematic, and the outcome less ambiguous, if there had been no conflict among government departments. Whether this was unavoidable or the result of a tactical error made by the Labour Department in its selection of members of the Royal Commission[9] makes little difference. The changing of the terms of reference allowed many other issues to be introduced, while giving room for maneuver to members of the legislature (particularly the Labour party). What initially passed into legislation was a victory for the perspective of the Labour and Justice Departments, in that it excluded those not injured in industrial or automobile accidents and returned control of the scheme to the minister of labour. The 1973 amendment extending coverage to nonearners was, however, a major victory for the income-maintenance orientation.

Finally, the importance of the relative ranking and influence of the government departments involved is highlighted in the return of control over

---

[9] Even that choice was an attempt at "secrecy," as the interest groups which had frustrated the previous reform attempt (the Wild Committee) were excluded from the commission.

the new body from the minister of social security (to whom it was delegated by the Woodhouse Report) to the minister of labour. The initially close ties between the Accident Compensation Commission and the Labour Department must be seen not merely as an overall growth of the bureaucracy but as a certain type of growth by one department at the expense of another.

The power and prestige of the departments involved seem to have had a major effect on the outcome of the accident compensation legislation. The importance of the Labour Department had grown considerably during the 1960s. It had previously been a rather low-ranking "social welfare" department, concerned primarily with controlling immigration and apprenticeships and inspecting factories. Semijudicial Arbitration Courts had played the main role in regulating industrial conflict. Over this period, however, the Labour Department's importance grew rapidly in areas of labor-force control, manpower planning, and, more recently, almost total responsibility for industrial relations (Jones 1973), to the extent that the arbitral functions of the court system were replaced by an "industrial commission" and Labour Department mediators. The reasons for this development almost certainly lie, at least on the highest level, with the increased importance of bureaucratic control of the labor force for monopoly industry.

In overall terms, what have been called the internal limits on state action on behalf of capital lie in the departmental divisions of the state apparatus itself. In this case they provided room for more recognizable forms of political struggle to develop and markedly modify the legislation.

EXTERNAL LIMITS: DEVIATIONS FROM THE NEEDS OF CAPITAL

The source and rate of payment to earners for the initial period after an accident and the reintroduction of a sliding scale of levies on employers are major features of the act which cannot be fully accounted for by the internal limits on the state. Both elements, as mentioned earlier, were contrary to the maximum possible perceived gains to monopoly capital, were marked changes to the suggestions in the original Royal Commission Report, and were among alternatives suggested by the White Paper prepared by the interdepartmental committee of public servants set up to consider the Royal Commission Report. The Royal Commission had recommended a very low rate of initial payment and a flat 1% levy on all employers, as we have seen. The Gair Committee had then suggested 100% payment by the employer for the first week for all accidents, whether occurring at work or not, and a graduated scale of levies according to the particular industry's accident rate. The first suggestion markedly improved the position of the workers, and the second placed significant limitations on the shifting of costs between various fractions of capital. Monopoly capital was disadvantaged by both proposals. Under intense pressure from the employers, however, the McLachlan Committee reduced the 100% payment to apply to work-related injuries only.

The central question for our purposes is why the civil servants proposed these changes. The reasons stated in the White Paper itself are a good place to start. That paper pointed out that the Royal Commission's proposal for an initial period of low payments would actually give workers less than they had received under the old workers' compensation scheme (White Paper 1969, pp. 58–59). It went on to suggest four possible changes. Two involved minor upward adjustments in initial payments, one suggested increasing the overall rate from 80% to 85% of earnings, after the initial four-week period, and one proposed the abolition of all time limits on compensation and the payment of 80% from the time of the injury.

Although the White Paper was written in the normal civil service style, providing a range of options for the political decision makers, there are clear reasons why civil servants would have preferred and informally supported the last option. The suggestion of a 5% increase did not address the issue of time limits at all. The two suggestions of minor upward adjustments in initial payments, while lifting the rate suggested by the Royal Commission, were a long way from what was originally desired by government departments, especially with respect to bringing New Zealand's workers' compensation in line with the ILO convention—the ostensible reason for raising the issue in the first place. Second, and perhaps more important, the civil servants in the Labour and Justice Departments, in view of the failure of the earlier attempt at injury compensation reform (the Wild Committee) and the trade unions' submissions to the Royal Commission, would have had no doubts about the reaction of the trade unions to the Royal Commission limits and would have realized that this could jeopardize the whole scheme. The trade unions had vigorously rejected a scheme which deprived them of all common-law rights and yet asked them to accept lower levels of payments for most injuries than they were already getting. They asked for, if not the retention of common-law rights, at least the minimum payment which they would receive if they had recourse to the legal system.

The civil servants were caught in something of a cleft stick, as they were also aware that their political "masters" were opposed to the involvement of extra taxation funds. Their proposal of 80% payment was therefore linked to the exclusion of nonearners. The White Paper went to some lengths to show that the costs involved would be bearable, especially if nonearners were excluded (1969, p. 75). Furthermore, the industrial relations experts, especially those from the Labour Department, because of their very expertise and the "harmonious cooperation" ideology of industrial relations theory, were somewhat sympathetic to the trade unions' position.

In the event, the Gair Committee's report excluded nonearners from coverage for any accidents except automobile and required direct 100% payment by employers for the first week, with the state paying 80% thereafter. The McLachlan Committee, however, was subjected to so much employer pressure that it reduced employer payments for the first week to payment for work-related injuries only.

The final result, then, must be attributed to the class struggle between employers and workers and the civil servants' sensitivity to and awareness of that issue within their overall objective of getting the scheme passed. However, the civil servants did not act automatically on behalf of monopoly capital; the point made in the previous section with respect to divisions between departments also applies here. Because civil servants tend to adopt views and propose solutions which are most favorable for the efficient management of their own substantive tasks, the bureaucracy's position is distinct from that of capital.

This perspective presents itself more clearly with respect to the second major example of the divergence of state policy and capital's needs: the graduated scale of levies on employers. The White Paper argues against the Royal Commission's rejection of the grade system, suggesting that a flat rate levy provided no incentive for accident prevention and quoting experts to prove that it taxed low-accident industry to subsidize high-accident industry. For a civil service document, the call for a risk-related levy is very strong indeed (pp. 86–87). With no evidence to the contrary, we should take seriously the stated objective of efficiency and equity in the scheme's operation. Once again, the "expert" mentality is evident.

The imperatives of the state bureaucracy differ from those of capital. The aim of the latter is capital accumulation or profit, and the criterion for evaluating change is the extent to which that change will aid or hinder the achievement of that objective. Bureaucratic thinking, in contrast, is more concerned with the logic of rational administration as perceived from a position of academic expertise. In this instance, therefore, the approach of the Labour Department was governed not only by the aim of continued accumulation but also by the aim of efficient management of the labor force. The difference in perspective is that between profit as such and profit as "reasonable," as seen from the perspective of industrial relations, with its ideology of "good on both sides" and harmonious cooperation. The profit or capital accumulation goal can thus be distinguished from the goal of "rational administration" which is proper to the state bureaucracy (that is, to the senior personnel). The two goals are often related and may coincide, but equally they may not.

We must stress that the specification of these two distinct goals goes beyond the traditional formulation of a conflict between the "legitimation" and "accumulation" functions of the state to suggest both a general logic of the state apparatus and a logic particular to different segments of that apparatus. The perspective proper to the state apparatus has two main elements: technical optimality and a public interest perspective.[10]

Technical optimality leads to a focus not only on what is technically possible but also on the most efficient and coherent means of achieving goals. This is a rational, ordered, coherent approach where objectivity, impartiality, and predictability are highly valued—very much the "academic" perspective. Thus, while the logic of capital accumulation in New Zealand outlined earlier did place major constraints on any change in the accident compensation system, it did not determine that tort law in this field be even partially abolished and replaced by an automatic administrative system.

The second element of rational administration follows more from the nature of the state apparatus itself. The logic here is one of expert impartiality, of occupying a position in the service not of capital or labor but of the "national interest." The divergences between bureaucratic action and the needs of monopoly capital cannot be explained by a cynical legitimation orientation but only by a perspective which sees the use of secrecy and the manipulation of politicians and interest groups as necessary to overcome narrow sectional interests for the good of the nation as a whole. This view, although relevant for many experts, is proper to the role of the expert in the state apparatus. For the interdepartmental committee which produced the White Paper, this rational[11] administration logic meant a unity at least partly opposed to the needs of capital, with respect to employer levies and payment of initial earnings.

CONCLUSION

In drawing together the threads of the above arguments, it is possible to reject the oversimplifications of traditional political analysis and of a functionalist Marxist approach. The former, in seeing the forms of political action as primarily significant, cannot explain why the Accident Compensation Act came about, why it happened in New Zealand, and why certain concessions rather than others had to be made. On the other hand, Marxist theories of the state have failed to recognize and incorporate the importance

[10] This interpretation may seem to be merely a revival of ideas about "managerial revolution." In fact, the argument over the managerial revolution was not whether managers had the ideas attributed to them, but whether such ideas overruled the profit motive. In the current instance, a "national interest" perspective may well conflict with supranational capital, acting against its interests. Location in the state apparatus provides an alternative power base.

[11] This does not, of course, mean that it is any more "rational" than the profit criterion, but that the criterion of rationality differs.

of specific features of the political process and how these interact with and develop the class content of state action. It is not enough to invoke relative autonomy or to assert that bureaucratic initiative is not antipathetic to Marxism. State initiatives are necessary for the reproduction of capitalism, particularly in the peripheral situation of dominion capitalism, but we must also specify how this occurs. Only a Marxist theory with a structurally adequate conceptualization of the capitalist mode of production can satisfactorily account for all these features.

In summary, this paper has approached the change in accident compensation policies by distinguishing the abstract structural requirements of capital accumulation in New Zealand and then by presenting a specific causal-historical analysis of the accident compensation change itself. At the structural level, the dominance of monopoly capital demands that, at worst, any change must not hinder accumulation by large-scale, capital-intensive industry and, at best, must advance such accumulation. We have seen that the Accident Compensation Act fulfilled these conditions. Specific causal investigation has indicated the act to be an initiative of the state bureaucracy, which was trying to reduce the cost of industrial accidents in a situation of chronic skilled labor shortage.

Analysis of the change process, however, has revealed that this was far from what was finally achieved. The new legislation can be seen as decidedly ambiguous and could potentially cause as many, if not more, problems for monopoly capital accumulation as it has solved. In locating effective control with the medical profession and the injured it has provided room for workers' control (which was clearly foreseen by the Woodhouse Commission); it has already led to much publicity about alleged abuse and at least one major special investigation. The scheme has had to bear exploding costs far above projections, which significantly increase the (socially defined) costs of the reproduction of labor power. And, finally, there are now obvious differences between those injured in accidents and those unable to work due to such things as illness. There is constant criticism, both academic and otherwise, of this dual arrangement, which appears markedly unjust.

The failure to achieve the desired goals has been seen to be the result of the change process itself; the analysis of that process has both methodological and theoretical implications.

Methodologically, while the distinction between structural requirements and historical process is heuristically useful, it is difficult to sustain. Close empirical investigation of the details of the change process has revealed that the contradictory nature of the actual legislation owes much to the process of change itself. Because the struggle was waged by the bureaucracy, on behalf of monopoly capital, the results are marked by the social democratic constraints on that bureaucracy. Furthermore, the division of labor within the bureaucracy and the nature of the expertise to which such division gives rise render the act's value ambiguous. These historical processes have left their mark on the act and have thus changed the structural requirements of monopoly capitalist accumulation in New Zealand. A more methodologically sophisticated approach, which takes account of the interaction between structural requirements and the historical process, must be developed.

Theoretically, this case study provides at least some suggestions as to how greater precision in the Marxist theory of the state may be achieved. It highlights the salience of the specific form of the New Zealand state, the limits imposed on state action by the conflicting rationalities of different departments, and the conflict between rational administration and the logic of capital accumulation.

We have seen that the ability of the state to initiate legislation depends on structural features of the state form (unicameral legislature, centralized system, and rigid party discipline, in this case) which provide ground rules for the intentional use of specific tactics by bureaucratic actors. The understanding of this dependence needs to be developed further in other areas of state action and for other states; it is no longer enough merely to dichotomize liberal-democratic and bureaucratic-authoritarian political forms. If we are to move beyond the very broad and crude categorization of states in terms of their effects, we must pay close attention to the structures which produce those effects. It can be hypothesized on the basis of this study that in liberal-democratic societies organized differently—for example, with federal systems, loose party discipline, a different division of labor within the bureaucracy, and so on (as in the United States)—the relative autonomy of the state would take different forms and have different outcomes. It should also be possible to map a continuum from liberal-democratic to bureaucratic-authoritarian forms of the state and to chart various points on that continuum and shifts from one point to another. New Zealand, for example, is closer to the bureaucratic-authoritarian end of the continuum than is a much less centralized system like that of the United States. The contribution of this case study has been to indicate that, by paying attention to such structures, we can explain precisely and determinately features which cannot be accounted for by a vague functionalist formulation.

Similarly, the relevance of the goals of bureaucratic initiative for the legislative outcome has been seen. Internally, conflicting rationalities based on the division of labor within the state enabled the process of class struggle to change markedly the range of people covered by the legislation. Externally, the limits on state action imposed by the state's own logic of rational administration, as opposed to that of capital accumulation, determined such features as initial payment levels, employer levies, and the abolition of the tort system. The implication is that capital's need to shift costs onto the state gives the logic of rational administration more freedom. The more state expertise is brought to bear, the more the administrative imperative takes over. In other words, the "ideology of the (tame) expert" and his "neutral objective" philosophy, which has served capitalist development so well when contained within industry, ultimately, via the state, becomes detrimental to that development. Clearly, the political economy of the state apparatus itself requires more attention.

CHRONOLOGICAL APPENDIX

1966   Woodhouse Royal Commission established.
1967   Woodhouse Report.
1968   Interdepartmental Committee of Civil Servants.
1969   White Paper (from the above committee).
1970   Parliamentary Select Committee (Gair Committee).
1971   Draft Bill: Second Parliamentary Committee (McLachlan Committee).
1972   Accident Compensation Act passed.
1972   Change of government (Labour party).
1973   New government passes amendment extending coverage to all persons injured in any accident.

REFERENCES

Armstrong, R. 1978. "New Zealand: Imperialism, Class and Uneven Development." *Australian and New Zealand Journal of Sociology* 14:297–303.
Ehrensaft, P., and W. Armstrong. 1978. "Dominion Capitalism: A First Statement." *Australian and New Zealand Journal of Sociology* 14:352–62.
Ellis, J. A. 1976. *Industrial Concentration*. Research Paper no. 20. Wellington: New Zealand Institute of Economic Research.
Gough, I. 1979. *The Political Economy of the Welfare State*. London: Macmillan.
Jackson, K. 1978. "Cabinet and the Prime Minister." Pp. 63–77 in *Politics in New Zealand*, edited by S. Levine. Sydney: Allen & Unwin.
Jones, P. E. R. 1973. "The Need for Manpower Planning." Pp. 64–78 in *Contemporary New Zealand*, edited by K. W. Thomson and A. D. Trlin. Wellington: Hicks Smith.
Kaim-Caudle, P. R. 1973. *Comparative Social Policy and Social Security*. London: Martin Robertson.
Kronick, J., N. Farley, R. Gaskins, J. Orbell, M. Vosburgh, and W. Vosburgh. 1978. "Community Responsibility: The New Zealand Accident Compensation Act as a Value Response to Technological Development. Final Report." Unpublished report, U.S. National Science Foundation grant no. OSS76-14794.
Lane, P. A. 1973. "Growth and Change." Pp. 1–14 in *Decade of Change: Economic Growth and Prospects in New Zealand, 1960–1970*, edited by P. A. Lane and P. Hamer. Wellington: Reed.
Miliband, Ralph. 1969. *The State in Capitalist Society*. London: Weidenfeld & Nicolson.
Palmer, G. W. R. 1979. *Compensation for Incapacity: A Study of Law and Social Change in New Zealand and Australia*. London: Oxford University Press.
Perez-Diaz, V. M. 1978. *State, Bureaucracy and Civil Society*. London: Macmillan.

Poulantzas, N. 1973. *Political Power and Social Classes,* translated by T. O'Hagan. London: New Left Books.

———. 1976. "The Capitalist State: A Reply to Miliband and Laclau." *New Left Review* 95:65–83.

Rosenberg, W. 1975. "Foreign Investment in New Zealand." Pp. 46–61 in *New Zealand Politics: A Reader,* edited by S. Levine. Melbourne: Cheshire.

Rowthorn, R. 1974. "Skilled Labour in the Marxist System." *Bulletin of the Conference of Socialist Economists* (Spring), pp. 25–45.

Shannon, P. 1980. "The New Zealand Accident Compensation Act, 1972: Towards an Historical Materialist Account of the Development of Public Legislation." Pp. 174–96 in *Legislation and Society in Australia,* edited by R. Tomasic. Sydney: Allen & Unwin.

Simpson, A. C. 1978. "Commissions of Inquiry and the Policy Process. Pp. 22–36 in *Politics in New Zealand,* edited by S. Levine. Sydney: Allen & Unwin.

Smith, T. B. 1974. *The New Zealand Bureaucrat.* Wellington: Cheshire.

Szakats, A. 1968. *Compensation for Road Accidents: A Study on the Question of Absolute Liability and Social Insurance.* Wellington: Sweet & Maxwell.

———. 1973. "Community Responsibility for Accident Injuries: The New Zealand Compensation Act." *University of British Columbia Law Review* 8 (1): 1–34.

Transcript of Royal Commission Hearings. 1967. "Submissions to the Royal Commission of Inquiry." Vols. 1–3. Unpublished documents. Wellington, General Assembly Library, Parliament Buildings.

White Paper. 1969. "Personal Injury: A Commentary on the Report of the Royal Commission of Inquiry into Compensation for Personal Injury in New Zealand." Pp. 431–51 in *Appendix to the Journals of the House of Representatives.* Vol. 4. Wellington: Government Printer.

Woodhouse Report. 1967. *Report of the Royal Commission of Inquiry: Compensation for Personal Injury in New Zealand.* Wellington: Government Printer.

Proletarianization in the Changing American Class Structure[1]

Erik Olin Wright
University of Wisconsin—Madison

Joachim Singelmann
United Nations, Population Division

This paper attempts to address empirically the debate between two opposed images of the transformation of work in contemporary capitalism. The first, commonly associated with "postindustrial theory," sees work as becoming more humanized, more autonomous, less routinized; the second image, associated with Marxist theories of proletarianization, sees work as becoming more routinized and degraded, with less autonomy and responsibility for the worker. The debate between these two perspectives has largely been waged at the theoretical level, with at best anecdotal evidence in support of one side or the other. This study uses national data to make a preliminary assessment of the adequacy of each perspective. The central analytical strategy is to decompose total changes in the degree of proletarianization into two components: an *industry-shift effect*, which measures the changes in proletarianization due to changes in the overall sectoral distribution of the labor force across industries; and a *class-composition-shift effect*, which measures the changes in proletarianization due to changes within given sectors. Contrary to the expectations of postindustrial theory, it is demonstrated that there is a strong and consistent proletarianization process within sectors. This proletarianization process is hidden from view because of the strength of a counteracting process in the industry-shift effect (i.e., the relatively more rapid expansion of those sectors which were relatively less proletarianized in the first place). The paper concludes with a discussion of the likely transformation of the class structure in the remaining part of the century. It is predicted that this counteracting tendency will weaken, and thus a clearer process of aggregate proletarianization should appear in the next decades.

Two radically opposed images have dominated discussions of the transformations of the labor process in advanced capitalism.[2] In the first, typified

[1] This research was supported in part by funds supplied through National Science Foundation grant SES-7812189, by funds granted to the Institute for Research on Poverty at the University of Wisconsin—Madison by the U.S. Department of Health and Human Services, and by funds granted from the Wisconsin Alumni Research Foundation. Requests for reprints should be sent to Erik Olin Wright, Department of Sociology, University of Wisconsin, Madison, Wisconsin 53706.

[2] We will use the term "labor process" to designate the totality of technical and social aspects of the activity of work.

by the works of "postindustrial" theorists such as Fuchs (1968), Bell (1973), Gartner and Reisman (1974), Richta et al. (1969), and others, the labor process is becoming increasingly less proletarianized, requiring higher and higher proportions of workers with technical expertise and demanding less mindless routine and more responsibility and knowledge. For some of these theorists, the central process underwriting this tendency is the shift from an economy centered on industrial production to one based on services. Thus, Fuchs contrasts industrialization with the service society by arguing that "industrialization has alienated the worker from his work, that the individual has no contact with the final fruit of his labor and that the transfer from a craft society to one of mass production has resulted in the loss of personal identification with work . . . [whereas] the direct confrontation between consumer and worker that occurs frequently in services creates the possibility of a more completely human and satisfactory work experience" (1968, p. 189). Other theorists have placed greater stress on the emancipatory effects of the technical-scientific revolution within material production itself. This position has perhaps been most eloquently elaborated by Radovan Richta and his associates. Automation, Richta et al. argue,

> relieves [the worker] of his role as a mere cog in the machine system and offers him the position of inspirer, creator, master of the technological system, able to stand apart from the immediate manufacturing process. . . . We may assume that the advance of the scientific and technological revolution will first engulf the operative type of work involving manual machine-minding and later the less sophisticated regulatory and control activities— in a word, the traditional simple industrial work, insofar as man does not need it and it is enforced by external necessity, or will cut it down to a degree not exceeding people's need for movement. Then, when man stops doing the things that things can do for him, he is offered the prospect of creative activity as the normal occupation through which he can exercise all his powers—activity imbued with scientific elements, discovery, invention, pioneering and cultivating human powers. [Richta et al. 1969, pp. 112–14]

Although Richta and his associates argue that such tendencies cannot reach full realization within the constraints of capitalist social relations, they nevertheless feel that changes in this direction are already characteristic of the transformations of work within capitalism itself.[3] The result is a trajectory of change that undermines the material basis of alienation within production by giving workers progressively greater control over their conditions of work and greater freedom within work.

The second image of transformation of the labor process is almost the negative of the first: work is becoming more proletarianized; technical

---

[3] It should be noted that Richta and his associates, like most of the more sophisticated theorists sharing this general position, explicitly discuss the countertendencies to this process of technological emancipation. However, they unambiguously insist that the emancipatory side of the process is the dominant one in the present era.

expertise is being confined to a smaller and smaller proportion of the labor force; routinization of activity is becoming more and more pervasive, spreading to technical and even professional occupations; and responsibilities within work are becoming less meaningful. This stance is particularly characteristic of Marxist discussions of the labor process. The argument usually runs something like this: because the capitalist labor process is a process of exploitation and domination and not simply a technical process of production, capital is always faced with the problem of getting workers to work (or, in more technical terms, of transforming labor power into labor). In the arsenal of strategies of social control available to the capitalist class, one of the key weapons is the degradation of work, that is, the removal of skill and discretion from the direct producers. The result is a general tendency for the proletarianized character of the labor process to be intensified over time.

This argument has been most clearly laid out in Braverman's *Labor and Monopoly Capital* (1974). Since its publication there has been an interesting and fruitful debate over various aspects of Braverman's account, particularly over his tendency to minimize the effectiveness of workers' resistance to degradation and to ignore various kinds of countertendencies to the general process of degradation.[4] In spite of these disagreements over the nuances of Braverman's analysis, however, there is a general consensus among Marxists about the systematic character of the tendencies toward intensified proletarianization in advanced capitalism. Far from undermining the material basis of alienation within production, the trajectory of changes in the labor process has, if anything, deepened alienation.

Clearly, the stakes in this debate are considerable at the theoretical, ideological, and political levels. Theoretically, the two images of the transformation of work reflect fundamentally different conceptions of the dynamics of social change. The first account sees change as emanating from an incremental process of technological change and adaptation; the second sees change as the result of struggle between antagonistic classes.

At the ideological level, much of the technocratic legitimation of advanced capitalism revolves around visions of technological liberation and postindustrial humanization. The specific application of this ideology to the case of work is part of a larger ideological system in which technology is seen as the solution to social problems and conflict is seen as irrational and counterproductive.

Finally, at the political level, the specific modalities of Marxist conceptions of socialist transformation within advanced capitalist society depend in important ways on the analysis of transformations in class relations, and

---

[4] For general Marxist discussions of Braverman's thesis, some of which are fairly critical of the simple, unilinear story he tells, see Burawoy (1978, 1979), Friedman (1977), and Edwards (1979).

the pivotal axis of such transformation is the problem of proletarianization. While it would be oversimplistic to claim that a socialist transformation requires ever-increasing levels of proletarianization, it is certainly the case that the forms of organization of socialist movements and socialist struggles, and the nature of the class alliances that would be necessary for a socialist transformation, depend to a large extent on the proletarianization process. If the postindustrial theorists are correct and advanced capitalism is witnessing a reverse of the historic process of proletarianization, then a fundamental rethinking of socialist strategies is necessary.

While there has been much energy put into this debate, there has been remarkably little systematic empirical investigation of the problem. Most of the debate has been waged through a combination of anecdotal evidence and formal census statistics. Anecdotal evidence is obviously inadequate, since within either perspective there is room for counterexamples. Census evidence, as Braverman (1974, pp. 424–49) demonstrates so well in his discussion of the category "semiskilled," is also almost useless since the contents of census categories may themselves change radically over time. Thus any shift in the population from one census occupational category to another may be more than compensated for by changes in the real attributes of the categories themselves. Unless we know explicitly what real changes are occurring within the census occupational categories, knowing that a greater proportion of the population is employed as "clerks" or "technicians" tells us nothing about the problem of proletarianization.

This paper attempts to present some provisional quantitative data which bear directly on the problem of proletarianization in contemporary American society. Our central conclusion is that the data support some of the main descriptive claims of both Marxist and postindustrial theories, but that overall they are more consistent with the explanatory logic of Marxist theory. In particular, the data indicate that observed changes in proletarianization should be understood as the outcome of two processes: a tendency for positions to be proletarianized within industrial sectors, and a countertendency for employment to shift from industries that are relatively highly proletarianized to industries that are relatively less proletarianized. Until recently, these two processes have resulted in an increase of both proletarianized and nonproletarianized positions among employees in the labor force (at the expense of self-employed positions). However— and this is the critical punch line of the analysis—there are good reasons to believe that the countertendencies are weakening. It is thus reasonable to predict that in the decade from 1980 to 1990 we may observe a relative decrease in nonproletarianized employee positions and an increase in proletarianized positions, that is, a net proletarianization process.

Those are our basic conclusions. Before we can examine the empirical material that supports them, it is necessary to define more rigorously the central concepts and questions that will guide the analysis. In particular, it is necessary to translate the categories used by the postindustrial theorists into the same conceptual space used by Marxist proletarianization theorists. Such a common theoretical terrain is essential if the two positions are to be operationalized in a way that makes it possible to assess their relative merits. On the basis of this common conceptual schema, we will then formulate the propositions of the two theories in terms of a set of empirical expectations about transformations in the class structure. This will be followed by a discussion of the problems in operationalizing the concepts necessary to test these divergent expectations and a presentation of the empirical results of the investigation.

1. THE CONCEPTUAL SCHEME

Within Marxist theory, proletarianization is essentially a process of transformation of the underlying class relations of capitalist societies. The problem of conceptualizing proletarianization, therefore, is closely bound up with the problem of conceptualizing the overall class structure of capitalist societies. If that class structure is viewed as a simple, polarized structure consisting of wage laborers and capitalists, then proletarianization is seen as a fairly simple process by which the self-employed become wage laborers. On the other hand, if the class structure is understood as a complex, articulated structure of relations in which workers and capitalists are defined not by polarization within a one-dimensional class relationship but by a structure of polarizations along a series of dimensions of class relations, then proletarianization itself becomes a much more complicated matter.

Since this more complex understanding of class relations has been elaborated in detail elsewhere (Wright 1976, 1978a, chap. 2; 1979, chaps. 1 and 2; 1980a, 1980b), we will only schematically present it here.[5] The specific strategy of decoding the class structure which we will adopt is based on a distinction between two kinds of locations within a class structure: *basic class locations* and what can be termed *contradictory locations within class relations*. To understand this distinction, we must first briefly discuss a second kind of distinction: between a *mode of production* and a *social formation*.

[5] All Marxists may agree that classes are, in the first instance, defined within the social relations of production, but there is no consensus at all about how to define the social relations of production in capitalist society or about the logic by which those relations actually determine the class structure. It is important to remember, therefore, that what follows is not *the* Marxist theory of class structure, but one contending Marxist account within an ongoing debate. For a detailed discussion of the alternative Marxist treatments of class and class structure, see Wright (1980b). For views which differ from the one advanced in this paper, see Carchedi (1977), Crompton and Gubbay (1978), and Poulantzas (1975).

A mode of production is defined by a coherent structure of production relations and forces of production (broadly: technology and other capacities for the transformation of nature). Concrete societies are always characterized by various combinations of different modes of production.[6] Even in the United States, the paragon of capitalist societies, the capitalist mode of production coexists with various kinds of noncapitalist production relations, in particular, simple commodity production (i.e., production for the market within which no wage labor is exploited—the direct producers own and control their immediate means of production).[7] The analysis of such concrete combinations of modes of production defines the social formation.

Now, basic class locations are classes defined within pure modes of production. In the pure capitalist mode of production there are only two classes: the bourgeoisie, which controls the flow of resources into and out of production, controls the means of production within production, and controls the labor of others within the labor process; and the working class, which is excluded from control on each of these dimensions.[8] These two classes exist in a relation of perfect polarization.

In concrete capitalist social formations, however, the model of a pure capitalist mode of production is no longer adequate as the basis for a map of the class structure. In the first place, as mentioned above, the capitalist mode of production coexists with various kinds of noncapitalist modes or forms of production. Thus, in American capitalism we must also include the petty bourgeoisie as a distinctive location in the class structure (i.e., self-employed producers who own their means of production and employ no labor of others). Second, there is no longer a perfect polarization along all of the dimensions of social relations of production that define the basic classes of the capitalist mode of production. This implies that certain positions within the class structure may partake of the relational characteristics of more than one class. In a sense such positions can be considered to be simultaneously in two classes. Such positions will be designated contradictory locations within class relations.

Figure 1 represents the interconnections between the basic class locations of a capitalist social formation and contradictory locations. (The spatial

[6] For an analysis of the meaning of combinations of modes of production in social formations, see Wright (1982).

[7] Strictly speaking, simple commodity production is not a mode of production but a form of production. The concept of mode of production is usually restricted to those forms of social organization of production which are capable of becoming the organizing principle of an entire society (i.e., becoming the dominant mode of production in a social formation). Simple commodity production has never been a dominant structure of production, and there are good theoretical reasons to suspect that it could not become a dominant mode of production. Thus, in most Marxist discussions, it is not referred to as a "mode" of production.

[8] The term "control" is being used as a convenient expression for the social relations of domination and subordination. Control is not an attribute of a position but, rather, a way of characterizing the relationship between positions.

Wright and Singelmann

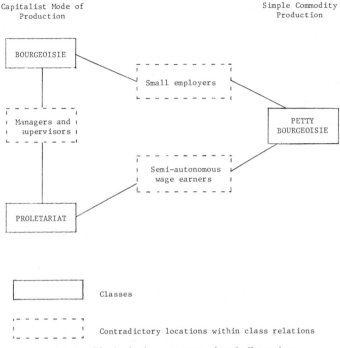

FIG. 1.—The basic class structure of capitalist society

metaphor in this figure may be somewhat misleading, since it suggests that contradictory locations are "between" basic classes rather than located simultaneously in two classes. Throughout this discussion it is important not to turn this relational concept into a gradational one by interpreting the figure too literally.) In many ways the most important of the contradictory locations illustrated in this figure is that of managers and supervisors, the contradictory location "between" the bourgeoisie and the proletariat. Managers occupy class locations within which they simultaneously dominate workers and are dominated by capital. Within the relations of domination and subordination that define the capitalist mode of production they therefore occupy both poles of the relationship. Managerial positions are thus simultaneously bourgeois and proletarian.

Two other contradictory locations are specified in figure 1. Both of these are contradictory locations that combine two different structures of production relations—capitalist production and simple commodity production. Small employers occupy a contradictory location between the petty bourgeoisie and the bourgeoisie. Like the petty bourgeoisie, they are direct producers who own their own means of production; like the bourgeoisie, they employ labor power and thus exploit the labor of workers. Semi-autonomous employees, on the other hand, occupy a contradictory location between the petty bourgeoisie and the working class. Like workers they are wage laborers, dominated by capital (or by state bureaucratic apparatuses), but like the petty bourgeoisie they have substantial degrees of real control over their immediate conditions of work, over what they produce and how they produce it. A good example is an engineer or a scientist who, within limits imposed by superiors, has considerable control over the immediate labor process but is excluded from any control over the apparatus of production.

Several brief comments on this scheme are necessary to avoid confusion. First, this is a typology of class structure, not class formation. That is, it is a strategy for decoding the "empty places" (Przeworski 1977) in the class structure, not for specifying the organized, collective class actors in a particular society. To be sure, the premise of the analysis of the structure of positions is that it will facilitate an understanding of the process of class formation; but the typology itself must not be confused with such an analysis.

Second, as specified in figure 1, this typology only decodes the class structure of the economically active labor force. A variety of locations in the social structure outside of the labor force are thus ignored: students, children, retired people, housewives, the permanently unemployed, etc. This is not to say that such locations have no class content, but simply that they are not directly organized within the structure of the social relations of production. Thus the decoding of the class nature of such positions requires additional theoretical arguments. For purposes of the analysis of transformations of the class structure we will limit ourselves to the simpler cases, those positions directly mapped by production relations.[9]

Finally, this strategy for decoding the class structure of contemporary capitalism must be seen as provisional. There are numerous areas of ambiguity, such as the specification of what is meant by "control over the immediate labor process" in the definition of the semiautonomous location, and it could well happen in the attempt to eliminate such ambiguities that the basic schema may itself be radically transformed. Nevertheless, this approach seems to us to be the most developed and useful map of class structure currently available, and thus we will use it in this empirical investigation of proletarianization.

2. CONTRASTING EXPECTATIONS OF POSTINDUSTRIAL AND MARXIST THEORY

Within the framework presented in figure 1, "proletarianization" designates the complex process by which non-working-class locations are destroyed or transformed and working-class locations created. The debate between

[9] For discussions of how such positions not directly in the labor force can be analyzed in class terms, see Wright (1978*b*, 1979, pp. 53–54; 1980*b*).

postindustrial and Marxist conceptions of transformations of the labor process can, then, be seen as a set of competing claims about the relative expansion and contraction of contradictory locations between the working class and other classes. In general terms, postindustrial theorists argue that such contradictory locations tend to expand in advanced industrial societies while the working class tends to contract. Marxist theorists, on the other hand, tend to argue that the semiautonomous-employee location will systematically contract, the managerial location will expand as production becomes more centralized and workers' skills become appropriated by management, and the working-class location will expand greatly as work becomes degraded. Both theories predict a decline in self-employed locations. These expectations are presented in table 1.

The hypotheses in table 1 center on overall outcomes for the expansion and contraction of class locations. The debate between Marxist and postindustrial theory, however, is as much a debate over the process which produces these outcomes as it is over the outcomes themselves. To adjudicate fully between the contending perspectives it would be necessary to study this process directly. The data for such an analysis simply do not exist. Short of that, however, it is possible to disaggregate the expectations in table 1 in a way which reflects more accurately the differing accounts of the underlying dynamics at work. We will briefly describe this strategy of data analysis and then formulate a more refined set of hypotheses which will differentiate more rigorously between the two theoretical arguments.

Strategy of Analysis

The strategy for disaggregating the overall expectations of the theories under consideration involves decomposing aggregate changes in the class structure into three analytically distinct components: (1) a component due to changes in the distribution of the population across economic sectors (referred to as the "industry-shift" component), (2) a component due to changes in the class distribution of the population within economic sectors (referred to as the "class-shift" component), and (3) a component due to simultaneous changes in the distribution of the population across and within sectors (referred to as an "interaction-shift" component).

TABLE 1

OVERALL EXPECTATIONS OF MARXIST AND
POSTINDUSTRIAL THEORIES

Locations within the Class Structure	Marxist Theory	Postindustrial Theory
Working class	Increase	Decrease
Semiautonomous employees	Decrease	Increase
Managers	Increase	Increase
Small employers and petty bourgeoisie	Decrease	Decrease

The technical details of this strategy are explained in Appendix A. In less technical terms, perhaps the easiest way to explain the strategy is to run through a hypothetical example. Let us suppose that, net of overall labor force population changes, there were 1.5 million more workers in the United States in 1970 than in 1960. (That is, after subtracting the number of additional workers that would have occurred simply from population increase in the labor force, there were still 1.5 million more workers.) Our task is to decompose this total net increase of the working class into the three components. This is done by playing a kind of counterfactual game. The first step is to ask the following question: How many workers would there have been in 1970 (net of overall population change) *if* the class structure within economic sectors had remained unchanged, but the distribution of people across sectors had changed in the way it actually did? Using these assumptions, we then add up the expected number of people in each class in each sector in 1970, and this gives us the expected number of workers, managers, petty bourgeois, and so forth, in 1970 as if the only thing that had changed was the distribution of people across sectors. This would constitute the industry-shift component for each class. In our example, if the sectors with the lowest concentrations of workers in 1960 happened to be the sectors which grew the fastest between 1960 and 1970 (e.g., education), then there could actually have been a negative industry shift for workers. Let us say that this negative shift was −300,000 workers. This would mean that, net of overall population changes, there were 300,000 fewer workers in 1970 than in 1960, owing to changes in the industrial structure, holding the within-sector class distributions constant.

The second step of the decomposition is to turn the counterfactual game on its head and ask: How many workers would there have been in 1970 compared with 1960 if the employment distribution across sectors had not changed but the class distributions within sectors had changed? This constitutes the class-composition shift for each class. In our example, if a process of proletarianization occurred within sectors, then the class-composition shift could be quite large and positive for workers, even though those sectors with relatively fewer workers expanded the most. Let us say that this positive class-composition-shift effect was 1.7 million. This would mean that, net of overall changes in the population, there were 1.7 million more workers in 1970 than in 1960 due to changes in the class structure within sectors, holding the distribution of the population across sectors constant.

The interaction-shift effect is mathematically a residual term. In our example it would be +100,000, since the total of the three components has to add up to the total net change in workers (1.5 million). Conceptually, the interaction effect represents changes in the class structure due to simultaneous movements from one class location within one sector to another class location in another sector. For example, in the Industrial Revolution, one of the pivotal forces changing the class structure was the simultaneous destruction of petty bourgeois positions in agriculture and the creation of working-class positions in manufacturing. This would appear as a large, positive, working-class interaction effect. Since we have no theoretical expectations about these interaction terms, and since they are quite small in the data we will be examining compared with the main effects, we will not give them any systematic discussion, although we will report the results in our tables.

This decomposition procedure is performed for each class location. The end result is a table in which the industry shift, class-composition shift, interaction shift, and total net shift are presented for each class. This kind of table will be at the heart of the results we will report. Let us now discuss briefly the expectations implicit in Marxist and postindustrial theory for each of the cells in this table.[10]

Detailed Expectations

Table 2 presents the specific expectations of the two theories for the industry shifts and class shifts for each of the class categories we have been discussing. In general only the direction of the expectation is given, but in a few cases the theories seem to suggest an order of magnitude as well.

1. *Small employers and petty bourgeoisie.*—Both Marxist and postindustrial theory would expect an overall decline in both categories of self-employment, and both theories would predict that there would be negative industry shifts as well as class shifts. That is, they would expect that self-employed-class locations would decline both because of the continuing shift of the economy away from those sectors of production, like agriculture, within which the petty bourgeoisie is most concentrated (the negative industry shift) and because of a continuing destruction of self-employed locations within most sectors of the economy (the negative class shift). Marxists are more likely to emphasize the class-shift dynamics, focusing on the ways in which multinational corporations are systematically entering agricultural production, fast-food restaurants, retail trade, and so on, whereas postindustrial theorists are more likely to emphasize the industry-shift processes. However, the two theoretical perspectives would not differ in the expected directions of changes in any of cells of the table for these two classes.

2. *Managerial contradictory class location.*—The two theoretical perspectives will also generally agree on the detailed expectations for managers,

[10] Neither Marxist not postindustrial theorists formalize their conceptions of transformations of the class structure precisely in terms of the schema of class relations presented in table 1 or in terms of the decomposition strategy presented above. The following discussion relies on drawing out the hypotheses which are implicit in the overall arguments of each of these theoretical traditions.

TABLE 2

HYPOTHESIZED CHANGES IN THE CLASS STRUCTURE WITHIN MARXIST AND POSTINDUSTRIAL THEORIES

CLASS LOCATION	MARXIST THEORY			POSTINDUSTRIAL THEORY		
	Industry-Shift Effects	Class-Composition-Shift Effects	Total Shifts	Industry-Shift Effects	Class-Composition-Shift Effects	Total Shifts
Small employers and petty bourgeoisie..	Negative	Negative	Negative	Negative	Negative	Negative
Managers/supervisors..............	Positive	Positive	Positive	Positive	Positive	Positive
Semiautonomous employees...........	Positive	Large Negative	Negative	Positive	Positive	Positive
Workers............................	Negative	Large Positive	Positive	Negative	Negative	Large Negative

NOTE.—No expectations for interaction effects are indicated since neither perspective discusses such effects for advanced capitalism.

although for somewhat different reasons. Both will expect a positive industry shift for managers, but their rationales are likely to be somewhat different. Marxists will stress the growth of the state as a source of employment and the tendency for state organizations to be more heavily bureaucratized than private capitalist organizations. Postindustrial theorists are more likely to emphasize the growth of services in general and the greater need for personal supervision in service-delivery systems than in manufacturing because of the less routinized character of the activity.

Similarly, in the class shifts for managers, the explanations for the expected positive shift will differ. Marxists would see the growth of managerial locations within given industries as the result of two main processes: first, the increasing concentration and centralization of capital, which results in the greater need for large administrative apparatuses;[11] and second, the continuing appropriation of skill and control from the direct producers, which requires an expansion of the agents of social control within production. The dynamics of the accumulation process and class struggle would thus provide the basic explanations for the expansion of managerial locations. Postindustrial theorists are much more likely to emphasize the imperatives of technological development. Because production in all sectors, including services, is based on increasingly sophisticated technologies and communications/information systems, an increasing proportion of the labor force has to be involved in the control and decision-making activities of these technical systems, and this will tend to increase the proportion of people involved in formal roles of supervision. Technocratic rationality rather than class conflict would constitute the basic explanation for increasing concentrations of managers within different sectors of production.

3. *Semiautonomous-employee locations.*—For the semiautonomous-employee and working-class locations we come to cases in which the detailed expectations of Marxist and postindustrial theories differ significantly. Although both perspectives would expect positive industry-shift effects for semiautonomous employees, for reasons parallel to the expectations for managers, they would have opposite expectations for the class shifts. On the basis of arguments about the degradation of labor, Marxists would expect a systematic and large decline in semiautonomous-employee locations within given labor processes. Although it might be the case that the technical qualifications for various jobs increase, the actual control over

[11] In the most recent period of American capitalist development, it would be expected that the expansion of the productive facilities of multinational corporations in the Third World will further intensify the concentration of managerial locations within the American class structure. In effect, the global accumulation process in the 1960s and 1970s has disproportionately increased proletarian class locations outside the boundaries of the United States, and it would thus be expected that managerial and administrative locations within the United States would tend to expand disproportionately, producing a positive class shift.

the conditions of work and the activity within work will tend—it is argued—
to be eroded as part of the general strategy of social control by capital (and
by managers). Postindustrial theorists would expect systematic tendencies
for semiautonomous locations to increase within most sectors of the economy. As in the case of the positive class shift for managers, the rationale
behind this expectation rests largely on technological arguments. Sophisticated technologies require less routinization and offer more possibilities
for autonomy and creativity within work; thus there should be a relative
expansion of nonproletarianized jobs within the labor process.

As a result of these specific expectations for the decomposed industry
and class shifts, postindustrialists would predict positive total shifts for
the semiautonomous-employee locations, whereas Marxists would tend to
predict negative shifts.

4. *Working class.*—The expectations for the working class are the inverse
of the expectations for the semiautonomous-employee category. Postindustrial theorists expect systematic deproletarianization to occur, both
because of shifts of the population out of the most proletarianized sectors
of the economy (heavy industry especially) and because of technological
changes within all sectors. Marxists expect the process of degradation of
labor to more than counteract whatever tendencies might exist for the less
proletarianized sectors to grow more rapidly than the more proletarianized
ones. A net expansion of the working class is thus expected.

These hypotheses, it must be emphasized, do not directly tap the differing
theoretical arguments of the underlying processes at work. By themselves
they cannot provide an adequate basis for adjudicating between accounts
of the labor process based on a logic of class struggle and accounts rooted in
arguments of technological determinism. But they will provide suggestive
support for one or the other view, since in the case of certain specific cells
of the table, the two contending theoretical perspectives would generate
opposing empirical expectations.

3. VARIABLES AND DATA

The two central variables in this research are economic sector and class
structure. All of the statistical analyses in this study are based on a 37-
sector division of the economic structure. This is a fairly refined disaggregation of the total economic structure; it certainly goes far beyond any
simple classification of sectors as primary, secondary, and tertiary. These
37 sectors have then been reaggregated into seven more general categories:
extractive, transformative, distributive services, business services, professional services, state-supported social services, and personal services.[12]

---

[12] This classification of economic sectors is a slight modification of the typology developed
by Singelmann (1978) and used in Browning and Singelmann (1978). A number of comments on the typology are necessary. First, the rubric "business services" was referred

Wright and Singelmann

These 37 sectors are listed in table 3. (All of the calculations used to decompose changes in the class structure are based on the 37-sector disaggregation, so the specific manner in which these have been reaggregated in table 3 will not affect the results.)

The class-structure variable is particularly problematic to measure adequately, given available data sources. Census data simply will not do by themselves, since the census is gathered in occupational rather than class terms, and no simple collapsing of occupational titles can generate an adequate operationalization of Marxist class categories.[13] Unfortunately, relatively few social surveys have asked the kinds of questions necessary to operationalize classes in a rigorous manner. The data which we have used in this study are derived from a social survey which does permit some fairly rough estimates of class structure, but the questions are not adequate for a precise operationalization.

Table 4 presents the operational criteria which we have used to define each class. Since the problems with these operationalizations have been discussed in some detail elsewhere (Wright 1980a, pp. 183–85), we will not dwell on them here. There are two main points to note: the criterion for being a manager is extremely broad and undoubtedly includes many nominal supervisors who probably should be classified as workers or semi-autonomous employees; and (2) the criterion for being a semiautonomous employee relies heavily on relatively subjective assessments of job characteristics by respondents. The net effect of these measurement problems is that our estimates of the size of both the managerial and semiautonomous-employee contradictory class locations are probably somewhat inflated. Thus, our estimates of the working class should probably be considered minimum estimates.

It is possible that these problems of adequately operationalizing class

to as "producer services" in earlier publications. We have changed the label in order to emphasize the specific role of these sectors in servicing capitalist business organizations rather than "production" abstracted from its capitalist context. Second, we have formed a separate sector for "professional services" since the status of these activities as the most important traditional "free professions" gives them a distinctive character for a class analysis. A good case could be made for including legal services in the business service category, since the legal profession is so closely tied to property law, but for present purposes we will combine them with the medical profession in the professional services category. Finally, given the dependence of medicine in general on state activity, medical services could have been placed under state-supported social services. We decided for the present to restrict this state-supported social service sector to those activities which are mainly organized directly by the state. Thus we included hospital services and excluded medical services (which remain largely private). A broader notion of the state sector which includes all activities closely tied to the state and state policy would certainly be worth exploring, but since we are unable to include such things as the armament and aircraft industries in such a sector with the present data, we decided that a narrower definition of the state sector would be better for this project.

[13] For a detailed discussion of the relationship between occupational categories and class categories, both theoretically and empirically, see Wright (1980a, pp. 177–88).

TABLE 3

PERCENTAGE DISTRIBUTION OF THE U.S. LABOR FORCE BY INDUSTRY SECTORS
AND INTERMEDIATE INDUSTRY GROUPS, 1940-70

Sectors and Industries	1940	1950	1960	1970
I. Extractive	21.3	14.4	8.1	4.5
1. Agriculture	19.2	12.7	7.0	3.7
2. Mining	2.1	1.7	1.1	.8
II. Transformative	29.8	33.9	35.9	33.1
3. Construction	4.7	6.2	6.2	5.8
4. Food	2.7	2.7	3.1	2.0
5. Textile	2.6	2.2	3.3	3.0
6. Metal	2.9	3.6	3.9	3.3
7. Machinery	2.4	3.7	7.5	8.3
8. Chemical	1.5	1.7	1.8	1.6
9. Miscellaneous manufacturing	11.8	12.3	8.7	7.7
10. Utilities	1.2	1.4	1.4	1.4
III. Distributive services	20.3	22.4	21.9	22.3
11. Transportation	4.9	5.3	4.4	3.9
13. Communication	.9	1.2	1.3	1.5
13. Wholesale	2.7	3.5	3.6	4.1
14. Retail	11.8	12.3	12.5	12.8
IV. Business services	4.7	4.4	6.1	8.0
15. Banking	1.1	1.1	1.6	2.6
16. Insurance	1.2	1.4	1.7	1.8
17. Real estate	1.1	1.0	1.0	1.0
18. Engineering	N.A.	.2	.3	.4
19. Accounting	N.A.	.2	.3	.4
20. Miscellaneous business services	1.3*	.6	1.2	1.8
V. Professional services	N.A.	1.5	1.9	2.7
21. Legal services	N.A.	.4	.5	.5
22. Medical services	N.A.	1.1	1.4	2.2
VI. State-supported social services	10.9	11.3	14.9	19.8
23. Hospitals	2.3†	1.8	2.7	3.7
24. Education	3.5	3.8	5.4	8.6
25. Welfare	.9	.7	1.0	1.2
26. Nonprofit	.9	.3	.4	.4
27. Postal services	.7	.8	.9	1.0
28. Government	2.6	3.7	4.3	4.6
29. Miscellaneous social services	N.A.	.1	.2	.3
VII. Personal services	14.0	12.3	11.3	10.0
30. Domestic services	5.3	3.2	3.1	1.7
31. Hotels	1.3	1.0	1.0	1.0
32. Eating and drinking	2.5	3.0	2.9	3.3
33. Repair	1.5	1.7	1.4	1.3
34. Laundry	1.0	1.2	1.0	.8
35. Barber and beauty shop	N.A.	N.A.	.8	.9
36. Entertainment	.9	1.0	.8	.8
37. Miscellaneous personal services	1.6‡	1.2‡	.4	.3
Total labor force	100	100	100	100

SOURCE.—Modified from Browning and Singelmann 1975.
NOTE.—Percentages may not add to 100% because of rounding; N.A. = not available.
* Includes legal, engineering, and accounting services.
† Includes medical services.
‡ Includes barber and beauty shops.

Wright and Singelmann

TABLE 4

OPERATIONAL CRITERIA FOR CLASS LOCATIONS

	Self-employed	Have Employees	Have Sub-ordinates*	Job Characterized by "a Lot" of Freedom and Decisions†
Employers‡.....................	Yes	Yes	...	...
Petty bourgeoisie...............	Yes	No	...	...
Managers/supervisors...........	No	No	Yes	...
Workers.......................	No	No	No	No
Semiautonomous employees........	No	No	No	Yes

* All teachers were classified as nonsupervisors regardless of their response to this criterion, since many teachers appear to have interpreted the question about supervision in the survey as referring to supervising students.

† Jobs which the respondent claims are characterized "a lot" by *both* of the following descriptions: (*a*) "a job that allows a lot of freedom as to how you do your work," and (*b*) "a job that allows you to make a lot of decisions on your own."

‡ Since 80% of all employers in the sample employed fewer than 10 workers, it was not possible to study a proper capitalist class location. Throughout most of the analysis which follows, therefore, I will treat all employers as occupying a contradictory location between the petty bourgeoisie and the capitalist class.

could undermine the meaningfulness of the results which we will report. However, we think that the results are sufficiently striking and consistent with our general theoretical expectations that they cannot be simply dismissed as artifacts of these difficulties. If anything, one might expect such weak measures of class to scramble the results rather than to strengthen them. In any event, these are the best data available, and thus for the moment this operationalization will have to suffice.

Two quite different data sources were used in this research: the Survey of Working Conditions (SWC) carried out by the Survey Research Center at the University of Michigan in 1969, and the U.S. censuses of 1960 and 1970. The SWC contained the questions presented in table 4 and provided the basis for operationalization of the class structure. But the SWC data were available for only one point in time, while the questions we were attempting to answer all concerned structural change over time. The censuses, of course, contain a great deal of information gathered at two time points but lack the necessary questions to operationalize class. The problem, then, was to devise a strategy for combining these two sets of data so that we could make reasonable estimates of the class structure in 1960 and 1970. This estimation procedure is described in detail in Appendix B and more briefly below.

Estimating the Class Structure in 1960 and 1970

On the basis of the SWC data we were able to construct a three-way table of class × occupation × economic sector. This means that we had estimates of the class distribution within occupations for each of the 37 economic sectors. For the 1960 and 1970 censuses we then constructed two-way tables of occupation × economic sector. The procedure was then to use the SWC table as the basis for apportioning the people within the cells of the census occupation × sector tables into classes. Thus, for example, if 70% of all craftsmen in the construction industry were workers in the SWC table, we allocated 70% of the individuals in the corresponding cells of the 1960 and 1970 census tables into the working class. In effect we are reallocating people within each of the 37 sectors from occupational categories into class categories on the basis of the empirical class distributions within occupations in the SWC data. This procedure enabled us to construct an imputed class distribution within each economic sector for 1960 and 1970 and, by aggregating these distributions, an overall imputed class distribution for the entire labor force for the two years.

This procedure involves an assumption which, according to the theory advanced in this paper, is probably incorrect—namely, that the class distributions within occupations (within economic sectors) remained unchanged during the decade, and thus such a distribution in 1969 could be used to estimate the class structure from census data for 1960. If it is the case that proletarianization occurred within specific occupations, then this assumption would be wrong. The result would be that we would have underestimated the working class for 1960, since the distribution used for the estimates came from the end of the decade (i.e., after a relative proletarianization of the 1960 occupational categories had occurred). This means that our estimates will tend to minimize the possible expansion of the working class over the decade. Since this bias works against the basic thrust of the theoretical arguments we have advanced, we feel that the data can still serve as a provisional basis for testing our hypotheses. (See Appendix C for a discussion of possible biases.)

Because of these problems in estimating the class structure, we felt that it was not feasible to carry the analysis back in time to the 1950 census. Whatever distortions occurred in imputing the class structure to 1960 would have been greatly exaggerated for earlier periods. As a result, the empirical analysis of structural transformations in this research will be limited to a single decade, 1960–70.

4. RESULTS

Before we discuss the results of the detailed decomposition of changes in the class structure it will be instructive to look at the overall changes. These are presented in table 5. Probably the most striking feature of this table is the relatively small magnitude of the changes. While some change did occur—both categories of the self-employed declined, managerial locations expanded the most, followed by working-class locations, while semiautonomous-class locations expanded only slightly—the essential

Wright and Singelmann

shape of the class structure did not change greatly over the decade. If the analysis were to stop here, one would probably conclude that there was not much of interest to explain and the results could hardly help clarify a significant theoretical debate. When we examine the decomposition of these changes, however, quite a different story can be told.

Table 6 presents the basic decomposition of changes in the class structure into the industry-shift component, the class-composition-shift component, and the interaction component. Table 7 presents these same results as percentages of the number of people in each class in 1960.

Before we discuss these results a word is needed on how to read the tables. The sum of the entries in any column of table 6 is zero. Since each of the entries is net of total population change, the sum of such shifts must be zero. The sum of the first three entries in any row equals the fourth entry in the row since the first three entries represent a decomposition of the fourth entry (total net change). Specific entries should be interpreted in the following way: the employer industry shift of −331,290 means that, net of any changes due to overall population change, there

TABLE 5

CHANGES IN THE AMERICAN CLASS STRUCTURE, 1960–70

	N		%	
	1960	1970	1960	1970
Small employers............	4,111,014	3,087,226	6.6	4.0
Petty bourgeoisie...........	3,753,212	2,859,979	6.1	3.7
Managers..................	20,293,995	27,291,760	32.7	35.6
Semiautonomous employees...	6,794,122	8,475,457	10.95	11.05
Workers...................	27,081,959	34,954,862	43.65	45.6
Total.................	62,034,302	76,669,284	100	100

NOTE.—See table 4 for operationalizations of class; percentages may not add to 100% because of rounding.

TABLE 6

DECOMPOSITION OF CHANGES IN THE AMERICAN CLASS STRUCTURE, 1960–70

	Industry Shift	Class-Composition Shift	Interaction Shift	Total Net Change
Small employers........	−331,290*	−1,659,392	−2,966	−1,993,648
Petty bourgeoisie.......	−498,285	−1,140,344	−140,053	−1,778,682
Managers.............	+722,088	+1,404,512	+83,455	+2,210,055
Semiautonomous employees..........	+383,823	−301,178	−4,163	+78,482
Workers..............	−276,336	+1,696,402	+63,727	+1,483,793

* All entries are changes in the number of people in a given category net of overall population changes in the labor force. Thus each column sums to zero.

S194

TABLE 7

DECOMPOSITION OF CHANGES IN THE AMERICAN CLASS STRUCTURE
AS PERCENTAGES OF 1960 CLASS POPULATIONS

	Industry Shift	Class-Composition Shift	Interaction Shift	Total Net Change
Small employers...............	−8.1*	−40.4	−.07	−48.5
Petty bourgeoisie..............	−13.3	−30.4	−3.7	−47.4
Managers.....................	+3.6	+6.9	+.4	+10.9
Semiautonomous employees......	+5.6	−4.4	−.06	+1.3
Workers......................	−1.0	+6.3	+.2	+5.5

* All entries are net shifts as a percentage of the 1960 population figures for the class.

were 331,290 fewer employers in 1970 than in 1960 because of changes in the overall industrial structure; the working-class class-composition shift of +1,696,402 means that, net of population change, there were 1,696,402 more workers in 1970 due to changes in the class structures within industries.

In table 7 the entries in table 6 have been divided by the 1960 populations of the relevant class categories. The entry of −8.1% for the employer industry shift thus indicates that, net of population changes, the employer category declined by 8.1% between 1960 and 1970 owing to changes in the industrial structure. The results in table 7 are thus made relative to the size of the classes involved.

Now let us examine the results themselves. The results for both categories of self-employed (small employers and petty bourgeoisie) are very much as both Marxist and postindustrial theories would expect. Small employers and the petty bourgeoisie were decimated in the 1960s, both because of changes in the industrial structure which undermined those sectors within which these classes were most concentrated and because of the continuing process of the destruction of small businesses within most sectors of the economy.[14] In a limited way one might want to argue that the fact that the class shifts are considerably larger than the industry shifts for these two classes is suggested more by Marxist theory than by postindustrial theory. In terms of the destruction of small businesses, Marxists are more likely to emphasize the effects of strategies of capital accumulation within sectors than overall shifts in the industrial structure.[15]

[14] If we perform an additional disaggregation of the data and examine the contribution of each of the economic sectors to the overall industry shift, we see that virtually all of the negative shift for these two classes can be attributed to the decline of the extractive sector. The negative shift from this sector alone is −508,705 for small employers and −1,004,671 for the petty bourgeoisie. See table 9 for these data represented as percentage shifts.

[15] It is interesting in this context to see in precisely which sectors the negative class-composition shift for these classes was greatest. For small employers by far the largest negative class shift was located within distributive services (−755,599), while for the

However, since the theoretical predictions in these terms are relatively weak, it seems more appropriate at this point to see the results as consistent with both perspectives.

The results for the managerial-class location are also basically in line with both theoretical expectations: the managerial location expanded greatly, owing to changes in the industrial structure and to the expansion of managerial positions within sectors. The magnitude of the class-composition shift, however, is somewhat more consistent with the postindustrial framework. While Marxists would generally expect an increase in managerial positions within given industries, the arguments about concentration and centralization of capital and social control would not suggest such a large increase in managerial positions attributable to the class-composition shift. These results, therefore, may indicate that at least part of the expansion of such positions is bound up with the technological changes emphasized by postindustrial theorists. However, as in the arguments about relative magnitudes of different shifts for the self-employed, the theoretical expectations about the relative size of these shifts are relatively underdeveloped, and thus it is probably safest to see these results as largely supportive of both theoretical stances.

By far the most interesting results in tables 6 and 7 occur for the semi-autonomous-employee-class and working-class locations. For these classes the data are clearly more consistent with the arguments of Marxist theory than with those of postindustrial theory. In the case of semiautonomous employees, the industry shift and class shift are almost of equal magnitudes but in opposite directions: the change in the overall industrial structure in the 1960s produced an expansion of this class location by just under 385,000 positions (an increase of 5.6%), whereas the change in the class structure within industries generated a contraction of just over 300,000 (4.4%). The net result was a modest increase in semiautonomous employees of about 80,000 positions between 1960 and 1970. For the working class, on the other hand, the industry shift produced a decline of just over 275,000 positions (1.0%), while the class-composition shift produced an expansion of nearly 1.7 million (6.3%). Overall, as a result, the working class expanded by just under 1.5 million positions during the decade.

These results are directly contrary to the expectations of postindustrial theory. The process of proletarianization within given sectors was large and consistent. This resulted in a substantial expansion of the working class in the decade, and it largely neutralized the effects of changes in the industrial structure for the expansion of the semiautonomous-employee

---

pure petty bourgeoisie it was in the extractive sector (−256,770). Both of these sectors are sectors in which considerable inroads of large-scale corporate capital occurred during the 1960s (retail chains and department stores within distributive services, and agribusiness within the extractive sector). See table 9 for these data represented as percentage shifts.

category. Although there was a net expansion of semiautonomous locations, as predicted by postindustrial theory and contrary to the expectations of most Marxist accounts, nevertheless the decomposition of this net shift is more consistent with the pattern expected within Marxist theory.

All of the above results are based on a decomposition of changes in the overall class structure of the United States. It could be objected that this is not the most appropriate decomposition for a comparison of the core expectations of postindustrial and Marxist theories of the labor process, since those theories are largely focused on changes in wage-earner positions rather than all positions in the class structure. This objection would suggest that the decline of self-employed positions (small employers and petty bourgeoisie) should be treated as a kind of exogenous source of labor supply similar to the entry of housewives into the wage-labor force. In this line of reasoning, the statistical decomposition of industry shifts and class-composition shifts should be restricted to the three categories of wage earners: managers, semiautonomous employees, and workers. The results of this alternative strategy are presented in table 8.

The pattern of net shifts is significantly different in this table, as would be expected: only managers showed a positive net expansion during the decade; there was a relative decline of both workers and semiautonomous employees. The basic pattern for the decomposition of shifts, however, remains essentially the same: on the one hand, there was a large negative industry shift for workers and positive industry shifts for managers and semiautonomous employees; on the other, there was a large negative class-composition shift for semiautonomous employees but a positive shift for workers and managers. Thus, even if the statistical analysis is restricted to wage earners only, the basic structure of the findings is still more consistent with the general expectations of Marxist theory than with those of postindustrial theory.

TABLE 8

DECOMPOSITION OF CHANGES IN CATEGORIES OF WAGE EARNERS ONLY, 1960–70

	Industry Shift (%)	Class-Composition Shift (%)	Interaction Shift (%)	Total Net Change (%)
Managers..................	+431,925* (2.1)†	+334,901 (1.7)	+29,983 (.1)	+796,809 (3.9)
Semiautonomous employees...	+326,656 (4.8)	−635,715 (−9.4)	−85,592 (1.3)	−394,651 (−5.8)
Workers..................	−758,581 (−2.8)	+300,814 (+1.1)	+55,609 (.2)	−402,158 (−1.5)

* All entries are changes in the number of people in a given category net of overall changes in the population of the wage-labor force (not the total labor force). Thus each column sums to zero.

† Entries in parentheses are the shifts expressed as a percentage of the 1960 population in the particular category.

5. CONCLUSIONS

The data presented in table 6 do not directly provide a definitive basis for adjudicating the theoretical debate between Marxist and postindustrial theories. On the one hand, the data do not explicitly tap the process of transformation as such but only its effects, whereas the heart of the theoretical debate centers on contending views of the dynamics of social change. On the other hand, like any robust paradigm, postindustrial theory is sufficiently flexible that it can provide post hoc interpretations of the data in table 6 consistent with its overall theoretical framework. The decline of semiautonomous employees due to the class-composition shift could be explained, for example, as the result of a new unity of autonomy and responsibility in advanced technologies in which managerial locations replace nonmanagerial semiautonomous locations. Rather than constituting a process of the degradation of semiautonomous locations, such locations are being integrated into the authority structure of postindustrial society. At most, therefore, the results reported in this paper provide only suggestive support for the Marxist stance in the debate.

Nevertheless, those suggestions are striking: within given economic sectors, there was a systematic tendency for those positions with relatively little control over their labor processes to expand during the 1960s and for those positions with high levels of autonomy to decline. This does not imply, of course, that there were no examples of technological change in specific labor processes which may have enlarged the scope of autonomy and self-direction within work. But such changes appear to have been the exception rather than the rule during the decade. Contrary to the arguments of most postindustrial theorists, therefore, a continuing process of proletarianization does characterize advanced capitalism.

The data reported in this study span only a single decade. Both Marxist and postindustrial theories, however, base their arguments on a much broader time frame. It is entirely possible that the specific patterns observed in our results are consequences of peculiarities of the 1960s. It is important, therefore, to attempt at least some speculative judgments about the likely trajectory of these transformations in the future.

In terms of the strategy of analysis presented in table 6, the attempt at forecasting future developments amounts to generating a set of expectations about the changes in the relative magnitudes of the class and industry shifts for each of the cells in the table. In order to do this in a reasonable way, it is necessary to perform one further disaggregation of the data on structural changes. Table 9 disaggregates the class-composition and industry shifts for each of the class categories into the specific contributions from each of the seven broad economic sectors. Thus, for example, the table indicates that of the 40.3% decline in small employers due to the class shift, 18.4% can be attributed to the decline of small employers within

TABLE 9

Disaggregation of Percentage Industry Shifts and Class-Composition Shifts into Contributions by General Economic Sectors

Class Category	Extractive*	Transformative	Distribution Services	Producer Services	Professional Services	State Services	Personal Services	Total†
Employers:								
Industry shift	−12.4	−1.2	2.3	.8	2.2	.1	.2	8.0
Class shift	−4.1	−8.0	−18.4	−1.7	−2.1	.0	−6.0	−40.3
Petty bourgeoisie:								
Industry shift	−26.8	−.3	.2	6.1	3.6	1.5	2.2	−13.5
Class shift	−6.8	−4.8	−3.0	−4.2	−4.4	−1.3	−5.9	−30.4
Managers:								
Industry shift	−2.2	−3.5	1.2	3.8	.9	4.8	−1.3	3.7
Class shift	1.4	1.8	1.0	.2	.9	1.2	.4	6.9
Semiautonomous employees:								
Industry shift	−1.0	−3.3	1.4	1.8	.6	9.5	−3.3	5.7
Class shift	−.1	−2.6	1.1	.0	−.1	−2.7	.1	−4.3
Workers:								
Industry shift	−2.5	−4.8	1.0	2.8	.5	4.6	−2.7	−1.1
Class shift	.6	1.2	2.2	.7	.2	−.1	1.4	6.2

Note.—The entries indicate the percentage change in the number of people in a given class that can be attributed to the class shifts and industry shifts for specific economic sectors. The entry of −12.4% for the employer industry shift in the extractive sector thus indicates that in the employer category a net decline of 12.4% between 1960 and 1970 is attributable to the contribution of the extractive sector to the industry shift for employers.

* See table 3 for the classification of sectors under these general headings.

† The entries in the "total" column correspond to the entries in table 7, cols. 1 and 2. The slight differences are due to rounding.

distributive services, 8% to the decline in small employers in transformative industries, and so on. This table can help us assess the likely impact of future changes in the industrial structure on the class and industry shifts we have been discussing.

The most striking entry in table 9 is the tremendous importance of the growth in the state for the expansion of the semiautonomous-class location in the 1960s. While the state also contributed to the expansion of working-class and managerial positions, it had a much larger relative impact on the semiautonomous-employee locations. As a proportion of the 1960 population in each class location, the expansion of state-supported services generated a 9.5% increase in semiautonomous-employee locations but only a 4.8% and 4.6% increase in manager and working-class locations, respectively. On the other hand, the decline of the transformative sector has had the greatest relative negative impact on the working class: the number of workers declined by 4.8% as a result of the decline of transformative industries, whereas manager and semiautonomous-employee positions declined by only 3.5% and 3.3%, respectively.[16]

The question, then, becomes: What are the likely future trends for the growth of the state and the decline of transformative industries? Until the early 1970s there was a general tendency for the state sector to expand and the transformative sector to decline. Since the mid-1970s, however, there has been a slight decline in the relative employment of the state sector, and at least a leveling off in the decline of the transformative sector. In 1947, approximately 9.6% of the civilian labor force was employed directly by government (federal, state, and local combined).[17] This figure

[16] The basic structure of this statistical decomposition remains unaltered when we restrict the analysis to wage-earner categories (as in table 8): the expansion of the state generated an 8.4% increase in semiautonomous employees, compared with only 3.9% and 3.8% for managers and workers, respectively, whereas the decline in the transformative sector led to a 6.6% decrease in the working class, compared with only 4.7% and 5.1% decreases for managers and semiautonomous employees.

[17] The figures reported here are derived from data reported by the U.S. Bureau of Labor Statistics (1980, tables B-1 and A-1). The categories used in this source do not correspond precisely to those used in the rest of this paper in several respects. First of all, the data for the transformative sector do not include utilities (which we did include in that sector) but do include mining (which we placed in the extractive sector). The data reported here are what the U.S. Bureau of Labor Statistics refers to as "goods-producing" industries. Second, the category "government" in the Bureau of Labor Statistics data is restricted to employees directly working for some governmental agency, whereas our "state-supported services" sector included all services within which the government played a predominant role. Third, the only annual time series by economic sector we could find was for employees only (thus excluding self-employed people in each sector). For the state sector this obviously does not greatly affect the results, but it probably does have some effect on the trends for the transformative sector since, presumably, there would have been more self-employed within that sector in the late 1940s than at present. The percentages reported are thus the number of employees in a sector divided by the total employed civilian labor force (i.e., employees and self-employed, but excluding unemployed). While these percentages do not correspond precisely to those found in the rest

increased steadily until 1975, when it reached a peak of 17.3%. In the following four years this figure declined every year, reaching 16.4% in 1979 (the most recent date for which annual figures are available).[18] In the transformative sector, on the other hand, peak employment was reached in 1953, with 34.5% of the employed civilian labor force being employees in transformative industries. With some fluctuations up and down, this figure declined until 1975, when it reached 26.7%. In the four years after that the figure has risen slightly each year, reaching 27.3% in 1979.

Are these recent trends likely to persist into the future? Given the fiscal crisis of the state, the general retrenchment of state programs, the tax revolt, and the call for restraints on state employment by virtually all major political figures in the United States, it seems likely that the stagnation and decline in state employment observed in the period after 1975 will continue into the 1980s and probably beyond. And it certainly seems quite implausible that we will witness a renewal of the expansion of state employment characteristic of the 1950s and 1960s at any time in the foreseeable future.

The fate of the transformative sector is less clear. The movement of industrial production beyond the borders of the United States may in fact accelerate in the years to come and thus initiate a further decline of this sector. However, the political discussions concerning the "reindustrialization" of America suggest that state policies may be introduced to counter this tendency for industry to move abroad. If this were to occur it would signal a stabilization of the transformative sector, perhaps even a modest expansion.

If these expectations are borne out, it will mean that the negative industry shift for workers should be reduced in the 1980s, perhaps even becoming positive if a genuine reindustrialization process should occur. However, the positive industry shift for semiautonomous employees should be drastically reduced as the expansion of the state is halted. Indeed, if state employment were to continue to decline proportionately, we might even witness a negative industry shift for semiautonomous employees.

There is less that can be confidently said about likely class-composition shifts. To the extent that capital faces a general stagnation and crisis of accumulation, it might be expected that there would be attempts at rationalizing the managerial structure and increasing the pressures for proletarianization within the labor process. This could lead to a thinning out of managerial ranks and to an increase in the degradation of semiautonomous-

---

of this paper, the discrepancies should not seriously distort the broad tendencies being discussed in the present context.

[18] Between 1947 and 1975 the percentage of the civilian labor force employed by the government increased in every year except 1953, when it declined to 10.9% from 11.0% in 1952, and in 1955, when it declined from 11.21% to 11.1%. The four consecutive years of decline from 1975 to 1979 are thus unprecedented in the postwar period.

employee locations. Under pressures of fiscal constraint in the state, we might also expect to see such tendencies in state-supported social services as well, resulting in a rationalization of state administration and a slowing down in the proportional growth of managers within the state sector.

There are very few data available which bear on these expectations, but some very rough indications can be derived from data gathered by Richard Sobel.[19] Sobel examined a series of social surveys, conducted in the 1970s, within which questions about being a supervisor were included. While there are only four data points in his analysis—1970, 1973, 1976, and 1977— they indicate a steady decline in the proportion of the labor force occupying supervisory positions: from 36.1% in 1970 to 34.1% in 1973, 31.4% in 1976, and 31.1% in 1977. Because of differences in sampling designs and the precise form of the questions asked, these data cannot be taken as a strong demonstration of the decline of managerial locations in the 1970s, but they may at least indicate that the powerful class-composition shift for managers which underwrote their relative expansion in the 1960s has been significantly reduced.

Taken together, these expectations suggest that the rest of the century is likely to be characterized by a continuing and perhaps intensifying process of proletarianization. The specific balance between tendencies and countertendencies mapped out in table 6 should therefore not be seen as immutable but, rather, as a historically specific consequence of the character of American capitalism in the 1960s. As conditions of accumulation change, the balance between these opposing tendencies is likely to change as well. Any serious discussion of transformations of the labor process, proletarianization, class structure, and similar problems must attempt to unravel the complexity of these opposing trajectories of change. On the basis of the most informed speculation we can make with the available data, it seems likely that in the next several decades the net result of these trajectories will be an expansion of the working class, a systematic decline of semiautonomous-employee positions, and a stagnation (and perhaps gradual decline) of managerial positions. If this turns out to be the case, it will directly contradict the central thrust of postindustrial theory.

APPENDIX A

The Decomposition of Change in the Class Structure

The basic method used to decompose the changes in the class structure of U.S. employment is a modified shift-share technique (see Huff and Sperr [1967] and Perloff et al. [1960] for other uses of this approach). In their study *The Emergence of a Service Society*, Browning and Singelmann (1975)

---

[19] Personal communication. For a discussion of data sources and measurement problems, see Sobel 1981.

adopted this approach, along with the technique developed by Palmer and Miller (1949) and Gnanasekaran (1966), to examine the relationship between the industry structure and the occupational structure. Following their procedure, it is possible to decompose changes in the class structure into these components: (1) an industry-shift effect, (2) a class-composition-shift effect, and (3) an interaction effect. For our purposes the industry effect refers to changes in the class structure that result from a changing industry structure. Since the petty bourgeoisie, for example, is strongly concentrated in agriculture, a decline of this industry is unfavorable to the growth of the petty bourgeoisie, *ceteris paribus*. The class-composition effect refers to changes in the class structure that result from a changing class composition within each industry, independent of changes in the relative size of these industries. Finally, some changes in the class structure can be attributed neither to changes in the industry structure nor to a changing class composition within industries; rather, they result from an interaction of these two forces or, accordingly, the interaction effect. This procedure is comparable to Kitagawa's (1955) approach of decomposing changes in rates into different components.

An application of this method is carried out in table A1. Columns 1 and 2 are the actual numbers in each class category in 1960 and 1970, respectively. The figures in column 3 would have been observed in 1970 had each class category grown at the same rate as total employment during the 1960s. In column 4, we assumed that there were no changes in the class composition within industries between 1960 and 1970 and, therefore, permitted only the industry structure to change as it did. Thus the actual 1970 employment in each industry was distributed according to its specific 1960 class composition. The summation of each class category across the 37 industries results in the figures that are given in column 4. Columns 5 and 6 refer to the actual change and the expected change, respectively, in each class category.

The key column in this table is that of the net shifts (col. 7), which indicate the growth of each class category independent of the growth of total employment. A positive figure indicates a relative expansion of this class category, whereas a negative figure indicates a relative decline; the net shifts thus are comparable to the percentage figures in table 5.

Column 8 gives the growth of workers in each class category if there had been only industry shifts but no shifts in the class composition within industries, with the growth rate of total employment controlled. We call this the industry-shift effect. Column 9 refers to the number of workers each class category would have gained (or lost) had there been no change in the industry structure but only changes in the class composition of industries and an interaction between the two. In order to separate the interaction effect from the class-composition-shift effect, the standardization was

TABLE A1

INDUSTRY SHIFT EFFECT AND CHANGES IN THE CLASS STRUCTURE OF THE U.S. LABOR FORCE, 1960–70

CLASS	EMPLOYMENT				CHANGE			CHANGE DUE TO		%	
	1960 (1)	1970 (2)	Expected 1970 (3)	Weighted 1970* (4)	Actual (5) = (2) − (1)	Expected (6) = (3) − (1)	Net (7) = (5) − (6)	Industry-Shift Effect (8) = (4) − (3)	Class-Composition- and Interaction-Shift Effects (9) = (2) − (4)	Industry-Shift Effect (10) = (8) ÷ (7)	Class-Composition- and Interaction-Shift Effects (11) = (9) ÷ (7)
Employers	4,111,014	3,087,226	5,080,874	4,749,584	−1,023,788	969,860	−1,993,648	−331,290	−1,662,358	16.6	83.4
Petty bourgeoisie	3,753,212	2,859,979	4,638,661	4,140,376	−893,233	885,449	−1,778,682	−498,285	−1,280,397	28.0	72.0
Managers	20,293,995	27,291,760	25,081,705	25,803,793	6,997,765	4,787,710	2,210,055	722,088	1,487,967	32.7	67.3
Semiautonomous workers	6,794,122	8,475,457	8,396,975	8,780,798	1,681,335	1,602,853	78,482	383,823	−305,341	489.0	−389.0
Workers	27,081,959	34,954,862	33,471,069	33,194,733	7,872,903	6,389,110	1,483,793	−276,336	1,760,129	−18.6	118.6
Total	62,034,302	76,669,284	76,669,284	76,669,284	14,634,982	14,634,982	0	0	0	…	…

SOURCE.—1960 and 1970 census data.

*Weighted by 1960 class composition within industries.

reversed; this is carried out in table A2. In that table, column 4 results from the assumption that there was no change in the industry structure between 1960 and 1970 and that only the class composition within industries changed as it did. This procedure now allocates the interaction effect to the industry-shift effect and thus yields the change in each class category, controlled for the growth of total employment, that would have occurred had there been only changes in the class composition within industries but no shifts in the industry structure (and its interaction). This change is referred to as the class-composition-shift effect, and it is given in table A2, column 8. By subtracting this class-composition-shift effect from the combined composition-shift and interaction effect (table A1, col. 9), the interaction effect is derived. The results of both tables in Appendix A are summarized in table 6.

APPENDIX B

The Method Used to Impute Class Structures Using Census Data

Since there exists no single data set that would permit an empirical investigation of the relationship between class structure and industry structure, we had to link two separate data sources and, in that process, make some rather sweeping assumptions. The two data sources employed in the analysis are (1) the 1969 Survey of Working Conditions (SWC), conducted by the Institute for Social Research, University of Michigan; and (2) the 1960 and 1970 population censuses. The SWC could not be used by itself because it was taken at one time only and thus does not yield any information about changes in the class structure or the industry structure. The Population Census (PC) reveals changes in the industry structure, but it does not contain any questions about social class (as defined in this paper). To link the two data sets, we therefore created identical cross-classifications of 37 industry categories and 11 occupational categories with the SWC and the two PCs. The industry and occupational categories represent the total civilian employment in the SWC and in the PCs (for an elaboration of these categories, see Browning and Singelmann [1978]). Using the SWC, we then specified the class distribution for each industry-specific occupation. Furthermore, two main assumptions had to be made. First, it was assumed that there is no difference between the SWC and the PC in terms of the class composition of each industry-specific occupation. And second, we assumed that the class composition of industry-specific occupations did not change between 1960 and 1970. Obviously, the second assumption is rather questionable, but it was necessitated by the nature of the available data (see Appendix C for a comment on the biases in the findings that result from these assumptions). Once these assumptions are made, the class composition of each industry-specific occupation as derived from the

TABLE A2

Class-Composition-Shift Effect and Changes in the Class Structure of the U.S. Labor Force, 1960–70

CLASS	EMPLOYMENT				CHANGE			CHANGE DUE TO		%	
	1960 (1)	1970 (2)	Expected 1970 (3)	Weighted 1970* (4)	Actual (5) = (2) − (1)	Expected (6) = (3) − (1)	Net (7) = (5) − (6)	Class-Composition-Shift Effect (8) = (4) − (3)	Industry-Shift and Interaction-Shift Effect (9) = (2) − (4)	Class-Composition-Shift Effect (10) = (8) ÷ (7)	Industry-Shift and Interaction-Shift Effect (11) = (9) ÷ (7)
Employers..........	4,111,014	3,087,226	5,080,874	3,421,482	−1,023,788	969,860	−1,993,648	−1,659,392	−334,256	83.2	16.8
Petty bourgeoisie..	3,753,212	2,859,979	4,638,661	3,498,317	−893,233	885,449	−1,778,682	−1,140,344	−638,338	64.1	35.9
Managers..........	20,293,995	27,291,760	25,081,705	26,486,217	6,997,765	4,787,710	2,210,055	1,404,512	805,543	63.6	36.4
Semiautonomous workers..	6,794,122	8,475,457	8,396,975	8,095,797	1,681,335	1,602,853	78,482	−301,178	379,660	−383.8	483.8
Workers..........	27,081,959	34,954,862	33,471,069	35,167,471	7,872,903	6,389,110	1,483,793	1,696,402	−212,609	114.3	−14.3
Total..........	62,034,302	76,669,284	76,669,284	76,669,284	14,634,982	14,634,982	0	0	0	...	...

Source.—1960 and 1970 census data.

* Weighted by 1960 composition within industries.

SWC can be imputed for each industry-specific occupation in the two censuses. Finally, by aggregating individuals of the same class in each industry, we eliminated the occupational categories. The result is the class composition of each industry. Before adding these results across industries to obtain the class structures for 1960 and 1970, we made one further refinement. Since the sum of the small employer and the petty bourgeois class locations has to equal the sum of the census category "self-employed," it was possible partly to eliminate the distortion that results from the assumption about a fixed class composition within industry-specific occupations. By using the census information about the distribution of employment among self-employed and employed as parameters, we correctly estimate the combined class locations of small employers and the petty bourgeoisie, on the one hand, and the combined class locations of managers, semiautonomous employees, and workers, on the other hand. Specifically, we divided the employment in each industry between the self-employed and the employed, as given by the census in 1960 and 1970. The self-employed then were allocated to the small employer and petty bourgeois class locations in the same proportions as the imputed proportions for these two class locations to one another. The same procedure was followed for the employed, which were allocated to the class locations of managers, semiautonomous employees, and workers. These adjusted class distributions for each industry were then added to obtain the overall class structures for 1960 and 1970. Comparing the 1960 and 1970 data, we can identify changes in the class composition within industries and changes in the overall class structure that resulted from a different industry structure.

APPENDIX C

Possible Biases in the Estimation Procedure

The strategy adopted for estimating changes in the class structure between 1960 and 1970, and then decomposing those changes into three different components, involved a number of assumptions which undoubtedly introduce various distortions. The following distortions seem particularly important.

1. Overestimation of the semiautonomous-employee category in 1970. The questions available for measuring the semiautonomous-employee-class location in the SWC were limited to subjective questions concerning "freedom on the job" and "decision making." While it is probably the case that most people in genuinely semiautonomous locations would respond "a lot" on the subjective questions, it is likely that many people who lack real autonomy might also respond on the high end of the subjective autonomy questions. This would be expected since it is likely that people answer the question in terms of the expectations of autonomy relative to some

abstract, absolute norm of autonomy. The result would be that we probably overestimated the 1970 level of autonomous locations.

2. Overestimation of the managerial category in 1970. Since each person who states that he or she is, even nominally, a supervisor is being placed in the supervisor/manager class location, we have undoubtedly included certain individuals who are mere conduits for information and lack any real "authority" in the sense of having the capacity to invoke sanctions on subordinates.

3. It is more difficult to say whether we have under- or overestimated the size of semiautonomous and managerial locations in 1960. *If* the Braverman thesis is correct and there has occurred a systematic degradation of work within industry-specific occupations, then our assumption that occupation-specific class distributions within industries have remained unchanged would imply that our estimated numbers of the managerial- and semiautonomous-class locations in 1960 are underestimates. However, since we have reason to believe that, in fact, we overestimated the size of these class locations in 1970, the actual estimate for 1960 may be closer to the true distributions than for 1970.

4. Underestimation of the working class in 1970. Since we used the 1960 and 1970 census information on self-employed/employed members of the labor force to adjust the combined size of the managerial, semiautonomous, and working class locations, an overestimation of the managerial and semiautonomous locations (see 1 and 2 above) in 1970 implies that we underestimated the size of the working class in 1970.

REFERENCES

Bell, D. 1973. *The Coming of Post-industrial Society.* New York: Basic.
Braverman, H. 1974. *Labor and Monopoly Capital: The Degradation of Work in the Twentieth Century.* New York: Monthly Review Press.
Browning, H., and J. Singelmann. 1975. *The Emergence of a Service Society: Demographic and Sociological Aspects of the Sectoral Transformation of the U.S. Labor Force.* Springfield, Mo.: National Technical Information Service.
———. 1978. "The Transformation of the U.S. Labor Force: The Interaction of Industry and Occupation." *Politics and Society* 8:481–509.
Burawoy, M. 1978. "Toward a Marxist Theory of the Labor Process: Braverman and Beyond." *Politics and Society* 8:247–312.
———. 1979. *Manufacturing Consent.* Chicago: University of Chicago Press.
Carchedi, G. 1977. *On the Economic Identification of Social Classes.* London: Routledge & Kegan Paul.
Crompton, R., and J. Gubbay. 1978. *Economy and Class Structure.* New York: St. Martin's.
Edwards, R. C. 1979. *Contested Terrain.* New York: Basic.
Friedman, A. 1977. *Industry and Labour.* London: Macmillan.
Fuchs, V. R. 1968. *The Service Economy.* New York: National Bureau of Economic Research.
Gartner, A., and F. Reisman. 1974. *The Service Society and the Consumer Vanguard.* New York: Harper & Row.

Gnanasekaran, K. S. 1966. *Interrelations between Industrial and Occupational Changes in Manpower, United States, 1950–1960.* Analytical and Technical Report no. 6. Philadelphia: University of Pennsylvania, Population Studies Center.

Huff, D. L., and L. A. Sperr. 1967. "Measures for Determining Differential Growth Rates of Markets." *Journal of Marketing Research* 4:391–95.

Kitagawa, E. 1955. "Components of a Difference between Two Rates." *Journal of the American Statistical Association* 50:1168–74.

Palmer, G., and A. Miller. 1949. *Industrial and Occupational Trends in National Employment.* Philadelphia: University of Pennsylvania, Wharton School of Finance and Commerce, Industrial Research Department.

Perloff, H., E. S. Dunn, Jr., E. E. Lampard, and R. F. Muth. 1960. *Regions, Resources, and Economic Growth.* Baltimore: Johns Hopkins University Press.

Poulantzas, N. 1975. *Classes in Contemporary Capitalism.* London: New Left Books.

Przeworski, A. 1977. "From Proletariat into Class." *Politics and Society* 7:343–401.

Richta, R., et al. 1969. *Civilization at the Crossroads.* White Plains, N.Y.: International Arts and Sciences Press.

Singelmann, J. 1978. *From Agriculture to Services.* Beverly Hills, Calif.: Sage.

Sobel, R. 1981. "White Collar Class: Educated Labor Re-evaluated." Ph.D. dissertation, University of Massachusetts—Amherst.

U.S. Bureau of Labor Statistics. 1980. *Employment and Earnings Monthly.* Washington, D.C.: Government Printing Office, October.

Wright, E. O. 1976. "Class Boundaries in Advanced Capitalist Societies." *New Left Review* 98:3–41.

———. 1978a. *Class, Crisis and the State.* London: New Left Books.

———. 1978b. "Intellectuals and the Working Class." *Insurgent Sociologist* 8:5–18.

———. 1979. *Class Structure and Income Determination.* New York: Academic Press.

———. 1980a. "Class and Occupation." *Theory and Society* 9:177–214.

———. 1980b. "Varieties of Marxist Conceptions of Class Structure." *Politics and Society* 9:323–70.

———. 1982. "Capitalism's Futures." *Socialist Review*, in press.

Reinventing the Bourgeoisie: State Entrepreneurship and Class Formation in Dependent Capitalist Development[1]

Peter Evans
Brown University

This study examines the attempts of the Brazilian state to promote the expansion of the role of local capital in the capital goods and petrochemical industries during the period 1974–79. In the capital goods industry the attempt was unsuccessful and generated serious political opposition to the regime among local entrepreneurs, thus illustrating the extent to which processes of class formation lie outside the control of even a relatively powerful state apparatus. In the petrochemical industry the existence of a powerful state enterprise within the sector was critical to the state's ability to restructure the industry. What resulted was neither a "reinvention of the bourgeoisie" nor the creation of a "state capitalist" sector but, rather, an interesting oligopolistic community in which state and private local capital are thoroughly integrated and similarly organized. It is suggested that focusing on the concrete forms of such oligopolistic communities represents the most promising strategy for understanding the local side of dependent capitalist development.

An industrial bourgeoisie should be the leading class in capitalist industrialization. Marxist and liberal theories of development use different terminology, but they share this assumption. So do policymakers in the Third World. Thus, when Gen. Ernesto Geisel initiated Brazil's second national development plan he proposed that "curing the deficiencies of local entrepreneurs" was one of the tasks which had to be accomplished in order for Brazil to "cross the frontier to full development" (Brasil, República Federativa, 1974, pp. 5, 51; hereafter referred to as II PND, 1974). Since the project of turning Brazil into a "developed" country required a local class of industrialists, the "creation of strong entrepreneurial structures" would take its place alongside the construction of hydroelectric projects among the responsibilities to be shouldered by the state.

The idea of a bourgeoisie being constructed through the conscious under-

[1] I would like to thank Guillermo O'Donnell, whose quick response to an earlier version of this paper was most helpful in improving some of my initial formulations. Requests for reprints should be sent to Peter Evans, Department of Sociology, Brown University, Providence, Rhode Island 02912.

taking of a state apparatus is obviously a contradictory one. Yet it is no more contradictory than the realities of Third World capitalist development. Most scholars would agree that capitalist industrialization has taken place in at least a few Third World countries, usually labeled "semiperipheral" or "newly industrializing." Few would argue that this industrialization has been dominated by a class that fits the classic description of an "industrial bourgeoisie." While some have followed Hobson in assuming that foreign capital may be the social agent for peripheral industrialization, most would agree with Cardoso and Faletto (1970) that it is the interaction of local social classes and their international environment, not external forces alone, that explains the movement of peripheral capitalism. Most would agree that, while the state plays a central role in peripheral capitalist development, its role can only be understood as part of a "triple alliance" which includes both international capital and the local bourgeoisie (O'Donnell 1978; Evans 1979). The role of the local bourgeoisie itself remains crucial, even if it does not conform to the classic pattern.

Because the central roles of international capital and the state represent a departure from the conventional paradigm of capitalist industrialization, most analysis of peripheral industrialization has been focused on these two actors. International capital, primarily as embodied in transnational corporations (TNCs), has been a major focus of recent work, especially work by North Americans (see Evans 1981b). The study presented here attempts to concentrate on the local side of dependent development. It focuses particularly on the local bourgeoisie and on relations between the local bourgeoisie and the state. Relative to the breadth of the theoretical issues involved, it is restricted in its empirical scope. It examines the attempt by the Brazilian regime presided over by General Geisel to "reinvent the bourgeoisie" (O'Donnell 1978, p. 22) during the period of the Second National Development Plan (II PND; see the Appendix for a glossary of acronyms and Brazilian terms), 1974–79. Within this period it focuses on relations between the state and local entrepreneurs in the capital goods industry[2] and in the petrochemical industry.[3]

The case of the capital goods industry illustrates the problematic nature of the attempt to "reinvent the local bourgeoisie." The economic constraints

[2] My discussion of the capital goods industry is based primarily on Carlos Lessa's (1979) elegant and provocative analysis of the Geisel regime's economic policies. Lessa has not, however, had the opportunity to correct the inevitable errors in my reading of his work. This is particularly unfair to both Lessa and North American readers, since the work is not available in English. I can only hope that I succeed in drawing attention to his contribution without burdening him with responsibility for my errors.

[3] The material on the petrochemical industry is based on interviews and other primary sources collected in Brazil in the spring and summer of 1979. It does not take into account developments in the industry since 1979 (except for some examples reported in the international press). Readers of my previous work (1977, 1979) will notice that additional fieldwork has produced certain changes in interpretation.

Evans

created by the regime's commitment to abide by the normal rules of internationalized oligopolistic competition made it difficult for the state to
promote the interests of local capital. This in turn meant that the program
to strengthen local capital had political consequences for the regime quite
the reverse of those that were intended. Thus, the case of the capital goods
industry is aimed at demonstrating the extent to which control over processes of class formation lies outside the capacity of even a relatively
powerful state such as the Brazilian one.

The discussion of the petrochemical industry offers some important
modifications of the conclusions derived from the capital goods case. It
suggests, first, that the state's capacity must be examined concretely in
terms of the institutional nature of its involvement in a given sector. In
particular, it is argued that the existence of powerful entrepreneurial organizations, "relatively autonomous" vis-à-vis the central bureaucratic apparatus itself, was a central element in the state's capacity to intervene
successfully in petrochemicals. It suggests, furthermore, that, to the degree
that such intervention is successful, the parts of the state apparatus that
are involved are likely to become even more "privatized," that is, even
more "relatively autonomous" vis-à-vis the central bureaucracy. Equally
important, the petrochemical case suggests that insofar as the state suc-
ceeds in strengthening local capital in a given sector, the local bourgeoisie
is not reinvented but rather transformed. The combination of the privatized entrepreneurial elements which emerge within the state apparatus
and the new corporate forms which develop in the private sector creates a
peculiarly modern form of capitalism, one which seems to bear a family
resemblance to the more "organized" sort of advanced corporate capitalism, such as the French and Japanese varieties.

The analysis of this particular moment in Brazil's industrialization can
be no more than suggestive for the formulation of more general propositions regarding the role of the state and class formation in dependent capitalist development. It does, however, provide evidence that fits aptly into
current theoretical debates, both those which are concerned with the nature of the local bourgeoisie in semiperipheral countries and those which
revolve around the role of the state in dependent development. In the
context of these general theoretical discussions the Brazilian capital goods
and petrochemical industries become relevant, even to those with no special interest in Brazil.

THE LOCAL BOURGEOISIE AND THE STATE IN THE PERIPHERY

For analysts of the original Industrial Revolution, the "conquering bourgeoisie" may be a useful ideal type. For students of peripheral capitalism,
it distracts attention from the actual role of local owners of capital and

leads to a focus on what the local bourgeoisie is not rather than on what it is (Diniz and Boschi 1977, p. 168). Anyone starting from the assumption that a bourgeoisie should consist of a class of individual owners of capital, so coerced by the competitive market that it "cannot exist without constantly revolutionizing the means of production," yet having "conquered for itself in the modern representative state exclusive political sway" (Marx and Engels 1969, pp. 19, 18), will find no class that fits the description in Third World countries.

Equally distracting is what O'Donnell has called "the central myth of populism: the feasibility of capitalist development undertaken by an entirely national coalition" (1978, p. 24). In this myth, the conquering bourgeoisie is replaced by the "national bourgeoisie," a class which retains the progressive economic role of the original bourgeoisie but has acquired a touching parochial loyalty to the political unit in which it resides. Rather than "eradicating national one-sidedness and narrow-mindedness" (Marx and Engels 1969) like the original bourgeoisie, the national bourgeoisie is willing to do battle with its cosmopolitan counterparts, joining together with other local classes in order to ensure that the local development of productive forces takes precedence over their global accumulation.

Empirical analyses of the local bourgeoisie—even in Brazil, where the local accumulation of capital is unquestionably taking place—have established that local industrialists boast neither the economic nor the political characteristics required by the ideal type. Economically, they have been displaced from dominance over leading industrial sectors by the "internationalization of the domestic market," that is, the rise of direct investment by multinational corporations (Cardoso and Faletto 1970; Evans 1979; Gereffi and Evans 1981; Newfarmer and Mueller 1975; Newfarmer 1980). Politically, they shared power, even before the extensive foreign penetration of the domestic market, with older agrarian elites and the representatives of the urban middle sectors (Cardoso and Faletto 1970; Martins 1976; Fausto 1970; Rowland 1974). In 1964 they allowed the destruction of parliamentary rule and its replacement by a "bureaucratic authoritarian" (BA) state. Studies of the self-perceptions of local industrialists confirm that subjectively as well as objectively they lack a "vocation for hegemony" or a "national project" (Cardoso 1964, 1971; Martins 1968; Diniz and Boschi 1977, 1978; Boschi 1980; McDonough 1981), perceiving themselves instead as politically subordinate to a state apparatus which they do not control.

Recognizing the weakness of local capital, one must still accept its essential role in capital accumulation on the periphery. The local bourgeoisie cannot be simply replaced by international capital. International capital shifts production to a peripheral region only when the configuration of local social forces creates an expectation of increased profitability.

Without pressure from local social forces, international capital has little impetus to construct a fully differentiated productive apparatus in each region. Some form of alliance between local and international capital is necessary for capitalist development to proceed at the local level. Thus, the "nonhegemonic" local bourgeoisie allies itself with international capital to form what Cardoso and Faletto (1970, pp. 130–34) call an "internationalized bourgeoisie."

The same international context that has weakened the local bourgeoisie increases the pivotal role of the state as an institution and social actor, making it either the most important ally of the local bourgeoisie or its potential replacement as an agent of capital accumulation. The centrality of the state to the structuring of domestic economic relations is a long-standing historical feature of Latin American economies. Their subordinate position internationally, while obviously making them susceptible to external manipulation and therefore "weak," has also had an opposite and contradictory effect on Latin American states. As Fitzgerald puts it, "The Latin American state has always been closely involved in the negotiation of the integration of the economy into the international division of labor. Indeed, a case can be made to the effect that this tradition stretches back to colonial times, when the state made grants of land, labor, minerals, import licenses and tariff protection" (1981, p. 10). More recently, the penetration of domestic economies by multinational corporations has had the same paradoxical effect. On the one hand, it diminishes sovereignty. On the other hand, precisely because sovereignty is at issue, the state becomes more thoroughly involved in negotiating the economic order.

Because it is the only domestic actor with the power to confront the multinationals, the state is pushed toward intervention in the affairs of private capital. In raw materials industries, state ownership is a common end point of bargaining between multinationals and the state (Moran 1974; Tugwell 1975; Becker 1981). For quite different reasons, the state is likely to end up replacing foreign capital in the ownership of public utilities (Tendler 1968; Singer 1975; Gereffi and Evans 1981). In the manufacturing sector the multinationals are more likely to retain control (Bennett and Sharpe 1979; Gereffi 1978; Evans 1979; Newfarmer 1980), but even here the process of bargaining in itself has the effect of increasing the capacity of the state as an economic actor. Some have gone so far as to suggest that the overall result of state/multinational bargaining is to make certain Third World states more adept at dealing with international capital than the core states themselves (Barnet and Müller 1974; Bergsten, Horst, and Moran 1978).

The pivotal role of the state is derived as much from the weakness of the local bourgeoisie as from the strength of international capital. The inability of local capital to push forward accumulation in key industries, most prominently intermediary goods like steel, along with the unwillingness of TNCs to move forward in these industries, created the impetus for the formation of state-owned firms (Baer 1969; Wirth 1970). When the state's role in these intermediate industries is combined with its role in petroleum and other extractive industries and its very important role in the financial sector, a formidable collection of state enterprises is the result.

The question which then arises is whether dependent development should be characterized as "state capitalist" (Fitzgerald 1976; Petras, Morley, and Smith 1977; Baer, Newfarmer, and Trebat 1977; Dupuy and Truchil 1979; Canak 1981). If the state were to become the dominant agent of capital accumulation, as the state capitalist label implies, then it would become the local bourgeoisie's replacement rather than its ally. Such a vision is, however, almost universally rejected.

The work of E. V. K. Fitzgerald perhaps best illustrates the reasons for this rejection. Fitzgerald concludes his analysis of Peru in the 1968–75 period by saying, "The most striking aspect of the Peruvian political economy has been the way in which the state has taken over so completely the functions of domestic capital—particularly the formation of capital, the coordination of production and relations with foreign enterprise" (1976, p. 95). Nonetheless, even Fitzgerald ends up rejecting the idea that the state is capable of acting as an independent demiurge of capitalist accumulation.

Starting from the premise that "for state capitalism to function as a distinct variant of the capitalist mode of production, it must be the dominant one in the economy," Fitzgerald goes on to argue that "if state capital is merely supportive to private capital it will not be able to articulate the necessary system of planning, capital finance and surplus extraction because these eliminate the market system necessary to private capitalism" (1977, p. 69). He concludes that "the characteristics of autonomous state accumulation do not obtain" in the major countries of Latin America (1977, p. 75). Either insufficient fiscal resources or the inability to institute efficient general planning, or both, preclude the possibility of the state being the dominant actor in capital accumulation. Consequently, "despite the large public sector share of investment, state capitalism is not an appropriate description of the Latin American experience of the large state" (1977, p. 78).

Political as well as economic reasoning can be used to argue for the primacy of the state, but here again even those theorists whose work puts the state most squarely at the center of dependent capitalist development conclude that a durable "pact of domination" requires the participation of the local bourgeoisie. The work of Guillermo O'Donnell is the prime example.

O'Donnell focused on the "dual alliance" of the state and the TNCs in his analysis of the emergence of the BA state. Arguing that the politics of import-substituting industrialization led to popular mobilization which eventually reached levels incompatible with the predictable investment climates required to induce TNC investment in vertically integrated industrial endeavors, O'Donnell saw the local bourgeoisie as unable to guarantee the political conditions necessary for capital accumulation. Economic problems exacerbated the political situation, leading to a situation in which the society's "continuity as a capitalist system was perceived as threatened" (O'Donnell 1979, p. 300). In the face of this threat, political power is turned over to "techno-bureaucrats" who must repress the popular sectors on the one hand and gain the confidence of international capital on the other. But in order to demonstrate its commitment to international capital's version of "rationality" and "efficiency," the BA state must go beyond repression of the popular sectors and become "almost deaf to the national bourgeoisie" (O'Donnell 1978, p. 19). It must introduce a range of measures including "the elimination of subsidies for the domestic bourgeoisie, the lowering of import tariffs, and other measures that reveal even further the weakness of national capital vis à vis international capital" (1978, p. 17). If such a pattern were to persist, the BA state would end up destroying its own local bourgeoisie, and the techno-bureaucrats in the state apparatus would become the local component of a dual alliance with international capital. In O'Donnell's view, however, such an outcome is not politically feasible.

O'Donnell argues that the dual alliance version of the BA state can exist only in that "particularly diaphanous moment" immediately following the elimination of the threat to "the capitalist parameters of society" (1979, p. 309). Once this moment has passed, the state must confront the fact that it is still a national state and as such "must present itself as the incarnation, as the political and ideological expression of the general interests of the nation" (1978, p. 20). It "lacks, both politically and ideologically, a crucial component—the national and private ingredient that only the local bourgeoisie can contribute" (1978, p. 22). The BA state now needs a viable local bourgeoisie in order to ensure its own political survival. Consequently, "the state must not merely offer itself passively to the reentry of the local bourgeoisie, but must actively tutor it . . . it once again must subsidize the activities of that bourgeoisie; it must reserve for itself and for the national bourgeoisie hunting ground forbidden to the direct access of international capital. . . . In other words the BA must come to restrict international capital to a degree almost unthinkable in the initial orthodox stage, making economic space for itself and for the national bourgeoisie, thus tutoring it and in doing so, virtually reinventing it" (1978, p. 22).

The literature, both economic and political, leads to a diagnosis quite similar to that proposed by the Geisel administration: the state must act as the ally of the local bourgeoisie. As Brazil's Council on Economic Development put it, the "tripod" consisting of international capital, local capital, and the state must be "equilibrated" by strengthening the weak leg which is local capital (Lessa 1979, p. 211). The reasons why the semiperipheral state might undertake to "reinvent the bourgeoisie" are clear. The consequences of such an undertaking have not, however, been the subject of the same sort of theoretical analysis. Understanding them requires, first of all, closer attention to the institutional character of the state apparatus in general and to the more entrepreneurial parts of it in particular.

THE BRAZILIAN STATE, CIRCA 1974

The Brazilian state in the mid-seventies had exceptional leverage vis-à-vis civil society. Centralization of political power began with the 1964 coup. By 1968, with the passage of the Fifth Institutional Act, political parties, the legislature, and popular organizations such as unions were essentially destroyed as effective political actors.[4] As Abranches summarizes the situation, "With civil society devoid of autonomous political organizations, all political transactions are mediated by the state structure. Thus, politics becomes an affair circumscribed to the bureaucracy of the state" (1978, p. 68).[5] Even within the bureaucracy, pressures emanating from the popular sector—for example, the influence of unions in the social security bureaucracy (see Malloy 1979)—had been essentially eliminated.

Even the dominant fractions of the bourgeoisie were not in a position to shape state policies systematically or control the actions of the central bureaucracy. Cardoso and Faletto characterize their control as "almost purely structural" (1970, p. 136), which is to say that, while the state continued to serve the interests of private capital, entrepreneurs had little direct say in its policies. Abranches elaborates the same perspective: "Although the state faithfully serves the general and most fundamental interests of the bourgeoisie and makes every effort to assure the advancement of private capital accumulation, it appears as a menacing Leviathan to most social forces as particular actors" (1978, p. 168). Interaction with incumbents in the state apparatus provided possibilities for individual members of the bourgeoisie to influence policy. But, as Cardoso points out (1975, pp. 201–9), the "bureaucratic rings" that result from the linking of public functionaries and members of the bourgeoisie only provide means of real-

[4] Those interested in the political history of the coup and the military regimes that ruled subsequently can turn to Skidmore 1967; Stepan 1971; Fiechter 1975; Fernandes 1975; Dreifuss 1981.

[5] The work of Sergio Abranches and Luciano Martins has been very influential in shaping my views on the structure of the Brazilian state apparatus. The caveats noted above in relation to Carlos Lessa again apply, especially in the case of Martins, whose work is, due to the irrational vagaries of the translation process, not available in English.

izing particular interests, not means by which class-wide demands can be articulated and imposed on the state apparatus.

The monopolization of the political process by the state apparatus was complemented by its increasing appropriation of the surplus. The share of public sector revenues rose by about 5% of the GDP between the premilitary period and the early seventies (Wells 1977, p. 327). At the same time, revenues were progressively shifted from the state and cities to the federal government. In the context of a rapidly increasing GDP, this meant that federal receipts almost quintupled in real terms between 1960 and 1974 (Martins 1977). Furthermore, these increased revenues were largely available for projects of accumulation and economic restructuring, since "welfarism" of the Western European sort was absent. Between 1968 and 1973, for example, while state receipts grew dramatically, state expenditures on health declined absolutely (Wells 1977, p. 325).

The increasing accumulation of resources by the state apparatus might have undermined its support among the local elite, had it not been for the regressive pattern in which they were extracted. The greatest increase in the state's revenues was provided by the various forced savings plans imposed on wage earners (Wells 1977, p. 327). Martins (1977) estimates that the resources garnered by means of these sources were almost as great as those generated by income taxes. At the same time, the tax burden on the bourgeoisie was substantially mitigated by the various "incentives" deducted from the tax obligations of both corporations and individuals which have been estimated as amounting to 50% of total direct taxes (Baer 1979, p. 98). Thus, the state was able to increase its revenues without antagonizing the local bourgeoisie.

The resources accumulated by the state had a substantial impact on the structure of economic power in part because they were applied through a diverse set of relatively decentralized organizations. From the beginning the military promoted the growth of the various autarkies and institutes which comprised the "decentralized administration" as opposed to the traditional central bureaucracy. In the case of capital formation within the federal apparatus, for example, the majority was undertaken by the centralized administration in the premilitary period (1959), but by the early seventies three-fourths was undertaken by the decentralized administration (Martins 1977). The financial autonomy of subunits was increased by the proliferation of "funds" which involved earmarking specific sources of revenue for the use of particular agencies and organizations, freeing them from having to negotiate their budgets with the central bureaucracy. Of the roughly 200 such funds in existence in the mid-seventies, two-thirds were created by the military regime (Martins 1977).

Even more insulated from the central bureaucracy are the state-owned enterprises, whose numbers increased dramatically under the military regime. Of the roughly 200 enterprises owned by the federal government, over half were created in the 10 years of military rule (Martins 1977). In addition, the autonomy of state enterprises was legitimated by the administrative reforms introduced by the military regime in 1967. According to Decreto Lei 200, state enterprises are "guaranteed conditions of operation identical to those of the private sector" (cited in Martins 1977).

Within the various entities in the orbit of the state but not directly under control of the central bureaucracy, the emergence of internal administrative cadres loyal to these organizations themselves and willing to defend them against encroachments by an "alien" central bureaucracy often reinforced other tendencies toward "decentralization." Luciano Martins's (1976, 1977) study of the National Bank for Economic Development (BNDE) provides a good illustration.

The economic impact of the state's activities might have been more limited if the military had concentrated on activities traditionally performed by the central state bureaucracy. Martins documents the evolution of the bank from, first, an institution designed to help international lending institutions control the implantation of externally financed infrastructure projects, to a major stockholder in state-owned enterprises, and still later to the "demiurge of local industry." Despite attempts by powerful opponents to reduce its role during the initial phase of the military government, the bank not only survived but managed substantially to enhance its autonomy vis-à-vis the central state apparatus. First it became a "state enterprise" and managed to gain substantial internal control over the appointment of its own directors; then, at the beginning of the Geisel administration, it was given control over the massive resources generated by the PIS-PASEP forced savings program, assuring it financial resources independent of the central budgetary process.

Petrobrás, the state-owned oil monopoly, is perhaps an even better example of the powerful organizations which have grown up in the ambit of the state apparatus. The fact that it was from the presidency of Petrobrás that General Geisel was recruited to the presidency of the Republic is indicative of the special nature of the relationship between Petrobrás and the central bureaucratic administration. Politically sacrosanct because of its nationalist origins (Cohn 1968; Martins 1976) and economically buttressed by the enormous profitability of oil refining in the post-1973 world, Petrobrás was the largest company in Brazil and one of the 50 largest in the world. In 1974 it was already diversified. By the end of the II PND the "Petrobrás system" would contain in the neighborhood of 70 different firms engaged in everything from exporting soybeans to building hotels in Iraq to making synthetic rubber in Brazil (Petrobrás, *Annual Report,* 1978, pp. 22–28).

The existence of organizations like the BNDE and Petrobrás gave the state the ability to undertake economic tasks which would otherwise have been beyond the capacity of the central bureaucracy and thereby enhanced the power of the state. At the same time, these organizations were "relatively autonomous" vis-à-vis the central administrative machinery of the state. Their position is symptomatic of what Abranches has called the "segmentation" of the Brazilian state apparatus, a lack of coherence in the relationships among the different organs of the state which must eventually have the effect of making policy "more and more conjunctural and less and less articulated" (1978, p. 751).

As important to the regime as the concrete organizational structures that had been built since 1964 was the legitimacy which had been generated by Brazil's economic performance during the period from 1968 to 1973, the period of the so-called Brazilian miracle. The first three years of the military regime (1964–67) had been a textbook example of the dual alliance phase of BA rule as predicted by O'Donnell. Stringent fiscal policies combined with classically liberal economic policies decimated the ranks of local industrialists. The next five years of rapid growth, however, were profitable for local and international capital alike.

Credit for the "economic miracle" was central to the legitimacy of the military regime in the eyes of the local bourgeoisie. It was also central to the confidence with which the Geisel administration approached its development plan in 1974. In the view of the regime, military rule had not just proved itself technocratically efficient; it had transformed the fundamental character of Brazilian society. On sending his development plan to Congress, Geisel explained that Brazil could look forward confidently to "crossing the frontier to full development" in the near future because 10 years of "renovating revolution" had produced "an elevated coefficient of rationality, acceptance of even difficult truths and a serene and responsible pragmatism, all of which are spreading through all levels of the population, from top to bottom of the social structure of this renewed Brazil" (II PND, 1974, p. 6). Needless to say, neither the situation confronting the regime nor its internal "coefficient of rationality" was as unambiguously positive as it sounded in Geisel's pronouncements.

A favorable external conjuncture combined with the cyclical nature of growth internally had been as responsible for the "miracle" as any elevation in the regime's level of rationality.[6] Consequently, the Geisel admin-

[6] In fact, the connection between the policies introduced by the regime and the growth rates of the 1968–73 period was at least in part coincidental. Both international liquidity and international trade were expanding rapidly during this period, helping to free Brazil from the foreign-exchange constraint that had traditionally limited its ability to grow. In addition, after the 1961–67 downswing the economy was poised for a cyclical upswing. Growth in the early years of the miracle could be achieved by utilizing excess capacity rather than increasing the share of the GDP going to investment, thus allowing output to expand without restricting the consumption of the elite. The administrative reforms and the concentration of income produced by the mili-

istration was much more vulnerable than it realized, both to changes in the international environment and to the exhaustion of the expansionary phase of the growth cycle internally. In addition, the "economic miracle" had produced a more highly internationalized economy, both in the sense of dependence on external financing and in the sense of having its internal market thoroughly penetrated by foreign subsidiaries. The "weak leg" of the tripod (local capital) could be strengthened only insofar as the rules of the game were maintained in a way that was satisfactory to the "external leg" of the tripod (the TNCs). The TNCs had to be allowed to compete with local capital in most sectors, and fundamental financial parameters such as the rate of inflation and the deficit in the balance of payments had to be maintained at levels considered tolerable by the international financial community.

The state apparatus over which Geisel presided was not simply a "strong state." Its apparent strength was derived from a number of contradictory features. It was both highly centralized and full of centrifugal tendencies. It was highly legitimate in the eyes of the local bourgeoisie, yet unconnected to it by any well-institutionalized system of linkages. It was not politically restricted by civil society, but it was critically constrained by its commitment to maintaining an international market economy. Once the interplay of these contradictory features is appreciated, the outcome of the state's efforts to "reinvent the local bourgeoisie" becomes more comprehensible.

STRENGTHENING LOCAL CAPITAL: THE MISADVENTURES OF
THE STATE AS TUTOR

The capital goods industry was the focus of a special effort to strengthen the position of the local industrial bourgeoisie, but the state's effort in this industry must be seen as part of a more general set of initiatives. According to the diagnosis of the Geisel regime, inadequate capitalization was what prevented local firms from growing into strong entrepreneurial structures. To remedy the problem, a three-pronged strategy was designed. First, the state would expand its role as the primary source of investment loans for industrial purposes. Second, for those local firms which were unable or unwilling to take on more debt, even at concessional interest rates, equity would be provided through the purchase of nonvoting preferential shares by one of the BNDE's three subsidiaries (FIBASE, IBRASA, and EMBRAMEC). Finally, private savings would be directed toward equity investments by fiscal incentives and improved legal protection for investors.

---

tary's policies no doubt contributed to the growth rate, but their effects were substantially enhanced by these conjunctural factors (Malan and Bonelli 1977; Serra 1979; Wallerstein 1980; Knight 1981).

The state's role as a source of capital for local industry was already well established at the time of the initiation of the II PND. Suzigan (1976, p. 113) estimates that state institutions were providing 70% of the loans made to the private sector for purposes of investment in 1974. Since three-fourths of the investment loans from private sources were oriented toward real estate, the predominance of the state in the provision of loans for industrial purposes was well over 70%. Even so, the activities of the state as banker were expanded. The resources available to the BNDE increased by more than two-thirds from 1974 to 1975 (Martins 1977). New programs such as the Program of Support for the Capitalization of National Private Firms (PROCAP) were added, and existing programs, like FINAME, were oriented more explicitly toward nationally owned firms.

While the availability of financing through the state obviously benefited local firms, it did not have the effect intended. The BNDE and its subsidiaries found themselves drawn more into the business of propping up weak firms than into "the creation of strong entrepreneurial structures." The BNDE's Fund for the Modernization and Reorganization of Industry (FMRI) continued to be used, as it had since 1970, mainly for rescue operations. In some cases (e.g., Fiação Lutfalla; see *Latin America Weekly Report* [*LAWR*] [March 6, 1981], p. 7) there was even the suspicion that local owners had essentially "unloaded" their investment on the BNDE in order to limit the damage to themselves. Likewise, IBRASA, designed to aid firms that wanted to expand, found itself primarily repairing the damage done by the recession of 1974–75 (Lessa 1979, pp. 214–17).

The attempt to stimulate the flow of private savings into risk capital also had unanticipated consequences. Legal reforms designed to protect the "small investor" had the effect of strengthening the hand of financial institutions vis-à-vis industrial capitalists rather than producing "people's capitalism." The heavily traded shares on the stock exchanges continued to be those of foreign subsidiaries or state-owned firms, while a surprising number of the most prominent local firms (e.g., Votorantim and Matarazzo) remained absent from the exchange altogether. In fact, during the period 1972–75, 75% of the volume on the stock exchanges was accounted for by shares in state-owned enterprises (Martins 1977).

One of the central difficulties with the regime's attempts to stimulate the flow of resources into risk capital was what Carlos Lessa (1979, p. 234) has called the "schizophrenic split" between measures of the II PND aimed at strengthening national firms and the financial and credit policies which were enacted simultaneously. In its attempts to deal with inflation and international financial balances the regime provided attractive interest rates and full indexing against inflation for those who wanted to invest in essentially risk-free fixed-income securities, such as treasury bonds. Complementing the attractiveness of the financial arena was the attractive possibility of selling out to a foreign firm. The local entrepreneur with possibilities for growth had to choose between trying to challenge the oligopolistic redoubts of the multinationals or selling out to them and moving his capital into the lucrative financial sphere. The possibility of getting capital through the state did little to change the difficulties of competing with larger, technologically better endowed firms, and therefore did little to diminish the attractiveness of selling out. Despite the ostensible focus on industrial capital, the overall configuration of the regime's policies was most clearly beneficial to members of the local bourgeoisie involved in the financial sector. Furthermore, the relative power of this sector grew in part at the expense of local industrialists.

The general incentives and support which the II PND had to offer local industrialists seem clearly inadequate in retrospect, particularly because the state had no way of controlling the market in which local firms operated. In the case of the capital goods industry, however, the state had special leverage. According to the II PND, the industrial sector was projected to grow at 12% annually between 1974 and 1979, creating a rapidly expanding market for capital goods. More important, the "new industrial profile" which the plan was intent on attaining involved a "new phase of import substitution" focused on capital and intermediary goods (II PND, 1974, p. 37). It was one of the "fundamental preoccupations" of the plan to reverse the tendency for firms to "import the maximum possible" in purchasing capital goods (II PND, 1974, p. 38).

Central to the possibility of achieving this "new phase of import substitution" was the fact that the state sector itself would become a major purchaser of capital goods. Suzigan (1976, pp. 117–18) estimates that capital goods expenditures projected for the state sector during the plan were equal to 35% of the industry's output on an annual basis, even without the assumption of a fall in the import coefficient. Local producers were to be given priority in the purchases of both the central government and the state enterprises and "special help" to insure their participation in major public projects (II PND, 1974, p. 38). In addition, there was a significant "carrot" offered to the private sector in the form of the BNDE's FINAME program, which provided medium- and long-term loans for the purchase of capital goods at extremely favorable interest rates (1%–7%, plus indexing) provided the capital goods were locally produced. Finally, there was the "stick" of tightening import restrictions on capital goods (Suzigan 1976, pp. 119–22).

With an expanding market assured by the plan, local capital goods producers needed only to expand their capacity rapidly enough to keep up with demand. Here, of course, the various measures designed to allow locally owned firms to increase their capitalization came into play. In addition to BNDE loans, one of the BNDE's subsidiaries, EMBRAMEC, was specially charged with assisting firms in the capital goods industry. Lessa (1979, p. 110) estimates that EMBRAMEC, together with the BNDE's other programs, gave a local firm the possibility of expanding without having to provide more than 21% of the investment itself.

The capital goods industry was doubly important. Its expansion was central to attaining an "industrial profile" compatible with "full development." No country could claim to be developed if it was unable to produce its own capital goods. At the same time, by promoting local capital in this expanding sector, the state could ensure that industrial transformation did not lead to denationalization and increasing penetration by TNCs, as it had in the previous development of the consumer durables sector (see Evans 1979; Gereffi and Evans 1981). Hence, the two-sided program for capital goods producers: a market assured by state purchases and special financing (FINAME) on the one hand, and a program of capitalization to allow local capital to take advantage of the market on the other hand.

Unfortunately for local capital goods producers, the strategy depended fundamentally on the regime's confident assumption that it could reproduce 1968–73 growth rates. Since the regime diagnosed the earlier period of growth as having been determined primarily by its own achievements, the expectation was consistent. Reality was less kind. The cyclical factors which had fed into the 1968–73 boom were exhausted (see n. 6 above), and Brazil was not able to "take advantage of the recent situation" internationally as the plan suggested (II PND, 1974, p. 36). Capital output ratios were rising instead of falling (Knight 1981, p. 21), making growth more costly. Rising debt service payments and oil bills, rather than opportunities for Brazil, were the main features of the international situation. Growth in the industrial sector fell to 6.2% in 1975 and, after achieving the 12% goal briefly in 1976, fell back again to 2.3% in 1977 (Baer 1979)—an enviable overall performance compared with that of most countries during the period, but significantly lower than the projections of the II PND. Inflation, which had been below 20% in the three years prior to 1974, immediately jumped to 30% and would reach 77% by the end of the II PND (Baer 1979, p. 173; *Economic Commission for Latin America* [ECLA] 1981, p. 112). The trade balance shifted from slightly positive in 1973 to a $4.6 billion deficit in 1974, while debt service grew from 30% of exports in 1974 to 70% in 1979 (ECLA 1980, p. 117; 1981, p. 127).

The regime found itself pressed to maintain fundamental economic parameters at what it (and its external allies) considered acceptable levels. While it never formally renounced plans for restructuring the industrial profile, policies introduced in order to cope with inflation and balance-of-payments problems increasingly contradicted plans for the transformation of the local capital goods sector. The Council for Economic Development (CDE) adopted resolutions limiting the price increases of public services to rates below the inflation rates. This in turn limited the ability of state enterprises to finance new investment and the purchase of capital goods. At the same time it was decided that a number of projects originally included in the central state budget must be cut in order to fight inflation, further reducing the rate of state investment and the demand for capital goods (see Lessa 1979, pp. 152, 159–63). Finally, pressure on the balance-of-payments front strengthened the hand of foreign lenders who wanted the capital goods for the projects they financed purchased abroad rather than in Brazil. The import coefficient for capital goods was higher in 1975 and 1976 than it had been during the boom years of 1968–69 (Bonelli and Façanha, cited in Abranches 1978, p. 292).

Those capital goods producers who had accepted the state's invitation and expanded their capacity now faced a market growing more slowly and more unpredictably. Even worse, the buoyant conditions and optimistic projections of the early seventies had attracted an influx of foreign subsidiaries to the sector. Local firms found themselves facing not only excess capacity but also "excessive" competition. One manufacturer of converters, for example, complained that there were seven firms competing for the domestic market in Brazil, while in Japan there were only two (Lessa 1979, pp. 138–39). The degree of competition in the industry gave purchasers of capital goods, usually large and powerful entities, the opportunity to resolve their own budgetary problems by negotiating lower prices. According to Bonelli and Façanha, capital goods evidenced "the smallest increase in prices among all categories of goods domestically produced" (cited in Abranches 1978, p. 293). The state could provide loans, but it could not change competitive conditions in the market without abrogating its general commitment to an internationalized market economy.

Facing a difficult competitive market in which their chances of survival were in doubt, rather than the guaranteed growth promised by the II PND, local capital goods producers were understandably disillusioned. Claudio Bardella, acknowledged leader of local industry, summarized the sector's grievances nicely in the spring of 1976. "No artifice created by the government, and I consider all these measures artificial, is going to resolve the issue," he said. "Our problem is profits" (quoted in Lessa 1979, p. 139). For some in the industry lack of profitability led to the opposite of strengthening the local bourgeoisie—denationalization. Perhaps most symbolic was the sale of Sanvas S.A., a leading local capital goods producer, to the German firm Linde. David Sanson, head of Sanvas, was a prominent figure among local industrialists and a vice-president of ABDIB (the association of local capital goods producers). As early as 1975 he was suggesting that the BNDE would have to make the terms of its loans to local firms even more concessionary if national capital were to survive. In 1979, when his firm was sold, he attributed its demise to "lack of official assistance in the face of the growing threat of denationalization" (*Gazeta Mercantil* [April 25, 1979], p. 6).

Exacerbating the disillusionment of local firms was their frustration at both the extreme centralization of policy decisions that characterized the Geisel regime and the "segmentation" that led to the appearance of different subunits of the state working at cross-purposes. As one executive put it, "The Geisel government finds itself substantially distanced from the entrepreneurial class. The President has absorbed all the decision-making power . . . you can discuss with everybody, but the decision is closed" (Diniz and Boschi 1977, p. 172). Another complained, "The BNDE has really supported the capital goods industry but other ministries and state organs take contradictory actions . . ." (1977, p. 173). And a third blamed state enterprises for the high import coefficient for capital goods, saying, "The state executive forgets that he too is the government" (1977, p. 181).

The leaders of the capital goods industry became leaders of what Lessa calls "the entrepreneurial rebellion." Beginning with "a growing wave of protests apparently against the role of the state in the Brazilian economy" (Lessa 1979, p. 129; cf. Evans 1979, pp. 268–73), this rebellion eventually moved to open questioning of the political structure of the regime. By 1978, Claudio Bardella was advocating not only a return to a more representative form of government but also the legalization of socialist parties and a free trade union movement (Lessa 1979, p. 131). Eventually he and a number of other local entrepreneurs joined several dissident members of the military in signing a manifesto entitled "In Defense of a Nation under Threat," which accused Geisel's successor of "selling out" Brazil's interests economically, politically, and culturally (*LAWR* [January 16, 1981], p. 7; *Business Latin America* [*BLA*], 1981, p. 13). The state's efforts at "reinventing the local bourgeoisie" not only failed to produce the sought after "re-equilibration of the tripod," but had the unintended consequence of generating serious elite opposition to the regime.[7]

RECONSTRUCTING LOCAL CAPITAL IN THE
PETROCHEMICAL INDUSTRY

Industries like petrochemicals which provided "basic inputs" shared the priority status of the capital goods sector in the economic restructuring proposed by the Geisel regime (II PND, 1974, pp. 38–39). As in capital goods, the state had special leverage in the petrochemical industry. Here, however, the leverage proved less ephemeral. The state did not control the

---

[7] It should be noted that the BNDE, the organization most closely identified with the "reinvention of the bourgeoisie" in capital goods, lost strength relative to other parts of the state apparatus as the drama unfolded in capital goods. It lost its control over the PIS-PASEP funds and suffered severe cuts in its share of the central budget (see *LAWR* [March 6, 1981], p. 7).

market for outputs in petrochemicals, but it did control the raw materials. Petrobrás, the state oil monopoly, controlled the local production, import, and refining of crude oil. If a company needed naphtha or natural gas to produce petrochemicals, it was dependent on Petrobrás. Control over raw materials meant that the state could control entry in a way that it could not in capital goods. Equally important, Petrobrás gave the state a direct entrepreneurial presence in the industry, a presence whose economic strength and ability to generate funds internally was unique among state enterprises.

By the end of the II PND, it was clear that the conjuncture in petrochemicals lent itself to the reinvention of the bourgeoisie in a way that the situation in capital goods had not. Brazil, which had virtually no petrochemical industry at the end of the sixties, had created by the end of the seventies a major, technologically sophisticated industry with substantial ownership participation by local capital. Even more clear was the extent to which "reinventing the bourgeoisie" meant transforming local capitalist structures. The result of the state's success in the petrochemical industry was not a set of individualistic, entrepreneurial capitalists bent on competitive struggle with one another. Instead, a set of corporate entities emerged patterned along cooperatively oligopolistic "managerial capitalist" lines. Not surprisingly, given the role of the state in the process, the industry was characterized by a tight integration of state and local private capital analogous to the French and Japanese patterns rather than the sort of separation of the two kinds of capital that characterizes Anglo-Saxon versions (cf. Katzenstein 1978).

Understanding the process through which the petrochemical industry was created requires an appreciation of the "decentralized" face of the Brazilian state apparatus. The segmented (Abranches 1978) nature of the state and the "relative autonomy" of organizations like Petrobrás and the BNDE vis-à-vis the central state bureaucracy created a space within which a modest network of midcareer technocrats, mostly chemical engineers, were able to construct a set of projects of impressive entrepreneurial boldness. Obviously the sanction of those at the top of the central state apparatus was necessary for such an endeavor to proceed, but entrepreneurship at lower levels was essential to both initiation and implementation of the overall project.

The formulation of plans for the Polo do Nordeste (Northeast Petrochemical Pole) is a good illustration. The first major feasibility study for the Polo was sponsored by local interests in the State of Bahia (Evans 1981a, pp. 95–96). Those who worked on the study included engineers "on loan" from Petrobrás and the BNDE (CLAN 1969, 1:4). Some of them, like Otto Perroni and Paulo Belotti, later became involved in an informal working group, coordinated out of the Ministry of Industry and Commerce, which further elaborated the definition of the pole in 1970 (Candal 1978). Perroni, who is sometimes referred to as the father of the Polo do Nordeste (Evans 1979, p. 327), went on to become president of COPENE (the Petroquisa subsidiary that ran the raw materials center in the Polo) and later executive vice-president of Petroquisa. Belotti ended up as president of Petroquisa and director of Petrobrás. Arthur Candal, another member of the informal working group, varied the pattern by moving from a directorship in COPENE to being director of one of the local capital groups involved in the Polo (Peixoto de Castro). A full description of the network involved in the creation of the Polo do Nordeste would obviously be much more complex than this brief sketch, but its essential character would not change. It would still be a set of individuals, moving through various positions, largely within the entrepreneurial part of the state apparatus but sometimes into the private sector, whose primary commitment is to a particular vision of sector development. It is this sort of network, not the centrally directed initiatives implemented by a monolithic bureaucracy which might seem to be implied by state-sponsored industrialization, that lies behind most of the projects in the petrochemical industry.

There is a second, even more important way in which understanding the decentralized nature of the state apparatus is a prerequisite to understanding the process of development in the petrochemical industry. Petrobrás is not just a part of the state apparatus relatively insulated from central control; it is an enterprise, legally guaranteed "conditions of operations identical to those of the private sector" (see above). Profit-making and protection of its own oligopolistic territory are among its primary goals (cf. Evans 1979, pp. 266–67). Its relationship to other corporations interested in petrochemicals must be seen in part as that of a dominant firm to smaller firms interested in one of its subsidiary markets. At the same time, oligopolistic control always involves political elements, and in the case of Brazilian petrochemicals the political elements were paramount. Petrochemicals were not oil refining. Petrobrás had no legal claim to dominate the industry, especially after the military regime specifically excluded petrochemicals from Petrobrás's monopoly. Within Petrobrás itself, there were some who felt that entry into petrochemicals would "dilute" the organization's effectiveness in dealing with its main task, providing Brazil with oil (cf. Martins 1977). For those within Petrobrás who wanted the company to become involved in petrochemicals, local capital represented two opposing potentialities: on the one hand, it could become a disruptive competitor; on the other hand, it could become a politically valuable ally in struggles against opponents both external and internal.

The complexity of Petrobrás's relation to the project of strengthening local capital is nowhere better illustrated than in its relation to the Soares/Sampaio or UNIPAR group. It was entrepreneurial initiatives of this group that resulted in the creation of the basic and intermediate petrochemical complex in São Paulo (see Evans 1979, pp. 229–33, 266). In one reading of the record, Petrobrás was simply supportive of UNIPAR. Petrobrás provided UNIPAR with the credible partner it needed to convince foreign capital of the viability of its pioneering venture. In taking over control of UNIPAR's naphtha cracker and refinery in 1974, Petrobrás was helping UNIPAR out of a difficult financial situation in a way that enabled UNIPAR to keep a share of the future profits of the complex. This reading is consistent with Petroquisa's subsequent supportive behavior with regard to local capital, both in going to substantial effort to make and preserve space for local groups in the Polo do Nordeste (see Araújo and Dick 1974; Evans 1981a) and in being willing to write new rules for the third pole which were even more favorable to local capital (see Evans 1981a, p. 101).

There is, however, an alternative reading in which Petrobrás's actions can be seen as aimed at eliminating UNIPAR as a potential rival. At the beginning of the period, the UNIPAR group was, after all, one of only four companies with private refineries in Brazil and the only one with a refinery in the key region of São Paulo. By the end of the period it had neither its refinery nor any operational control in basic petrochemicals. According to this reading, Petrobrás is seen as having squeezed out UNIPAR by refusing to support either an expansion of its allowed refining capacity, or a renegotiation of the terms under which Petroquímica União (PQU) purchased its naphtha, or an increase in the prices for which PQU's output could be sold. This latter reading is consistent with UNIPAR's apparent difficulties in gaining a position in the Polo do Nordeste. The group was involved in plans for a joint venture making polypropylene (which eventually ended up in São Paulo), but the local capital slot went instead to a group involved in ranching and construction (*Dirigente Industrial* 1979 [1], p. 10). UNIPAR was also a potential participant in a toluene di-isocyanate (TDI) plant, but was not included in the final construction of the company. Petrobrás/Petroquisa may be innocent of any role in UNIPAR's difficulties, but it does seem that, if they had been committed to strengthening this particular bundle of local capital, its fortunes would have been different.

The ambiguous relation between the state and local capital that is illustrated in the UNIPAR case arises directly from the fact that the state apparatus must act in a way that appears consistent with its general commitment to supporting the local bourgeoisie even though its immediate presence in the sector is as an enterprise. For Petrobrás/Petroquisa the "strong entrepreneurial structures" created when the local bourgeoisie is strengthened are not abstract "local capital"; they are co-participants in an oligopolistic community. As such, they will either be political allies and collaborators or mavericks, threats to the maintenance of a stable, profitable oligopolistic structure. Those in the state apparatus have a strong interest, as co-participants in the community, not just in strengthening local capital but in making sure that the local capital groups which participate will be good members of the community. Cooperative relations are particularly important in an industry, like basic and intermediate petrochemicals, in which there are only a few firms whose fates are closely bound together by the technological and economic character of the industry (see Evans 1981a). The process of strengthening becomes, then, one of selecting certain capital groups rather than others and of fostering the transformation of corporate structures or the structures of the groups themselves to create good community members. This selectivity is likely to occur despite the state's ideological commitment to universalistically sponsoring local capital.

A quick look at a few of the other local participants in petrochemicals should make the selective nature of the strengthening process clearer. For a comparison to the UNIPAR group, the best example is the Grupo Ultra (see Evans 1979, pp. 242–43). Like UNIPAR, Ultra began in petrochemicals with participations that were eventually sold to Petroquisa.[8] Its subsequent expansion, however, is marked by successful collaboration with Petroquisa and suggests strong support from the state apparatus.

Ultra's "tri-pé" (three-way joint venture involving state, TNC, and local capital) in São Paulo, Oxiteno, was the only São Paulo tri-pé allowed to set up a subsidiary in the Polo do Nordeste. A participant in both of the first two poles, Ultra then gained an unprecedented victory by securing a place for itself in the southern pole as well. Including Oxiteno, Ultra was, as of 1979, involved in a total of six projects in the Polo do Nordeste, more than any other local capital group. It is the only group in the Polo to have a project in which neither Petroquisa nor a multinational has equity, an accomplishment made possible by capital from FIBASE; FIBASE has also provided capital for Ultra's engineering subsidiary, Ultratec. In addition, the Ultra group was the beneficiary of a major loan from the BNDE (Ultra, *Annual Report*, 1977).

Another group which appears to have enjoyed unreserved sponsorship is the Mariani group. No local firm has a larger stake in the downstream companies of the Polo do Nordeste than Petroquímica da Bahia, the group's holding company.[9] The Mariani group was chosen as the local partner in the Polo do Nordeste's TDI plant, a project in which UNIPAR had orig-

[8] In the late sixties, Ultra had minority shares in PQU and a major fertilizer company. Petroquisa bought out its PQU holding completely, as well as some of its shares in the fertilizer company, Ultrafertile. In neither case, however, did the shift in ownership represent the kind of strategic blow that UNIPAR's loss of its refinery plus control of PQU represented.

[9] Founded by Clemente Mariani, a prominent lawyer and politician in Bahia, the group's economic base was built around the Banco da Bahia. Its involvement in petrochemicals began in the late sixties when some of its customers expressed an interest in using their regional incentives in petrochemicals. After investigation the bank

inally been interested. It also participates in two other major plants making intermediates for synthetic fibers. The group could not have maintained its position without the support of the state apparatus. When two of its TNC partners decided to pull out of its joint ventures, the group was in no position to buy up their shares (Evans 1981*a*, p. 100). The problem was solved by FIBASE, which essentially doubled the group's equity base through the purchase of nonvoting preferential shares in its holding company in an amount equal to the company's voting shares.

UNIPAR, Ultra, and Mariani are all family-owned groups. Why should the latter two get stronger support than the first? A look at the current executive leadership of the Grupo Ultra offers a starting point for an explanation. Helio Beltrão, who was asked by Peri Igel, scion of the group's founding family,[10] to become the group's president, was Costa y Silva's planning minister and the author of Decreto Lei 200 which guaranteed state-owned enterprises treatment "identical to the private sector" (see above). Beltrão's career is as much that of a public administrator as it is that of a private entrepreneur. Paulo A. G. Cunha, president of Oxiteno and executive vice-president of the group, was recruited by Igel from Petrobrás. His background makes him even better suited to building cooperative relations with executives from the state sector. Trained as an engineer, he combines technocratic expertise with a familiarity with the Petrobrás system and operating experience in the context of a partnership with Petroquisa.

The case of the Mariani group is less clear-cut. Carlos Mariani, who oversees the group's petrochemical operations, does have technocratic training (as an engineer) as well as industrial operating experience (in Magesita). The Mariani family has a long tradition of political sophistication. But perhaps the most important characteristic of the group is its clear commitment to collaboration. Coming into the industry with a much less powerful base than either UNIPAR or Ultra began with, it has staked its future on ventures in which Petroquisa is, at least for the present, the dominant partner operationally.

The leadership of UNIPAR, at least in the early seventies when the Polo do Nordeste was being defined without its participation, presents a very different picture. Paulo Geyer, the dominant figure in the group at that time as well as its controlling owner, had neither technocratic nor industrial background. His experience with bureaucratic organizations was as an

---

decided that it was an area worth going into. Later, the bank itself was sold to one of Brazil's largest banks, Bradesco, giving the group sufficient funds to capitalize Petroquímica da Bahia.

[10] The Ultra group began with the founding of Ultragaz by Ernesto Igel in 1937. Ultragaz became Brazil's largest distributor of bottled gas and remains the mainstay of the family empire (*Exame* [August 3, 1978], pp. 20–26).

owner rather than as an executive or administrator. Essentially an individualist entrepreneur, he was a fine candidate for strengthening if the aim was reinvention of a classical bourgeoisie, but more likely to be a maverick than a quiet collaborator in the oligopolistic community. All of this is, of course, in addition to Geyer's semiantagonistic historical relation to Petrobrás as the owner of one of the exceptions to the state's refining monopoly.

A final case will serve to reinforce the contrast between the kind of bourgeoisie that is constructed through the selective participation of local groups in petrochemicals and the bourgeoisie as traditionally defined. The Votorantim group is Brazil's largest and most successful private industrial group. Antonio Ermírio de Moraes, the current head of the group, is practically a one-man national bourgeoisie. One of the groups' companies, Nitroquímica, is Brazil's principal producer of artificial fibers (rayon) and also produces substantial amounts of traditional chemical products. Votorantim might seem an obvious candidate for participation in petrochemicals. In fact, no candidate was less likely.

When it became clear that the refining industry would be a state monopoly, Antonio Ermírio de Moraes, "not wanting to become a public functionary,"[11] switched from training to be a petroleum engineer to a course in metallurgical engineering. Ermírio de Moraes focused Votorantim's expansion on nonferrous metals (like petrochemicals, a priority basic input according to the II PND) and found little evidence in that area of efforts to strengthen local capital. Refused loans by the BNDE, he embarked on a project to produce zinc "without incentives, without a penny in loans," and went on to produce "more than 85% of Brazil's national output of zinc." Antonio Ermírio de Moraes may be Brazil's best candidate for membership in a classic conquering bourgeoisie, but he is a poor one for participation in the sort of collaborative project that is entailed in the strengthening of local capital in petrochemicals.

This detailed comparison between the local capital that was integrated into the process of state-sponsored industrialization in petrochemicals and local capital that was included only partially or not at all should serve to reinforce a very simple point. State initiatives came not from a central bureaucracy interested only in fostering general goals like those set out in the II PND, but instead from a network of individuals with an intimate interest in the operation of the sector. Because Petrobrás was centrally involved in the sector, the kind of local capital that would be strengthened became as important as strengthening per se. In short, the structure of the state apparatus as it impinged on this sector not only made strengthening the local bourgeoisie possible but also helped to determine what kind of local bourgeoisie would emerge as a result of strengthening.

[11] Quotations from Antonio Ermírio de Moraes are taken from an extensive interview published in the *Estado de São Paulo* (May 29, 1979), pp. 12–13.

THE TRANSFORMATION OF CORPORATE STRUCTURES

Ten years of state-sponsored expansion in petrochemicals has changed more than the relative position of different local capital groups. New organizational structures have also emerged. New structures can be seen at three levels: in the new operating companies that have been set up, in the administrative structure of the holding companies that tie local capital groups together, and in the character of the industry association that ties the sector together.

In the joint-venture operating companies that surround the new petrochemical complexes (the *tri-pés*), the main feature of change has been a gradual increase in the integrity of internal administrative structures. Consequently, the linkage between operating executives and owners has become less immediate. When first created, the *tri-pé* firms represented simply the intersection of their owners' interests, a way station for their operating executives who remained Mitsubishi men, Dupont men, Petroquisa men, and, to a lesser extent, Grupo Ultra or Petroquímica de Bahia men. It followed that the interests of individual shareholders would take precedence when it came to decisions about output, capitalization, or product line. A finance director chosen by the local partner would have to take the local partner's cash-flow problems into account when deciding on capitalization. A marketing manager on loan from the multinational partner would have to consider the position of this subsidiary in the parent's global marketing strategy before recommending production for export.

As the *tri-pés* matured, there has been more concern with establishing operational maneuvering room for their executives, more discussion of the necessity of having executives who are willing to fight with the owners when the owners' interests appear to conflict with the interests of the firm itself. At the same time, there has been the gradual emergence of cadres, trained within the *tri-pés*, who see their careers as primarily determined by the future performance of the *tri-pé* itself.[12] No firm exemplifies this process better than Oxiteno, the model *tri-pé*.

Oxiteno had the advantage of an ownership structure which lent itself to independence from individual shareholders (Evans 1981a, p. 109).[13] It

[12] As the case of Oxiteno implies, the strength of internal administrative autonomy is likely to be inversely related to the degree to which the TNC partner, as opposed to Petroquisa or the local partner, dominates the company operationally.

[13] Oxiteno's ownership is split among five owners (six if the International Finance Corporation's portfolio interest is counted). In addition to Ultra, local groups include Lokab, one of the holding companies of Ralph Rosenberg's formidable petrochemical empire, and the Monteiro Aranha group, a very sophisticated and successful group though not one directly involved in petrochemicals. While Ultra has an "inside track," given Cunha's presidency of Oxiteno, none of these groups is likely to allow Oxiteno to be used simply as a vehicle for the others. Even more important is the fact that the multinational partner, Halcon/Scientific Design, was not itself an operating com-

has also had the advantage of 10 years of successful operating experience. Together, these factors have generated an exceptional corporate esprit de corps, hard to measure except by recounting corporate mythology (see Evans 1981a, p. 110), but quite palpable nonetheless. Executives talk of the "Oxiteno system" as a distinctively efficient way of doing business. Directors are characterized as "professional," by which it is meant that they are not simply the creatures of the shareholders. A typical story involves a manager who, after working a number of years at Oxiteno "on loan" from Petrobrás, decided to resign from Petrobrás and become a full-fledged member of Oxiteno. The point of the story is that he considered Oxiteno a corporation with future prospects and organizational solidity to rival that most solid of all Brazilian organizations, Petrobrás.

Corporate esprit de corps may have nothing to do with Oxiteno's tremendous economic and technical success over the last 10 years (Evans 1981a, p. 109). The fact remains that this hybrid corporate form—linked to the state yet insulated from control by the state apparatus, linked to foreign capital yet without any operational control by the foreign partner, owned in the majority by local capital yet insulated from the particularistic demands of individual owning families—has become a powerful factor in a strategic industry and a model for entrepreneurially oriented technocrats, both inside and outside the state apparatus.

Perhaps more surprising than the corporate evolution of the *tri-pés* is the parallel transformation among state-owned firms. Perhaps the best example is COPENE, formed as a subsidiary of Petroquisa to play the central entrepreneurial role in the formation of the Polo do Nordeste (Evans 1981a, pp. 88–99). In order better to integrate COPENE with its downstream customers, about half the firm's stock was sold to the *tri-pés* that surrounded it. Later, a small amount of stock was sold to the public (including COPENE's management), making it, formally at least, a privately owned company.[14] The "private" nature of the company is reinforced by the fact that the directors elected to its board by the downstream *tri-pés* tend to come from local private capital groups (COPENE, *Annual Report*, 1978).

For COPENE's executives, the firm's not being state owned is important. It signifies being able to operate and expand as a firm rather than being

---

pany at the time Oxiteno was formed. It accepted equity because it wanted to sell its technology, but it never played any operating role in the company. Petroquisa, while an important partner, also seems to be a relatively unobtrusive one in the case of Oxiteno.

[14] The semifictitious quality of COPENE's private status is obvious in a number of respects. First, Petroquisa holds its stock as a block, while other holdings are dispersed. Second, the private owners are themselves owned in part by Petroquisa. Finally, Petroquisa and Petrobrás are the major holders of COPENE's debt. Nonetheless, its privateness is real in comparison to Petrobrás or the BNDE.

a creature, however indirect, of the central bureaucracy. Traditional state-owned public service enterprises, like the railroads, are the model of what COPENE does not want to become. The responsibility to make a profit for private stockholders is a form of protection against the possibility of "political control." For COPENE's management, political control means the possible imposition by the state apparatus of policies incompatible with getting the best return on the firm's capital. It might also mean that returns generated by the firm were appropriated by the state for use elsewhere.

The operating executives of COPENE and Oxiteno have similar organizational goals. What is sought is quite like the "autonomy" granted to operating executives by owners in the ideal typical managerial capitalism of core countries. Failure to deliver an acceptable rate of return curtails both autonomy and careers, but, barring such failure, considerable operational flexibility is allowed (cf. Zeitlin 1974). Owners have ultimate control, but executives are "agents of capital," not simply employees. In the petrochemical case, the heterogeneous nature of the capital involved (state, foreign, and local) increases the degree to which managers have a relation to capital in the abstract rather than to owners. In this sense, these new corporate forms might be considered more "modern" than the variety of managerial capitalism found in the United States.

The more modern, impersonal nature of the reinvented bourgeoisie is less evident in the administration of local capital groups than in the organization of the operating companies. At the group level, personal and familial control are much more the rule. Nonetheless, the trend is in the same direction. The recent evolution of the UNIPAR group provides a case in point. Looking at UNIPAR at the end of the seventies, one would have found Paulo Geyer playing a relatively unobtrusive role, not dissimilar from the role of Peri Igel in the Grupo Ultra. Shares in UNIPAR are publicly traded and have been very active on the stock exchange. A substantial administrative structure has been set up, and a number of more technocratically trained executives, such as Michel Hartveld, head of UNIPAR's development department, play a leading role in defining the group's future. Fueled by the cash flow from its original ventures in São Paulo, the group has been able to diversify. Perhaps most significant, it has finally been brought into a partnership with Petroquisa in the Polo do Nordeste, and current relations with Petroquisa are described by one of its directors as "excellent" (*formidável*). In short, the group looks less like a maverick and more like "reconstructed" local capital.

Changes at the level of the industry association were the last to emerge. In 1979, Paulo A. G. Cunha (of Oxiteno and the Grupo Ultra) and a slate of executives with similar orientation were elected to the leadership of ABIQUIM (the chemical industry association), breaking a long tradition of domination by representatives of multinational subsidiaries. The new leadership vowed to turn ABIQUIM into an instrument for the effective representation of the sector's interests. Their first campaign was aimed at trying to convince the central state apparatus (more precisely, the Price Control Commission) that return on investment should be calculated on replacement cost of assets, not their (inflation-corrected) historical cost.

The interesting thing about this campaign was that the proposed change would have raised the value of assets (and thereby the prices and profits allowed by the commission) most of all for those firms which were installed prior to 1973, which is to say primarily multinational subsidiaries. Why should the new, supposedly nationalist, slate promote such a policy? Quite simply because it was seen as the most likely strategy for increasing returns on capital for the sector as a whole. Whether local or foreign capital would benefit more was secondary to the overall interest of the capital employed in the sector.[15]

The point is nicely reinforced by Paulo A. G. Cunha's reaction to tentative approval by the Economic Development Council of a proposal by Dow Chemical to export vinyl chloride monomer (VCM). In what might have appeared a burst of xenophobia, he threatened to withdraw Oxiteno's commitment to build a plant in the Polosul if approval was not rescinded (*BLA*, 1980, pp. 209–10). Again, the underlying aim was the preservation of the return on capital in the sector. Approval would have allowed Dow to expand substantially its own 100% foreign-owned "northeast pole." Increasing domestic capacity to produce VCM, especially with the domestic market growing less rapidly, was a potential threat to the stability of an important product market. If Dow was unable profitably to place the VCM internationally, there would be strong pressure to throw it onto the domestic market. In an industry where fixed operating costs are high and marginal costs low, the possibility of overproduction threatens the general rate of return in the sector, especially if the "extra" capacity is in the hands of a company like Dow, which is known as a maverick and a loner.

The development of private sectoral political organization in the form of a revitalized ABIQUIM will be an important complement to the organization of sector interests which already existed within the central state apparatus. In his study of the CDI, the major industrial policymaking body within the central state bureaucracy, Abranches concluded that the CDI was primarily "a privileged institutional focus for articulations and negotiations involving several state agencies and entrepreneurial groups" (1978, pp. 256–57). Most relevant for the petrochemical industry is the CDI's Sectoral Group for the Chemical Industry. Abranches notes (1978, p. 263) that the actors involved in this group tend to be technocrats

---

[15] This campaign was eventually made mute by Planning Minister Delfim Neto's decision to remove price controls, but it remains a useful example of the approach of the new ABIQUIM leadership.

trained at the Escola Nacional de Química (National Chemistry College), which has close ties to the state entrepreneurial apparatus. The sectoral coordinator at the time of Abranches's study, for example, was also chair of the office for the implantation of the third petrochemical pole. The previous coordinator had moved on to become a director of Petroquisa.

From the organization of operating companies to the organization of the sector as a whole, there is a consistency to the social organization of capital. Control of capital in the sector is increasingly in the hands of individuals who have a technocratic bent but are at the same time conscious of the extent to which theirs is a politically shaped market in which the return on capital depends on their ability to collaborate with other members of the oligopolistic community and collectively defend its interests, whether against the central regulatory apparatus or against the potentially disruptive actions of mavericks within the industry. This organizational consistency includes state capital as well as private capital. State capital has not become the "private property" of individual owners any more than it was before. Nor is there a dramatic change in the degree to which decisions are dictated by impersonal market forces. What has happened is that state capital, like private capital, has become more thoroughly integrated into the oligopolistic community of firms that controls the sector. For private capital this has meant some insulation from the demands of individual owners; for state capital it has meant a strengthening of the extent to which behavior is insulated from the control of the central bureaucracy.

THE LIMITS OF RECONSTRUCTION

Despite the degree to which the sector has been transformed, there are clear limits to the capacity of the state to "reinvent the bourgeoisie" in petrochemicals just as there were in capital goods. The source of these limits is essentially the same: the state's commitment to the maintenance of an internationalized market. As in capital goods, TNCs must be allowed some space in which to operate. As the chain of petrochemical products moves from basic feedstocks to the diversity of final consumption items based on petrochemicals, entry becomes more difficult to control and problems of excessive competition reemerge. The experience of the petrochemical sector does not, in short, belie the contradictory nature of the project of "reinventing the bourgeoisie"; it only makes clearer the structural boundaries within which such a project may succeed.

A concrete example of the contradictions between maintaining good relations with international capital and strengthening the local bourgeoisie is provided by the recent controversy over who would produce methyl diisocyanate (MDI). Isocianatos, the *tri-pé* controlled by the Mariani group and Petroquisa, put forward a proposal in 1979. BASF (the German chemical giant) was persuaded to join the project and provide the technology. Bayer (BASF's larger German rival) did not like the idea of getting shut out of this market and proposed its own project. It was assumed that Bayer's project, which was wholly owned by Bayer, would be turned down in order to protect the market for the *tri-pé* proposal. Instead, the CDI gave Bayer permission to go ahead, and BASF immediately dropped out of its joint venture with Isocianatos (*LAWR* [June 19, 1981], p. 3; [June 26, 1981], p. 3).

In order for the *tri-pé* firms that have been created in petrochemicals to become "strong entrepreneurial structures," they must in the long run become multiproduct firms. The decision in favor of Bayer was a blow to the development of the Mariani group and therefore to the whole project of sponsoring local capital in petrochemicals. Camilo Penna, minister of trade and commerce, is reputed to have opposed the Bayer proposal on nationalist grounds, while planning minister Delfim Neto, more attentiive to the perceptions of West German bankers, is said to have been behind its approval (*LAWR* [June 26, 1981], p. 3). Thus, we see Abranches's (1978) segmented state in action and another case of the kind of schizophrenic split (Lessa 1979) that was discussed earlier in relation to policies toward local capital in general.

As production moves from basic feedstocks to more specialized downstream products, the increasing leverage of the TNCs can also be seen in the ownership structure of new projects in the northeast pole (planned but not yet under construction as of 1979). Three of seven were wholly owned by TNCs (Evans 1981*a*, p. 105).[16] Despite the success of the state in helping to build an integrated oligopolistic community in basic petrochemicals, local capital still faces the competitive pressures of an internationalized market as it tries to diversify and move downstream. The TNCs are still powerful actors in the industry, and their power constitutes a very tangible limitation on the ability of the state to build strong, locally controlled entrepreneurial structures.

The continuing strength of TNCs in the sector does not, of course, negate the tendency for the emergence of some features of the oligopolistic, managerial-capitalist organization of the market that have already been discussed. It does, however, limit both the degree to which operating companies are likely to develop more autonomous internal administrative structures and the degree to which ABIQUIM can focus the political energies of the sector around a nationalist project. Perhaps most important,

[16] It must also be noted that the other four are wholly owned by local capital, resulting in a substantial shift toward a diminished presence of the *tri-pé*. Nonetheless, insofar as both local private capital and the TNCs are allowed to operate independently, the result is to increase the sphere in which the TNCs can bring their market power to bear.

it impedes the synthesis of state and private capital into a single oligopolistic community. Where the TNCs remain in control, integration of Brazilian operations into an international organization of production will take
precedence over the creation of a locally integrated oligopolistic community.

Another way in which market structures impose limitations on the reinvention of the local bourgeoisie is illustrated by the difficulties that have
arisen in the creation of a "third generation" of locally owned firms around
the two new petrochemical poles. Tremendous effort has been made, both
in Bahia (Polo do Nordeste) and in Rio Grande do Sul (Polosul) to create
a set of manufacturing firms to transform the raw materials produced by
the poles into consumer goods. One local planner involved with this effort
in the southern pole said, in a confidential interview, "Everything the pole
represents depends on the third generation [the transforming companies]."
"Without the third generation," he went on, "we lose from the pole instead of gaining." In Bahia, as well, the transforming companies are seen
as essential if the pole is not to become simply another mode for exporting
raw materials from the northeast to São Paulo. It is the transforming companies that will generate employment, and it is also the transforming companies that will provide the basis for developing entrepreneurs at the regional as opposed to the national level.

To elicit interest from local entrepreneurs, an array of incentives even
more extensive than those available to Brazilian capital in general were
set up. To begin with, the state governments (Bahia and Rio Grande do
Sul) have taken responsibility for the investment in infrastructure necessary to prepare plant sites surrounding the poles. In addition, they have
set up agencies to explain the various incentive programs to potential investors, match up raw materials producers within the poles with appropriate
manufacturers, and generally facilitate the entry of small firms (cf. COPEC
1978; Maisonnave 1978). In the case of Polo do Nordeste, regional incentives are available. A would-be entrepreneur with a project approved by
the appropriate agencies can rely on loans through one or more of the 18
lines of credit available from the state development bank (COPEC 1978,
sec. 8.5) and the possibility of FINOR (an agency involved in regional incentives) participating in the project up to 75% of the total cost of the investment (COPEC 1978, sec. 8.1.1); he can also deduct 42% of any
equity investments from his personal income tax (up to a maximum of 60%
of the amount due) (COPEC 1978, sec. 1.6). One member of the staff of
the agency most involved in trying to promote small undertakings specu-
lated that an entrepreneur who fully utilized all the programs available
could start a project by providing as little as 2% of the capital himself.

Despite the efforts and the incentives, the search for the small regional
entrepreneur has been most frustrating in both poles. In Bahia in 1979
there were four industrial companies in operation in the area designed for

transforming firms. Three of them were engaged in the production of concrete. The one plant using raw materials from the pole was owned by a company based in São Paulo. One economist, after attempting to assist would-be entrepreneurs with a number of projects, commented in a confidential interview that "the small entrepreneur is the hardest person in the world to work with." In the South, where the aim is to attract enough transforming plants to employ 24,000 people directly (Maisonnave 1978, p. 71), a staff member described the job of bringing in entrepreneurs from the local area as "most painful." The agency involved has even considered trying to lure disillusioned small capitalists from Argentina and Italy to fill out the sparse ranks of the local volunteers.

The root of the problem probably lies less in the character of the local upper class than in the nature of the market. Regardless of the incentives and subsidies, what is being offered is an invitation to join a highly competitive branch of industry with low barriers to entry. An entrepreneur trying to mold plastic in the Northeast or the South must confront dozens of firms in São Paulo that can make whatever he can make and probably make it more efficiently. He has no equivalent to the market provided by the automobile industry in São Paulo, nor can he count on his regional market (insofar as one develops) being protected from firms in other regions. Clearly it is easier to speculate on the increase in real estate values created by the influx of affluent managers and skilled workers coming to work in the central plants of the poles.

We are back then to one of the fundamental lessons from the capital goods industry. Without a reliable market structure as a base, the state's efforts to strengthen the national bourgeoisie are likely to be fruitless. When a stable oligopoly is possible, as in basic and intermediate petrochemicals, efforts at reconstructing the local bourgeoisie reinforce the natural tendencies of the market itself, tightening interdependence and integration within it. When TNC entry cannot be effectively regulated, or when the market in question is one which requires a bourgeoisie more in the classic mold— small, individualistic entrepreneurs willing to brave a situation of atomistic competition—"reinventing the bourgeoisie" becomes a quixotic endeavor.

CONCLUSION

A dependent capitalist state, even one unconstrained by representative politics, enjoying exceptional credibility based on prior performance, and endowed with considerable fiscal strength, cannot restructure capital as it chooses, at least not without giving up its loyalty to market forces. While it may seem trivial to point out that members of a bourgeoisie allocate their capital first of all in response to the structure of the market, such an observation goes to the heart of the problems of the Geisel regime.

Capital and incentives from the state are not enough to make the risks of unequal competition attractive, whether the competition is between national capital and the multinationals or involves regional entrepreneurs fearful of national competition. Only when there is a reasonable expectation of a stable oligopoly does the state's invitation to increase capitalization become attractive.

By attempting to "reinvent the bourgeoisie" in circumstances where a stable oligopoly cannot be provided, the state runs the risk of revealing its inadequacy as a patron and thereby losing the loyalty of its clients. When the state failed to provide the local bourgeoisie in the capital goods industry with the means necessary to achieve hegemony over the sector, it contributed to local capital's rediscovery of its affinity for representative government and politics conducted in civil society rather than inside the state apparatus. By failing to "deliver the goods" economically, the state undercut the political basis of its own "relative autonomy."

Within the limits imposed by its commitment to an internationalized market, the Brazilian state has had substantial effects on the structure of the local productive apparatus. The state's efforts have affected both the character of the local industrial bourgeoisie and the character of the state apparatus. If an understanding of the state's difficulties must start from an analysis of market structures, an understanding of the changes it has wrought must begin with a closer look at the state apparatus itself.

The broad outlines of the projected "reinvention of the bourgeoisie" may have come from the pinnacles of the central state bureaucracy, but the implementation of this project clearly depended on the decentralized nature of the state apparatus. The possibility of constructing a stable oligopoly in which space could be created for local capital depended, in petrochemicals, not just on the structure of the market itself, but on the strong entrepreneurial presence of Petrobrás/Petroquisa in the sector.

A network of entrepreneurial technocrats, based largely within Petrobrás/Petroquisa, was the catalyst for the creation of the *tri-pé* ventures which made possible the expansion of local capital's role in petrochemicals. By the same token, Petrobrás/Petroquisa's role as a co-participant in the oligopolistic community that controlled the sector gave it a strong interest in the selective participation of local capital. Good collaborators, not individualistic competitors, are necessary if an oligopolistic community is to run smoothly. In addition, the very combination of capital of diverse origins to form the *tri-pé* joint ventures had consequences for corporate organizational structures, pushing them in a managerial capitalist direction.

Many of the features of the resultant industrial structure are those generally associated with oligopolistic markets. Just as the capital goods case illustrates that the state's efforts to support local capital are likely to fail if they fly in the face of market logic, the petrochemicals case suggests that the state's successes have the effect of reinforcing tendencies toward integration and interdependence that occur generally as capitalist markets mature. Nonetheless, what has emerged is not simply another oligopolistic industry. It is an industry permeated by the presence of the state. Any analysis of the industry's behavior will have to start from the fact that local capital in the sector consists largely of a synthesis of state and private capital. The key to such an analysis is taking the presence of state capital seriously without characterizing what is going on in the sector as "state capitalism."

If "state capitalism" means anything, it must mean that control over the reproduction of capital is vested in a chain of command that leads back to the central bureaucracy of the state. The accumulation process is then directed either toward what is structurally required by the logic of capital or toward whatever will enhance the particularistic interests of the bureaucratic apparatus itself, or toward some compromise between the two, depending on one's interpretation of the "relative autonomy" of the state. The convergence of state and local capital around a common managerial-capitalist model implies a quite different structure of control. Return on capital and its expansion are the aim, but the firm and the sector provide the frame of reference. If the logic of capital or the interests of the central bureaucracy dictated a shift from plastic resins to cellulose-based substitutes, those in control of the conglomerate of state and private capital in petrochemicals would in all likelihood resist, and resist effectively.

Linking state managers to local capital reinforced the "relative autonomy" of the entrepreneurial part of the state apparatus vis-à-vis the central state bureaucracy. Nominally state-owned capital and nominally private capital converged around a single organizational mode, one in which capital is operationally controlled by executives whose primary aim is expanding the capital over which they preside and who see this task as requiring a combination of technical efficiency and collective efforts at the political protection of the sector.

This hybrid sort of oligopolistic community is a powerful one. Being able to invoke "private" political pressure through the newly revitalized industry associations, while at the same time using sectoral networks internal to the state apparatus, gives the petrochemical sector good leverage vis-à-vis the central bureaucracy. At the same time, the insulation of the sector's corporate actors from both bureaucratic controls and the idiosyncratic demands of individual owning groups increase its flexibility at the entrepreneurial level. All of this in combination with concrete connections to international capital (provided by the multinational *tri-pé* partners) puts a rather formidable set of political-economic machinery behind the expansion of capital in the sector.

It is tempting to hypothesize that the synthesis of state and private capital creates an instrument for capital accumulation superior to either kind of capital individually. The sector gains a more general, long-term sense of a common project than would be the case if only private capital were involved but does not experience the loss of flexibility and entrepreneurship that would result if it were under the aegis of a centralized bureaucracy. What must also be recognized, however, is that, insofar as the integration that has occurred is primarily at the sectoral level, it may pose a serious threat to rational planning at a more general level. If, for example, Brazil's long-run development were to require a reorientation away from petroleum-based chemical products, the political and economic strength of the sector could be considered a disadvantage rather than an advantage (see Evans 1981a, pp. 121–22). In this sense the synthesis of state and private capital that has occurred in Brazilian petrochemicals may have disadvantages relative to the less sector-specific kind of integration that is found in the Japanese case. Such speculation, however, goes beyond the legitimate aims of this paper.

The aim of this analysis has not been to pass judgment on the long-run efficacy of the industrial structures that have emerged as a result of the Brazilian state's efforts to "reinvent the bourgeoisie." Its aim has been to show that those trying to understand the local component of dependent development should focus on the concrete forms of oligopolistic community that are created and particularly on the way in which state and private capital are synthesized in different sectors. If the Brazilian case is any test, such a strategy will be far more fruitful than dwelling on the inability of the local bourgeoisie to fulfill its classic role or trying to fit the complex structure of local capital onto the procrustean bed of "state capitalism."

APPENDIX

Glossary of Acronyms and Brazilian Terms

ABDIB:	Industry association for the capital goods industry.
ABIQUIM:	Industry association for the chemical industry.
BNDE:	National Bank for Economic Development.
CDE:	Council for Economic Development, the highest state policymaking body on economic issues.
CDI:	Council for Industrial Development, state policymaking body for industrial issues.
COPEC:	State agency attached to the Northeast Petrochemical Complex and charged with planning and coordination.
COPENE:	Petroquisa subsidiary for the Northeast Petrochemical Complex; owns the basic feedstock plant.

EMBRAMEC:	Mecânica Brasileira S.A., subsidiary of the **BNDE** designed to help local capital goods firms producing machinery.
FIBASE:	Subsidiary of the BNDE charged with assisting **firms** in industries producing basic inputs, for example, petrochemicals and nonferrous metals.
FINAME:	Program under the BNDE to provide financing for the purchase of capital goods.
FINOR:	Program for assisting firms making investments in the Northeast region.
FMRI:	Program for helping local firms to modernize and reorganize.
IBRASA:	Subsidiary of the BNDE designed to assist in the expansion of local firms.
Petrobrás:	State-owned oil monopoly.
Petroquisa:	Wholly owned subsidiary of Petrobrás charged with operating in the petrochemical industry.
PIS-PASEP:	Compulsory retirement funds contributed to by employees and employers.
II PND:	Second National Development Plan, 1974–79.
Polo do Nordeste:	Second petrochemical complex, constructed in the northeast state of Bahia.
Polosul:	Third petrochemical complex, constructed in the southernmost state, Rio Grande do Sul.
tri-pé:	Three-way joint venture in which ownership is divided among state, multinational, and local capital.
Grupo Ultra:	Large locally owned group of chemical companies, founded by the Igel family, heavily involved in petrochemicals; owns Oxiteno.
UNIPAR:	Large locally owned group which pioneered the first petrochemical complex in São Paulo.

REFERENCES

Abranches, Sérgio. 1978. "The Divided Leviathan: State and Economic Policy Formation in Authoritarian Brazil." Ph.D. dissertation, Cornell University.

Araújo, José Tavares, and Vera Dick. 1974. "Governo, emprêsas multinacionais, e emprêsas nacionais: O caso da indústria petroquímica." *Pesquisa e planejamento* 4 (3): 629–54.

Baer, Werner. 1969. *The Development of the Brazilian Steel Industry.* Nashville, Tenn.: Vanderbilt University Press.

———. 1979. *The Brazilian Economy: Its Growth and Development.* Columbus, Ohio: Grid.

Baer, Werner, R. S. Newfarmer, and T. Trebat. 1977. "On State Capitalism in Brazil: Some New Issues and Questions." *Inter-American Economic Affairs* 30 (3): 69–96.

Barnet, Richard, and Ronald Müller. 1974. *Global Reach: The Power of the Multinational Corporations.* New York: Simon & Schuster.

Becker, David G. 1981. "The New Bourgeoisie and the Limits of Dependency: The Social and Political Implications of the Mining Industry in Peru since 1968." Ph.D. dissertation, University of California, Los Angeles.

Bennett, D., and K. Sharpe. 1979. "Agenda Setting and Bargaining Power: The Mexican State versus the Transnational Automobile Corporations." *World Politics* 32: 57–89.

Bergsten, C. Fred, T. Horst, and T. Moran. 1978. *U.S. Multinationals and American Interests.* Washington, D.C.: Brookings Institution.

Boschi, Renato. 1980. *Elites industriais e democracia.* Rio de Janeiro: Edições GRAAL.

Brasil, República Federativa. 1974. *II Plano Nacional de Desenvolvimento (1975–1979).* Rio de Janeiro: IBGE.

Business Latin America: Weekly Report to Managers of Latin American Operations (BLA). New York: Business International.

Canak, William. 1981. "The Peripheral State Debate: Bureaucratic Authoritarianism and State Capitalism." Mimeographed.

Candal, Arthur. 1978. "Problemas e perspectivas de comercio exterior para o setor de petroquímica." Paper presented at the Fundação Centro de Estudos do Comercio Exterior, Rio de Janeiro, October 12, 1978.

Cardoso, Fernando. 1964. *Empresário industrial e desenvolvimento econômico no Brasil.* São Paulo: Difusão Europeia do Livro.

———. 1971. *Política e desenvolvimento em sociedades dependentes.* Rio de Janeiro: Editora Zahar.

———. 1975. *Authoritarianismo e democratização.* Rio de Janeiro: Paz & Terra.

Cardoso, Fernando, and Enzo Faletto. 1970. *Dependência e desenvolvimento na America Latina: Ensaio de interpretação sociológica.* Rio de Janeiro: Editora Zahar. (*Dependency and Development in Latin America,* translated by Marjory M. Urquidi. Berkeley and Los Angeles: University of California Press, 1979.)

CLAN, S. A. 1969. *Desenvolvimento da indústria petroquímica no estado da Bahia.* Bahia: Conselho de Desenvolvimento do Recôncavo.

Cohn, Gabriel. 1968. *Petróleo e nacionalismo.* São Paulo: Difusão Europeia do Livro.

COPEC. 1978. *Guia empresarial.* Camaçari, Bahia: COPEC.

Diniz (Cerqueira), Eli, and Renato Boschi. 1977. "Elite industrial e estado: Uma análise da ideologia do empresariado nacional no anos 70." Pp. 167–88 in *Estado e capitalismo no Brasil,* edited by Carlos Estevan Martins. São Paulo: Editora Hucitec-CEBRAP.

———. 1978. *Empresariado nacional e estado no Brasil.* Rio de Janeiro: Editora Forense Universitária.

Dreifuss, Rene. 1981. *1964: A conquista do estado: Ação política poder e golpe de classe.* São Paulo: Editora Vozes.

Dupuy, A., and B. Truchil. 1979. "Problems in the Theory of State Capitalism." *Theory and Society* 8:1–38.

Economic Commission for Latin America (ECLA). 1980. *Economic Survey of Latin America, 1978.* New York: United Nations.

———. 1981. *Economic Survey of Latin America, 1979.* New York: United Nations.

Evans, P. B. 1977. "Multinationals, State-owned Corporations, and the Transformation of Imperialism: A Brazilian Case Study." *Economic Development and Cultural Change* 26 (1): 43–65.

———. 1979. *Dependent Development: The Alliance of Multinational, State and Local Capital in Brazil.* Princeton, N.J.: Princeton University Press.

———. 1981a. "Collectivized Capitalism: Integrated Petrochemical Complexes and Capital Accumulation in Brazil." Pp. 85–125 in *Authoritarian Capitalism: The Contemporary Economic and Political Development of Brazil,* edited by T. C. Bruneau and P. Faucher. Boulder, Colo.: Westview.

———. 1981b. "Recent Research on Multinational Corporations." *Annual Review of Sociology* 7:199–223.

Evans

Fausto, Boris. 1970. *A revolução de 1930.* Rio de Janeiro: Editora Zahar.
Fernandes, Florestan. 1975. *A revolução burguesa no Brasil.* Rio de Janeiro: Editora Zahar.
Fiechter, Georges-Andre. 1975. *Brazil since 1964: Modernization under a Military Regime.* New York: Wiley.
Fitzgerald, E. V. K. 1976. *The State and Economic Development: Peru since 1968.* Cambridge: Cambridge University Press.
———. 1977. "On State Accumulation in Latin America." Pp. 65–90 in *The State and Economic Development in Latin America,* edited by E. V. K. Fitzgerald, E. Floto, and A. D. Lehmann. Occasional Paper no. 1. Cambridge: University of Cambridge, Center of Latin American Studies.
———. 1981. "The New International Division of Labour and the Relative Autonomy of the State: Notes for a Reappraisal of Classical Dependency." Paper presented at *Millenium* Conference on Political Development in Latin America, London School of Economics, April 30, 1981.
Gereffi, Gary. 1978. "Drug Firms and Dependency in Mexico: The Case of the Steroid Hormone Industry." *International Organization* 32:237–86.
Gereffi, Gary, and Peter Evans. 1981. "Transnational Corporations, Dependent Development and State Policy in the Semi-Periphery: A Comparison of Brazil and Mexico." *Latin American Research Review* 16 (3): 31–64.
Katzenstein, Peter, ed. 1978. *Between Power and Plenty: The Foreign Economic Policy of Advanced Industrial States.* Madison: University of Wisconsin Press.
Knight, Peter T. 1981. "Brazilian Socioeconomic Development: Issues for the Eighties." *World Development,* in press.
Latin America Weekly Report (LAWR). London.
Lessa, Carlos. 1979. *A estratégia de desenvolvimento, 1974–1976: Sonho e fracasso.* Rio de Janeiro: Reproarte.
McDonough, Peter. 1981. *Power and Ideology in Brazil.* Princeton, N.J.: Princeton University Press.
Maisonnave, Banco. 1978. *Perfil: Polo petroquimico do Rio Grande do Sul.* Porto Alegre: Editora Intermedio.
Malan, Pedro, and Regis Bonelli. 1977. "The Brazilian Economy in the Seventies: Old and New Developments." *World Development* 5 (1/2): 19–45.
Malloy, J. 1979. *The Politics of Social Security in Brazil.* Pittsburgh: University of Pittsburgh Press.
Martins, Luciano. 1968. *Industrialização, burguesia nacional e desenvolvimento.* Rio de Janeiro: Editora Saga.
———. 1976. *Pouvoir et developpement economique: Formation et evolution des structures politiques au Bresil.* Paris: Editions Anthropos.
———. 1977. "A expansão recente do estado no Brasil: Seus problemas e seus atores." Mimeographed.
Marx, Karl, and Fredrich Engels. 1969. *The Communist Manifesto.* Chicago: Regnery.
Moran, T. 1974. *Multinational Corporations and the Politics of Dependence: Copper in Chile.* Princeton, N.J.: Princeton University Press.
Newfarmer, R. S. 1980. *Transnational Conglomerates and the Economics of Dependent Development.* Greenwich, Conn.: JAI.
Newfarmer, R. S., and W. Mueller. 1975. *Multinational Corporations in Brazil and Mexico: Structured Sources of Economic and Non-economic Power.* Prepared for the Subcommittee on Multinationals, Committee of Foreign Relations, U.S. Senate. Washington, D.C.: Government Printing Office.
O'Donnell, Guillermo. 1978. "Reflections on the Patterns of Change in the Bureaucratic-authoritarian State." *Latin American Research Review* 13 (1): 3–38.
———. 1979. "Tensions in the Bureaucratic-authoritarian State and the Question of Democracy." Pp. 285–318 in *The New Authoritarianism in Latin America,* edited by D. Collier. Princeton, N.J.: Princeton University Press.
Petras, J., M. Morley, and S. Smith. 1977. *The Nationalization of Venezuelan Oil.* New York: Praeger.

Rowland, R. 1974. "Classe operária e estado de compromisso." *Estudos cebrap* 8:1–40.
Serra, José. 1979. "Three Mistaken Theses Regarding the Connection between Industrialization and Authoritarian Regimes." Pp. 99–163 in *The New Authoritarianism in Latin America*, edited by D. Collier. Princeton, N.J.: Princeton University Press.
Singer, Paulo. 1975. "O Brazil no contexto do capitalismo mundial, 1889–1930." Pp. 345–90 in *Brazil republicano: Estructura de poder e economia*, edited by Boris Fausto. Historia Geral do Civilização Brasileira, tomo 3, vol. L. São Paulo: Difusão Europeia do Livro.
Skidmore, Thomas. 1967. *Politics in Brazil, 1930–1964: An Experiment in Democracy.* New York: Oxford University Press.
Stepan, Alfred. 1971. *The Military in Politics: Changing Patterns in Brazil.* Princeton, N.J.: Princeton University Press.
Suzigan, W. 1976. "As emprêsas do governo e o papel do estado na economia brasileira." Pp. 77–134 in *Aspectos da participação do governo na economia*, edited by F. Rezende et al. Rio de Janeiro: IPEA.
Tendler, J. 1968. *Electric Power in Brazil: Entrepreneurship in the Public Sector.* Cambridge, Mass.: Harvard University Press.
Tugwell, F. 1975. *The Politics of Oil in Venezuela.* Stanford, Calif.: Stanford University Press.
Wallerstein, Michael. 1980. "The Collapse of Democracy in Brazil: Its Economic Determinants." *Latin American Research Review* 15 (3): 3–40.
Wells, John. 1977. "State Expenditures and the Brazilian Economic 'Miracle.' " Pp. 315–34 in *The State and Economic Development in Latin America*, edited by E. V. K. Fitzgerald, E. Floto, and A. D. Lehmann. Occasional Paper no. 1. Cambridge: University of Cambridge, Center of Latin American Studies.
Wirth, John. 1970. *The Politics of Brazilian Development.* Stanford, Calif.: Stanford University Press.
Zeitlin, M. 1974. "Corporate Ownership and Control: The Large Corporation and the Capitalist Class." *American Journal of Sociology* 79 (5): 1073–1119.

ADDITIONAL REFERENCES

Baer, Werner, I. Kerstenetsky, and A. Villela. 1973. "The Changing Role of the State in the Brazilian Economy." *World Development* 1 (11): 23–44.
O'Donnell, Guillermo. 1973. *Modernization and Bureaucratic-Authoritarianism: Studies in South American Politics.* Berkeley: Institute of International Studies, University of California, Berkeley.
Sercovich, F. 1980. "State-owned Enterprises and Dynamic Comparative Advantages in the World Petrochemical Industry: The Case of Commodity Olefins in Brazil." Development Discussion Paper no. 96. Cambridge, Mass.: Harvard Institute for International Development.

The Political Economy of Food: The Rise and Fall of the Postwar International Food Order[1]

Harriet Friedmann
University of Toronto

The widespread perception of a "food crisis" since the early 1970s reflects a real turning point in the global structure of production and distribution of food grains. Scarcity is always an aspect of capitalist relations, but its specific form is determined historically through the international food order. The latter is a stable set of complementary state policies whose implicit coordination creates specific prices relative to other prices, a specific pattern of specialization, and resulting patterns of consumption and trade. The social consequences of those orderly international arrangements make sense within a Marxist conception of accumulation and class formation on a world scale. I present a historical analysis of the rise of an international food order after World War II whose principal axis was food aid from the United States to formerly self-sufficient agrarian societies. This order had contradictory effects, both economic and political, leading to a reorganization of aid and trade, higher prices, and a possible shift of grain specialization within the international division of labor. The postwar international food order left specific legacies for classes and nations. For example, the low prices of the postwar order contributed to both agricultural underdevelopment and urban concentrations of dispossessed people in the Third World in the 1950s and 1960s as a particular form of capitalist penetration. The elements left by the decomposition of the postwar order, however, are much broader and allow for alternative paths to the construction of a new international food order.

1. IS THERE A FOOD CRISIS, AND FOR WHOM?

Since the early 1970s a perception of scarcity has been the refrain of most commentaries on the food situation. Grain prices soared and world reserves plummeted in 1973 and 1974, ushering in a new period of instability and the recurrent possibility of shortages (Hopkins and Puchala 1980, pp. 4–9). In the major grain-exporting countries, food price inflation in the 1970s for the first time equaled or outpaced the consumer price index (Organization

[1] I am grateful to Fred Block for extensive critical suggestions for revision of an earlier draft. I also benefited from (but sometimes rejected) specific suggestions by Nancy Howell, Michael McMahon, Göran Therborn, Barry Wellman, and Irving Zeitlin. I also owe much to general discussions with Susan George, Geoffrey Kay, and Rianne Mahon. Requests for reprints should be sent to Harriet Friedmann, Department of Sociology, University of Toronto, 563 Spadina Avenue, Toronto, Ontario M5S 1A1, Canada.

for Economic Cooperation and Development [OECD] 1980, p. 90). Agrarian countries, formerly self-sufficient in food, had come increasingly to depend on grain imports during the 1950s and 1960s, and the leap in prices of the 1970s added pressure to their balances of payments and domestic programs (Janvry 1980). In the Soviet Union and some Eastern European countries, political pressures to increase meat consumption required imports of grain (Morgan 1979, pp. 139–40), despite—at least for the Soviet Union—a "respectable" rate of growth in domestic production (Paarlberg 1978, p. 670).

Although the scarcity of food appears to be new, it is not. It is true that the preceding decades were characterized by chronic surplus stocks of grain in the United States, by low world prices (except in Europe behind its high protective trade barriers), and by imports of subsidized food into underdeveloped countries. Yet even in that period, millions were starving in various parts of the world. Not only in the underdeveloped world, but also for the "third world within America" (Weatherby 1980, p. 9), hunger and malnutrition were present (Citizens Board of Inquiry into Hunger and Malnutrition in the United States 1968). Scarcity has taken a new form, affecting different groups of people with different intensities. It may well have increased absolutely, to judge by the higher prices of grain relative to other commodities, but it was not invented in 1973.

If there was a crisis, then, it was not the sudden scarcity of world food supplies but a structural turning point, a reorganization of production and distribution of grains in the world economy. Specifically, as I shall argue at length, a stable set of international arrangements was constructed during the 1950s, which I shall call the international food order of the postwar era. For two decades it operated in ways that maintained grain surpluses, especially American grain surpluses, well above effective world demand. At the same time, however, the order produced specific effects in each of the major export countries and in many of the new import countries in the underdeveloped world, some of which were inconsistent with the initial arrangements. As a result, the order became increasingly unstable, and with it the existence of world surpluses in excess of effective demand.

The international food order collapsed when a variety of events occurred to concentrate the impending disappearance of grain surpluses into a brief period. Some events were natural, such as the failure of the Peruvian anchovy harvest, an important source of protein in the area. But of greater long-term significance were events which signaled the end of the old order. The most dramatic of these was the Soviet-American grain deal of 1973, a main feature of détente (Destler 1978; Dittmer 1977). This represented a break from the trade isolation between East and West which had been part of the international food order. The other elements of the order broke down, too, though less conspicuously. This was not a temporary failure of the order, even though neither Soviet-American trade nor anything else at the moment shows much promise of providing the stable basis for a new order.[2] It was the dramatic end of a period in which international grain policies were shaped by the weight of chronically accumulating surpluses, particularly in the United States (McLin 1979). Stability and mountains of grain disappeared together.

The crisis of the early 1970s, continuing into the present, was the collapse of the set of orderly international arrangements which had maintained grain surpluses and depressed prices. Yet most talk of crisis suggests absolute scarcity. The perception of a new period of scarcity rests on real change in the scope of the circulation of food as a commodity. The international food order encouraged a massive increase in the numbers of people in all countries separated from direct ties to agriculture. This change is what makes an increase in grain prices also an increase in scarcity—not in what can technically be produced,[3] but in what people with constant or declining real monetary incomes can buy. Furthermore, the concentration of so many of these people in underdeveloped countries, where manufacturing employment is so scarce and where the balance of payments is so tenuous, creates problems for nations as well as for classes.

For people separated from the land, an increase in the price of food threatens a crisis in a different sense, a crisis of subsistence. For national economies in the particular bind of dependence on food imports without compensatory manufactured exports—that is, for most countries of the underdeveloped world—the increase in the price of food contributes to still another crisis, that of the balance of payments. After two decades of taking for granted plentiful supplies of cheap—indeed, subsidized—food, governments and international agencies are at last attending to agricultural production. Turns toward simple solutions, such as national self-sufficiency,[4]

---

[2] At its peak, Soviet-American trade was the largest single international grain transaction.

[3] Scarcity of food is socially organized (see Johnson 1975, pp. 1–12). Its sudden appearance takes the form of a bigger gap for more people between income and food prices. Certainly the limits to food supply are not simply technical. Less than half the available fertile land of the world is being used for any type of food production (U.S. Congress 1975; Cochrane 1974; United Nations 1974; Johnson 1973), and cereal yields from lands being cultivated in most of the world, including some major export countries, are less than half those in the United States and Europe (U.S. Congress 1975). For the near future, at least, the supply of grain from current sources will meet demand. In the longer run, the vast virgin lands of South America and Africa await colonization, and the low yields in historic agricultural regions await the application of scientific methods. To be sure, the longer run may also present dangers. The U.S. Department of Agriculture (USDA) has recently attended to the possible ecological dangers of modern farming methods (Crittendon 1980a). Similar problems of monocropping and chemical fertilizers seem inherent in Green Revolution technologies.

[4] For autarky as the implicit solution to world hunger, see Lappé and Collins (1979) and George (1976). Similar understandings are implicit in the economic press: e.g., in a recent article on the Philippines, the *Economist* (October 13, 1979) counterposes statistics on the desperate state of malnutrition with those on the amount of land used by agri-

alternate with a debilitating sense of the complexity, even the intractability, of the problems. To understand the international food order of the postwar era, and the pieces left by its dissolution, is to begin to understand the food crisis and its possible resolution.

In what follows I offer an account of the rise and fall of the international food order between the early 1950s and the early 1970s. The principal features of that order were (1) surpluses of grain, sustained primarily for domestic political reasons by the American government; (2) American policies, particularly food aid, designed to dispose of these surpluses abroad, necessarily in quantities above effective demand and within the constraints of European protection and restriction of trade to the "free world"; (3) the consequent increase of the historically large American share of world grain exports; (4) a consequent downward pressure on world prices and, therefore, on grain production in other export and import countries; (5) the opening of new grain markets, notably in the underdeveloped world; (6) "cheap food" policies of many Third World governments, encouraging the growth of urban populations dependent on food as a commodity; and (7) the resulting contribution to one condition for the penetration of international capital into previously self-sufficient agrarian societies.

Before the historical analysis can be presented, a conceptual framework is necessary. This is the subject of the next section.

2. CONCEPTUAL OUTLINE: STATES, CLASSES, AND THE INTERNATIONAL FOOD ORDER

The international food order developed as part of the larger economic and political arrangements of the postwar period. The immediate pressure on American food policy came from the costs of maintaining mounting grain surpluses arising from domestic farm-subsidy programs. In the formative years of the postwar order, however, grain surpluses came to be not simply an economic burden but also a resource in international relations. Specific policies to find customers for American grain in an impoverished world became entwined with attempts to solve complex political and military problems abroad. From the Marshall Plan through the Vietnam War, objectives came to shift, blur, and conflict, as American largesse was dispensed with a discriminating eye for building international alliances. Even the strictly economic pressures to solve the grain surplus problem at home quickly came to be interpreted within the language of the Cold War. American food aid, as Emma Rothschild writes, went "to an idiosyncratic ideal, of remaking the world in the image of wheat-eating and Americanism: an ideal

---

businesses to produce sugar, coconuts, bananas, rubber, pineapples, coffee, and cocoa for export. It also points out, however, that the Philippines exported 48,000 tons of rice that year and 90,000 tons the next; food is produced in the Philippines, but Filipinos cannot afford to buy it.

of feeding the hungry and selling wheat" (1976, p. 304). American farmers were simultaneously encouraged to restrict production at home and presented abroad as models of independence and initiative.[5] American food aid dispensed judiciously to Poland and Yugoslavia was intended both to corrode economic ties within the Soviet bloc and to underscore the relative success of capitalist agriculture.

The period between the late 1940s and the early 1970s was characterized by several overlapping sets of orderly international arrangements. The linchpin of the general postwar stability was the international monetary order centered on the dollar. This monetary order was intimately bound up with the U.S.-centered project to establish an open world economy for the free movement of commodities and capital. Cold War alignments, particularly trade barriers between East and West, defined the boundaries of the open order as the free world (Block 1977, esp. p. 10). The penetration of self-sufficient agricultural societies by commodity relations was part of the project to incorporate them within the open world economy. Nationalist movements threatening to restrict trade and capital movements thus seemed as dangerous to the free world as Soviet political influence. The American government often confused the two in rhetoric, economic policy, and military intervention.[6]

Orderly international arrangements are difficult to achieve in a world economy with many states. The existence of sovereign, though unequal, states, each subject to domestic and foreign pressures on economic policy, means that international order must depend on complementary national policies. The international order may be explicit, as in the Bretton Woods monetary arrangements (Block 1977; Keohane and Nye 1977, pp. 61–162), or implicit, as in the de facto unilateral importance of American policy in the international food order (McLin 1979, p. 38; Hopkins and Puchala 1978). Neither complementarity nor formal agreement implies equal weight or equal advantages for the nations involved, nor indeed that all of them benefit. And within each nation, policies which form part of an international order benefit classes and economic sectors differentially. As Gourevitch

---

[5] The glorification of the family farm, quite without evidence or analysis, as the "backbone of democracy," took its most dramatic form at the height of the Cold War. The U.S. Secretary of Agriculture wrote in 1951, "The love of freedom is deeply rooted in the family farm community. . . . This love of freedom is the real backbone of democracy. . . . [There is] a world reason . . . why the family farm system . . . is a vital force in American democracy. . . . The ideas—democracy and communism—are pitted against each other in a vast world struggle. . . . Farm families have moral values to offer that are of great importance to American democracy" (USDA 1951, pp. ii–iv).

[6] The rhetorical response to Cuban trade policies between 1959 and 1961, followed by cancellation of sugar imports, contributed to the feared condition of Cuban dependence on the Soviet Union. Another economic response to national economic policies—socialist but not involving Soviet influence—was the successful attempt to undermine the Chilean economy under Allende. And, of course, there was no Soviet presence in cases of U.S. military intervention such as Guatemala in 1954 and the Dominican Republic in 1965.

argues, "The international system is not only a consequence of domestic politics and structures but a cause of them" (1978, p. 911; see also Friedmann 1980, p. 249).

The analysis of both international order and international disorder, then, requires examination of three mutually dependent but analytically distinct factors: (1) state-to-state, or international, relations; (2) transnational economic processes, such as commodity circulation and capital movements; and (3) changing class and sectoral structures within nations.

The importance of state-to-state relations in the genesis and operation of international economic orders suggests the need for major modifications of economic theories. It is odd that neoclassical economics should for the past century have considered the distribution of economic power irrelevant. That it should have done so in the field of international economics is astonishing (Strange 1975). While international trade theory assumes free trade and perfect competition among large, developed economies in its analysis of comparative advantage, these conditions are even approximated only as a special case (Krasner 1976, p. 319). Most economists characterize all other cases negatively as "deviations," often abandoning explanation and blaming policymakers for their manifest irrationality or irresponsibility (Strange 1975, pp. 214–15; Krasner 1976, p. 319).[7] Such reasoning is backward and needs correction through a model in which power is intrinsic.

At the same time, analyses of state-to-state relations have all too often reduced transnational economic processes to a simple derivative of international power. For the world-system approach (Wallerstein 1974, 1979, 1980), and indeed for most of the dependency school, a hierarchy of nations emerged with and has reinforced the international division of labor since the 16th century (Gourevitch 1978, pp. 888–91). Their account is the mirror image of the comparative advantage account. They contend that market relations accentuate differences of power—and therefore of wealth—among countries because strong states "interfere" to produce "unequal exchange" (Wallerstein 1979, pp. 274–75). This formation emphasizes international power but leaves little space for explicit analysis of the mechanisms of price formation governing specialization, trade, and specific productive relations. In contrast to Emmanuel's model of unequal exchange, in which states play no role, Wallerstein's model of state interventions does not lend itself to analysis of relative prices. The world market retains little autonomous existence (Friedmann 1980, p. 248).[8]

[7] In her excellent essay, Strange (1975) gives proper due to the exceptions among neoclassical economists—Galbraith, Kindleberger, Kaldor, Phelps-Brown, and Perroux—and recognizes the potential importance of Marxist theory in addressing economic power.
[8] Arghiri Emmanuel (1972) produced the purely economic concept of "unequal exchange" among countries without reference to either states or power. By appropriating the term uncritically, the dependency school deprives it of its content. In fact, Wallerstein in particular cites Emmanuel to support conclusions derived from opposite premises (see Friedmann 1980).

Analysts of the world economy have had difficulty proposing consistent interpretations of state-to-state relations and transnational economic processes. A promising way out of the impasse is to focus on one commodity or sector of the world economy. Whatever the complex mechanisms of determination—economic and political, national and international—prices are the immediate signals guiding and constraining states, enterprises, and individuals. Deeper processes determine the international division of labor and international class formation. Yet these processes, no matter how complex the mediations, must work through prices—ultimately, through changes in relative prices.

Analysis may be simplified in a more useful way than usual if we can understand the price of one commodity in relation to the international specialization, trade, and productive relations of that same commodity, including class politics affecting its production and consumption in various countries (Friedmann, in press).[9] The international food order is an appropriate case for developing this strategy of analysis to the extent that it operates through an identifiable price. Fortunately for this analysis, wheat has been the overwhelmingly important staple food in world commerce throughout modern history (Ashley 1921; Fairlie 1969). Within the postwar food order, it has progressively replaced rice and corn in Asia and Latin America as food grains have become commodities (see Rothschild 1976, p. 304).[10] This must not be assumed to be a simple economic phenomenon, since it includes power and culture, yet it reinforces the case for using wheat to analyze the international food order. Moreover, wheat prices interacted with feed grain and other food grain prices. Yet the centrality of wheat in both aid and trade allows for relative simplicity of analysis of prices within the international food order.

The international food order reflects international power through the

[9] This approach is parallel to the "issue areas" within the study of "international economic regimes" but seeks to avoid its typically normative emphasis. The political science literature on international regimes is ambiguous about the relation between international power and international economics. Its virtue is that it proposes concepts for analysis of issue areas rather than constructing a formal model of the global "system" based primarily on international power, as does Wallerstein. Keohane and Nye (1977) provide a clear statement of the approach. Its commendable modesty, however, leaves the area without much coherence. There is no theory systematically appropriating economic concepts. Research on a single issue area, such as the international food regime, indicates the conceptual gap between economics and political science (see the special issue of *International Organization* [Summer 1978] devoted to the topic and the critique by Bergeson [1980]). Since the definition of the regime relies heavily on normative agreement (Hopkins and Puchala 1978), those studies emphasizing production and distribution (e.g., Christenson 1978) are not easily incorporated within the analysis of actual regime changes.

[10] Most grain, of course, is not traded internationally at all. The proportion has been increasing rapidly since World War II: from 6%–7% of world production in the 1950s to 8%–10% in the 1960s. After reaching a peak of 12% in 1972–74, it fell back somewhat (Nau 1978, p. 780). With the breakdown of the food order, other food grains, especially rice, have become more important. In this case, U.S. dominance was still greater in the small world trade but was recently surpassed by Thailand as an exporter.

complementary national policies that constitute it. In this case, the arrangements were implicit: within the context of European protection and Cold War trade restrictions, the main complementary policies were American food aid and the cheap food policies (to promote industrialization) of many underdeveloped states which led them to welcome this aid. The order which emerged from these policies was centered on aid as a key mechanism for trade and had price effects with consequences throughout the international food order.

This formulation specifies structural equivalence of states within the international food order (White, Boorman, and Breiger 1976) according to the totality of relations of each state with other states.[11] Positions within the order derive from patterns of wheat movement: exports and imports through trade and aid. Structural equivalence implies equivalent national policies. However, some national policies are more important than others in producing and sustaining the international order. The weight of the United States within the international food order requires special attention to its domestic structures and politics.

But what are the economic bases and the consequences of these arrangements? I use a particular version of Marxism to situate the rise and fall of the international food order within a theoretical project to understand the recent history (and possible future directions) of accumulation on a world scale. The main concept is class formation, with origins in the world economy, but a location and political expression within national economies (see Palloix 1973; Michalet 1976). In particular, the significance of the international food order lies in its contribution to the widening and deepening of capitalist relations within the world economy, by shifting vastly more of the world's population away from direct access to food and incorporating it instead into food markets.

Food has a special conceptual status within political economy. The commodification of food is a crucial aspect of proletarianization: the extension of markets in food grains to populations formerly engaged in subsistence and barter relations.[12] The construction of the international food order of the postwar era, therefore, occupied a specific place within the dynamics of global accumulation. Extension of capitalist relations to the former colonies was part of the general American strategy of constructing the free world as an arena for the open flow of goods and capital. The extension of commodity relations to the food supply became an intrinsic part of the project

[11] Wallerstein's formulation of structural equivalence in the world system (1974, 1979, 1980) seems premature and has generated considerable confusion in assigning nations to the core, periphery, and semiperiphery. At the lower level of abstraction of a single international economic order, the relations defining national positions are more limited and precise.

[12] This is true of all means of subsistence insofar as they exist in precommodity economies; e.g., see Meier's (1981) excellent study of the transformation of cloth production in rural Ecuador.

of capitalist industrialization and shaped its course (see Fröbel, Heinrichs, and Kreye 1980; Wood 1980).

At the same time, commodification of food involves specialization of agriculture and competition among producers. It has been a peculiarity of grain production for more than a century that the successful commercial enterprises are family farms (Friedmann 1978). In those countries specializing in wheat production within the world economy, therefore, there develop large classes of simple commodity producers, using primarily family labor to produce grain for the world market. These producers enter into national politics, just as do capitalists and proletarians. So, for that matter, do grain producers within subsistence economies who face the competitive onslaught of imports (Bernstein 1979).

At this point it is possible to introduce the third crucial factor in the analysis of international orders, the changing class and sectoral structures within nations. The internal structures of nations initially contribute to the policies constituting an international economic order. The order then operates in ways which produce differential effects both within nations and among them. The operation of the international order, therefore, may change the relations, both domestic and international, that originally produced it. If it creates new relations inconsistent with the original policies, one should expect to see struggles to change both national policies and international arrangements. The fall of an international economic order, then, is the result of internal contradictions (cf. Strange 1975, p. 218) which operate principally through the interaction between national orders and the irreducible international order. This occurred for the postwar food order.

This section has presented an analytical summary of the rise and fall of the postwar international food order. In what follows I add flesh and, if all goes well, also life to the skeleton. Section 3 shows the elements for the construction of the postwar food order left by the collapse of the prewar order, especially the domestic- and foreign-policy possibilities of the United States. Section 4 interprets the state-to-state relations and global economic dynamics of the postwar food order. Section 5 focuses on the contradictory consequences of the order, both for relative power among states and for domestic politics within nations. Section 6 identifies the specific elements produced by the breakdown of the order and the possibilities for construction of a new international food order. Finally, Section 7 draws theoretical conclusions in terms of global class formation and the international division of labor.

3. THE LEGACY OF THE PREWAR FOOD ORDER

An aspect of the crisis of the 1930s was a decomposition of the international food order which had begun to emerge around 1870. Since the late 19th century, trade had been relatively free[13] and conducted through the gold standard. Competition within the boundaries of the international food order promoted the realization of comparative advantage in both relations of production (family farms) and the international division of labor (Friedmann 1978). Falling prices reflected greater efficiency on more fertile soil.

While wheat production was maintained in Europe as a whole, imports almost sextupled between 1870 and 1929 (Friedmann 1976, p. 94). This growing demand resulted in the specialization of wheat production in the United States, Canada, Australia, and Argentina, whose aggregate wheat production almost tripled while population doubled (Malenbaum 1953, pp. 238–43). The prewar international food order was increasingly restricted to these major trading countries. Formerly important export countries, such as Russia, Austria-Hungary, Rumania, and India, became increasingly marginal (Olson 1974; Friedmann 1976).[14] The European colonies in Asia and Africa, as well as most of Latin America, remained largely self-sufficient in food grains.

This trade had important consequences for class composition and politics. In Europe, it facilitated the development of the working classes by lowering the cost of basic foods. In the wheat-exporting countries, it contributed to the development of large and politically significant classes of independent commodity producers concentrated in agriculture. And in both the major import countries and the declining export countries, falling grain prices entered into agrarian politics (Gerschenkron 1943; Walter 1963; Tracy 1964).

The prewar international food order, along with the gold standard and free trade, collapsed during the 1930s and World War II. National policy responses created three crucial conditions for postwar reconstruction: the political importance of export-dependent farmers, especially in the United States; the revitalization of European agriculture and agrarian classes; and the shift in international power, creating new possibilities for U.S. relations with Africa, Asia, and Latin America.

Family farmers in the wheat-exporting countries had emerged as regionally concentrated classes through supplying foreign demand. Their vulnerability to external conditions was already clear from the agricultural depression following the post–World War I boom. All hope of spontaneous recovery and market adaptation was lost with the general economic collapse of the

[13] There were, of course, tariffs in continental Europe, and trade was disrupted during World War I. For the classical account of variations in European national responses to foreign competition, see Kindleberger (1951). But these tariffs worked as they were theoretically supposed to do, namely, increase domestic prices as a function of the world price plus the tariff, and thus maintain domestic production. As we shall see, the different effects of state policies in the postwar order justify calling this a period of relatively free trade (see Friedmann, in press).

[14] Prior to World War I exports also increased from Russia, the Danubian countries, and India. See Olson (1974).

thirties. In these countries, trade was less amenable than domestic conditions to policy intervention. Policies introduced in major export countries attempted to support farm incomes through regulation of the supply and prices of agricultural commodities. State marketing boards were established in Canada, Australia, and Argentina.[15] In the United States, more comprehensive policies were central components of the New Deal.

The political coalition constructed by the Democratic party in the early 1930s depended heavily—and for the first time—on votes won through farm policy.[16] The Agricultural Adjustment Administration (AAA) and the Commodity Credit Corporation (CCC) were both established in 1933. The CCC made loans to farmers against their crops, at a rate calculated to create a specific ratio between farm and other prices. The loan rate worked as a minimum price, and when agricultural prices were below the intended ratio, the CCC accumulated agricultural commodities. The AAA regulated production through acreage allotments but failed to prevent the accumulation of stocks by the CCC (cf. Finegold and Skocpol 1980). By 1942, although wheat acreage was reduced by 13%, production had increased by 21% (Schultz 1945, pp. 166–80).[17] As a result, the CCC wound up holding 519 million bushels of wheat, or 70% of the average annual crop during the previous decade (Schultz 1945, p. 177).[18] Although war bailed out the CCC temporarily, agricultural experts, such as Theodore Schultz, were concerned that "rising prices, unprecedented droughts, and a world war once each decade [would be] required for [the CCC] to succeed" (1945, p. 161–62).

Trade did not promise a solution to the problem of American surpluses. Depression and war brought increased wheat production in Europe. The collapse of trade and impending war led to policies of self-sufficiency in food, especially in Germany and Italy. The annual average production of wheat in Western Europe increased by almost 20% by the end of the thirties (Malenbaum 1953, pp. 238–39). In Britain, the thirties saw the first tariff protection outside of wartime since the abolition of the Corn Laws almost a century before, and production of wheat went up by about a third. War-

[15] Argentina is an exception in both the class relations of wheat production and state policy regulating prices and trade. Its difference on both counts supports the general argument for the relationship between simple commodity production and price support policies. Its subsequent decline as a major exporter also supports the argument. For Argentine agrarian class relations, see Scobie (1964), and for policy see Martinez de Hoz (1967).

[16] The content of the policy, however, was not what farm organizations initially demanded. For insightful analyses of the complex politics behind the AAA in particular, see Finegold (1982) and Finegold and Skocpol (1980). The CCC, more central to the argument here, was more closely related to the earlier McNary-Haugen plan, supported by farm organizations and twice vetoed by Coolidge (Finegold 1982, pp. 7–12).

[17] The Department of Agriculture was, moreover, unable to overcome farmers' resistance to taking Great Plains land out of wheat production for ecological reasons (Bonnifield 1979, pp. 169–84).

[18] The CCC also held large stocks of corn and cotton.

time controls led to the reorganization of wheat production on a new technical and social basis (Tracy 1964).

After the war foreign exchange was scarce, requiring tariff protection. Moreover, the Marshall Plan included significant support for the reconstruction of agriculture. Reconstruction changed the balance of political forces in Europe: rising wages in industry tended to reduce the importance of the political trade-off between high food prices for farmers and low food prices for industrial employers, and agricultural development strengthened the political presence of farmers. This shift in political pressure favored agricultural support.

While European policies prevented the reestablishment of the prewar international food order, postwar changes in international power opened possibilities for a new order. One element of the new order was the economic and political centrality of the United States. Its new world position, and that of the dollar, allowed for creative simultaneous solutions to domestic farm surpluses and the extension of the free world beyond the countries of the wartime alliance.

It is impossible to know what would have happened to American farm policy in a different international context. In the event, however, domestic politics and foreign relations converged. The farm lobby, child of the New Deal coalition in the 1930s, achieved adulthood in the two decades after World War II. Its strength was not tested, as was that of its counterparts in the other major export countries, because the United States continually found means to send its surpluses abroad: first in immediate war relief, then during the Korean War and under the Marshall Plan, and finally as aid to underdeveloped countries. This is not to say that farm surpluses did not present themselves as a chronic problem. It was just the constant search for solutions to this problem that produced the step-by-step construction of food aid policy. This process was uniquely available to the American state, which alone could afford to subsidize exports of its own stocks and of commercial transactions. The particular mechanism of food aid that became so important to the postwar order was concessional sales in inconvertible currencies. This extended to the Third World in the 1950s and 1960s a means to overcome dollar shortages that had been invented for the Marshall Plan in Europe for similar reasons. It was to have different consequences.

The other element left by the old order and crucial to the new one was the breakdown of the colonial empires of Europe. Most were agrarian societies, self-sufficient in food grains. The countries of Latin America, often more industrial, were also generally self-sufficient in food, if not exporters. Politically, the United States was in a position to try to incorporate them into the free world as formally independent states. Economically, foreign aid—and especially food aid—was a way to facilitate industrial development policies (Wood 1980). The policies of the United States and of many new states of the Third World provided the asymmetrical nexus of the post-war food order.

4. THE INTERNATIONAL FOOD ORDER OF THE POSTWAR PERIOD

The international food order had a specific logic within the dynamics of postwar accumulation and Cold War politics. Even though it had to accommodate the reduced role of European wheat imports, it was constructed on the premise of severely restricted trade with the socialist bloc. Food aid was an important means by which free trade within the free world was extended to underdeveloped nations, solving American surplus wheat problems. Bilateral arrangements between the United States and Third World governments became the typical transaction of the international food order. These were at individually negotiated prices in inconvertible national currencies. Subsidies on this scale presupposed American economic strength and the centrality of the dollar internationally. The price effects went beyond specific bilateral aid and trade agreements; continually reproduced surpluses created a chronic downward pressure on the residual "world price." On their side, many Third World states welcomed American subsidized wheat as an immediate political aid and as a potential way out of one of the impasses of late capitalist development. The low prices and international trade patterns established by the international food order created food import dependence and contributed to agricultural underdevelopment in the Third World.

American food aid was conceived simultaneously as a solution to domestic farm-support problems and as a part of Cold War economic and political strategy. The wheat surpluses engendered by New Deal policies had become an overwhelming burden by the end of the war. Getting rid of them through food aid was one alternative which emerged through Cold War economic and military policies. The specific form of this aid was suggested by the experience of the Marshall Plan.

The Marshall Plan itself was debated as a crucial aspect of American foreign policy. Henry Wallace, former secretary of agriculture and midwestern farmer, was the major spokesman for the position that Russia should be included in the Marshall Plan. This position was also espoused by corporate leaders interested in maximal expansion of trade, and it reflected the belief that American participation in Russian reconstruction would lead eventually to the reestablishment of capitalism there (Schurmann 1974, pp. 117–23). Immediate and long-term expansion of trade was a focus entirely compatible with a concern with mounting grain surpluses and support for farm incomes.

In the event, the Marshall Plan actually developed in the context of the formation of NATO and the economic isolation of the Soviet Union. American policy was immediately directed toward the reconstruction of Europe and Japan and the containment of political movements which threatened both capitalist relations of production and the emerging NATO alliance. The weakened position of the European countries relative to the United States, and later the Soviet Union, was gradually realized on a world scale through the breakup of the old European empires. As one former colony after another established itself as an independent national state, each became a terrain of national and international struggle within the context of the Cold War. Latin America, too, rapidly became a terrain of this struggle.

The food aid component of the Marshall Plan sacrificed immediate American trade interests to the global strategies of the Cold War. Marshall Plan aid in the form of food, feed, and fertilizers constituted 29% of the total aid of $13.5 billion between 1948 and 1952 (U.S. Congress 1977, p. 23). It was geared both to providing immediate consumption needs during economic reconstruction and to rebuilding agriculture. Support for the reconstruction of European agriculture sacrificed historic import demand for American wheat[19] to larger strategies for strengthening the European economies on a capitalist basis and incorporating them within the American alliance.[20]

The immediate economic effect of fostering European agricultural self-sufficiency was to increase the magnitude of U.S. surplus disposal problems. Government purchases for the Marshall Plan and other foreign aid subsidized a ninefold growth of wheat exports between 1945 and 1949, to 505 million bushels, a quantity far in excess of prewar exports. Aid funds financed over 60% of all American agricultural exports in 1950 (U.S. Congress 1977, pp. 23–24). Added to this were export subsidies begun under the International Wheat Agreement of 1949. During the first four years of the program, negotiated export prices averaged around 62 cents a bushel less than American support prices and cost the government $546.5 million (Benedict and Stine 1956, p. 23). Meanwhile, increased yields more than compensated for acreage controls.[21] The U.S. government spent almost $2 billion in various subsidies in attempts to reduce stocks between 1932 and 1953. By 1954, when European agricultural production had recovered

[19] The rising standard of living in Europe led to increased meat consumption, and while wheat surpluses developed, feed grains (maize and soybeans) were imported in increasing quantities. Still, the U.S. share of total European agricultural imports fell from 11.9% in 1954 to 9.9% in 1969 (USDA, *Agricultural Statistics*, 1971).

[20] The relative importance of geopolitical considerations immediately after the war is underlined by the food donated for famine relief to Yugoslavia during Tito's pending split with the Soviet Union. At the same time, humanitarian motivations—somewhat mitigated by the unprecedented form of aid as a loan—underlay the India Emergency Food Act of 1951 (U.S. Congress 1977, p. 24).

[21] Acreage controls tended to lead to increased yields, since farmers concentrated production on their best lands and sought to maximize income through substitution of machinery for land as well as labor. The latter had been occurring already (Heady et al. 1965, pp. 1–44).

Friedmann

and peacetime trade prevailed, total CCC stocks were 903 million bushels, equivalent to a year's production (Benedict and Stine 1956, pp. 125–27).

The pressure of accumulating wheat surpluses and the experience of the Marshall Plan and ad hoc foreign aid led to Public Law (PL) 480, the Agricultural Trade Development and Assistance Act of 1954. Title I of PL 480 and section 402 of the Mutual Security Act of 1954 (an extension of the 1953 act) both provided for sale of surplus agricultural stocks for foreign currencies (OECD 1974, p. 77). This provision was designed to allow American grain to be imported by countries lacking foreign exchange for commercial purchases. Title II of PL 480 provided for grants to combat famine and Title III for the barter of food for other raw materials. Title I sales rapidly became the largest component of American food aid. Between the first and second years of the program total wheat disposal increased 45%, and Title I sales increased from 27% of the total to 42% (National Planning Association 1957, p. 36). By the late 1970s, Title I sales over the whole period accounted for more than 70% of food aid, most of this wheat (USDA 1978).

American food aid drew on the experience of European reconstruction, but the complex interplay of economic and Cold War policies was to be different for the Third World. The main purpose of PL 480 was surplus disposal, with the long-term goal of economic development in recipient countries to create new markets for American wheat. In contrast to conflicting American objectives earlier in Europe, in the underdeveloped countries, extension of wheat markets dovetailed with extension of the free world. Food aid quickly came to occupy a key place in the total foreign aid program. By 1956 food aid under PL 480 and the Mutual Security Act accounted for almost half of all economic aid (National Planning Association 1957, pp. 8–11).

The foreign-exchange bind of capitalist development in the Third World was superficially similar to that of war-devastated Europe. The Marshall Plan had been part of the general construction of an open world economy instead of the independent national development advocated by Keynes and others (Block 1977). American foreign aid was intended to assist capitalist development in the Third World just as it had effected recovery in Europe and Japan, on an open model. However, because of different political histories, food aid to agrarian societies did not have to include aid to agricultural development, as it had had to do in Europe, and could accommodate the long-term pressure for surplus disposal. Although this was to change later, initial decisions prohibited PL 480 assistance to countries, such as Spain, which might produce competitive wheat exports.[22] In contrast to the Marshall Plan (and to later amendments to PL 480), food aid in the

[22] The contradiction between surplus disposal and price maintenance was recognized in the provision of the foreign aid legislation requiring that precautions be taken to ensure that foreign disposal programs would not supplant normal sales (National Planning Association 1957, p. 128, n. 81).

heyday of the international food order was entirely directed toward feeding potential wageworkers during industrialization, not toward agricultural development.

But foreign aid generally, including food aid, was designed to promote trade and capitalist development in agrarian societies as part of the construction of the free world. Title I worked through "concessional sales" at negotiated prices in the currencies of recipient countries. The United States made concessional sales under Title I of $9.3 billion between 1955 and 1965 alone (U.S. Congress 1977, p. 25). This meant that the U.S. government paid this amount to private grain companies and held an equivalent amount of foreign currencies, mostly inconvertible, at the nominal rate of exchange.[23] It was then able to spend or lend this money in recipient countries without special appropriations from Congress.

The PL 480 aid was restricted to "friendly" countries and included among its official purposes the promotion of U.S. foreign policy (U.S. Congress 1977, p. 25). A presidential executive order gave the State Department responsibility for negotiation and final approval of PL 480 sales. In the early years of the program, 92% of local funds acquired through PL 480 sales were used as loans to recipient governments for approved development projects, for payment of U.S. obligations to them, and for procurement of military equipment, materials, and facilities (National Planning Association 1957, pp. 8–11).[24]

These transfers of commodities without convertible payments were made possible by the U.S. payments surplus and the central role of the dollar in the international monetary system. Food aid under Title I was both a transfer of commodities without dollar equivalents and a transfer of investment capital by the American state. Significant military expenditures abroad and more modest foreign economic aid were financed by PL 480 currencies.[25]

[23] For the role of the merchant grain companies during this period and the crisis of the seventies, see Dan Morgan's (1979) fascinating account.

[24] Until the Vietnam War, which induced dramatic policy changes, food aid was directed less to specific foreign policy objectives than to a general policy of extension and consolidation of the free world. Yet for some recipient countries aid and politico-military alliances were very significant. U.S. holdings of national currencies contributed to military and other expenditures in such key countries as Turkey, South Korea, and South Vietnam, three of the 11 countries which accounted for two-thirds of all PL 480 aid between 1954 and 1975. Sometimes shifts in policy or regime coincided with changes in food aid: Indonesia began to receive aid in 1966, the year after a bloody anti-Communist coup d'etat; Egypt's large receipts of the 1960s were abruptly cut off after the 1967 Middle East War and resumed only in 1974; Israel has consistently received aid; Yugoslavian aid between 1954 and 1960 was explicitly tied to support for Tito. At the same time, India and Pakistan, the two largest recipients, are probably representative of the general policy of promoting capitalist development and combating Soviet influence (U.S. Congress 1977, pp. 27–28).

[25] In 1955–56, $304 million of PL 480 foreign currencies were used for the acquisition of strategic raw materials alone, compared with $11.3 million for economic development loans and related purposes (National Planning Association 1957, p. 18).

This use of foreign currencies facilitated U.S. government expenditures abroad at the expense of forgoing dollar expenditures by foreign countries in world trade (National Planning Association 1957, p. 24).

Aid quickly restructured trade. The United States replaced Europe as the center of international trade. As exchange came to be centered on a dominant source of export supply instead of a dominant source of import demand, multiple new import markets were a necessary complement. Necessity does not produce reality, however. Aid was the mechanism for overcoming social and national limits to the transformation of self-sufficient agrarian societies into consumers of commercial wheat.

American food aid to underdeveloped countries accounted for an impressive proportion of world trade. Table 1 shows that between 1956 and 1960, in the early years of PL 480, American aid accounted for almost a third of world wheat trade. Between 1961 and 1965, it had increased to more than a third. Aid was redirecting trade to underdeveloped countries. Moreover, aid gave the United States an advantage relative to competing export countries. In 1965, more than 80% of U.S. wheat exports were financed by food aid funds (U.S. Congress 1977, p. 4), and during these years the American share of wheat exports increased from just over a third in the years preceding PL 480 to more than half in the first half of the sixties (USDA, *Agricultural Statistics*, 1961, 1971).

The importance of aid in trade led to a complementary concentration of wheat exports from the United States and diffusion of imports to many new nations. Table 2 shows, on one side, that between 1950 and 1974 the surplus regions of Asia and Latin America became deficit regions. (Africa accounts for a smaller proportion of total trade, though the importance—and irony—of import dependence is no less for the countries concerned.) On the other side, the United States took a radically increasing share of world exports, Canada and Australia remained significant, Argentina declined in importance, and France took its place as the third largest exporter of wheat. Understated in the table, but of interest in the light of events of the 1970s, was the erratic recovery of Soviet wheat exports during the fifties and

TABLE 1

U.S. AID SHIPMENTS OF WHEAT AND WHEAT FLOUR* AS
A PERCENTAGE OF TOTAL WORLD TRADE, 1956–65
(in Millions of Bushels)

	1956–60	1961–65
World exports	4,918	7,203
U.S. aid	1,564	2,564
Line 2 as a percentage of line 1	31.8	35.6

SOURCES.—USDA, *Agricultural Statistics*, 1971, 1976; USDA 1967; FAO, *Trade Yearbook*, 1960, 1964, 1970, 1974, 1977.
* Measured in grain equivalents.

TABLE 2

Net Quantities of Wheat and Wheat Flour Equivalents Exported
and Imported by Principal Countries (in Millions of Bushels)*

	1950–54†	1960–64†	1972–74‡
Principal exporters:			
United States............................	310	711	1,112
Canada..............................	300	405	472
Australia	98	224	236
Argentina.............................	79	97	78
France.............................	20	89	299
USSR..............................	30	51	Net imports
Turkey, Syria, and North Africa..........	30	Net imports	Net imports
Bulgaria/Rumania.....................	8	Net imports	6
Uruguay.............................	6	Net imports	Net imports
Principal importers:			
EEC countries........................	190	125	154
United Kingdom......................	168	113	384
Other Europe (including Yugoslavia)*......	85	63	41
Japan..............................	62	113	198
Latin America (except Argentina)*........	n.a.	484	168
Asia (except Japan)*....................	91	251	306
Middle East (Lebanon, Egypt, and Israel)*..	26	75	140

Source.—USDA, *Agricultural Statistics*, 1961, 1971, 1976.

Note.—n.a. = not applicable.

* Regional quantities understate the amount, since they are the sum of only the major import countries. Small countries in all regions, of course, account for the bulk of the remaining trade not shown in the table.

† Five-year averages, 1950–54 and 1960–64.

‡ Three-year averages, 1972–74.

sixties. In 1958 and 1959, Soviet net exports were again larger than those of Argentina, and the fifth largest in the world. Even at the time of the imports that shook the foundations of the international food order, the USSR had net exports of 167 million bushels in 1973 and 55 million in 1974.

Japan became an important new source of world demand. By 1959, Japanese net imports of grain accounted for 5% of the world total, net imports of wheat for 8%; in 1972, they accounted for 12% and 9%, respectively (Food and Agriculture Organization [FAO], *Trade Yearbook 1950, 1974*).

But the more spectacular aggregate growth of import dependence by underdeveloped countries became the complement to the increasing export dominance of the United States. Gross imports of the countries of Latin America, Asia, and Africa, excluding Argentina and Japan, had risen to more than a third of the world total by 1959. These accounted for almost half of world imports in 1971, on the eve of the first large Soviet purchases (FAO, *Trade Yearbook*, 1960, 1974). These countries were even more important for American exports. At their peak in 1968, the poor countries of the world took 78% of U.S. exports and, even with the drastic changes of the early seventies, still bought 56% of U.S. exports in 1973 (U.S. Congress 1977, p. 8).

The weight of American food aid in world wheat trade created a strong downward pressure on the world price. Under the weight of American subsidized exports, prices of wheat generally declined during the fifties, though they began to rise somewhat in the early sixties. Table 3 shows the spread between prices in the United States and those in Canada and Australia. Prices maintained by the American government were between a quarter and a third higher than the export prices of the other two countries. At the same time, CCC holdings remained at around 1 billion bushels throughout the period; again, this was equivalent to about a year's domestic production (USDA, *Agricultural Statistics*, 1961, 1971). The CCC periodically sold wheat at world prices, absorbing the difference, but contributing further to world supply. If this were not enough downward pressure on prices, the CCC made sales for dollar credit, and the Export-Import Bank, though dealing more with cotton, also gave credit for wheat purchases. Together, these credit sales totaled $166.5 million by 1966 (USDA 1967). Beyond this were the export subsidies for private transactions of the grain companies. Thus, American policies supporting domestic production and subsidizing exports, both commercial and concessional, increased world supplies and depressed world prices (Nau 1978, p. 797).

It is, of course, impossible to know what world prices would have been in the absence of this aid. To begin with, legislation constantly stressed the importance of not interfering with commercial trade and prices. At the

TABLE 3

PRICES OF WHEAT IN THREE MARKETS, 1951–64
(in Dollars per Bushel)

Year	Average U.S. Price (All Grades)*	Manitoba Price†	Sydney Price‡	Spread
1951	2.40	2.28	2.31	.12
1952	2.45	2.21	2.37	.24
1953	2.47	1.89	1.86	.61
1954	2.57	1.72	1.61	.96
1955	2.40	1.72	1.49	.91
1956	2.38	1.72	1.49	.89
1957	2.29	1.64	1.62	.67
1958	2.15	1.68	1.56	.59
1959	2.23	1.70	1.49	.74
1960	2.11	1.64	1.51	.60
1961	2.13	1.65	1.51	.62
1962	2.34	1.78	1.61	.73
1963	2.41	1.81	1.62	.60
1964	2.22	1.85	1.69	.53

SOURCE.—USDA, *Agricultural Statistics*, 1961, 1971.

* Average of Portland, Oregon, No. 1 Soft White; Minneapolis, No. 2 Hard Amber Durum; St. Louis, No. 2 Red Winter; Kansas City, No. 2 Hard and Dark Hard Winter; Chicago, No. 2 Soft Red Winter; New York, No. 2 Hard Winter.

† Canada No. 2 Northern, export price for sale outside the International Wheat Agreement (IWA).

‡ Basic selling price of the Australian Wheat Board f.o.b., both within the IWA and outside. For 1951–52, outside the IWA.

beginning of this period it is plausible to assume that aid did not displace trade but was an addition to it. If food aid made possible sales to consumers who would not otherwise have been able to purchase wheat, it would not have had a depressive effect on world prices. Moreover, productivity was increasing during the period: production increases of 2.7% per year in developed capitalist countries and of 3% per year in centrally planned economies were mostly due to increased yields.[26]

However, as aid had its intended effect of market development, low world prices, and especially the high level of production maintained in the United States and the increasing share of U.S. exports in world trade, must indicate trade displacement and consequent oversupply relative to a hypothetical, unhindered market. Although the development of the world market ultimately became accessible to all exporters, in the early stages other wheat-exporting countries, which initially could not finance similar programs, objected to American food aid policies as an unfair trading practice (Michigan State University 1964, p. 9).[27] At the time, export subsidies, through PL 480 sales or otherwise, constituted dumping.

Secondary pressure on world prices came from European protection, which raised the internal price of soft wheat to a level almost double the world price during the 1960s (Johnson 1973, pp. 46–49). The resulting surpluses, and exports by France, added to world supply. The maintenance of world wheat prices since 1972 at about double their sixties' level, together with a drastic decline in both food aid and the necessity for export subsidies, indicates their previous depression. At the same time, the link between the dollar and the wheat order was dramatically revealed by the coincidence—in the literal sense—of devaluation and the food crisis.[28]

The counterpart to American policy was the willingness of Third World states to accept food aid. The desperate appeals for aid since the 1973 "crisis" reflect a dependence on cheap food which grew out of the postwar international food order. The transformation of self-sufficient agrarian populations into mass consumers of commercial food was the prelude to the foreign grain dependence now manifest in the underdeveloped world. That transformation was accelerated by industrialization policies premised on the importation of cheap, often subsidized food. Many Third World states welcomed food aid, thereby playing their role in establishing the international food order. The consequences were extraordinary growth of urban

[26] By contrast, production increases of 2.7% per year in Africa and Latin America were due almost totally to increased acreage, and in Asia, North Africa, and Mexico to a combination of the two (U.S. Congress 1975, p. 18).

[27] In the longer run, of course, they were able to benefit from the market expansion American aid was facilitating and even to introduce their own aid programs. See Sec. 5.

[28] Johnson suggests that "overvaluation of the dollar during the 1960's and early 1970's probably depressed grain prices in international markets by 10 to 15 percent" (1975, p. 4).

populations—an aspect of proletarianization—and agricultural under-development.

The societies which rapidly came to account for the bulk of wheat imports after World War II were faced with unprecedented dilemmas of capitalist development.[29] Capitalist industrialization involves a double transformation: the population separated from the land must have income to purchase food, and agriculture must become specialized. This need not happen *within* a society and typically does not: commodity relations extend across national boundaries as they deepen within them. In the late 19th and early 20th centuries, commercial wheat production was concentrated in the Americas and Australasia. Efficiently produced food lowered the reproductive costs of expanding working classes, in Europe through imports and in the export countries through domestic supplies. At the same time, agricultural specialization in the countries of new European settlement complemented industrial specialization in Europe. Each required a specific national strategy of capitalist development.

The postwar world economy prevented the underdeveloped countries from following either the European/Japanese path of capitalist development through food imports or the New World path through food exports. Food imports require foreign exchange, earlier generated through industrial exports. After 1945, however, capital had become much more mobile and larger in scale than before the war. Foreign direct investment and competition from large-scale foreign enterprises limited late industrialization through the development of handicrafts (cf. Meier 1981). Producing manufactured exports to pay for food imports was thus implausible.

At the same time, a world market in basic foods already existed. The agricultural productivity of some advanced capitalist countries matched that of industry and implied devastating competitive pressure on potential Third World exports. This means of generating foreign exchange for industrial imports was also unpromising. Exports of nonfood raw materials, too, were generally not sufficient to buy industrial means of production.

In the context of an open world economy, U.S. food aid, working through the relation of the dollar to local currencies, was appealing to poor countries. Food aid reduced the necessity to choose among difficult alternative development strategies: investment in increasing agricultural productivity, which both uses scarce capital and expels the rural population; higher food prices or rationing, which increases the costs of reproduction of the labor force or creates political and administrative problems; or the use of foreign exchange for food imports, which limits import of investment goods and

---

[29] The other important new import country was Japan. Japan's capitalist economy, reconstructed under the Allied Occupation, provided wages for mass food consumption. Agricultural development, including both increased productivity and reduction of the rural population, could occur, as in prewar Europe, in conjunction with large imports (Johnston and Kilby 1975). Oil now provides foreign exchange for a few countries.

contributes to balance-of-payments difficulties (Michigan State University 1964, p. 13)

Most countries attempting to industrialize adopted cheap food policies (Nicholson and Esseks 1978). These were made possible by cheap imports with minimal drain on foreign exchange. The policy was economically rational within the international food order and politically pressing as population growth outstripped industrial employment. However, its effect on domestic agriculture could be severe.

Colombia illustrates the potentially extreme consequences of PL 480 imports for domestic agriculture. Even though Colombian imports were not important in total U.S. wheat exports, they were crucial in shifting the sectoral balance within that country. Between 1955 and 1962, concessional sales were made in pesos (overvalued in relation to the dollar) and accounted for 53% of total Colombian imports (Dudley and Sandilands 1975, p. 327).[30] Table 4 shows that between 1951 and 1971 domestic prices were cut in half, and wheat production fell by almost two-thirds. Domestic production as a proportion of consumption fell from 78% to 11%. These data do not represent a shift from wheat to other crops; the total area for wheat and the other climatically suitable commercial crops, barley and potatoes, declined by 54.6%. Dudley and Sandilands suggest that "much of the labor formerly used in wheat production must have been directed into areas of low productivity or into further increases in the number of unemployed" (1975, p. 332). The authors conclude that Colombian state pricing policy for imported food was about 20% below the optimum, leading to imports of 1.4 million tons of wheat "which could have been produced domestically at a lower opportunity cost" (p. 336).[31]

Colombia may be an extreme case (Isenman and Singer 1977), and countries with still less commercial development of agriculture, such as Pakistan, may be less affected by cheap food imports. But failure to develop commercial agriculture, no less than absolute reduction, reinforced the general tendency of the postwar food order toward increasing specialization of wheat production in the advanced capitalist countries—beyond comparative

[30] More than half the pesos were reloaned to the Colombian government for development projects, mainly in agriculture, and the rest were lent to American business in Colombia or spent in lieu of dollars by the American government. After 1963, in keeping with new policy, sales were for long-term dollar credits, and success in the development of the Colombian market meant that aid fell from 53% of total imports between 1955 and 1962 to 30% from 1963 to 1971 (Dudley and Sandilands 1975, p. 327).

[31] American aid not only increased Colombian imports through a disproportionate reduction in domestic production, but also increased the U.S. share. A rough calculation from Dudley and Sandiland's data and the U.S. export data indicates that the U.S. share of increased Colombian wheat imports went from just over 20% in the years before PL 480 to almost 40% in the late fifties and early sixties. (Colombian imports are from table 4 below; U.S. exports to Colombia, comparable for 1950–54, but averaged for the second period from 1958 to 1964, are from USDA [Agricultural Statistics, 1961, 1971].)

TABLE 4

DOMESTIC AND IMPORT PRICES, DOMESTIC PRODUCTION, IMPORTS, AND CONSUMPTION
OF WHEAT IN COLOMBIA, ANNUAL AVERAGES, 1951–71

	Price Received by Producers (A) (1958 Pesos/Ton)	c.i.f. Price of Imports (B) (1958 Pesos/Ton)	A ÷ B	Production		Imports		Consumption (Tons)
Period				Tons	% Consumption	Tons	% Consumption	
1951–54.....	1,031	464	2.22	139,750	78	38,900	22	178,700
1955–62.....	841	453	1.86	145,400	60	97,200	40	242,600
1963–70.....	709	390	1.82	99,000	33	205,500	67	304,500
1971........	514	345	1.49	49,000	11	384,900	89	433,900

SOURCE.—Dudley and Sandilands 1975, pp. 331–32.

advantage—and toward the shift of underdeveloped countries to dependence on wheat imports.

The operation of the international food order, therefore, tended to contribute to key Third World problems. Cheap foreign wheat facilitated the growth of urban populations and contributed to underemployment and poverty in the countryside. Dependence on commercial food was a necessary condition for capitalist industrialization, which indeed began to occur in historically new forms in some countries of Asia and Latin America. But it was not a sufficient condition. Many new customers for wheat were created, but at a rate that outstripped the growth of employment. Capitalist penetration increased the absolute level of effective demand for wheat but also increased the gap between the numbers needing wage employment and the number of jobs available. The demise of precapitalist self-sufficiency has created problems which remain in different measure unresolved in various nations of the Third World.

5. CONTRADICTIONS AND CRISIS IN THE EARLY SEVENTIES

The disappearance of surpluses and dramatic shift to high prices in the early 1970s indicated a crisis in the strict sense—a turning point in the international order. Contradictions within the postwar international food order began to emerge in the late 1960s. The order had emerged on the basis of constantly reproduced American wheat surpluses, maintained on behalf of American farmers and disposed of through various subsidies centered on American food aid. The success of American food aid in developing commercial markets progressively made the policies redundant (see table 5; note

TABLE 5

U.S. WHEAT AID IN U.S. AND WORLD WHEAT* EXPORTS, 1956-77
(in Millions of Bushels)

	1956–60	1961–65	1966–70	1971–75	1976–77†
World exports	4,918	7,203	10,068	12,640	5,235
Total U.S. exports	2,251	3,607	3,459	5,012	1,939
U.S. exports as % of world exports	45.8	50.1	34.4	39.7	37.0
U.S. aid‡	1,564	2,564	1,704	661§	302§
U.S. aid as % of U.S. exports	69.5	71.1	49.3	13.2	15.6
U.S. aid as % of world exports	31.8	35.6	16.9	5.2	5.8

Sources.—USDA 1967; USDA, *Agricultural Statistics*, 1971, 1976; FAO, *Trade Yearbook*, 1960, 1964, 1970, 1974, 1977.

* Including wheat flour in grain equivalents.

† Two years only.

‡ Government aid under PL 480 and Mutual Security Act (A.I.D.) only. Does not include subsidies for commercial exports. These were an average of $0.17 per bushel between 1967 and 1970.

§ For 1975, 1976, and 1977, Title I and II of PL 480 only.

that the last column refers to two years only). The costs of the program, and of other foreign expenditures by the U.S. state, were also increasingly difficult to sustain. Meanwhile, the operation of the international food order as a whole gradually changed the relations, both national and international, on which the order had been premised. As a result a new relation began to emerge between supply and demand, leading to higher prices and to the collapse of the arrangements constructed over two decades.

On the demand side, the commodification of food proceeded rapidly in underdeveloped countries, and détente expanded trade to the socialist countries, whose increasing meat consumption meant an increasing demand for grain imports.

The international food order induced a spectacular transformation of much of the Third World from self-sufficient agrarian societies to national economies dependent on wheat imports. Concessional sales of American surpluses were always intended to develop new commercial markets. They did so, though at considerable social and national cost to the recipient countries. First of all, although unemployment and poverty began to increase, too, in advanced capitalist countries in the 1970s, the scale of the aggregate gap between the human need for food and the ability to purchase it was vastly greater in the huge urban conglomerations of the underdeveloped world, created in part by the international food order. These concentrations of people were in advance of industrial employment. The numbers who *could* buy wheat increased sufficiently to solve much of the world problem of commercial surpluses but insufficiently relative to the numbers who *needed* to buy it but could not. Second, imported food was much more significant for the payments position of the underdeveloped countries than of the advanced capitalist ones. In conjunction with spiraling oil prices, crucial to both sets of economies, the effect on the underdeveloped world was devastating.

As the commercial goals were progressively reached, food aid legislation changed. A 1959 amendment to PL 480 made possible sales in dollar credits. In 1966, during the Vietnam War, PL 480 was extended and renamed "Food for Peace"—an irony which will be clear shortly. The goals of the act were redefined, deemphasizing surplus disposal and directing the president gradually to convert to sales in dollars or in convertible local currency credits.

An original condition of the international food order was the exclusion of trade beyond the boundaries of the free world. Détente allowed socialist countries to increase world demand for wheat dramatically. Other wheat-exporting countries preceded the United States in trade with socialist countries, but it was the enormous American sales to the Soviet Union in 1972 and 1973 that tipped the balance of the international food order. Détente represented an attempt to supersede the free world project of which the construction of the international food order was a part.

Finally, détente had such a significant effect because increased meat consumption in Eastern Europe and the Soviet Union contributed to their demand for grain. In the late sixties and early seventies, the Soviet Union adopted a policy of increasing the standard of living of the population on the American dietary model. The Soviet commitment to increase livestock production greatly—there was a 40% increase in the use of feed grains between 1968 and 1971—was probably reinforced by the Polish riots of 1970, after which "consumerism" became a general Eastern European demand (Morgan 1979, pp. 139–40). Soviet grain production in fact increased during that period, but not nearly in keeping with the demands of increased meat consumption. Trade with the West made consumerism possible.

On the supply side, the U.S. balance of payments made foreign aid more difficult to sustain; the domestic changes required by international pressures on U.S. expenditures were possible because of the diminished political importance of American wheat farmers; and similar support and aid programs emerged in other wheat-exporting countries, making general the problem of oversupply and leading to general attempts to reduce acreage. While it did not yet have significant supply effects, the introduction of Green Revolution technologies promised to reverse the tendency toward agricultural underdevelopment in at least some Third World countries.

The American shift away from surpluses was a matter of both policy and international political economy. Aid programs, together with other foreign expenditures and capital exports, developed new markets in the Third World at the expense of the U.S. balance of payments and the supreme role of the dollar (Mandel 1972, pp. 36–40).[32] While food aid undercut the U.S. payments position, food exports became potentially more important in improving it. However, competition became more intense among export countries to meet the new commerical demand.

In the early seventies aid became less important as an instrument of trade and Cold War policy, and domestic economics came to overshadow foreign policy in trade decisions. On one side, in the aftermath of the Vietnam War, food aid legislation shifted to a humanitarian focus. Food aid had been increasingly directed to Vietnam and Cambodia and much of the local currency given back as economic and military aid beyond that explicitly appropriated by Congress. At the same time, military expenditures for the war had contributed significantly to the deteriorating U.S. payments position. Amendments to the Foreign Assistance Act and to PL 480 itself between 1973 and 1975 prohibited "mutual defense" uses of food aid funds, gave priority to countries with a per capita gross national product below $300,

[32] Cf. USDA (1967, p. 3): "The balance-of-payments benefit derived from foreign currency usage in lieu of dollars has resulted in a total saving (1954–66) of $1,452.6 million." The foreign expenditures themselves hurt the U.S. payments. The use of foreign currencies reduced the pain.

and directed that more aid take the form of grants under Title II (U.S. Congress 1977, pp. 25–26). On the other hand, trade as a key to détente became subordinated to domestic economic policy. Mounting inflation in the United States for the first time included food prices. The growing weakness of the U.S. economy dictated its priority over détente in the policy governing wheat exports (Destler 1978, p. 629).

Just as the position of the United States in the world order declined, so did the position of farmers in the United States. Changes in domestic agricultural policy were politically possible because of the declining power of farmers. Partly through success of support policies, their numbers declined considerably. Table 6 shows that the number of people working in agriculture fell by more than half between 1950 and 1972. This represents a fall in the proportion of the farm population in the total from 15% to 5% (Destler 1978, p. 620). However, farming continued to be characterized by family labor,[33] and the organization of the class temporarily offset its numerical decline. The farm lobby remained significant beyond its numbers for several years. The differential price rises of the early seventies finally split apart the crucial alliances among lobbies for various supported commodities (Meier 1978, p. 43). More important, the alliance between the wheat lobby and consumer groups, based on a shared interest in the food stamp program, foundered with increased prices and government costs. Subsidies and high prices came eventually to pit consumers against producers (see King 1978), and consumer politics became more significant. The operation of the international food order helped to undercut the position of the group whose interests it had initially served.

Meanwhile, the growth of wheat surpluses in other countries transformed the unilateral problem of American disposal into a general problem of reduction of supply. Although exports remained concentrated in the advanced capitalist countries, American predominance declined as trade supplanted aid (U.S. Congress 1975, p. 45). As American stocks were diminishing, sup-

TABLE 6

FARM EMPLOYMENT BY KIND OF WORKER, UNITED STATES, 1950–72
(in Thousands)

	1950	1955	1960	1965	1970	1971	1972
Total workers...	9,926	8,381	7,057	5,610	4,523	4,436	4,373
Family workers..	7,597	6,345	5,172	4,128	3,348	3,275	3,228
Hired workers...	2,329	2,036	1,885	1,482	1,175	1,161	1,146
Hired workers as % of total....	23.5	24.3	26.7	26.4	26.0	26.2	26.2

SOURCE.—OECD 1974, p. 24.

[33] Since these aggregate statistics include capitalist fruit and vegetable farming in the Far West and South, they understate the importance of family enterprises in other sectors, particularly grain.

plies were increasing elsewhere: by the late sixties, Canada and Australia had adopted modest subsidy programs, and European surpluses were mounting under the Common Agricultural Policy (CAP). Although food aid was more generally adopted, it was no longer an effective means of surplus disposal. Most countries undertook acreage reduction. Between 1968 and 1970, the combined wheat area of the United States, Canada, Australia, and Argentina declined from 50 million to 30 million hectares, causing wheat production in these countries to fall from more than 80 million to less than 60 million tons. Had the area remained unchanged at existing yields, the production in the period 1968–72 would have been 90 million tons greater than it was (U.S. Congress 1975, p. 21). By the early seventies, the main downward pressure on prices came from Europe (Johnson 1973, p. 138).

The growth in demand and decline in supply led to modest price rises in the late sixties and thus reduced the extreme competitive pressure on Third World commercialization of agriculture. The new high-yielding varieties of wheat promised increased production with minimal expenditures of labor. They required expensive imports, especially of chemical fertilizers, and to the extent that investment was organized privately, generally required higher prices than those of the late sixties.[34] Between 1964 and 1970, however, fertilizer was overproduced and its world price fell by one-half. By 1973, when wheat prices were rocketing, fertilizer prices were three to four times the 1964 price (U.S. Congress 1975, pp. 60–62). In the meantime, a modest start had been made in introducing Green Revolution techniques. Although not contradictory in themselves, techniques for improved commercial agriculture in the Third World emerged at the same time as the contradictions described above. They provide one of the elements for the potential construction of a new order.

6. COLLAPSE: LEGACIES FOR CONSTRUCTION OF A NEW ORDER

A long path toward construction of a new order lies ahead. While trade has lost its central connection to food aid, no new set of complementary national policies has yet emerged to constitute a new international food order. The eventual shape of a new order and the character of the intervening period depend on national agricultural and trade policies, each of which will develop in the context of new class forces and changing international relations. Just as the international food order of the postwar period played a special role in global accumulation, its breakdown has specific effects, and reconstruction will both depend on and influence the dynamics of international capital.

The fall of the postwar order has involved a separation of aid from trade and a change in the character of aid. American aid rapidly became marginal

[34] International agencies applied pressure for private organization of agriculture. For an excellent discussion of World Bank policy for India as a condition for aid, see Frankel (1968, pp. 269–71).

to both world trade and American exports in the decade after 1965. Table 5 shows that the proportion of American food aid in world wheat trade declined steadily from more than a third in the early 1960s to between 5% and 6% in the 1970s. As a proportion of American exports, it fell from more than 70% to about 15%. Meanwhile, the U.S. share of world wheat exports fell markedly in the late sixties, but then leveled out in the seventies at just under 40%. The American position in the world wheat trade was adjusting from an advantage based on subsidies to a less dominant, though still leading, competitive edge.

As aid became separated from trade, more countries became donors, and donations ceased being exclusively American. Throughout the sixties the United States provided more than 90% of all food aid (see table 7). In 1970 this figure fell to 76.1% and in 1973 to 58.0%, remaining at a little over half of the total. The next largest donor over the whole period was Canada, whose aid contributions generally increased (apart from the special famine appropriations to India in the mid-sixties). European, Japanese, and Australian aid also increased. The new noncommercial role of aid is underscored by Japan: a large net importer, the country nonetheless gave 8.5% of food aid in 1973, more than Canada and much more than Australia.

The new humanitarian focus of aid was reflected in a shift from bilateralism to multilateralism and from loans to grants. The change away from aid overwhelmingly in the form of bilateral loans by the United States is clear from table 8. In 1973, more than a fifth of all aid passed through multilateral organizations, the most important being the food programs of the European Community and the United Nations. Among the new aid-giving countries, only Japanese food aid was in the form of bilateral loans. European bilateral contributions were consistently smaller than contributions to multilateral agencies, and all were grants. Canadian and Australian aid were both still mainly bilateral, though less so for Canada, and for both countries grants almost completely displaced earlier loans. Although bilateral loans still accounted for 58.2% of U.S. food aid, this represented a significant decline from the fifties and sixties.

This shift reflects less a new humanistic bent in capitalist foreign policy than a response to the breakdown of the postwar food order. Food aid no longer plays a central role in trade and may now take its place within the complex of objectives served by foreign aid in general.

The aftermath of the collapse of the aid-centered international food order is anarchy in world grain trade and high prices. The general movement toward a new international food order must be in the direction of either more openness or greater autarky. In either case prices will remain high: free trade will reflect the absence of downward price pressure from postwar surpluses, and autarky will produce high prices for those countries which forgo the efficiency that comes with specialization. Whatever their effects on

TABLE 7

VALUE OF ALL FOOD AID CONTRIBUTIONS BY COUNTRY, 1960–73 (in Millions of Dollars)

Country	1960	1965	1966	1967	1968	1969	1970	1971	1972	1973	Total, 1965–73
Australia	2.0	10.2	12.6	15.6	8.8	15.1	20.9	12.6	18.5	19.6	133.9
Austria	0	0	0	0	0	1.0	.5	.8	.8	.8	3.9
Belgium	.1	.3	.2	.2	.2	2.9	3.3	7.4	11.1	16.0	41.6
Canada	40.8	57.3	138.3	117.5	63.2	63.3	98.2	88.5	87.8	95.9	810.0
Denmark	.1	.2	.9	1.6	2.5	8.4	6.7	7.3	8.0	13.9	49.5
France	.4	.7	1.0	1.0	1.0	15.1	14.6	34.8	32.3	66.0	166.5
Germany	0	2.6	2.6	2.7	2.7	36.6	29.2	46.9	58.4	91.9	273.6
Italy	0	0	1.5	1.0	.5	4.5	17.8	24.0	20.0	27.4	96.7
Japan	.1	.4	.4	.5	.5	2.0	23.8	134.5	34.6	105.8	302.5
Netherlands	0	1.1	.4	.9	.1	13.8	17.1	15.7	20.3	33.0	102.4
New Zealand	N.A.	N.A.	N.A.	N.A.	N.A.	N.A.	N.A.	N.A.	N.A.	1.2	1.2
Norway	.3	.6	2.0	1.2	8.5	4.5	6.1	4.1	2.5	3.9	33.4
Portugal	0	0	0	0	0	.1	0	0	.1	.1	.3
Sweden	0	0	1.2	2.9	4.2	4.7	9.9	9.4	6.5	11.2	50.0
Switzerland	.5	1.1	1.1	3.1	4.1	6.8	6.4	4.1	7.6	8.5	42.8
United Kingdom	1.0	1.4	2.3	1.0	1.9	17.4	16.0	17.3	2.7	14.3	74.3
United States	901.0	1,234.4	1,213.0	1,007.0	1,060.0	907.0	860.0	826.0	978.0	730.0	8,815.4
Total, non-U.S.	45.3	75.9	164.5	149.2	98.2	196.2	270.5	407.4	311.2	509.5	2,182.6
Total, developed countries	946.3	1,310.3	1,377.5	1,156.2	1,158.2	1,103.2	1,130.5	1,233.4	1,289.2	1,239.5	10,988.0

SOURCE.—U.S. Congress 1975, p. 54.
NOTE.—N.A. = not available.

TABLE 8

BILATERAL AND MULTILATERAL FOOD AID CONTRIBUTIONS OF ADVANCED CAPITALIST COUNTRIES, ESTIMATED DISBURSEMENTS, 1973 (in Millions of Dollars)

COUNTRIES	BILATERAL			MULTILATERAL				TOTAL: BILATERAL AND MULTILATERAL
	Grants	Loans	Total	European Community	World Food Program	Other	Total	
Australia	18.7	0	18.7	0	.9	0	.9	19.6
Austria	0	0	0	0	.8	0	.8	.8
Belgium	5.0	0	5.0	10.7	.3	.9	11.0	16.0
Canada	65.3	9.8	75.1	0	19.9	0	20.8	95.9
Denmark	2.6	0	2.6	1.7	9.6	0	11.3	13.9
France	30.3	0	30.3	35.6	.1	0	35.7	66.0
Germany	37.5	0	37.5	41.8	12.6	0	54.4	91.9
Italy	0	0	0	27.4	0	0	27.4	27.4
Japan	7.5	97.0	104.5	0	1.3	0	1.3	105.8
Netherlands	6.1	0	6.1	16.0	10.9	0	26.9	33.0
New Zealand	.8	0	.8	0	.4	0	.4	1.2
Norway	.2	0	.2	0	3.7	0	3.7	3.9
Portugal	.1	0	.1	0	0	0	0	.1
Sweden	0	0	0	0	6.6	4.6	11.2	11.2
Switzerland	5.5	0	5.5	0	2.6	.4	3.0	8.5
United Kingdom	0	0	0	12.6	1.7	0	14.3	14.3
United States	251.0	425.0	676.0	0	27.0	27.0	54.0	730.0
Total	430.6	531.8	962.4	145.8	98.4	32.9	277.1	1,239.5

SOURCE.—U.S. Congress 1975, p. 56.

international specialization, high prices mean more hunger for the dispossessed poor.

The emergence of a new order depends both on state-to-state relations and on national policy responses to new international and domestic conditions. The postwar food order extended trade from advanced capitalist countries to the emergent Third World, and the breakdown of the order involved the extension of trade to the socialist countries. Wheat imports are now a condition of survival in much of the underdeveloped world and of higher consumption policies in socialist countries. They are expensive and contingent on unstable international politics. Wheat exports are increasingly important for the balance of payments of many advanced capitalist countries. However, high prices yield export earnings at the expense of domestic food price inflation and provide new incentives for competition from some Third World countries.[35] Since there is no return to the old order, each type of economy faces new difficulties whose resolution depends in part on the policy adaptations of the others.

The future of détente is crucial to the emergence and character of a new international food order. For the socialist countries, domestic pressures seem to point consistently in the direction of increased standards of consumption and therefore of grain imports. However, for countries such as Poland, foreign exchange limitations also come into play. Beyond this, the building up of animal stocks is slow and their depletion swift. Increased meat consumption predicated on imports requires international stability. The long-term agreement to stabilize the American/Soviet grain trade, after the turbulence and scandals surrounding the initial sales, seemed to promise such stability (Morgan 1979). The promise was short lived: trade was suspended by embargo in response to the Soviet invasion of Afghanistan, and later reinstated in response to American farmer protest. At one moment, however, Russian-American trade constituted the largest single set of transactions in world wheat commerce.

For the major export countries, policy pressures are less consistent. The initial American grain sales to the Soviet Union were an instrument in the construction of the policy which came to be called détente (Destler 1978, p. 621). At the time, the sales—which spurred the price leap of 1972–74—sacrificed domestic inflation and Third World development to the convergence of farm and foreign policy interests (Destler 1978, pp. 622–27). If a potentially drastic decline in American production does occur (Crittendon 1980a), there will continue to be opposition between farm and foreign exchange interest in large exports and control of domestic inflation. In any

---

[35] Thailand recently succeeded the United States as the leading exporter of rice, and Brazilian exports of soybeans and other grains have become significant. Wheat may well cease to be a monopoly of the advanced capitalist countries, as argued below. Meanwhile, for related reasons, wheat should cease to dominate the commercial grain trade.

case, a permanent revival of Cold War trade restrictions is facing powerful domestic economic resistance (Crittendon 1980*b*).

Moreover, the American monopoly of the grain trade ended with the collapse of the postwar food order. New competition makes unilateral American trade policy counterproductive. This was revealed as early as 1973 by the brief American soybean embargo: grain companies were forced to cancel contracts, including those with Japan; the U.S. share of world soybean exports fell from 92% in 1972 to 67% in 1975, the difference coming mainly from Japanese investment in Brazil (U.S. Congress 1977, p. 42). Other countries faced with an American call for solidaristic economic isolation of the Soviet Union must choose between free world alliances and export earnings. The idea of using food as a political weapon to restore declining American power is itself a reflection of that decline (Rothschild 1976).

A minor factor in the future of orderly international arrangements is the EEC's CAP. Europe largely insulated itself from the wheat-centered international food order and, therefore, from the effects of its collapse (Johnson 1975, p. 34). Europe's role in the postwar international food order was largely negative: its protection of wheat contributed to the potential importance of Third World markets; and its support policies—at triple the world wheat price in 1977 (Feld 1979, p. 339)—eventually contributed somewhat to world surpluses. European surpluses are now in stark contrast to global scarcity, but their effects are much more important for the CAP than for world supplies. Indeed, the crises of the CAP are in some respects a miniature of the contradictions of the international food order: a series of complex adjustments to exchange rates, beginning in 1968, ultimately led to nullity of common prices and serious disparities between costs and benefits among member countries (Feld 1979, pp. 339–42). Since all agricultural subsidies now account for three-quarters of the EEC budget, internal disputes focus increasingly on the CAP. Though there is general agreement that reform is necessary, protection remains firmly entrenched (Davidson 1980). European contribution to construction of a new international food order seems likely to remain minor.

Finally, the countries and populations of the Third World, which were most transformed by the postwar food order, are likely to play as passive a role in the construction of a new order as they did in the last. However, this will not be apparent in national terms as food sufficiency increases. The relation between urban and rural sectors tends to be reversed with the shift from low to high prices. Import dependence makes attempts at national self-sufficiency mandatory, and high prices encourage commercial transformation in place of rural underdevelopment. In fact, wheat production increased greatly in some countries during the seventies: compared with the average annual production between 1961 and 1965, production in 1977 was

159.9% higher in India, 120.4% in Pakistan, 94.7% in Turkey, and 46.6% in Mexico (FAO, *Production Yearbook*, 1972–77).

National self-sufficiency is won at the expense of much of the population. International and national planners in India knew, for example, that competitive modernization of agriculture would increase rural inequality (Frankel 1978, pp. 269–71). Those expelled from the land will join the urban masses already formed by the workings of the postwar food order and impoverished still further by its collapse. Even within those Third World countries able to achieve greater self-sufficiency in food, in the absence of increased employment and wages, or of alternative distributive mechanisms, starvation must increase (Christensen 1978). In the Philippines, for example, impressive rice exports have grown in tandem with high rates of deaths related to malnutrition (*Economist*, October 13, 1979).

The postwar international food order contributed to a particular structure of global accumulation. Low food prices in the postwar era reduced the cost of reproduction of free laborers throughout the free world. They encouraged the formation of new populations separated from the means of production in underdeveloped countries and contributed to increased real wages in advanced capitalist countries.

Industrial employment is growing in some Third World countries, just as it is beginning to decline in the advanced capitalist countries. Although many factors limit the mobility of industrial capital, that part of it encouraged by the low wages of newly formed working classes is directly affected by changes in grain prices. For new proletarians, staple grains are a central component of consumption. Since wages must in the long run reflect the cost of reproduction of the working class, higher food prices should put an upward pressure on wages in underdeveloped countries. But, as in Europe a century and a half ago, this will not happen by itself, but only through working-class struggle to achieve subsistence. The experience of 19th-century England shows the possibility for a prolonged period of rapid destruction of individual workers, continually replaced by new recruits from the countryside (Marx 1967, pp. 264–302). This is more likely if agricultural transformation increases the rate of expulsion of the rural population to urban slums. If wages in the industrializing countries of the underdeveloped world do increase to accommodate higher food prices, and if food price inflation contributes to declining real wages in advanced capitalist countries, even a modest reduction in wage differentials could slow industrial relocation. But in the context of the 1980s, prolonged wage struggles in the Third World may be less likely than political explosion.

The organization of the food supply is central to the formation and reproduction of proletariats in various parts of the world. The international food order of the postwar era made the decline of agricultural self-sufficiency and increased poverty of the underdeveloped world seem a matter of

Friedmann

rich and poor countries. The breakdown of that order reveals the deeper process of class formation in a world of unequal nations.

7. CONCLUSION: TOWARD A THIRD ESSAY ON POPULATION

The fall of the international food order is the underlying cause of the sudden growth in hunger in the Third World and in food price inflation in the advanced capitalist world. The order and its collapse make sense as part of a complex of international orders that structured global accumulation in the postwar period. The central role of the United States and of the dollar underlay food aid as a critical mechanism of trade and price formation. The order collapsed with the decline of American hegemony, and its legacy is high prices and Third World dependence. The study of the international food order shows the importance of sectoral analysis of the world economy, both as an approach combining economics and international power and as a substantive contribution to understanding postwar accumulation and its consequences.

New shortages and high prices raise the specter of widespread starvation. Almost 200 years ago, a similar specter appeared in England, accompanied by growing enthusiasm among the common people for the ideas of the French Revolution. In 1798 and 1803, Malthus published his two essays on population, offering what he claimed to be "conclusive [proof] against the perfectibility of the mass of mankind." He argued that redistributive reform was softhearted and softheaded, encouraging the poor to increase their numbers and hence their misery. His writings were influential in the passage of the Poor Law of 1834, which placed responsibility for poverty firmly on the poor and enforced this responsibility through the workhouse (Meek 1971, pp. 3–9). Similar arguments are being advanced today, though they are not yet accompanied by analogous concrete proposals.

The contemporary specter of starvation and popular unrest assumes a global dimension. The Brandt report (1980, p. 90) estimates that 800 million people in the Third World cannot afford an adequate diet. The poor were rapidly dispossessed and were barely sustained through the aid-centered international food order. The end of the surpluses of the old order is implicated in the recession of the world economy. After staying well below other price rises for two decades, food price inflation is now 30% higher (Janvry 1980, p. 8). For the few who are employed, wages buy less; for the rest, the seventies have dashed modest hopes for increased employment.

As starvation mounts, so do fears of political unrest. Third World states are in the front line, facing the consequences of two decades of the formation of urban masses dependent on cheap imported food. From the other side, they face increasingly costly imports of food on increasingly difficult terms. For the first time these states have joined together to give voice to protests against international inequality. The World Food Conference of 1974 was an important forum for demands for a new international economic order, and voices in the advanced capitalist world have joined in. But as the Cancun conference of 1981 revealed, starvation is still an amorphous political problem.

Most contemporary analysts of the world economy implicitly recall Marx's response to Malthus: poverty results not from a universal tendency of population to outstrip food but from a historically specific tendency of employment to lag behind population. By itself, no amount of food will end world hunger. The poor simply have insufficient incomes to buy food. The solution lies in employment and income redistribution (Brandt 1980, p. 98; Rothschild 1976; Nicholson and Esseks 1978), perhaps in complete reorganization of social production (Christensen 1978).

The crisis of subsistence now appears on a vaster canvas than that at the turn of the 19th century, but both are rooted in accumulation. The capitalist mode of production has its particular laws of population. The extension of capitalist relations to subsistence societies destabilizes the old population balance and promotes overpopulation relative to rural social organization (Caldwell 1978). The intensification of capitalist production continually produces more commodities per employed worker. In periods of contraction, laborers made redundant by increased productivity in one industry are not employed in other industries. Marx (1967, pp. 612–48) called this the production of relative surplus population. His description of the ensuing wretchedness in 19th-century England may now be modified to encompass those regions newly integrated into the sphere of global accumulation.

The dynamism of the postwar period simultaneously promoted the growth and concentration of populations in the Third World and increased wages in advanced capitalist countries. Despite the many barriers to the international mobility of capital, industrial relocation has begun to create employment in some Third World countries as it has begun to decline in advanced economies (Fröbel et al. 1980). Misery in the Third World and recession in the First are now intimately connected.

REFERENCES

Ashley, William. 1921. "The Place of Rye in the History of English Food." *Economic Journal* 31:285–308.
Benedict, Murray R., and Oscar C. Stine. 1956. *The Agricultural Commodity Programs: Two Decades of Experience.* New York: Twentieth Century Fund.
Bergeson, Helge Ole. 1980. "A New Food Regime: Necessary but Impossible." *International Organization* 34 (2): 285–305.
Bernstein, Henry. 1979. "Concepts for the Analysis of Contemporary Peasantries." *Journal of Peasant Studies* 6 (4): 421–23.
Block, Fred L. 1977. *The Origins of International Economic Disorder.* Berkeley and Los Angeles: University of California Press.

Friedmann

Bonnifield, Paul. 1979. *The Dust Bowl*. Albuquerque: University of New Mexico Press.
Brandt, Willy. 1980. *North-South, a Program for Survival*. Cambridge, Mass.: MIT Press.
Caldwell, John C. 1978. "A Theory of Fertility: From High Plateau to Destabilization." *Population and Development Review* 4 (4): 553-77.
Christensen, Cheryl. 1978. "World Hunger: A Structural Approach." *International Organization* 32 (3): 745-79.
Citizen's Board of Inquiry into Hunger and Malnutrition in the United States. 1968. *Hunger, U.S.A.* Boston: Beacon.
Cochrane, W. 1974. *Feast or Famine*. Washington, D.C.: National Planning Association.
Crittendon, Ann. 1980a. "Soil Erosion Threatens U.S. Farms' Output." *New York Times* (October 26).
———. 1980b. "Warfare: Trade as a Weapon." *New York Times* (January 13).
Davidson, Ian. 1980. "First Moves Towards Reform of the CAP." *Financial Times* (December 4), p. 19.
Destler, I. M. 1978. "United States Food Policy, 1972-1976: Reconciling Domestic and International Objectives." *International Organization* 32 (3): 617-53.
Dittmer, Lowell. 1977. "The World Food Problem: A Political Analysis." In *International Resource Flows*, edited by G. Garvey and G. Garvey. Lexington, Mass.: Lexington.
Dudley, Leonard, and Roger J. Sandilands. 1975. "The Side Effects of Foreign Aid: The Case of Public Law 480 Wheat in Colombia." *Economic Development and Cultural Change* 23 (2): 325-36.
Emmanuel, Arghiri. 1972. *Unequal Exchange: A Study of the Imperialism of Trade*. New York: Monthly Review Press.
Fairlie, Susan. 1969. "The Corn Laws and British Wheat Production, 1829-76." *Economic History Review*, 27th ser. 22:88-116.
Feld, Werner J. 1979. "Implementation of the European Community's Common Agricultural Policy: Expectations, Fears, Failures." *International Organization* 33 (3): 335-63.
Finegold, Kenneth. 1982. "From Agrarianism to Adjustment: The Political Origins of New Deal Agricultural Policy." *Politics and Society* 11 (1): 1-27.
Finegold, Kenneth, and Theda Skocpol. 1980. "Capitalists, Farmers, and Workers in the New Deal—the Ironies of Government Intervention." Paper presented at the American Political Science Association, Washington, D.C.
Food and Agriculture Organization (FAO). Various years. *Production Yearbook*. Rome: Food and Agriculture Organization.
———. Various years. *Trade Yearbook*. Rome: Food and Agriculture Organization.
Frankel, Francine R. 1978. *India's Political Economy, 1947-1977: The Gradual Revolution*. Princeton, N.J.: Princeton University Press.
Friedmann, Harriet. 1976. "The Transformation of Wheat Production in the Era of the World Market, 1873-1935: A Global Analysis of Production and Exchange." Ph.D. dissertation, Harvard University.
———. 1978. "World Market, State and Family Farm: Social Bases of Household Production in the Era of Wage Labor." *Comparative Studies in Society and History* 20 (4): 545-86.
———. 1980. "Review of *The Capitalist World Economy*, by Immanuel Wallerstein." *Contemporary Sociology* 9 (2): 246-49.
———. In press. "Foreign Trade Policy and World Commerce: The Case of Wheat, 1815 to the Present." In *The Sage International Yearbook of Foreign Policy Studies*, vol. 7, edited by Pat McGowan and Charles W. Legley, Jr. Beverly Hills, Calif.: Sage.
Fröbel, Folker, Jurgen Heinrichs, and Otto Kreye. 1980. *The New International Division of Labour*. London: Cambridge University Press.
George, Susan. 1976. *How the Other Half Dies: The Real Reasons for World Hunger*. London: Penguin.
Gerschenkron, Alexander. 1943. *Bread and Democracy in Germany*. Berkeley and Los Angeles: University of California Press.
Gourevitch, Peter. 1978. "The Second Image Reversed: The International Sources of National Politics." *International Organization* 32 (4): 881-911.

Heady, Earl O., Edwin O. Haroldsen, Leo V. Mayer, and Luther G. Tweeten. 1965. *The Roots of the Farm Problem*. Ames: Iowa State University Press.

Hopkins, Raymond F., and Donald J. Puchala. 1978. "Perspectives on the International Relations of Food." *International Organization* 32 (3): 581–616.

———. 1980. *Global Food Interdependence: Challenge to American Foreign Policy*. New York: Columbia University Press.

Isenman, Paul J., and H. W. Singer. 1977. "Food Aid: Disincentive Effects and Their Policy Implications." *Economic Development and Cultural Change* 25 (2): 205–39.

Janvry, Alain de. 1980. "Agriculture in the Crisis and the Crisis of Agriculture." *Society/Transaction* 17 (6): 36–39.

Johnson, David Gale. 1973. *World Agriculture in Disarray*. London: Macmillan.

———. 1975. *World Food Problems and Prospects*. Washington, D.C.: American Enterprise Institute for Public Policy Research.

Johnston, Bruce F., and Peter Kilby. 1975. *Agriculture and Structural Transformation*. Oxford: Oxford University Press.

Keohane, Robert O., and Joseph S. Nye. 1977. *Power and Interdependence: World Politics in Transition*. Boston: Little, Brown.

Kindleberger, C. P. 1951. "Group Behavior and International Trade." *Journal of Political Economy* 59:30–46.

King, Seth S. 1978. "Carter's Farm Hand." *New York Times* (May 14).

Krasner, Stephen D. 1976. "State Power and International Trade." *World Politics* 28 (April): 317–47.

Lappé, Frances Moore, and Joseph Collins. 1979. *Food First: Beyond the Myth of Scarcity*. New York: Ballantine.

McLin, Jon. 1979. "Surrogate International Organization and the Case of World Food Security." *International Organization* 33 (1): 36–55.

Malenbaum, Wilfred. 1953. *The World Wheat Economy, 1885–1939*. Cambridge, Mass.: Harvard University Press.

Mandel, Ernest. 1972. *Decline of the Dollar*. New York: Monad.

Martinez de Hoz, Jose Alfredo. 1967. *La agricultura y la granaderia en el periodo 1930–1960*. Buenos Aires: Editorial Sudamericano.

Marx, Karl. 1967. *Capital*. Vol. 1. New York: International Publishers.

Meek, Ronald L., ed. 1971. *Marx and Engels on the Population Bomb*. Berkeley, Calif.: Ramparts.

Meier, Kenneth John. 1978. "Building Bureaucratic Coalitions: Client Representation in USDA Bureaus." Pp. 57–75 in *The New Politics of Food*, edited by Don F. Hadwiger and William P. Brown. Lexington, Mass.: Heath.

Meier, Peter. 1981. "Peasant Crafts in Otavalo: A Study in Economic Development and Social Change in Rural Ecuador." Ph.D. dissertation, University of Toronto.

Michalet, Charles-Albert. 1976. *Le Capitalisme mondiale*. Paris: Presses Universitaires de France.

Michigan State University. 1964. *The Effects of United States Agricultural Surplus Disposal Programs on Recipient Countries*. East Lansing: Michigan State University, Agricultural Experiment Station, Department of Agricultural Economics.

Morgan, Dan. 1979. *Merchants of Grain*. New York: Viking.

National Planning Association. 1957. *Agricultural Surplus Disposal and Foreign Aid*. Washington, D.C.: Government Printing Office.

Nau, Henry R. 1978. "The Diplomacy of World Food: Goals, Capabilities, Issues, and Arenas." *International Organization* 32 (3): 775–809.

Nicholson, Norman K., and John D. Esseks. 1978. "The Politics of Food Scarcities in Developing Countries." *International Organization* 32 (3): 679–719.

Olson, Mancur. 1974. "The United Kingdom and the World Market in Wheat, 1885–1914." *Explorations in Economic History* 11 (4): 325–55.

Organization for Economic Cooperation and Development (OECD). 1974. *Agricultural Policy in the United States*. Paris: OECD.

———. 1980. *Review of Agricultural Policies in OECD Member Countries, 1979*. Paris: OECD.

Paarlberg, Robert I. 1978. "Shifting and Sharing Adjustment Burdens: The Role of the Industrial Food Importing Nations." *International Organization* 32 (3): 655–77.

Palloix, Christian. 1973. *Les Firmes multinationales et le procès d'internationalisation.* Paris: Maspero.

Rothschild, Emma. 1976. "Food Politics." *Foreign Affairs* 54 (2): 285–307.

Schultz, Theodore W. 1945. *Agriculture in an Unstable Economy.* New York: McGraw-Hill.

Schurmann, Franz. 1974. *The Logic of World Power.* New York: Random House.

Scobie, James R. 1964. *Revolution on the Pampas: A Social History of Argentine Wheat, 1860–1910.* Austin: University of Texas Press.

Strange, Susan. 1975. "What Is Economic Power, and Who Has It?" *International Journal* 30 (2): 207–24.

Tracy, Michael. 1964. *Agriculture in Western Europe: Crisis and Adaptation since 1880.* London: Jonathan Cape.

United Nations, World Food Conference. 1974. *World Food Problems. Proposals for National and International Actions.* Rome: Food and Agricultural Organization.

U.S. Congress, House, Committee on International Relations. 1977. *The Use of Food for Diplomatic Purposes.* Washington, D.C.: Government Printing Office.

U.S. Congress, Economic Research Service. 1975. *The World Food Situation and Prospects to 1985.* Washington, D.C.: Government Printing Office.

U.S. Department of Agriculture (USDA). 1951. "Family Farm Policy Review." Provisional Report and Tentative Recommendations of the Department of Agriculture's Family Farm Policy Review Subcommittee. June 11.

———. 1967. *Twelve Years of Achievement under Public Law 480.* Washington, D.C.: Government Printing Office.

———. 1978. *Food for Peace: Annual Report on Public Law 480.* Washington, D.C.: Government Printing Office.

———. Various years. *Agricultural Statistics.* Washington, D.C.: Government Printing Office.

Wallerstein, Immanuel. 1974. *The Modern World System.* Vol. 1, *Capitalist Agriculture and the European World-Economy in the Sixteenth Century.* New York: Academic Press.

———. 1979. "The Emergence of the New International Order." In *The Capitalist World-Economy.* London: Cambridge University Press.

———. 1980. *The Modern World System.* Vol. 2, *Mercantilism and the Consolidation of the European World-Economy.* New York: Academic Press.

Walter, Gerard. 1963. *Histoire des paysans de France.* Paris: Flammarion.

Weatherby, M. J. 1980. "America's Forgotten Time Bomb: The Poor." *Manchester Guardian Weekly* (November 9), p. 9.

White, Harrison C., Scott A. Boorman, and Ronald L. Breiger. 1976. "Social Structure from Multiple Networks. I. Blockmodels of Roles and Positions." *American Journal of Sociology* 81 (4): 730–80.

Wood, Robert E. 1980. "Foreign Aid and the Capitalist State in Underdeveloped Countries." *Politics and Society* 10 (1): 1–34.

The Intelligentsia in the Class Structure of State-Socialist Societies[1]

Ivan Szelenyi
University of Wisconsin—Madison

The paper describes the class structure of East European state-socialist societies, positing the existence of a class dichotomy between the working class and the intelligentsia. This thesis challenges those theories which claim that the importance of class conflicts declined under state socialism and that therefore such societies should be described as containing nonantagonistic classes or strata. It also challenges the critical theories which acknowledge the existence of a new dominant class in Eastern Europe, but which describe that class as the bureaucracy or technobureaucracy. This paper attempts to base its class analysis on the exploration of the mechanisms and institutions of expropriation of surplus under state socialism. It is suggested that in contemporary Eastern Europe private ownership and market mechanisms of expropriation have been replaced by central planning and redistribution of the economic surplus. All those who have vested interests in the maximization of redistributive power are members of a new dominating class. If we define the new class this way it will include more than just the bureaucracy; potentially, it includes the whole intelligentsia. The paper describes the new dominant class of intelligentsia as a class *in statu nascendi*. The formation of this class takes a whole historical epoch. In the first stage of state-socialist development the Djilas thesis is basically accurate: under Stalinism and in the early post-Stalinist years the bureaucracy had the monopoly of power. During the last two decades, on the other hand, the social base of power holders has broadened, especially in those countries which experimented with economic and political reforms. The formation of a new dominant class which incorporates the whole of the intelligentsia is now under way.

In this paper I will describe the class structure of the East European state-socialist societies, positing the existence of a class dichotomy between the working class and the intelligentsia. It will be argued that the power to which intellectuals aspire in a state-socialist redistributive economy derives from the basic institutions of social reproduction and, more specifically,

[1] This paper has been substantially revised from my article which appeared in *Critique*, nos. 10–11 (Winter–Spring 1978–79), pp. 51–76. Requests for reprints of the present paper should be sent to Ivan Szelenyi, Department of Sociology, University of Wisconsin, Madison, Wisconsin 53706.

from the institutions which guarantee the expropriation of surplus from the direct producers; consequently, that power is of a class nature.

The thesis is a highly provocative one, challenging all academically respectable theories of East European social structure and of the structural position of the intelligentsia. Those schools of thought which acknowledge the existence of class relations in contemporary Eastern Europe posit class dichotomies radically different from the one I suggest. Official Soviet Marxism distinguishes between two "nonantagonistic" classes, the working class and the peasantry;[2] those who build their arguments directly or indirectly on Trotsky's critical analysis of Soviet society suggest that a class antagonism exists between the working class and the bureaucracy or technobureaucracy (Kuron, Modzelewski, and Djilas are the best-known examples).[3] Most East European sociologists since Ossowski have tended to disagree both with the official Soviet Marxist position and with the Trotskyist position.[4] During the last two decades empirical sociologists have questioned whether class analysis indeed has any relevance to the study of East European societies, and they have tried to describe the East European social structure in terms of social stratification (e.g., Wesolowski, Ferge, and Hegedus).[5] All these schools of thought would object to defining the in-

[2] The so-called two-class, one-stratum model of social stratification under socialism is usually attributed to J. V. Stalin (1972).

[3] Milovan Djilas developed the concept of the bureaucracy as a new ownership class under socialism. According to Djilas, "The bureaucrats in a non-Communist state are officials in modern capitalist economy, while the Communists are something different and new: a new class" (1957, p. 44). Djilas does acknowledge that the intellectual roots of his criticism of socialism can be found in the work of Trotsky, but he also correctly notes that Trotsky did not acknowledge the class character of the bureaucracy. "Attacking the party bureaucracy in the name of the revolution, he attacked the cult of the party and, although he was not conscious of it, the new class" (p. 50). In fact, the Trotskyist analysis—contrary to the intentions of Leon Trotsky himself—was always very close to different versions of a bureaucratic class theory; the writings of Shachtman and Burnham are well-known examples of an extension of the theories of Trotsky into a new class theory (Shachtman 1962; Burnham 1962). The strength of Djilas's analysis is that it ties his concept of the new class to the political and historical realities of Eastern Europe; he is not venturing into a general theory of a new managerial or bureaucratic class. Another influential application of the Trotskyist critique of the bureaucracy in Eastern Europe is the "open letter" by Kuron and Modzelewski (1966). Kuron and Modzelewski in this article are rather orthodox Trotskyists; they do not develop a bureaucratic class theory, but their analysis points in that direction. Kuron has since moved significantly from this orthodox Trotskyist position, but even in his recent work he did not develop a bureaucratic class theory (Kuron 1978).

[4] Stanislaw Ossowski presented the first comprehensive and devastating criticism of the Soviet Marxist class theory from Eastern Europe (1963, pp. 110–13).

[5] Hegedus (1977) and Ferge (1973) build on the theories of Ossowski. Both Hegedus and Ferge want to replace the Soviet Marxist theory of class under socialism with an analysis of the social structure in which the division of labor is of central importance (Hegedus 1977, pp. 47–57; Ferge 1973, pp. 77–116). They actually replace class analysis with stratification analysis, but while doing so they avoid the theoretical question of whether socialist societies are class societies. (The terminological shift from the concept of "class"

telligentsia as a class; there would even be some disagreement whether intellectuals form a homogeneous stratum. Finally, those who have looked on the East European intelligentsia as a class have rarely used the term "class"; more frequently, they have simply described how the East European radical intelligentsia strives for a power monopoly (e.g., Berdyaev and Machajski)[6] or for what probably can be called "class power." They have not attempted to define the economic foundations of this class or penetrated beyond a description of its ideology.

When I started my work 15 years ago I, like most empirical sociologists in Eastern Europe, was highly critical of official Soviet Marxist theory. Following the example of Ossowski and Hegedus, I spent about 10 years in empirical work, describing different aspects of the East European stratification system, measuring and explaining the extent and nature of social inequalities; in fact, my empirical findings were further proof of the purely apologetic nature and scientific inadequacy of official Soviet Marxism. Thus I had to look for alternative theoretical tools. The Trotskyist frame of reference was obviously more relevant to the study of East European social structure than official Soviet Marxism or stratification theory, but I was not convinced of the theoretical accuracy of the definition of the bureaucracy as an ownership class, and even less so of the empirical validity of the crucial distinction made between bureaucrats and the rest of the intelligentsia (or the "intelligentsia proper").

I found that it might be necessary to go beyond the fairly rigid and orthodox official Soviet or Trotskyist interpretation of the Marxist notion of class, but not by accepting the superficial critique of Marxist class analysis contained within bourgeois stratification theory—which, despite the obligatory Marxist jargon of East European sociology, had had a major impact on the methodology and way of thinking of my fellow East European

---

to the concept of "social structure" is significant.) The main value of that kind of work in Eastern Europe was empirical—it prepared the ground to make empirical research on social stratification and social inequality legitimate in Eastern Europe. The task which was performed by Hegedus and Ferge in Hungary was done by Wesolowski in Poland (1970). Even Soviet sociologists conducted researches of this kind, describing stratificational inequalities, but they did not use their results to confront the official class theory (Shkaratan 1970).

[6] Nicolas Berdyaev, a former Marxist, in exile in the West after the October Revolution, suggests in an impressive study that in order to "understand the sources of Russian communism . . . one must understand that singular phenomenon which is called 'intelligentsia' " (1972, p. 19). He reconstructs the intellectual history of the Russian intelligentsia and argues that the "whole history of the Russian intelligentsia was a preparation for communism" (p. 122). Berdyaev does not develop anything like a class theory of the intelligentsia; he only suggests that the agent in Russia which was ready to absorb the Russian version of communism was not the proletariat but the intelligentsia. As Gouldner points out, the Polish-born Russian revolutionary Waclaw Machajski also claimed that socialism was an ideology of the intelligentsia (Gouldner 1975–76, 1979, p. 99).

empirical sociologists. I became convinced that Marxist class analysis could be a powerful tool for understanding structural conflicts under state socialism, but only if we tried to adapt it to the radically changed socio-economic conditions which now prevail: that is, to the conditions of industrial societies which operate without the institution of private ownership and which consequently, at least according to this crucial criterion, should be accepted as socialist. If a society no longer legitimates the expropriation of surplus through private property, then we should move toward a substantive analysis of the mechanisms and institutions of expropriation of surplus which *are* characteristic of this society. If we can define antagonistic interests focusing on these institutions, we can explain them as class interests and remain within the framework of Marxist class analysis, broadly defined, even if we do not base our definition of class on ownership relations as Marx did. It will be suggested in this paper that redistribution is the main mechanism which guarantees expropriation in state-socialist societies. All those who have a vested interest in the maximization of redistributive power are members of a new dominating class, since their interests are antagonistic to those of the direct producers. If we define the new class this way it obviously includes more than just the bureaucracy or even the technobureaucracy. It potentially includes the whole intelligentsia.

Finally, I would like to make clear in this introduction that the class I am talking about is still *in statu nascendi*. I am describing a process, not a static situation. The intelligentsia as a group, from the priests and monks of the Middle Ages to the anarchist and Bolshevik revolutionaries of the 19th and early 20th centuries and to the scholar-planner-technocrats of the late 20th century, has no doubt always had aspirations toward power monopoly, but this claim became realistic only with the institution of state-socialist redistributive economics. The East European intelligentsia still has a long way to go before it becomes an integrated class with its own class consciousness—the state-socialist societies are still at a very early stage of their development. All that I am suggesting is that there is a historical tendency for the power exercised in Eastern Europe to be increasingly the class power of the intelligentsia.

In *The Intellectuals on the Road to Class Power* (Konrad and Szelenyi [1979]; the book was written in 1974 and published in English in 1979), George Konrad and I attempted to document more fully the signs of the formation of the class power of the intelligentsia. In this paper I can do no more than describe the inadequacies of alternative theories of socialist social structure; analyze briefly the institutions of social reproduction and expropriation found under state socialism to show what kind of antagonism of interest is built upon them; and, finally, document some of the limitations of the definition of the intelligentsia as a class and define more precisely the intelligentsia as a class *in statu nascendi*.

NOTES ON DIFFERENT THEORIES OF EAST EUROPEAN CLASS STRUCTURE

The official Soviet Marxist theory of socialist social structure dominated East European social science literature for three decades, from the early thirties until the late fifties. It is no doubt superfluous to mention that this domination was not purely a product of the intellectual strength of the argument; those with scholarly doubts were constantly reminded of the necessity of ideological discipline by other than purely academic methods. Even today this theory is officially unchallenged in the ideologically more conservative countries like East Germany and the Soviet Union. To see this, it is sufficient to look at any recent edition of a Soviet textbook on historical materialism. Granted, German and Soviet ideologues no longer object when in empirical research sociologists "absentmindedly" forget about official class distinctions and use occupation as a variable in explaining the distribution of their data, as long as they do not draw theoretical conclusions. In the more liberal countries of Eastern Europe, like Hungary and Poland, no one with any academic prestige seriously pretends to accept the old Soviet Marxist dogma, but few people openly challenge it. One is simply no longer supposed to talk about class.

Official Soviet Marxist class theory has pretensions to rigid orthodoxy. It is argued that, because Marx defined classes on the basis of ownership, the same methodology should be applied in contemporary socialist societies; thus, because there are two forms of ownership—state and cooperative—there are two classes as well, the working class and the peasantry.

It should be clear from the beginning to everybody familiar with the logic of Marxist class analysis that, despite the formal orthodoxy, this is quite a flexible interpretation of Marx. Marx did not define his basic class dichotomy in terms of forms of ownership. The basic class antagonism in Marx's formulation exists between those who own the means of the production and those who are deprived of ownership. It is not the form of ownership, but ownership as such (or lack of ownership), which constitutes the class. On the other hand, it is possible to argue that Marx himself attributed class-forming force to forms of ownership. In *Capital* (vol. 3, chap. 52) he defines landowners as a separate class simply because they own something other than "capital," and in the "Eighteenth Brumaire" he uses forms of ownership as the basis for further differentiation between classes, especially differentiation inside the ruling class.[7] What I want to show is simply that

---

[7] In *Capital*, vol. 3, chap. 52, Marx adds a third class, the class of landowners, to his basic class dichotomy between owners of capital and owners of labor power. By adding this third class to his scheme he changes the criteria which supposedly constitute classes. In this text he considers that it is probably not ownership or nonownership which generates classes, but the identity of revenues and sources of revenues. Unfortunately, as he enters this discussion the manuscript breaks off (Marx 1974, pp. 885–86). In "The Eighteenth Brumaire of Louis Bonaparte," where Marx offers his most complex map of class rela-

the official Soviet Marxist dogma is not such a rigorous interpretation of Marx as it claims; in fact, it shifts from the main thrust of Marxist class analysis into a fairly marginal area (as we will see, the Trotskyists' claim to be rigorously Marxist is more justified).

There is another methodological trick built into this theory: namely, on the formal level it operates only with forms of ownership, but when the empirical relevance of the theory is tested we are referred to a distinction between industry and agriculture. It obviously appeals to our common sense that there are workers and peasants in contemporary East European societies, and a distinction between them sounds like a meaningful one. But if it is really the form of ownership that matters, then classes cannot be defined this way; it is not the peasantry which is the other class, but those industrial and agricultural laborers who are employed by cooperatives, and all agricultural laborers who work in the state-owned agricultural categories belong to the working class. Consequently, the industrial worker should belong to the same class as the industrial manager, or even the minister of heavy industry; but the peasant who works in a cooperative should belong to a different class than his neighbor, who is also an agricultural laborer doing the same type of work, having roughly the same income, education, and so forth, merely because he is employed on a state farm. This is obvious nonsense. Thus, what makes sense in the official Soviet Marxist class dichotomy is not the distinction between two ownership classes, but a stratificational distinction between people employed in the main sectors of the economy.

This official Soviet Marxist class theory has very little to do with Marxism; it has even less to do with the empirical realities of contemporary Eastern Europe. In fact, the unknown soldiers of the first silent revolution against this theory were the statisticians who were expected to use "Marxist class theory" in analyzing official statistics, especially population censuses. By 1960, at least in countries where statisticians and demographers had some self-respect, as in Hungary, they silently forgot their *histomat* seminars: in the population census volumes "class" no longer appeared, and statisticians used occupation as a variable to explain the distribution of data. In fact they had to do so, since "classes" as defined by the official dogma explained nothing, from the distribution of income to the allocation of housing. The significant difference was to be found between the major

---

tions, he also makes a class or classlike distinction between "capital" and "landed property," but this time not on the grounds of source of income but on the basis of the difference in the "kind of property" the two classes respectively own (1970, p. 117). In this later essay Marx seems to work with many classes. The petty bourgeoisie as a potential ally of the workers is regarded as a class (p. 119); Marx also spends quite some time analyzing the lumpen proletariat (pp. 136, 144), and he explicitly considers the possibility of the development of the peasants into a class (pp. 170–71). It is quite possible to find textual evidence from this essay for a five- or possibly seven-class model.

occupational groups, especially between white- and blue-collar workers. In a way we might argue that sociologists have undeservedly claimed the honor of being the champions in the struggle against the *histomat* class dogma. It was already practically destroyed by unknown civil servants in Central Statistical Offices. Ossowski and others only offered an ideological justification for an already existing statistical practice. Stratification theory has had a very different history in Eastern Europe and in the West. Critiques of stratification analysis from very early times emphasized its inbuilt conservative character. In the West stratification theory was a conservative weapon against "subversive" class analysis. But in Eastern Europe during the late fifties and early sixties, the discovery of social stratification was quite a subversive activity, subversion against an apologetic and conservative class theory. Those who nowadays criticize people like Ossowski from the ideological Left do not appreciate the intellectual and political courage he needed to challenge Soviet Marxism. The *histomat* class dichotomy served only one purpose: to justify the existing monopoly of power.

By defining the state and Party bureaucracy as the "working class," the official theory offered a convenient solution to the delicate question of the "dictatorship of the proletariat." Stratification analysis, however, at least proved that social inequalities did indeed exist and that the "physical workers" (probably not identical with the ideologically defined working class) were systematically the negatively privileged group in the East European "people's democracies." As time passed, the inherent limitations of stratification analysis came to the fore in Eastern Europe as they had in the West. Stratification analysis, by distinguishing between white-collar and blue-collar workers, between physical workers, clerical workers, professionals, and "professionals in leading positions" (using this polite term for highly placed Party and state bureaucrats), could statistically demonstrate the separation of white-collar workers, and especially the power elite, from the actual workers. But it could not offer any theory to explain the statistically observed differences. Most empirical sociologists used the term "working class" to describe manual workers, those directly involved in the production process, but they carefully avoided using any structural term for the upper half of the social hierarchy. We called them "people higher up in the social hierarchy," the higher-income group, higher social groups or strata—and no one seemed to pay much attention to the theoretical significance of this terminology.

Ossowski, the main theorist of social stratification, proposed that, since ownership had lost its explanatory importance with the elimination of private ownership, position in the social division of labor explained social structure and social inequalities.[8] But it was unclear what the theoretical

---

[8] In Ossowski's view, the importance of the ownership relationship radically declined in societies in which the means of production have been nationalized (1963, p. 182); he also mentions the importance of the emergence of a new class, or "stratum," of non-

significance of this thesis was: did it suggest that class relations no longer existed and that socialist social structure could only be explained by inequalities between different occupational groups, or did it mean that we should define classes in terms of the division of labor? Marx himself obviously flirted with the idea of basing class analysis on the division of labor as far back as the "German Ideology"[9] and Ossowski, a well-trained Marxist, could claim still to be a Marxist while rejecting ownership classes and using division of labor as the main variable for structural analysis. But as stratification research developed, it became clearer that East European empirical sociologists, by emphasizing the importance of the division of labor, wanted to replace class analysis with stratification analysis and were not interested in developing a new class definition. For East European empirical sociology, contemporary socialist society was a classless society, a thesis which did not bother the official ideological censors much and which also pleased Western anti-Marxists, who found it amusing that the first accomplishment of "Marxist sociology" was to get rid of the concept of class. The most consequential stratification theorist in Poland, Wesolowski, was even to question whether a working class existed at all in Eastern Europe, and he proposed

---

manual white-collar workers (p. 183). This new class or stratum (interestingly, he does not seem to attach much importance to the terminological distinction) is, on the other hand, constituted by the nature of its work and not according to ownership relations. Ossowski also suggested that Marx himself cannot be interpreted as a theorist who worked only with a single class dichotomy based on ownership. In Ossowski's view, Marx combined at least three dichotomies to develop a complex map of class relations (Ossowski 1974, p. 82). Hegedus agrees with this, and he adds the "position in the division of labour" and the "sector of the economy" to "property relations" as the "independent variables in the mathematical model of the structure of socialist societies" (Hegedus 1977, p. 70).

[9] Those East European sociologists who attempt to replace or at least combine ownership with "division of labor" frequently quote the "German Ideology." Indeed, in the "German Ideology" Marx and Engels still seemed to assume that the historical development of class relations directly corresponds to the evolution of the division of labor (1972, pp. 18–21). Marx and Engels go so far as to suggest that "the existing stage in the division of labour determines also the relations of individuals to one another with reference to the material, instrument and product of labour" (p. 19). But probably already while writing the "German Ideology" Marx and Engels began to see problems with this proposition. In particular, when they attempt to describe the transition to feudalism, it becomes clear that quantitative indicators of the division of labor are not sufficient to explain the differences in class relations between a slave and a feudal mode of production. It might not be accidental that the manuscript breaks off at this point and that the authors do not even attempt to continue the analysis and to describe the transition from feudalism to capitalism (p. 21). I would suggest that Marx should have developed the concept of "relations of production" first, which would have provided more sophisticated instruments for discussing the issues of transition of modes of production and transformation of class relations. It is interesting, however, that neither Hegedus nor Ferge seems to notice that from the point of view of class theory the "German Ideology" is still an early work—and indeed without the concept of relations of production it cannot be regarded as a mature statement of Marxist class theory (see Ferge 1973, pp. 77–78).

that theoretically it might be more accurate to call workers a "stratum."[10] Suddenly we find the originally subversive stratification analysis turning out to be even more apologetic than Soviet Marxism. At least Soviet Marxists acknowledged that contemporary socialist societies were class societies (although composed of nonantagonistic classes—quite a squaring of the circle) and that classless "communist society" was still to come.

But this question of "classlessness" is not a purely ideological one. Wesolowski and the stratification school of sociology in Eastern Europe, by rejecting the applicability of class analysis to socialist societies, were in fact suggesting that it was impossible to define structural economic conflicts in these societies. Consequently, it was also impossible to explain existing social inequalities from structural economic conflicts. This has far-reaching consequences for empirical research and for the interpretation of empirical facts. If contemporary socialist societies are classless—that is, free from structural economic conflicts—then the inequalities we can observe and measure are not inherent characteristics of these societies. They are inherited from the capitalist past or, alternatively, are consequences of nonsocial factors (e.g., the ideologues of stratification theory would argue that inequalities will be overcome under socialism by the gradual development of productive forces or technology). If this theory stands, then the structure of inequalities could not reflect the socioeconomic laws of these societies and, historically, inequalities should decline. In my empirical work I found none of these assumptions to be true. The main inequalities which I observed in the fields of housing and urban structure or in the regional system were not inherited. They were emerging from the East European socialist strategy of economic growth. They were structured by the redistributive mechanisms of the socialist economy and not by surviving market forces. And, finally, there was little evidence that inequalities were declining. (It is not the purpose of this paper to elaborate this point, which was documented in my earlier publications on housing and urbanization in Eastern Europe.) Since I found the inequalities I observed to be inherent in East European societies and to be structured by basic state-socialist economic institutions, it was logical to assume that class antagonism lay behind these inequalities.

It was Leon Trotsky who first suggested the existence of antagonistic interests in the Soviet Union, when he analyzed the nature of conflict between the bureaucracy and the working class. Trotsky himself never

[10] In Wesolowski's formulation: "The proletarian revolution abolishes the class structure thus conceived. . . . Deprived of their 'opposed role,' the workers cease to be a class in the traditional sense of the term. . . . In the Marxian sense, they are no longer a 'true class,' but rather an 'ex-class' . . . we continue to call them 'workers,' but not the working class in the Marxian sense of the term. Perhaps it would be convenient to call them 'the stratum of workers' " (1974, p. 123).

Szelenyi

went so far as to call the bureaucracy a class. Sociologically speaking, he defined the bureaucrats as a ruling elite alien from the working class.[11] The theory that Trotsky developed concerning the Soviet social structure is a curious one. It is basically a class theory since it assumes a class antagonism, but it operates with a one-class model. The oppressed class is opposed only by a political elite. But this contradiction is quite understandable. Trotsky as a scholar was more a political scientist than a sociologist. He did not show a great deal of interest in the critical examination of the economic institutions of the Soviet system. He in fact assumed that the economic revolution was accomplished and that the Soviet system needed only a new political infrastructure. Later theorists were less restrained than Trotsky himself, and those trying to elaborate the sociological nature of the antagonism discovered by Trotsky became interested in the definition of the other class, the new dominating or ruling class of Soviet-type societies. All those who either followed Trotsky directly or were influenced by him described the bureaucracy as the new class. These theorists—Djilas is the most influential among them—used the classical Marxist tools of class analysis and defined the bureaucracy as an ownership class, arguing that under state socialism the bureaucrats monopolized the disposition of the means of production.[12]

Undoubtedly we can learn more from Trotsky or from Djilas about the

[11] Trotsky explicitly rejects attempts to define the Soviet bureaucracy as an ownership class. "The attempt to represent the Soviet bureaucracy as a class of 'state capitalists' will obviously not withstand criticism. The bureaucracy has neither stocks, nor bonds. . . . The individual bureaucrat cannot transmit to his heirs his rights in the exploitation of state apparatus" (1972, pp. 249–50). But Trotsky very clearly sees that the bureaucracy which emerged in Stalinist Russia is a historically new phenomenon. "In its intermediary and regulating function, its concern to maintain social ranks, and its exploitation of the state apparatus for personal goals, the Soviet bureaucracy is similar to every bureaucracy, especially the fascist. But it is also in a vast way different. In no other regime has a bureaucracy achieved such a degree of independence from the dominating class. . . . The Soviet bureaucracy has risen above a class which is hardly emerging from destitution and darkness. . . . Whereas the fascists, when they find themselves in power, are united with the big bourgeoisie . . . the Soviet bureaucracy takes on bourgeois customs without having beside it a national bourgeoisie. In this sense it is something more than a bureaucracy" (pp. 248–49). He defines the bureaucracy as a "stratum" (p. 249), but this term certainly would not suit his aim of describing the parasitism (p. 250) of the bureaucracy, its bourgeoisie customs, etc.; therefore, he will often refer to a ruling Soviet caste (p. 253). In fact, in Trotsky the terms "ruling stratum" and "ruling caste" are used interchangeably. The Trotskyist concept of bureaucratic caste is a very insightful one, since it (unlike the concept of stratum) does emphasize the qualitatively new feature of the Soviet bureaucracy. However, the application of the concept to the Soviet bureaucracy does not seem to be very fortunate. Max Weber is very precise when he defines caste as a special case of "status groups" or "estates," as a position in traditional social structures. Weber is also persuasive when he suggests that caste differs from ordinary status order because caste is oriented religiously and ritually (1958, p. 44). None of these criteria seems to apply to the Soviet bureaucracy.
[12] Djilas states: "The specific characteristic of this new class is its collective ownership" (1957, p. 54).

real nature of social structure under state socialism than from the official Soviet Marxists or from the stratification theorists, but I have serious doubts—both theoretical and empirical—that the dominating class of state-socialist societies can be identified with the bureaucracy. The fundamental theoretical dilemma is whether the bureaucracy can be defined as an ownership class. Such a definition equates the right of disposition with ownership, which is more than questionable. It hardly requires textual proof that Marx himself clearly distinguished between ownership and disposition, and without this distinction it would be impossible to understand the bureaucratic and technocratic phenomena of capitalist society. If we define the socialist bureaucrat as a member of an ownership class because he has the right to dispose of the means of production, why not apply the same logic to modern capitalism and call the technobureaucracy found in the latter a new dominating class? In my understanding, the strength of Marxist class analysis is its emphasis on mediations. It is a powerful theory because it explains why those who formally exercise power act in the interest of a ruling class which may itself be less visible. If we equate ownership with the right of disposal, then we make the concept of ownership so abstract and general that it loses all its theoretical strength.

Furthermore, if we define the dominating class as those who dispose of the means of production, then we make an empirically unjustified distinction between the technobureaucracy and the rest of the intelligentsia. I do not want to repeat here the well-known arguments as to how difficult it is to determine accurately who in fact has the right to dispose of the means of production in a state-socialist society. It is well known how limited the rights of a factory manager are. Strictly speaking, any ownership class which could be defined in terms of a real monopoly of the right of disposal might be as exclusive as the Politburo, which would mean restricting the membership of the new class to 10–20 individuals—an obvious nonsense. But even if we treat these problems of operationalization generously, we would still have to explain why a minor bureaucrat in an economic ministry or in the Central Planning Office is a member of the dominating class and why an influential professor of economics is not.

One empirical difficulty connected with this crucial distinction between the bureaucracy and the intellectuals is created by the relatively fast circulation of the intellectual elite in Eastern Europe. The present director of one of the comedy theaters in Budapest is a former high-ranking officer of the political police. His former boss in the Hungarian equivalent of the KGB is today the manager of a big salami factory. Today one may be an officer in the political police, but tomorrow one might be the only person licensed to produce political jokes, or one might supervise salami production or sociological research, as a manager or an academic. The line between intellectuals and bureaucrats is a very shaky one in terms of personal career patterns. Many university graduates with academic ambitions enter the Party bureaucracy immediately after graduation, since they know that a few years in the Party bureaucracy is the most powerful recommendation to university chairs and other high academic positions. The intellectual elite circulates rapidly. It is stratified according to the levels of power rather than segmented into a bureaucracy/intellectuals dichotomy. It may well be more difficult to jump from the local level into the national power elite than to shift from the Academy of Science into the Central Committee of the Party or vice versa.

I would also argue that the bureaucratic class theory overemphasizes the power of bureaucrats and underestimates the impact of nonbureaucratic intellectuals on societal decision making. The bureaucrat in the Central Planning Office who allocates a few hundred million zloty or levas may not exercise a great deal of power, since the rules of the game are strictly set. However, those who have an impact on the formation of these rules, from the expert economics professor to the ideologically influential movie director or poet, may in fact have more power than the bureaucrat without having any right of disposal. Finally, I would like to add that from the point of view of material privilege it is practically impossible to distinguish between the technobureaucracy and the intelligentsia. Their living standards are practically identical. It is the level of power which stratifies them, not the bureaucracy/intellectuals dichotomy.

THE ECONOMIC FOUNDATIONS OF CLASS ANTAGONISMS UNDER STATE SOCIALISM

I found that existing class and stratification theories do not explain the nature and dynamism of social conflicts and inequalities in state-socialist societies. Despite their diverging political and ideological overtones, they all espouse "formal Marxism." They define class relations as ownership relations. I will propose first that in state-socialist societies, which by definition have abolished the institution of private ownership, we have to go beyond this formal Marxism and beyond the analysis of ownership if we want to find the economic foundation of class antagonisms.

Marx himself undoubtedly explained class relations from facts about ownership, but Marxist theory was a reaction to capitalist society, and even Marxist methodology may need crucial modifications when applied to the substantive analysis of noncapitalist socioeconomic formations. Marx himself became increasingly aware of the limitations of his own methodology, whereby the structure of different modes of production was derived from ownership relations. Already in the *Grundrisse* he proved to be highly flexible when analyzing non-Western societies. He seriously considered the possibility that the institutions of the village community were as important for the understanding of Asiatic societies as the forms of relations of owner-ship, and it is clear from his later correspondence that he understood the significance of the *obshchina* in the Russian model of development.[13] He started to differentiate between socioeconomic formations on the basis of criteria other than ownership. Generally speaking, I would argue that ownership played the crucial role it did in Marxist theory only because Marx developed his methodology in the course of his study of Western societies, where—already in the precapitalist stage of development—private owner-ship was the major socioeconomic institution around which social conflicts were structured. But this methodology will not explain much about the functioning of societies where private ownership does not exist and where we cannot find inherent forces which would lead to the development of private ownership. When Marx inclined to accept Vera Zasulich's proposi-tion that in Russia socialism might emerge directly from the village com-munity, he had to give serious thought to the possibility that societies might bypass the development of private ownership.[14] Consequently, the history of mankind could not be explained simply in terms of how private ownership developed and why this institution would in the future cease to exist.

If this is true for non-European precapitalist formations, then the empha-sis on ownership relations in the analysis of socialist societies is even more misleading. A formally applied orthodox Marxist methodology which assumes that socioeconomic antagonisms can emerge only from ownership relations loses all scientific strength and may well become pure apologetics when applied to state-socialist societies—societies which consciously abolished private ownership in the belief that this single historical act would generate the establishment of a nonantagonistic society. This may well explain how the most revolutionary theory of all time came to be a conservative state religion in all those countries which accept the ideological papacy of Moscow. Most contemporary Marxists try to solve this paradox

[13] As Perry Anderson points out, in his early correspondence with Engels, Marx around 1853 assumed that a separate "Asiatic mode of production" should be identified (Ander-son 1974, pp. 476–83) due to the domination of state ownership of the land under Asiatic feudalism. Later he changed his mind, and in the *Grundrisse* the "self-sustaining village community" seems to be the major variable which explains the existence of a separate "Asiatic mode of production" (Marx 1975b, pp. 66–70). In the light of Marx's early correspondence with Engels and the analysis of the *Grundrisse*, it seems clear that Marx could not decide what sort of ownership existed in the East, and from this we might safely conclude that therefore ownership cannot be all that important to identify "modes of production."

[14] In 1881, in letters drafted to Zasulich, Marx goes so far as to suggest that "Russia is capable of developing and transforming the archaic form of its village community, instead of destroying it." In these letters he clearly hesitates to decide whether the development of private ownership is an absolute necessity and if it would not be possible to maintain the "collective element" that he finds so attractive in the Russian communes. At the end he explicitly rejects a deterministic position and describes an alternative: "either the property element in it will overcome the collective element or the other way around" (1975b, pp. 142–45).

by questioning whether Soviet Marxism is "real" Marxism, but not even the most sophisticated talmudic argument could explain why orthodox Soviet ideologues claim to be Marxist, even though when they are weighed on the scales of real Marxism they are found wanting.

I would argue that Soviet ideologues chose and cling to Marxism because they found something in its orthodox teaching that suited them in their effort to build an apologetic ideology of state socialism, and this is precisely the assumption that class antagonism can emerge only from conflicts related to ownership. Consequently, if we want to develop a critical theory of any of the phenomena of state-socialist societies, we have first to fight the myth of the all-importance of ownership and develop a substantive understanding of the economic institutions and mechanisms of such societies. The last half-century has proved that Marx let himself be misled by his own methodology. He attached exaggerated hopes to the abolition of private ownership, and he failed to foresee that the new society would create its own mechanisms of economic exploitation and political oppression, that the abolition of the class power of the bourgeoisie would lead to the emergence of a new, similarly alienated, and politically—at least for the time being—even more oppressive class power. But if this is indeed a new class power and not merely the political totalitarianism of a ruling elite, then we should be able to find its roots in specific state-socialist economic institutions, and obviously in something other than the state ownership of the means of production. In this way we might be able to go beyond the formal analysis of ownership relations but still stay within the general framework of a historical materialist perspective.

In attempting to broaden the frame of reference of class analysis sufficiently to make it applicable to state-socialist societies, I would suggest that the purpose of class analysis is to explain rationalized forms of economic exploitation and the forms of political and social oppression built on these. When Marx and Engels developed their theory of the class dichotomy of capitalist society, they were first of all interested in the capitalist system of economic exploitation to be found in the institutions and mechanisms which guaranteed the expropriation of surplus from the direct producer by the owner of capital. The crucial task of class analysis is, then, to understand the institutions of expropriation of surplus; and if around these institutions an antagonism of interests is to be found, then one may be justified in talking about class relations. Furthermore, I would argue that Marx defined his classes on the basis of ownership relations because in a capitalist market economy it was the private ownership of the means of production which legitimated expropriation. Following this logic, I suggest that to test whether class analysis is applicable to state-socialist societies at all, we first have to understand the state-socialist institutions of expropriation of surplus and define the principles which legitimate expropriation under state socialism.

Then we need to find out whether the direct producer is in a position to challenge this system of legitimation and whether his interests are systematically in conflict with those who expropriate or who legitimate the state-socialist form of expropriation.

State-socialist societies developed and legitimated institutions of expropriation which are specifically state socialist, which are not known in other socioeconomic formations—and these are the institutions of state-socialist rational redistribution. In a recently published paper on the social inequalities engendered by state-socialist redistributive economies (Szelenyi 1978), I tried to contrast the redistributive institutions of state-socialist societies with mechanisms of redistribution of real income in welfare capitalism. I do not want to, and due to the limitations of space I cannot, repeat the arguments developed there. Here I merely want to emphasize that, despite the increasing role of redistributive mechanisms in contemporary welfare capitalism, modern capitalist economies can still be distinguished as "late market economies" from "state-socialist redistributive economies." The redistributive intervention of the welfare state did not overrule the market logic of the economy in any of the contemporary Western capitalist societies. In all these societies the state only redistributes incomes. The incomes themselves are defined on the market. Furthermore, the economic surplus that can be used for extended reproduction is not allocated by the welfare redistributors; the key investment decisions are made according to the logic of profit maximization by the owners of capital or their representatives. Under welfare capitalism the basic class division is still, therefore, the division between the capitalist (who disposes of the surplus available for investments) and the wage laborer or direct producer. The welfare redistributor plays only a mediating role in this basic class dichotomy. In state-socialist societies redistribution is not limited to the reallocation of incomes: under state socialism it is the very surplus which is redistributed. If the main task of the redistributor is to allocate surplus, then this redistributor does not mediate between the owner of capital and the seller of labor power; he replaces the owner of capital. While contemporary welfare capitalism is a market economy modified by welfare-oriented income redistribution, state socialism is a redistributive economy. It is a new type of economy. While contemporary capitalism still can be characterized by the class dichotomy between capital owners and wage laborers, contemporary state socialism might be characterized by the antagonism between redistributors and direct producers. I claim that this analysis is a quite consistent adaptation of the Marxian methodology: the basic class distinction is established around the processes of production and expropriation and the allocation of surplus, around the key relations of production.[15]

[15] My distinction between "contemporary welfare capitalism" and "state-socialist redistributive economies" is a distinction between two ideal types. I am aware that empiri-

If we define a new dominant class according to its relation to the institutions of redistribution in a state-socialist society, don't we necessarily agree with Djilas or with Dahrendorf? If the new dominant class is constituted by the institution of redistribution of surplus, is it not identical with the bureaucracy which makes the actual planning decisions? If the new class is constituted on redistributive power, don't we agree with Dahrendorf that in modern economies economic class is replaced by political power?[16]

It is central to my analysis that the new dominant class is neither bureaucratic in the precise Weberian sense of the term nor based on political power, as Dahrendorf suggested. The class which is organized around redistributive power is far from being bureaucratic, at least if we use the term "bureaucratic" in a precise Weberian sense. Both Weber and Marx[17]

---

cally identifiable systems—say, the Swedish economy in 1980, or the Polish or Hungarian economy in any given year—might be to a degree mixtures of these ideal types. One might find examples in Sweden when the state does not limit itself to income redistribution, but might significantly affect investment decision, or one might be able to observe certain market mechanisms to be at work even in the crucial spheres of investments or trading of labor power in East European socialist societies. But these empirical "mixtures" do not make the construction of ideal types unnecessary or invalid: it can still be claimed that Sweden is predominantly ruled by the ideal type of "welfare capitalism," Poland by "state-socialist redistributive economy."

[16] According to Dahrendorf, "From the point of view of social structure of industrial enterprises, this means a significant change in the basis of legitimacy of entrepreneurial authority. . . . The old style capitalist exercised authority because he owned the instruments of production. By contrast to this legitimation by property, the authority of the manager resembles in many ways that of the heads of political institutions. . . . The right of the manager to command and expect obedience accrues in part from the property rights delegated to him. . . . But besides these . . . the manager . . . has to seek a second, and often more important, basis of legitimacy for his authority, namely, some kind of consensus among those who are bound to obey his commands. . . . The manager, unlike the 'full capitalist,' can ill afford to exercise his authority in direct and deliberate contravention to the wishes and interests of his subordinates" (1959, pp. 44–45). Dahrendorf here suggests that even in the case of the industrial manager it is political power which constitutes class position—economic power based on ownership is replaced by political power based on consensus. My analysis is rather different. I suggest that economic power based on ownership is replaced by economic power based on the teleological knowledge of the redistributor.

[17] Despite the fundamental differences in the Marxian and Weberian theories of bureaucracy, Marx and Weber both emphasize the executive nature of bureaucratic power and its dependence on modern capitalism and civil society. Probably the fullest and most interesting discussion of the bureaucracy by Marx can be found in his "Contribution to the Critique of Hegel's Philosophy of Law." Here Marx attempts to prove that Hegel is wrong in assuming that the bureaucracy is a "universal class." For Marx the basic classes are formed within civil society and the political state. The state bureaucracy is far from being the universal class; the state is not above civil society. In the light of this analysis the state bureaucracy rather appears as the executive arm of the bourgeoisie (Marx 1975a). From this analysis of Marx it follows that it is in fact quite problematic for Marxists whether a bureaucracy can exist under socialism, when civil society and, more specifically, the class antagonism of the bourgeoisie and proletariat have been abolished. For Weber bureaucratic domination is the purest type of legal authority. Of course, Weber does not think that the bureaucracy is an executive arm of the bourgeoisie, but he

would agree that bureaucracy—at least in its pure form—is the product of civil society. Civil society is integrated by formal rationality; it is the first societal formation which separates ends and means, the telos and techne, and subordinates telos to techne.[18] Civil society emerged when the rationality of goal setting, or teleological thinking, was questioned, and rationality was more narrowly defined as the "optimal choice of means leading to a given end." Marx with critical and Weber with apologetic overtones state that in civil society goal setting is referred to the "irrational," to the sphere of beliefs, to bourgeois politics. In civil society a separate sphere of politics exists, where goal setting is ideally done in a pluralistic political system and executive functions are reserved for bureaucratic organizations. When Weber defined bureaucratic power he identified it with executive tasks, and he believed that it was rooted in the expert knowledge of the bureaucrat. Weber strongly believed that experts are unable to tell people what they ought to do, that they can only tell them how to reach goals they have selected for themselves according to criteria not susceptible to judgment in terms of "rationality." For societal analysis this means that bureaucracy only executes goals set by a separate political mechanism. Bureaucrats will always try to extend their power. They will claim that goal-setting functions are basically technicalities; that the only possible course of action is the one that they predict with their "scientific methods"; and that, since no alternatives are open, no political decision is required or possible. But even the

finds formalism or formal rationality the most crucial criterion of rational bureaucracy. The bureaucracy for Weber is efficient as long as it operates within formal rationality, as long as it uses technical knowledge, as long as it does not have to set goals but can execute goals set by a separate political mechanism. Weber is quite aware that the socialist project intends to transcend bourgeois formal rationality, and he very clearly sees the explosive contradiction between the substantive rationality socialism represents and the formal rationality of legal authority and bureaucratic domination. "For socialism would ... require a still higher degree of formal bureaucratization than capitalism. If this should prove not to be possible, it would demonstrate the existence of another of those fundamental elements of irrationality—a conflict between formal and substantive rationality of the sort which sociology so often encounters" (Weber 1978, pp. 217–26, esp. p. 225). See also, about Marx's theory of the bureaucracy, Perez-Diaz (1978, esp. pp. 10–11).

[18] In the work of Marx the critique of bourgeois rationality, the critique of capitalism as the system in which techne dominates telos, is implicit. Marx did not develop any systematic theory of rationality, and this is only implied in his critique of political economy. The problematic of the relationship between telos and techne, teleological and technical rationality, will mostly appear only as the subordination of use value to exchange value, as the subordination of human need to profit interests, as the problem of production for profit rather than for the satisfaction of human needs. It is the Frankfurt School which develops the Marxist critique of capitalism as a critique of technical or instrumental rationality, as a critique of rationality which accepts the domination of telos by techne. This type of critical Marxism finds its roots in the early works of Horkheimer and Adorno (Horkheimer 1978; see also Connerton 1976, esp. pp. 27–28; Arato and Gebhardt 1978, esp. pp. 8–12) and is later more fully developed in Habermas (see esp. Habermas 1974, pp. 195–252, 268–76; also see Habermas 1970).

most power-hungry bureaucrat operates within the framework set by the civil society. He can claim power only on the basis of his expert knowledge. He cannot claim to have the scientific, rational knowledge to set goals. I would argue that redistributive power under state socialism is basically of a different nature. It is not based on "expert knowledge." It is not based on the assumption that goal setting is something irrational and that only the choice of means can be considered as, properly speaking, rational activity. The bureaucrat of civil society has to operate in the sphere of "formal rationality." The redistributor of state socialism claims to operate within the framework of "substantive rationality" (to use again Weber's terminology).[19] He claims a monopoly of rational choice among goals. He claims a monopoly of technical knowledge. Thus the orthodox Soviet Marxist view that under socialism bureaucracy does not exist makes sense in a way. The teleological redistributor is of a different social nature from Weber's bureaucrat. The Weberian bureaucrat's claim to power does not challenge the fundamental power structure of civil society based on private ownership; the bureaucrat may have certain particularistic interests, but he cannot strive for his own class power.[20] Bureaucratic power, properly defined, can exist only in a world where techne dominates telos, in a world which is split into economy and politics, means and ends, subject and object; and this is the world of market capitalism, the world of private ownership, which is basically structured into a class dichotomy between owners and nonowners. Under these circumstances the bureaucrat of civil society will mediate conflicts between the basic classes, but his main interest is in the maintenance of the status quo of class relations, since by challenging it he would undermine the very basis of his existence.

The Marxist ideal of socialism is an attack not only on capitalism narrowly

[19] It is interesting to note that Weber does not develop his distinction between formal and substantive rationality in his general theory of types of rationalities, but only in his sociology of economic systems (1978, pp. 85–113). The need to develop the concept of substantive rationality arises for Weber when he begins to analyze the problems of planning and especially planning under socialist economies. When I am using the term "substantive rationality" to describe the specific nature of knowledge of the "teleological redistributors" I follow closely Weber's own logic. As Weber states, "Where a planned economy is radically carried out, it must further accept the inevitable reduction in formal, calculatory rationality. . . . Substantive and formal . . . rationality are . . . after all largely distinct problems. This fundamental and, in the last analysis, unavoidable element of irrationality in economic systems is one of the important sources of all 'social' problems, and above all, of the problems of socialism" (p. 111). This quotation, together with the one from n. 17 above, allows us to conclude that, since formal rationality is the rationality of the bureaucracy, the teleological redistributor and planning guided by substantive rationality do not fit the Weberian ideal type of bureaucracy.

[20] For Marx it is obvious that the bureaucracy does not represent such a separate set of interests which would allow us to define the bureaucracy as a class. The bureaucracy only expresses as general interests the particularistic interests of the dominant class, of the bourgeoisie. What is peculiarly bureaucratic interest is nothing more than the transformation of the particular interests into universal ones (1975a, pp. 44–48, esp. p. 46; see also Perez-Diaz 1978, pp. 28–32).

defined but also on the very principles on which civil society is built. All previous critical theorists criticized capitalism from the standpoint and values of civil society. Marx and Engels were the first to claim that the radical revolutionary transformation of the capitalist mode of production is impossible without the rejection of civil society and its values, without the rejection of bourgeois humanism and bourgeois democracy.[21] The ideal society they proposed would reunite a world split into separate, alienated spheres of existence. It would be a society in which telos again dominated techne, a society ruled by substantive rationality. When I suggest that the intelligentsia is a class *in statu nascendi* in contemporary state socialism, what I am saying is that in this new society, which is the negation of civil society, the intellectuals attempt to monopolize this substantive rationality. And if they succeed in doing so the power they claim will be of a class nature, since it is based on the dominant principle of legitimation.

It would be wrong, on the other hand, to believe that this new class (and the new society) is the product of the Marxist ideal. On the contrary, it would be more realistic to say that intellectuals have used Marxist ideals in order to grasp class power. They had been unable to do this successfully in previous socioeconomic formations. Marx believed that his teachings would become a material force through the revolutionary praxis of the proletariat, but things happened otherwise. It was the Russian intelligentsia which realized the potential of Marxist ideology and transformed it into a powerful weapon of class struggle.[22]

Neither was it accidental that this happened in Russia and that Russia's example was followed first by other East European countries. The new society in which telos dominates techne emerged from societies where there existed an "intelligentsia" properly speaking, where intellectuals consciously articulated their aspirations to occupy a dominant position in the social structure.

In other words, state socialism and its new dominant class emerged in

[21] Marx formulates clearly that the purpose of his materialism is to transcend civil society in thesis 10 on Feuerbach: "The standpoint of the old materialism is 'civil' society; the standpoint of the new is human society or socialised humanity" (1972, p. 13). When Marx emphasizes that the standpoint of his new historical materialism is *socialized humanity*, he rejects the individualism of civil society, which is a clear indication that he does not limit his project to the critique of capitalism and its political economy but intends more: to develop a comprehensive critique of civil society too.

[22] Gouldner does not believe that the proletariat came to power in the so-called socialist revolutions, or that it is likely for the proletariat ever to come to power: "The Communist Manifesto had held that the history of all hitherto existing society was the history of class struggles: freeman and slave, patrician and plebian, lord and serf, guildmaster and journeyman, and, then, bourgeoisie and proletariat. In this series, however, there was one unspoken regularity: the slaves did not succeed the masters, the plebians did not vanquish the patricians, the serfs did not overthrow the lords, and the journeymen did not triumph over the guildmasters. The lowliest class never came to power. Nor does it seem likely to now" (1979, p. 93).

Eastern Europe because two sets of conditions met there. On the one hand, a redistributive economic system was created, and this system served as an objective base for class power rooted in the teleological knowledge of planners and redistributors. On the other hand, in this part of the world a new type of intellectual, the intelligentsia, developed prior to the socialist revolutionary transformation. This East European intelligentsia was distinguished from other types of intellectuals precisely by the importance it attached to the teleological component of its knowledge. In 1917 in Russia and following the Second World War in Eastern Europe, when the objective position of a new class was created with the abolition of private ownership and the creation of a centrally, "scientifically" planned economy, the "agents" to fill these positions—the intelligentsia—were also ready for their new historical task.

The central hypothesis of my analysis, therefore, is that the new class in Eastern European state socialism is broader than the bureaucracy: it is composed of all those who have a vested interest in the production and reproduction of a certain type of intellectual knowledge—teleological knowledge—which is legitimating redistributive power under socialist redistributive economies. The new dominant class is composed, therefore, of a type of intellectual, the intelligentsia.

In this paper I use the concept of intellectuals as a generic concept. Unlike Gouldner,[23] I do not claim that all intellectuals in all modern societies are on the road to class power. My hypothesis is a more modest one. All that I suggest is that one type of intellectual, the intelligentsia, gains class power under state-socialist redistributive economies. I disagree with Gouldner concerning the possibilities of class formation of the other major modern type of intellectuals, the professionals. While Gouldner maintains that professionalism leads intellectuals into the new dominant class position,[24] I propose that professionalism integrates intellectuals into the basic class structure of market capitalism. As long as intellectuals accept their

[23] Gouldner, unlike most left-wing theorists of the new class (e.g., Djilas, Burnham, or Shachtman), does not exclude from the new class the "proper intellectuals": ideologues, social scientists, etc. While left-wing theories mostly limit the new class to managers and/or technocrats and bureaucrats, Gouldner uses a broad concept which includes all intellectuals: "In all countries . . . in the twentieth century . . . a New Class composed of intellectuals and the technical intelligentsia . . . enter into contention with the groups already in control of the society's economy, whether these are businessmen or party leaders" (1979, p. 1). I want to note here that Gouldner is using the concept "intelligentsia" rather differently than I do in this paper. I think my usage is closer to the conventional one (see Gella 1976, esp. pp. 9–27). It is also interesting that Gouldner, while using a broad definition of "intellectuals," still excludes from this the Party leaders, but he never explains why he does that.

[24] Gouldner believes that the vehicle by which the new class replaces the rule of money capital with the rule of "cultural capital" is professionalism: "Professionalism in effect devalues the authority of the old class" (1979, p. 19). I think Gouldner is wrong: professionalism, by emphasizing the significance of technical knowledge, does not represent any challenge to the ideological and cultural hegemony of the bourgeoisie.

definition as professionals—what market capitalism offers them—they cannot claim class power of their own. They will remain only a semiautonomous stratum—or, to use Erik Olin Wright's more precise terminology, they will remain in a contradictory class location.[25]

At this stage I have to offer at least a working definition of the concepts of "intellectuals," "professionals," and "intelligentsia."

I will follow Gouldner in defining intellectuals as those who are bound together by the "culture of critical discourse" (CCD).[26] The CCD, according to Gouldner's definition, is a "speech community"[27] which has been developed since the Enlightenment by the modern "men of idea." These modern men of idea, whom I will call intellectuals, within the CCD do gain monopoly of a kind of knowledge which has two main characteristics: it is secular (in Gouldner's definition, it does not accept any authority but reason) and it is theoretical. The theoreticity of the knowledge intellectuals monopolize is sometimes also linked by Gouldner to its "context-variability."[28] The CCD is common to all modern intellectuals, under both market capitalism and state socialism. But in its historical evolution the CCD takes two different forms. Where modernization coincides with the development of market capitalism, the CCD leads to professionalization. Professionalism is the form of knowledge within the CCD in which the technical component, the know-how, dominates the teleological component. In those social-historical contexts where attempts to modernize do not coincide with market capitalism—already in prerevolutionary Eastern Europe and more so in this area after the socialist transformation—the teleological component of intellectual knowledge is not subordinated to technical know-how: intellectuals are not defined as professionals but, rather, as intelligentsia.

[25] Erik Olin Wright introduced the concept of "contradictory class locations" to describe positions in the class structure that more conventional orthodox Marxists would call "strata." According to Wright, "An alternative way of dealing with . . . ambiguities in the class structure is to regard some positions as occupying objectively contradictory locations within class relations. . . . (In a sense, of course, all class positions are 'contradictory locations' in that class relations are intrinsically antagonistic, contradictory social relations. The point is that certain positions in the class structure constitute doubly contradictory locations: they represent positions which are torn between the basic contradictory class relations of capitalist society. . . . I will for convenience simply refer to them as 'contradictory class locations'.)" (1978, pp. 61–62).

[26] Gouldner defines the culture of critical discourse this way: "The culture of critical discourse (CCD) is an historically evolved set of rules, a grammar of discourse, which (1) is concerned to justify its assertions, but (2) whose mode of justification does not proceed by invoking authorities, and (3) prefers to elicit the voluntary consent of those addressed solely on the basis of arguments adduced" (1979, p. 28).

[27] Gouldner calls the CCD a "grammar of discourse" and therefore the new class of intellectuals is a "speech community" (1979, p. 28).

[28] Gouldner uses the concept of context-variability to describe the CCD. "Here, good speech is speech that can make its own principles explicit and is oriented to conforming with them, rather than stressing context-sensitivity and context-variability. Good speech here thus has theoreticity" (1979, p. 28).

My basic typology therefore is the following:

Intellectuals
= those modern men of idea who are
bound together by the CCD.

Professionals
= intellectuals under
market capitalism in
whose knowledge
technical know-how
dominates the
teleological component.

Intelligentsia
= intellectuals who
maintain the domination of the
teleological component of
knowledge above technical
know-how, intellectuals in
pre- and postrevolutionary
Eastern Europe, in societies
where modernization does
not coincide with the
development of civil society and
market capitalism.

It is not accidental that most of the sociological and philosophical literature on intellectuals concerns Eastern Europe (publications on the Russian
and Polish intelligentsia, particularly, dominate the field).[29] I would
attribute a symbolic importance to the fact that the very term "intelligentsia" is of Russian origin. Anglo-Saxon authors, when they had to go
beyond the notion of "professionals," needed to transliterate a Russian
expression into English. Capitalism in England produced professionals.
Eastern Europe, fluctuating between Asiatic and European feudalism,
between feudalism and Western capitalism, between East European
absolutism and civil society, gave birth to an intelligentsia. For a genuine
empiricist (who is by definition a product of a "pure" civil society), trained
in Anglo-Saxon pragmatism and positivism, the notion of an intelligentsia
is an obscure, prescientific (or nonscientific) one. The scientific category is
"professionals," which includes a group of occupations: people with certain
qualifications performing social and economic functions for which these
qualifications are necessary. Professionals are people who have a monopoly
of knowledge of how to choose means to reach already selected goals. They

---

[29] Aleksander Gella emphasizes the uniqueness of the concept of intelligentsia for Eastern
Europe: "While all other classes and strata of Eastern Europe have had their counterparts
in the West, the intelligentsia, strictly speaking, did not" (1976, p. 10). He suggests that
one should make a clear distinction between the concepts of intellectuals and intelligentsia (p. 11) and should locate the intelligentsia in the mid-19th-century East European context. Interestingly, he notes that the use of the term "intelligentsia" first occurs
at almost the same time in Germany, Russia, and Poland (in 1849, 1846, and 1844,
respectively) (p. 12).

are experts whose services are bought by those who set the goals. Professionals are the product of civil society and of market capitalism. The very basis of their existence—like the basis of the existence of the bureaucracy—is the definition of "expert knowledge" as knowledge relating to means and a market demand for this knowledge from those who set goals.

The history of Western intellectuals is a continuous struggle against this definition. The best Western intellects never accepted this subordinate social role. They reserved their right to make judgments about the goals they were hired to execute. Among left-wing theorists, the belief prevailed that genuine intellectuals were more than professionals: they were social critics.[30] But despite such reservations, most of those with rare intellectual skills were continuously "corrupted" by Western capitalism. High wages were offered for their executive skills, and they were increasingly allowed to wield bureaucratic power in compensation for their intellectual frustration.

This mass transformation of intellectuals into professionals simply did not occur in Eastern Europe. The numerical expansion of intellectuals from the 18th century onward was not followed by a similar increase in market demand for professionals. For many decades—in the late 18th and early 19th centuries—the intellectuals were in the vanguard of the fight for the Westernization of Eastern Europe, but by the mid-19th century, especially in Russia, Western professionalization looked less and less attractive to many of them. East European intellectuals increasingly realized the advantages of not being professionals. They defined themselves as intelligentsia, people with not only executive skills but also moral commitment and historical vision. This late 19th-century East European intelligentsia was open to ideologies which projected new "teleological societies," societies ruled by substantive rationality. The East European intelligentsia was ready to bypass Western professionalization, which had proved a historical dead end for intellectuals in their long march to power. It was ready for the Bolshevik call to form a historical vanguard to lead the revolutionary transformation of society and create a new rational order based on the principles of scientific socialism. The Leninist emphasis on superrationality in organization, the fight against any form of anarchism and spontaneity, the skepticism concerning bourgeois electoralism as a legitimate way to choose among alternatives, appealed not only to those who shared Bolshevik values but to all intellectuals who believed they knew how a rational society should be organized. Lenin argued on the eve of the October Revolution that the Bolsheviks were ready to take power, not because they could count on the support of the majority of the population, but because they

[30] Paul Baran (1961) makes a crucial distinction between "mental workers" and "intellectuals" which is typical of most left-wing ideologues. For Baran, to be an intellectual means to be a "social critic." Those who fall short on this criterion—however competent they might be in their professions—can only be defined as "mental workers."

had enough cadres to fill all major decision-making positions.[31] What the new society needed first of all was cadres armed with the tools of scientific socialism, cadres with teleological knowledge, to lead society and to run the state-socialist redistributive economy.

It should be clear from this short and necessarily superficial argument that the class which is organized around the position of teleological redistributor stretches beyond those who make the immediate redistributive decisions. It is integrated by the ethos of state-socialist rational redistribution, and it includes all those who claim power—not only economic power but, for example, cultural or administrative power—on the basis of their monopoly of teleological knowledge. It potentially integrates the whole intelligentsia into a dominating class. The main thrust of this analysis is the rejection of the bureaucratic class concept, but without the acceptance of Dahrendorf's proposition that in modern societies economic class power is being replaced by political class power. The intelligentsia's claims under state socialism are legitimated in the same way as is the expropriation of surplus. The class power of the intelligentsia stretches beyond the economic sphere, but its foundations are in the basic institutions which guarantee social reproduction in state-socialist societies. Critics of Dahrendorf[32] rightly point out that he is basically rejecting class analysis. He calls the political elite a class and argues that classes proper—that is, classes emerging from economic antagonisms—no longer exist. When I suggest that the intelligentsia is in the process of becoming a class, I am not describing the political or bureaucratic elite of state socialism; I am using a broad, economically based category.

Here I have to acknowledge one major theoretical problem all attempts—including mine—which try to offer a class analysis of state socialism are

[31] Lenin, in September 1917, when he tried to convince his fellow Bolsheviks that the Party was ready to take state power, clearly indicated that for such a move the Party does not need the vote of the majority of the population, or even that of the working class. The Party will be ready to govern as soon as it can produce enough cadres to rule. In Lenin's own words, "The proletariat, we are told, will not be able to set the state apparatus in motion. Since the 1905 revolution, Russia has been governed by 130,000 landowners. ... Yet we are told that the 240,000 members of the Bolshevik Party will not be able to govern Russia. ... These 240,000 are already backed by no less than a million votes. ... We therefore already have a 'state apparatus' of one million people devoted to the socialist state ... " (1970, p. 413).

[32] Giddens claims that Dahrendorf does not actually reformulate the concept of class, but replaces class with authority. "Indeed, Dahrendorf might be accused of escaping from the issues involved by the same sort of terminological speciousness of which he accuses Marx: 'for while private property may disappear (empirical hypothesis), this can have no possible bearing upon the existence or disappearance of classes (trick of definition).' In attempting to reformulate the concept of class, Dahrendorf throws out the baby with the bath water ... by substituting 'authority' for 'class.' We already possess in sociology a reasonably adequate conceptual framework with which to analyse systems of authority, and there is little purpose served in confusing this with the terminology of 'class' " (1973, pp. 74–75).

confronted with. When I suggest that those who rule in Eastern Europe are not members of an elite constituted by political power, but that they form a class which is based in the system of economic reproduction, I have to justify why the concept of class is applicable to socioeconomic systems like state socialism where the separation of political and economic instances is much more limited than under market capitalism. Most class theorists would agree that the concept of class is applicable only in social-historical contexts where the political and economic instances are separated.[33]

I would try to defend my position and the applicability of the concept of class for contemporary Eastern Europe by claiming that under state socialism at least a relative separation of the "economic" from the "political" can be observed. Historically speaking, with the consolidation of the new socialist economic and social system this separation in fact increased. Following the revolutions the "political instance" seems to have a "primacy." This will later be criticized as "Stalinist voluntarism" in economic policy. With post-Stalinist "liberalization" this primacy of the political is reduced, and the need for scientific planning is emphasized. The "making of the new dominant class" of state socialism can be understood only in the historical process of this relative separation of the economic from the political. In the very first stage of state socialism those who rule do not yet appear as a class. The ruling Party and state apparatus appear to be constituted outside the economic system, constituted simply by coercive political power. (In this perspective the concept of "caste" of Trotsky is imprecise, but insightful.) We can understand only in the light of the later development that the main historic function of this Party and state apparatus is to facilitate the emergence of the new dominant class of intelligentsia as soon as the old social system is defeated politically and a relative separation of the economic instance becomes possible again. In this perspective the Party and state apparatus, which in the early stages of socialist develop-

[33] Bauman, in the most original analysis, suggested that state socialism produced a new system of authority which he, with a sense of humor, calls "partynominal authority" (1974, p. 136). He suggested that this partynominal authority is different from legal authority since it is "intimately attached to *Wertrationalität*" (p. 136). From this it follows that under partynominal authority neither the concept of "class" nor the notion of "bureaucracy" is applicable; both class and bureaucratic relations assume legal authority and *"Zweckrationalität."* Bauman proposes the concept of "officialdom" to describe the distribution of power under partynominal authority. The notion of officialdom is a very insightful one and an interesting candidate to replace class for the analysis of the social structure in state-socialist societies. Balint Balla offered an analysis similar in many respects to that of Bauman. Balla documented in great detail why the Weberian concept of bureaucracy is inapplicable to Soviet-type societies, and he proposed the notion of *"Kaderverwaltung"* (administration by cadres) to describe the system of domination of state socialism (1972, esp. pp. 47–62, 173–204). One ought to consider the need, following the analyses of Bauman and Balla, to try to develop a completely new terminology to describe structural positions under state socialism. For some sociologists this might be a more attractive attempt than my analysis which, more modestly, tries only to reinterpret the concept of class for state-socialist conditions.

ment appears as a bureaucratic elite, caste, or—to put it probably more precisely—estate, is actually a sort of vanguard of the new dominant class, the intelligentsia. This function of the early Party and state apparatus is obscured by the fact that the political history of state socialism can be described in terms of political struggles between the Party and state apparatus, which is constituted by the primacy of the political instance, and the technocratic and liberal and ideological intelligentsia, which represents the interest of the relative separation of the economic from the political.

The making of the new dominant class of intelligentsia is therefore identical with the historical process of relative separation of the economic from the political, the relative decline of the primacy of the political. From this proposition it follows that what Dahrendorf supposed to happen— namely, the replacement of "economic class power" by "political class power"—did not occur even under state socialism. A new dominant class emerged under state socialism only to the extent to which economic power can be conceived as relatively autonomous. The economic class was not replaced by a political class. However, Dahrendorf's analysis still offers insights for the understanding of social structures under state socialism. It is true that the separation of the economic and political instances declines with the transition from capitalism into state socialism. In this sense I would like to acknowledge that "class" under state socialism is a somewhat different concept than under market capitalism. While under capitalism class appears as economic class, under state socialism the classes which are formed probably should be called political-economic classes to acknowledge that, besides economic factors, political forces also play a role in constituting them.

The empirical and historical analysis of the complex interplay of political and economic forces in constituting the new class is important to explain the internal differentiation and dynamics of the new dominant class of the intelligentsia. It ought to be clear from the above analysis that I do not try to describe the new dominant class as a homogeneous one. The main fractions within the new class probably could be defined by the relative importance of political power in constituting them. The Party apparatus, more clearly constituted by political power, is a distinct fraction of the new class. The Party apparatus is in conflict—both historically and in contemporary struggles—with the planning-technocratic intelligentsia, which is more clearly constituted by the economic system. Most of political history is the struggle of the planning-technocratic intelligentsia (often articulated by their ideologues, the "liberal intellectuals") for economic reforms. On the surface it appears that the history of state socialism can be described as the struggle of liberal intellectuals against the Party apparatus. These conflicts between Party apparatus and rational planners and their liberal ideologues are real but not basic. The liberal, planning-technocratic intelligentsia gradually shares power with the Party apparatchik intelligentsia. The major economic antagonism is not between liberal intellectuals and the Party bureaucrats, but between the two classes, between the intelligentsia and the working class.

As was suggested earlier, if a class dichotomy exists in society, it must be rooted in the antagonism of interests with respect to the institutions which guarantee expropriation in the economic system. This antagonism under state socialism can be described in terms of conflicts between redistributive power and the interests of the direct producers—the antagonism on which the class dichotomy between the intelligentsia and the working class is based.

But does such an antagonism in fact exist? Is there a structural conflict of interest between the direct producer and the teleological redistributor? I would argue that such an antagonism does in fact exist and that the working class has an alternative system of legitimation. The dominating power under state socialism is challenged in a de facto way from time to time by attempts at self-determination by the working class, by the steadily re-emerging vision of self-managing socialism as an alternative to state-socialist redistributive economy. Yugoslavia, with her highly questionable claim to be the only country which has realized "self-managing socialism," is only one instance, but it can be shown that in political crises spontaneous working-class movements emerge unexpectedly, attempting to bring the economy more directly under workers' control. (Probably the classic example is the workers' councils formed in 1956 in Hungary without intellectuals or ideologues, on the initiative of the workers and under workers' control, but similar developments occurred in Czechoclovakia around 1968 and in Poland more recently.) These two alternative conceptions of socialism are already present in the classical theories.

Marx and Engels originally emphasized only that socialism would be that form of social organization which abolished the institution of private ownership, without specifying what the economic institutions of socialist society would look like. But later Engels, in particular, tried to define the *differentia specifica* of socialism as the self-determination of direct producers.[34] The

---

[34] Even the classics of Marxism seem to operate with different "models of socialism"; they seem to present different views of what constitutes the essence of a revolutionary socialist transformation of capitalism. In the "Communist Manifesto," Marx and Engels seem to assume that the socialist transformation is identical with the abolition of private ownership and the introduction of state ownership of the means of production—or, in more contemporary terminology, they see the essence of socialism in "nationalization of the means of production." Marx and Engels clearly state in the "Communist Manifesto": "The theory of Communists may be summed up in a single sentence: abolition of private property" (Marx and Engels 1970, p. 47). Then they add, "The proletariat will use its political supremacy . . . to centralise all instruments of production in the hands of the State . . . " (p. 52). But in other works the emphasis is on the socialization rather than simply on the nationalization of the means of production. Engels, in "Socialism: Utopian and Scientific," written more than four decades after the manifesto, strongly argues that

Szelenyi

Bolshevik fixation on discipline and order subsequently omitted all content from this concept and transformed it into a pure slogan, a pure ideology of state-socialist redistribution which served to deprive the working class of all power and to make workers far more powerless than workers in a capitalist factory or in a capitalist economy at large.

A socialist counterethos based on the principle of self-determination of the direct producer is highly underdeveloped and unarticulated and in fact is more evident in spontaneous opposition movements by the workers of Eastern Europe than in codified ideologies. I would argue that one reason for the underdeveloped nature of this alternative vision of socialism is the class nature of the intelligentsia under state socialism.

The emergence of "organic intellectuals" of the working class, intellectuals who articulate working-class interests from within the ranks of a class *in statu nascendi*, is far less likely here than it is under capitalist conditions where intellectuals, after all, do not occupy a major position of their own in the class structure, but are by definition between classes. Furthermore, I am inclined to believe that the counterethos of self-determination will remain in the long run only an opposition ideology in Eastern Europe. It cannot replace the ethos of rational redistribution, only continuously challenge it, at most limiting redistributive power slightly and forcing redistributors to consider more seriously the interests of the direct producer. It is difficult to imagine a modern noncapitalist industrial society without strong redistributive mechanisms. A certain degree of expropriation from the direct producer may be unavoidable, and I have little doubt that if an opposition movement based on the ideology of self-management succeeded in coming to power its leaders would still have to exercise a certain degree of redistributive power. When in August 1980 the Polish working class won major concessions, Lech Wałęsa, the chief negotiator of Solidarity, summed up the working-class victory this way: From now on we are co-owners. This is possibly the most realistic formulation of the challenge which the direct producer can pose to the teleological redistributor. What Wałęsa put forward was not a program to "abolish" teleological redistribution or central planning. In a sense, Wałęsa proposed a sharing of powers between two "owners," the acceptance of two principles of legitimation, the establishment of a dual power system. Realistically, it might be very difficult to go much beyond this; it might not be possible to imagine a society based only on the "immediate power of the direct producer" in an anarchosyndicalist fashion. Nonetheless, spontaneous working-class move-

"state ownership does not do away with the capitalistic nature of the productive forces" (1970, p. 422). Here Engels emphasized that the criterion of socialist transformation is the replacement of the capitalist mode of appropriation with a "direct social appropriation" (p. 423). This is more than a terminological difference. Two different visions of socialism (one based on state ownership, the other based on the principle of direct power of the immediate producer) find their roots here.

ments toward self-determination and workers' control and intellectual attempts to develop a counterideology based on the principles of self-management are highly important; they challenge the dominating ethos, and they represent forces which might transform contemporary socialist societies into articulated conflict systems. If we understand working-class interest in terms of a class hostility to redistributive power, then it becomes clear that self-determination is something qualitatively different from decentralization of administration, an easily acceptable concept for any teleological redistributor. The requirements of decentralization of administration, a central theme in most socioeconomic reforms in Eastern Europe during the last two decades, correspond to the spirit of redistributive power. Struggles between decentralization and centralization reflect conflicts between different levels of redistributive power. Real movement toward self-determination can only occur with the development of the countervailing power of the direct producer, a power which could force redistributive power into compromises. Decentralization in itself is only the delegation of power to lower echelons of the power structure and does not affect the relationship between the powerful and the powerless. (Probably Yugoslavia—at least if we can believe its internal left-wing critics—is merely a more decentralized version of the state socialism found in other East European countries.)

The purpose of the arguments above is to show that it may be meaningful to assume that a crucial structural antagonism exists within state-socialist redistributive economies between the class which is organized around the redistributor and the class which is to be found in the position of direct producer. It is to be hoped that any existing lack of theoretical sophistication and empirical documentation will only serve to stimulate both theoretical and empirical work in this direction, which may well be of crucial importance for the further development of socialist theory.

THE DOMINANT CLASS OF STATE SOCIALISM *IN STATU NASCENDI*

The intelligentsia is on its way to becoming the dominant class of East European state-socialist societies, but we are still only at the beginning of an obviously long historical process. Consequently, if we call the intelligentsia a class, we should be aware of a number of limitations in the use of this concept for the analysis of contemporary East European societies. The intelligentsia in many respects forms a different kind of class from the bourgeoisie, and it is not clear that all the connotations attached to the notion of a dominant class will ever be applicable to the intellectuals. First of all, the intelligentsia not only is not an ownership class; it is not an inheritance class either. Despite the laborite reform of inheritance laws which has taken place in countries ruled by social democratic parties for decades, the bourgeoisie is still an inheritance class: bourgeois wealth and, to a large extent, power are passed from one generation to the next. No doubt from a purely political economic point of view this does not make a great deal of difference: the class power of the bourgeoisie is based on its right to expropriate surplus. With the legitimation of private ownership of the means of production, the roots of class conflict lie in the antagonism between capital and labor. In other words, if a social democratic party ever succeeded in abolishing inheritance of the means of the production, this ideal capitalism would still be capitalism as long as private ownership entitled anyone to expropriate surplus. What really matters is the nature of exploitation. On the other hand, it would be foolish to deny that inheritance is very important when it comes to judgments about the morality of capitalism. Societies which limit the inheritance of wealth and power are perceived to be "better" than those which do not do so. The East European intelligentsia, at least at present, is a noninheritance class. The intellectuals are unable to pass their power position to their children. This is especially true at the highest echelons of power. At these highest echelons of power "socialist nepotism" is not unheard of, but it is relatively infrequent. (Interesting exceptions are Rumania and North Korea.) The intelligentsia is also a fairly open class. It receives new members from the "dominated class." You do not have to be the son or daughter of an intellectual to enter the class. It is possible to argue, on the other hand, that the intelligentsia is slowly losing its open character. A significant proportion of university graduates in Eastern Europe are still from nonintellectual backgrounds, but the proportion is steadily declining.[35] It is also possible to argue that this open character was always a relative one. The intelligentsia received new members, but only very rarely did these intellectuals let their own sons or daughters leave the dominant class. In other words, upward mobility into the intelligentsia is high, but downward mobility is quite insignificant, and even if crucial positions are not transferred along family lines, those who are born into the families of the powerful are significantly privileged. They usually start their careers in higher positions, and they climb the ladders of power faster. As state socialism matures, the inheritance of wealth also plays a more important role than formerly. Even if it is incomparable with inheritance in capitalist society, the inheritance of flats, dachas, cars, and so forth is clearly and increasingly a privilege. Finally, one could argue that the open character of the dominant class was only a temporary phenomenon and that any new and numerically expanding dominant class is "open." There are simply not enough sons and daughters to occupy the new positions.

[35] According to Zsuzsa Ferge, the proportion of children of whom at least one parent is a manual worker in institutions of tertiary education increased dramatically with the socialist transformation. This proportion increased in Hungary from 3.5% in 1938 to 48.5% in 1950. Over the next 20 years this proportion declined, to 37.1% by 1970 (1979, p. 145). Hungary does not seem to be atypical of Eastern Europe; see Walter D. Conner's quite similar data on the USSR and Poland (1979, pp. 177–214, esp. p. 206).

In fact, even if the *numerus clausus* had not operated and all children of the intelligentsia had been admitted straight into the university, enough places would still have remained for the children of blue-collar families simply because the university population expanded so rapidly. (I think few children of the intelligentsia were kept out in the long run. The *numerus clausus* guaranteeing a certain proportion of non-white-collar children at the universities usually placed children of intellectuals on a waiting list. After one or two years all who really wanted to enter the university could do so.) But despite all this evidence we should acknowledge that the intelligentsia, compared with the bourgeoisie, is basically a noninheritance class and that this may be significant for those who wish to make moral judgments concerning its rise to power.

Furthermore, the intelligentsia is not a "selfish" class. It does not expropriate surplus in order to consume it. The selfishness of the bourgeoisie, the conspicuous consumption of the leisure class, the extent of inequality in terms of consumed and personally possessed material goods, are important criteria in moral judgments of capitalism. Theoretically, selfishness is not a crucial criterion; the dominant class can be ascetic—and in fact, if we can believe Benjamin Franklin, the bourgeoisie has been highly ascetic in the past. It is also important to remind ourselves that in modern capitalism, with progressive taxation, absentee ownership, and so forth, most of the surplus is not consumed by the owners of capital. It is reinvested or allocated through the state budget. We could imagine an egalitarian capitalism, with ascetic capitalists who only expropriate in order to reinvest, which would not be less capitalistic as long as the exploitation was of a capitalist nature. We also should not overemphasize the unselfishness of the East European intelligentsia. There is a significant degree of inequality between the intellectuals and the working class. Wage differentials in Eastern Europe between a university professor and a plumber or taxi driver are frighteningly similar to those in a Western welfare society.[36] Eastern Europe is only more equal in terms of the extremes—it does not know the extreme rich and does not allow the existence of the extreme poor—but the gap of inequality for the overwhelming majority is nonetheless significant, and it follows in direction the class distinction between intellectuals and workers.[37]

[36] Reliable data from Eastern Europe are not easily available. To the best of my knowledge, Zsuzsa Ferge offers the most reliable and comprehensive data for Hungary. According to her figures (based on investigations carried out in the mid 1960s), in Hungary the top 20% of the income earners earned 36.2% of the total income, the top 5% earned 11.8%. Comparable figures for a group of countries composed of the United States, Sweden, and Denmark were, according to Ferge, 42.7% and 16.4% (1979, p. 169).

[37] According to Ferge, in Hungarian state-owned firms in 1975 the ratio of total monthly income of top management to the income of workers was 2.5:1. The same ratio for middle-level mangement was 1.5:1. She also claims that the ratio is steadily declining. For the top management the above ratio in 1968 was 3.0:1; in other words, she reports a decline of almost 20% over less than 10 years (1979, p. 180).

The intelligentsia, furthermore, is privileged not only in terms of income distribution. For example, the intellectuals have a better chance of getting a highly subsidized state flat; they fill trade union vacation homes during peak seasons; they are the only people who have access to the well-equipped Party hospitals and who can shop in the tax-free hard currency shops. Wherever the analyst looks in the East European redistributive economy he will find the intellectuals in a privileged situation, even in those spheres where, in a capitalist welfare state, socialist policy counteracts inequalities.[38]

But it is still true that intellectuals not only cannot pass on to their children the surplus which is expropriated under their power, but they are by and large unable to use it for their personal purposes. A capitalist, despite trade union and state control, even today can commit economic suicide, can overconsume and underinvest, but the redistributor of state socialism does not own the surplus which flows through his hands. He only administers it. However, it is crucial to emphasize that this unselfishness of the intelligentsia is only true in terms of material goods, not in terms of power. The chances for the redistributor to increase his personal wealth are very limited, but he is not only permitted but also structurally motivated to maximize his redistributive power. If the law of capitalism consists in the striving for more profit, the law of state socialism consists in the striving for the maximization of redistributive power, and from this point of view the teleological redistributor—with, of course, evangelistic zeal—will be as ruthless as any capitalist could ever be.

Furthermore, the East European intelligentsia, at least at present, is only a "class in itself"—it has not developed a class consciousness.

One could argue that, at least according to orthodox Marxist class theory, "class" does not have a sociological meaning without class consciousness. Class, properly speaking, is always "class for itself." The East European intelligentsia is obviously not a class in this sense. Not only does it not recognize the class nature of its own power, but it promotes the ideology of classlessness and consensus and, even more paradoxically, claims that the power exercised by the intellectuals is in fact the power of the proletariat. The revolutionary intelligentsia interprets itself as the tool of the dictatorship of the proletariat. Dominating classes are not usually very keen on promoting the development of class consciousness. Dominating classes always promote ideologies of consensus, while dominated classes have a vested interest in becoming classes for themselves and in emphasizing the conflictual nature of social relations. However, I am ready to acknowledge that class consciousness or even, more generally speaking, social consciousness in contemporary Eastern Europe exists at a very low level. Social

[38] For inequalities in administrative and redistributive allocation, see Szelenyi (1978) and Ferge (1979, pp. 233–73).

consciousness is less articulated than that in bourgeois society at a very early stage of its development. On the level of political analysis one can see this in the vulnerability of state-socialist societies when confronted with significant changes. The events of 1956 were totally unexpected in Hungary. No one was able to predict the rapid rise and fall of the "Prague Spring" or the more recent working-class opposition movements in Poland. The East European societies know less about themselves, despite fairly well-developed sociological and public opinion research, than bourgeois societies did even in times when the terms "sociology" and "opinion poll" did not exist. I would argue that the inarticulate nature of social consciousness is one of the main social and political problems East European societies are faced with today. It produces political and economic instability. It is partially responsible for the repressive political infrastructure, since the dominating class overestimates the forces which threaten its power monopoly and may feel it necessary to eliminate by administrative measure critics who in bourgeois political systems would be peacefully coopted by means of sheer "repressive tolerance." On the other hand, the inarticulate nature of social consciousness is the direct product of the class formation of the intelligentsia. The fact that the intelligentsia for the first time in the history of mankind is becoming a dominating social class prevents the development of opposing class ideologies, prevents the emergence of organic intellectuals of oppressed classes. Bourgeois society was able to produce conflicting class ideologies because intellectuals, the potential ideologues, occupied an intermediary position between two basic classes and could become organic intellectuals of one or the other of them. The fact that the intelligentsia is not a class in capitalist society, but only a stratum (and this means that intellectuals do not have a system of interests antagonistic to other major components of the social structure), is the precondition for the development of class consciousness. It is a precondition of the development of the proletariat as a class for itself. As the principle which legitimates the claim of the intellectuals to power becomes the main principle of legitimation of social and economic power in society, the intelligentsia loses its potential to produce organic intellectuals of the dominated classes. It only promotes ideologies which are in its own basic class interest, the most important being the ideology of classlessness.

The state-socialist redistributive economy represents a new system of economic exploitation. Under this economic system the immediate producer has no more control over the product of his labor than the worker in a capitalist economy. But in state-socialist societies the cultural deprivation of the working class is probably more serious than the economic—the worker is deprived not only of the products of his labor, but also of his social identity. Curiously enough, one of the first measures of the so-called dictatorship of the proletariat was the abolition of all working-class organizations.

The authorities outlawed not only political organizations such as parties, trade unions, and youth groups, but even workers' choirs and hiking clubs. Since the working class has ultimate power in society—argued the official ideologues of state socialism—there is no longer any need for specifically worker organizations. The trade unions were transformed into worker-management corporations (in all East European societies managerial and engineering staff belong to the same union as workers), and the same logic was applied to "innocent" cultural and sporting organizations or clubs.

Not only are the workers deprived of the opportunity to associate with their fellow workers, but their quest for identity as workers is also continuously questioned. The worker is replaced with an ideological notion, that of the proletariat—the worker who is aware of his historical mission. The worker finds himself labeled as "petty bourgeois" or "lumpen proletariat" if he tries to live up to his immediate values and aspirations, and he is accused of lacking proletarian consciousness. The empirically identifiable values, aspirations, and ways of life of the actual physical workers are confronted with the ideals of "socialist man," who socially and in class terms is a faceless creature devised by Soviet Marxist ideologues. If someone were to analyze carefully the ideal type of socialist man—a test still to be done— he would find striking similarities with the values and tastes of the high-brow upper middle class of any advanced industrial society. Socialist man should read books, listen to music, be dressed like, and behave with his children as doctrinaire left-wing academics do. If a semiskilled factory laborer in Prague does not match this ideal, then he should be ashamed of himself. State-socialist society does not permit self-identification in terms of position in the social structure. One cannot be proud of being a worker or peasant: the cultural image is a homogeneous one, and conflicting or competing values simply do not exist. There is only a single hierarchy of values.

The ideology of classlessness of state socialism could not suppress all expressions of working-class consciousness. Haraszti's powerful book *A Worker in a Worker's State* (1977) offers convincing evidence of the existence of a significant degree of "class identity" and "conflict consciousness," to use Michael Mann's terminology,[39] among workers. The workers Haraszti worked with in the Red Star Tractor Factory in Budapest could draw as clear a distinction between a "we" and a "they" as any "traditional worker" can under capitalism.[40] Haraszti found that a strong identity among blue-

---

[39] Michael Mann distinguishes among four elements of consciousness—identity, opposition, totality, and alternative. According to Mann, these four elements are separate in reality and any can occur without the others. However, he claims that revolutionary class consciousness can develop only if all four elements are present in the consciousness of the working class (1973, pp. 68–73).

[40] The development of workers' consciousness of class identity and even of some perception of opposition and totality is powerfully argued by Haraszti in his discussion of

collar workers on the production line was reinforced by a perception of an antagonism between workers and all those who work in the office rather than on the shop floor. "They" were the enemy. It is worth noting that for the workers Haraszti described, this "enemy" was not only high-level management but included the lowest echelons of salaried supervisory personnel: the night guard who searched the workers at the factory gate after their shifts was one of "them," was also an enemy. Haraszti empirically identified a perception by the workers of a dichotomic class structure in the Red Star Tractor Factory, a strong feeling of identity among blue-collar workers and an ability to perceive the conflictual nature of class relations. What Haraszti could not document, in Michael Mann's terminology, was a sense of class totality; the vision of an "alternative" was rather naive. From the Haraszti study we can establish the existence of a conflict consciousness, but we still do not have proofs of the existence of a class consciousness.

The recent events in Poland, especially since August 1980, are of major importance for the understanding of class dynamics under state socialism.[41] Since August 1980 one can find signs of development of a consciousness among the Polish working class which may point beyond a simple class identity and conflict consciousness. In orthodox Marxist language, one can suggest the transition from a "trade union consciousness" to "class consciousness" among the Polish working class during August 1980. It would be premature even to attempt to offer a full analysis of the present Polish struggles; without aspiring to draw far-reaching conclusions, I would like to

---

how workers distinguish between "we" and "they": "They, them theirs: I don't believe that anyone who has ever worked in a factory . . . can be in any doubt about what these words mean. In every place of work . . . them means the same thing: the management, those who give orders and take the decisions, employ labour and pay wages, the men and their agents who are in charge. The word lumps together those whom one knows and those whom one does not know, those whom one likes and those whom one hates, the foreman with whom one is on friendly terms, the design engineer whom one addresses formally, the manager whom one approaches with obsequious respect, the secretaries, the time-keepers, the inspectors, the factory journal and the guards. Although we mainly talk about factory matters, them transcends the walls of the factory and encompasses . . . everything which is above, far away, outside the power of whoever is speaking. . . . I have also worked in offices in which, just like here, they had directors and subordinates, some of whom were privileged and others on low salaries. . . . But nowhere, except among factory workers, have I heard this absolute them, peremptory, exact, and crystal clear. This usage not only differentiates industrial workers from others, even within the factory it traces a subtle demarcation line between the majority and those whose posts and quali-fications are such that they lost sight of the distance which divides the common destiny: dropping them is the first sign that someone really wanted to start climbing the ladder" (Haraszti 1977, pp. 71–72).

[41] For rich documentation of the Polish events see the special issue of *L'Alternative* (no. 7), November–December 1980. This special issue published the full text of the "Information Bulletin" of the Solidarity movement from August 23, 1980, until August 31, 1980 (*L'Alternative* 1980). For an interesting theoretical analysis see Arato (1981).

point to a few interesting new elements in the development of class consciousness of the Polish working class.

It is of theoretical importance that the first six of the 21 demands formulated by the Solidarity movement on August 24, 1980 (*L'Alternative* 1980, pp. 14–15), are political, and only the rest can be called "normal" trade union demands. It is probably even more important that the very first demand is for unions which are independent from management, which are genuine organizations of workers rather than worker-management corporations. The striking workers of the Gdansk shipyard put the "question of organization" first in this list of demands, before the trade union issues. In fact, in the agreements later reached with the government, Solidarity compromised on many trade union–type demands but was unwilling to compromise on the question of organization. Under some government pressure, Solidarity accepted that the unions are not political in nature (*L'Alternative* 1980, p. 44) and agreed that the movement would not play the role of a political party. But this concession was significantly less than the acceptance of a "proper trade union" role for Solidarity. The intention of the Polish Communist Party and government was to limit the activities of Solidarity to "bread and butter" issues, but—as Kania, the first secretary of the Polish CP, noted with disquiet—with the establishment of Solidarity Poland moved rather toward a "dual power" system (Arato 1981). It is probably true that, in the early stages at least, when Solidarity was virtually identical with the striking shipbuilders of Gdansk and had not become an occupationally highly heterogeneous body, the movement's main aim was not to challenge the existence of the Party and/or the government. Even the issue of the composition of the Party and government appears to be secondary. The main objective was to establish the "countervailing power" of workers. The editors of the "Information Bulletin" of Solidarity expressed this in the following way in their declaration dated August 28, 1980: "Malheureusement certaines pertes dues à la mauvaise gestion . . . ne pourront être récupérées. . . . Nous ne cherchons pas de coupables. . . . Il s'agit avant tout de créer les conditions qui garantiront la non-reproduction de ces pertes. Cela sera possible quand le monopole du pouvoir ne sera plus transformé par ce pouvoir en monopole de l'intelligence, du savoir et de la rationalité. On ne pourra y parvenir sans décentraliser le pouvoir, sans créer les conditions qui permettront l'utilisation du savoir professionnel des savants et l'intelligence collective de la classe ouvrière" (*L'Alternative* 1980, p. 29).

What the movement is seeking to achieve, therefore, is not a change of personnel in the existing power structure, but a new system of power in which the "collective intelligence of the working class" can be utilized side by side with the professional knowledge of scholars. According to the authors of the declaration, the decentralization of power, the reform of the planning system (and a "better utilization of the professional knowledge of scholars"), is necessary, but not sufficient. In addition to decentralization of the planning system, they insist that the right of the producers to dispose of the products of their labor be respected. In the wording of the declaration: "Nous faisons confiance aux militants sociaux et aux spécialistes qui insistent sur la nécessité de réformes fondamentales dans le système de planification et de gestion de l'économie. . . . Cela n'est certes pas facile . . . mais il faut entamer le processus de changement . . . en créant les conditions d'une authentique participation de tous ceux qui travaillent et qui ont le droit d'attendre des effets de leur activité, à l'élaboration du destin de notre pays" (*L'Alternative* 1980, p. 29). Unlike Hungary in 1956 and Czechoslovakia in 1968, where the opposition was initiated and led by sections of the intelligentsia, in Poland in 1980 the movement emerged from the working class directly. Unlike 1970 and 1976, in 1980 the Polish workers were no longer willing to restrict their struggles to bread-and-butter issues; they moved beyond conflict consciousness, and one can identify elements of class consciousness in their actions. In this sense Poland in 1980–81 represents an important further stage in the unfolding of the new class structure of state socialism.

But even in the light of the Polish events of 1980–81 the analyst can identify only elements of this new class structure: the new class regulations and the new dominant class of state socialism are still in the making, still *in statu nascendi*.

As I proposed above, the new relations between the rulers and ruled will appear in class relations only after the political and economic instance becomes relatively separated, after civil society gains a significant autonomy from the political state.

As long as the civil society is penetrated by the totalitarian political state, all political movements in Eastern Europe will aim first at the establishment of basic civil liberties. The Polish working class—and the workers of other East European nations—obviously cannot articulate successfully the interests of workers' self-determination as long as basic civil liberties are not guaranteed to all, as long as at least a relative autonomy of civil society from the political state is not achieved. Both the rationalization of the central planning and management of the economic (and cultural-political) system and the aspiration to workers' self-determination require the relative autonomy of civil society, guarantees of civil liberties. At this stage it appears that the only conflict is the one between the state and civil society, between the "powers" and "society." The central thesis of this essay is that, as the relative autonomy of civil society is achieved, this ideologically constructed facade of consensus of the whole society against the powers disappears, and the new and now class type of conflict between intelligentsia and the working class becomes obvious.

Szelenyi

In a sense this paper does not therefore reject Djilas. Djilas offered a theory that probably accurately described the agents who first held power under state socialism, under the conditions of total penetration of civil society by a totalitarian state. Under these circumstances—under Stalinism—state socialism indeed is dominated by the party and state apparatus. Unlike Djilas, I would not call this apparatus a class, since I could not locate it in an identifiable economic structure. My main claim is that during the last 20 years, since the publication of Djilas's work, profound changes have taken place under state socialism. Stalinist economic voluntarism is gradually replaced with a more rationalized system of planning whose claim to be "scientific" must be taken more seriously, and there has been some tendency toward an increase in the autonomy of civil society. As these processes continue the circle of the power holders gradually opens up, the power monopoly of the party and state apparatus declines. The apparatchiks gradually begin to share power with the intellectuals, and the power of apparatchiks is gradually replaced with the class power of the intelligentsia. My claim is that, while Djilas accurately identified the power holders prior to the 1960s, since then analysts have noted the emergence of a genuinely new class of intelligentsia. This intelligentsia is broader than the "new class" of Djilas, and it is also more clearly of a class nature. As one can see from the example of Poland in 1980–81, and especially from the events following the imposition of martial law on December 13, 1981, these apparatchiks still hold on to their power. But in this later stage of development of state-socialist societies we can already see what Djilas could not notice in the late 1950s: the replacement of a conflict between the apparatchiks and the society by conflicts between a new dominant class of intelligentsia and the working class as the most likely outcome of political and economic developments in contemporary Eastern Europe.

REFERENCES

L'Alternative: Special Issue on Poland. 1980. (November–December.)

Anderson, Perry. 1974. *Lineages of the Absolutist State.* London: New Left Books.

Arato, Andrew. 1981. "Civil Society against the State." *Telos,* no. 47 (Spring), pp. 23–47.

Arato, Andrew, and Eike Gebhardt, eds. 1978. *The Essential Frankfurt School.* Oxford: Basil Blackwell.

Balla, Balint. 1972. *Kaderverwaltung.* Stuttgart: Ferdinand Enke.

Baran, Paul. 1961. "The Commitment of the Intellectuals." *Monthly Review* 13 (May): 8–18.

Bauman, Zygmunt. 1974. "Officialdom and Class—Bases of Inequality in Socialist Society." Pp. 129–48 in *The Analysis of Class Structure,* edited by Frank Parkin. London: Tavistock.

Berdyaev, Nicolas. 1972. *The Origins of Russian Communism.* Ann Arbor: University of Michigan Press.

Burnham, James W. 1962. *The Managerial Revolution.* Bloomington: Indiana University Press.

Connerton, Paul, ed. 1976. *Critical Sociology*. London: Penguin.
Connor, Walter D. 1979. *Socialism, Politics and Equality*. New York: Columbia University Press.
Dahrendorf, Ralf. 1959. *Class and Class Conflict in Industrial Society*. London: Routledge & Kegan Paul.
Djilas, Milovan. 1957. *The New Class*. New York: Holt, Rinehart & Winston.
Engels, Frederick. 1970. "Socialism: Utopian and Scientific." Pp. 375–428 in *Karl Marx and Frederick Engels: Selected Works*. Moscow: Progress Publishers.
Ferge, Zsuzsa. 1973. *Tarsadalmunk Retegzodese*. Budapest: Kozgazdasagi & Jogi Konyvkiado.
———. 1979. *A Society in the Making*. New York: Sharpe.
Gella, Aleksander, ed. 1976. *The Intelligentsia and the Intellectuals*. London: Sage.
Giddens, Anthony. 1973. *The Class Structure of the Advanced Societies*. London: Hutchinson University Library.
Gouldner, A. W. 1975–76. "Prologue to a Theory of Revolutionary Intellectuals." *Telos*, no. 26 (Winter), pp. 3–36.
———. 1979. *The Future of Intellectuals and the Rise of the New Class*. New York: Seabury.
Habermas, Jürgen. 1970. *Toward a Rational Society*, translated by Jeremy J. Shapiro. Boston: Beacon.
———. 1974. *Theory and Practice*, translated by John Viertel. London: Heinemann.
Haraszti, Miklos. 1977. *A Worker in a Worker's State*. London: Penguin.
Hegedus, Andras. 1977. *The Social Structure of Socialist Society*. London: Constable.
Horkheimer, Max. 1978. "The End of Reason." Pp. 26–48 in Arato and Gebhardt, eds., 1978.
Konrad, George, and Ivan Szelenyi. 1979. *The Intellectuals on the Road to Class Power*. New York: Harcourt Brace Jovanovich.
Kuron, J. 1978. "Pour une platform unique de l'opposition." In *La Pologne: Une société en dissidence*, edited by Z. Erard and G. M. Zygier. Paris.
Kuron, J., and K. Modzelewski. 1966. "An Open Letter to the Party." *New Politics* 5 (2): 5–47.
Lenin, V. I. 1970. "Can the Bolsheviks Retain State Power?" Pp. 393–434 in *Selected Works*, vol. 2. Moscow: Progress Publishers.
Mann, Michael. 1973. *Consciousness and Action among the Western Working Class*. London: Macmillan.
Marx, Karl. 1970. "The Eighteenth Brumaire of Louis Bonaparte." Pp. 96–179 in *Karl Marx and Frederick Engels: Selected Works*. Moscow: Progress Publishers.
———. 1972. "Theses on Feuerbach." Pp. 11–13 in *On Historical Materialism*, by K. Marx, F. Engels, and V. I. Lenin. Moscow: Progress Publishers.
———. 1974. *Capital*. Vol. 3. Moscow: Progress Publishers.
———. 1975a. "Contribution to the Critique of Hegel's Philosophy of Law." Pp. 5–129 in *Karl Marx and Frederick Engels: Collected Works*, vol. 3. New York: International Publishers.
———. 1975b. *Precapitalist Economic Formations*. New York: International Publishers.
Marx, Karl, and Frederick Engels. 1970. "Manifesto of the Communist Party." Pp. 31–63 in *Karl Marx and Frederick Engels: Selected Works*. Moscow: Progress Publishers.
———. 1972. "The German Ideology." Pp. 14–76 in *On Historical Materialism*, by K. Marx, F. Engels, and V. I. Lenin. Moscow: Progress Publishers.
Ossowski, Stanislaw. 1963. *Class Structure in the Social Consciousness*. London: Routledge & Kegan Paul.
———. 1974. "Old Notions and New Problems—Interpretations of Social Structure in Modern Society." Pp. 79–89 in *Social Inequality*, edited by André Beteille. London: Penguin.
Perez-Diaz, Victor M. 1978. *State, Bureaucracy and Civil Society*. London: Macmillan.
Shachtman, M. 1962. *The Bureaucratic Revolution*. New York: Donald.
Shkaratan, O. I. 1970. *Problemy sosial'noi struktury rabochego klassa SSSR*. Moscow: Mysl.
Stalin, J. V. 1972. *Economic Problems of Socialism in the USSR*. Peking: FLP.

Szelenyi, Ivan. 1978. "Social Inequalities in State Socialist Redistributive Economies." *International Journal of Comparative Sociology* 10:63–87.

Trotsky, Leon. 1972. *The Revolution Betrayed*. New York: Pathfinder.

Weber, Max. 1958. *The Religion of India*. New York: Free Press.

———. 1978. *Economy and Society*. Berkeley and Los Angeles: University of California Press.

Wesolowski, Wlodzimierz, ed. 1970. *Zroźnicowanie spóleczne*. Warsaw: Wydownictwo Polskiej Akademii Nauk.

Wesolowksi, Wlodzimierz. 1974. "The Notion of Strata and Class in Socialist Society." Pp. 122–45 in *Social Inequality*, edited by André Beteille. London: Penguin.

Wright, Erik O. 1978. *Class, Crisis and the State*. London: New Left Books.

CONTRIBUTORS

MICHAEL BURAWOY, one of the editors of this Supplement, wrote the Introduction while he was assistant professor of sociology at the University of California, Berkeley. He is the author of *Manufacturing Consent* and of the forthcoming book *Politics of Production*.

THEDA SKOCPOL, the other editor of this Supplement, is associate professor of sociology and political science at the University of Chicago. She is the author of *States and Social Revolutions: A Comparative Analysis of France, Russia, and China* (1979). Her current research focuses on the political formation of the American welfare state in historical and comparative perspective.

JULIA WRIGLEY is an associate professor in the Departments of Education and Sociology at the University of California, Los Angeles. She has written a book, *Class Politics and Public Schools: Chicago, 1900–1950*, on conflicts between working class and capitalist groups over the control, curriculum, and funding of the public schools. She is currently studying the relation between England's industrial decline and its lack of a developed technical or scientific education system. She is also studying contemporary antibusing movements in the United States.

DWIGHT B. BILLINGS is associate professor of sociology at the University of Kentucky. He is a specialist in class analysis, modernization, and regional American political economy. Among his interests are Southern and Appalachian regional development and the application of critical theory to American neo-evangelical movements. In 1980 his book *Planters and the Making of a "New South"* won a Distinguished Scholarly Achievement Award from the North Central Sociological Association.

ROBERT J. THOMAS is assistant professor of sociology and a faculty associate of the Center for Research on Social Organization of the University of Michigan. He is currently completing revisions of a manuscript on the labor process in industrial agriculture and (with William H. Friedland) is preparing an extensive work on the United Farm Workers union. His present research is focused on a comparative analysis of class struggle and the labor process in the U.S. and Japanese automotive industries.

LARRY J. GRIFFIN is associate professor of sociology at Indiana University at Bloomington. His current interests include political economy, macro-level stratification processes and outcomes, and the analysis of social change in capitalist economics. In addition to the article included in this Supplement, he and his coauthors have written the forthcoming article "On the Economic Determinants of Welfare Spending in the Post–World War II Era." Other recent publications include "Class, Occupation, and Inequality in Job Rewards" and "Stratification and Meritocracy in the United States," both coauthored with Arne Kalleberg. He is currently analyzing the economic consequences of the American labor movement since the turn of the century, the linkages between income distribution and fis-

Contributors

cal policy in the United States, and the growth and demise of European Social Democratic parties during the period 1880–1920.

JOEL A. DEVINE is assistant professor of sociology at Tulane University. His dissertation, "Capitalist Development, State Expenditures, and Economic Inequality: Historical and Quantitative Analyses of the United States in the Post–World War II Era," assesses the sociopolitical determinants and economic consequences of fiscal policy. At present he is continuing these investigations in fiscal sociology and political economy with Larry Griffin and Michael Wallace. In addition, he has recently undertaken an empirical analysis of the fiscal crisis in American cities.

MICHAEL WALLACE, scheduled to receive his Ph.D. from Indiana University late in 1982, is joining the Department of Sociology at Yale University early in 1983. His substantive interests include the political economy of American capitalism, social stratification, the sociology of work and industrial organization, and time series analysis. His dissertation, a quantitative historical analysis, is entitled "Working Class Organization and Labor Militancy: A Comparative Analysis of the United States and Canada in the Twentieth Century." Among his publications is the 1982 article "Industrial Transformation and the Decline of Craft: The Decomposition of Skill in the Printing Industry, 1931–1978."

PAT SHANNON is a lecturer in applied social studies in the Community Studies Centre of Otago University Extension in New Zealand. He works as a member of a team in adult education and social action; the centre attempts especially to develop a cohesive community effective in decision making. He has been both an editor of and a contributor to two recent publications: *Unemployment and New Zealand's Future* and *The Rights of the Child and Social Policy*.

ERIK OLIN WRIGHT is associate professor of sociology at the University of Wisconsin and an active member of the class analysis and historical change program in that department. He is author of *Class, Crisis, and the State* and *Class Structure and Income Determination*. His current research involves a comprehensive comparative study of class structure, class biography, and class consciousness in the United States and seven other countries.

JOACHIM SINGELMANN is a demographer working in the United Nations Population Division. His major research has centered on transformation of the industrial and occupational structures. He is the author of *From Agriculture to Services: The Transformation of Industrial Employment*.

PETER EVANS is associate professor of sociology at Brown University. His major research interests are multinational corporations, the comparative study of development, and the state. He is the author of *Dependent Development: The Alliance of Multinational States and Local Capital in Brazil*.

HARRIET FRIEDMANN is associate professor of sociology at the University of Toronto. She is currently investigating the politics of food and agriculture in Western Europe immediately after World War II on a grant from the German Marshall Fund of the United States. A book entitled *The Political Economy of Food: Farmers, States, and the International Division of Labor* is also in preparation.

IVAN SZELENYI is professor of sociology at the University of Wisconsin—Madison. He is author of *The Intellectuals on the Road to Class Power* (with George Konrad, 1979) and *Urban Social Inequalities under State Socialism* (1982) and has contributed articles to *American Sociological Review, Telos, Sociological Review, Australian and New Zealand Journal of Sociology,* and *Revue française de sociologie.*

The editors gratefully acknowledge the assistance of the following advisors and referees:

Editorial Advisors

FRED BLOCK, University of Pennsylvania
PETER EVANS, Brown University
ANTHONY GIDDENS, Cambridge University
TEMMA KAPLAN (History), University of California, Los Angeles
IRA KATZNELSON, New School for Social Research
MAGALI SARFATTI LARSON, Temple University
JOAN SCOTT (History), Brown University
ERIC WOLF (Anthropology), City University of New York
ERIK OLIN WRIGHT, University of Wisconsin—Madison
MAURICE ZEITLIN, University of California, Los Angeles

Additional Referees

HARRIET FRIEDMANN, University of Toronto
TODD GITLIN, University of California, Berkeley
STANLEY GREENBERG (Political Science), Yale University
CLARENCE LO, University of California, Los Angeles
CHRISTOPHER JENCKS, Northwestern University
JOHN MOLLENKOPF (Political Science), City University of New York
JOHN PADGETT, University of Chicago
CHARLES RAGIN, Northwestern University
DAVID STARK, Duke University
JONATHAN WIENER (History), University of California, Irvine